Psychological Illusions

Explorations of the G. I. Gurdjieff
Fourth Way Teaching

Christopher P. Holmes

ZERO POINT
Institute for Mystical and Spiritual Science
Box 700, 108 Clothier Street East
Kemptville, Ontario, Canada K0G 1J0
zeropoint@bell.net
(613) 258-6258
www.zeropoint.ca

Zero Point Publications 2010

Cover illustration: Anita J. Mitra
Graphic Design and Prepress: Željka Županić

1st Printing - 2002

National Library of Canada Cataloguing in Publication

Holmes, Christopher P
Psychological illusions : explorations of the G. I. Gurdjieff fourth
way teaching / Christopher P. Holmes.

Includes bibliographic references.

ISBN 978-0-9689435-2-6

1. Fourth Way (Occultism). 2. Gurdjieff, Georges Ivanovitch, 1872-1949.
3. Consciousness. 4. Mysticism. I. Title.

BP605.G92H64 2002   197   C2002-901748-3

G. I. Gurdjieff

"A man may be quite alone in the desert
and he can trace the enneagram in the
sand and in it read the eternal laws of
the universe."

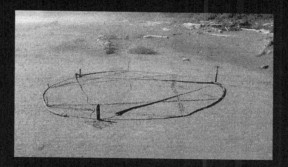

"the teaching whose theory is here being
set out is completely self-supporting
and independent of other lines and it
has been completely unknown up to the
present time. "

- 1916 -

G.I. Gurdjieff

"... every man should strive to have his own "I" ... ."

- Beelzebub's Tales to His Grandson -

- 1950 / p.1201 -

"Both states of consciousness, sleep and the waking state, are equally subjective. Only by beginning to remember himself does a man really awaken. And then all surrounding life acquires for him a different aspectand a different meaning. He sees that it is the life of sleeping people, a life in sleep. All that men say, all that they do, they say and do in sleep. All this can have no value whatsoever. Only awakening and what leads to awakening has a value in reality."

- 1949 / p. 143 -

Gurdjieff

P.D. Ouspensky

"Ordinary psychology is very far from reality.
... We ascribe to ourselves many qualities we do not possess."

- 1957 / p. 27 -

"(One) illusion is that we are awake. When we realize that we are asleep
we will see that all history is made by people who are asleep. Sleeping
people fight, make laws; sleeping people obey or disobey them. The worst
of our illusions are the wrong ideas among which we live and which govern
our lives. If we could change our attitude towards these wrong ideas and
understand what they are, this in itself would be a great change and would
immediately change other things."

-1957 / p.29 -

"... until we begin to understand our illusions we can never see truth."

- 1957 / p. 18 -

Table of Content

X - XI   **Preface**

I /
2   **Self knowledge**
Mystical Teachings and the Fourth Way

3   1. "Know Self"
7   2. Mysticism
10   3. The Fourth Way
17   4. The Psychopathology and Sleepwalking State of Humanity
23   5. Beelzebub's Tales to his Grandson

23   5a. A New Language   20
24   5b. About the Strange Psyche of the Three-Brained Beings on Planet Earth
26   5c. Similitudes of the Whole

II /
30   **The Fourth Way**
Definitions of psychology

31   1. The Two Psychologies
32   2. The Psychology of A Human's Possible Evolution
36   3. The Study of Language
39   4. The Study of Oneself
41   5. The Study of the Centers
44   6. The Study of Consciousness
49   7. Self-Remembering: A Key, a Door, a Missing Link
54   8. The Study of Lying
56   9. The Study of a Human and the Cosmos
62   10. An Overview

III /
68   **Enumerating the Whole**

69   1. Enumerating the Whole
70   2. The Dualities of Formatory Mind and Formatory Psychology
74   3. The Three, Five & Seven Brained Being

75   Thinking or Intellectual Center
77   Emotional or Feeling Center
80   Moving Center
82   Instinctual Center
83   Sexual Center
86   Higher Emotional and Higher Intellectual Centers

88   4. Essence, Personality & the Organic Body
93   5. Humans Number One, Two and Three & the Higher Types
96   6. The Question of the Soul & the Alchemy of the Higher Being-Bodies

IV /

104   **The Psychopathology of Humanity**

105   1. A Portrait of "Man" in Quotation Marks
109   2. The Wrong Work of Centers

109   2a. The Wrong Work of Intellectual or Thinking Center
109   The turning of the mind
110   Unnecessary talking
111   Internal and External considering
112   Imagination
113   Lying and Formatory thinking

115   2b. The Wrong Work of the Emotional Center
115   Negative Emotions
119   Mr. Self-Love and Madame Vanity

121   2c. The Moving and Instinctual Life
123   2d. The Misuse of Sexual Energy

126   3. False Personality, Buffers and Chief Features
132   4. Lunatics, Tramps and Hasnamuss Individuals
134   5. A Human Being as a Chemical Factory
137   6. A View on the Sleeping World
140   7. Beelzebub's Tales: Human Psychopathology
       and the Processes of Reciprocal Destruction

V /

146   **Psychological illusions**
     The Illusions of Consciousness, Will and Unity

147   1. The Illusion of Self Knowledge
148   2. The Illusion of a Unified and Permanent 'I'
150   3. The Illusion of Will
154   4. The Illusions of Consciousness

154   4a. The Invisibility of Consciousness
156   4b. Normal States of Consciousness
159   4c. Nature's Very Funny Trick
162   4d. The Tricks of Thought and Self-Analysis
164   4e. The Centering of Consciousness

166   5. The Study of the Consciousness

166   5a. Self-Observation &Self-Consciousness
169   5b. Identification and Attachment
171   5c. Self-Observation & Self-Remembering
173   5d. Self-Remembering & the Illusions of Self Knowledge

174   6. The Dual Consciousness
176   7. Illusions of Freedom, Souls and Immortality

VI /

180   **Towards awakening**
Objective Knowledge & Higher States

181   1. The Inner Work: Order in the Household
185   2. Being-Partkdolg-Duty
187   3. Consciousness, Light and Knowing Together
190   4. The Awakening of Conscience: the Sacred
         and Divine Being-Impulse in the Subconscious
195   5. Glimpses of Mystical States of Consciousness

195   5a. Science #4 & Supernormal Psychology
199   5b. Glimpses of Self-Consciousness
204   5c. From Personal to Impersonal Emotions & Sacred Being-Impulses
207   5d. Ouspensky on Great Beings & Higher Mind
211   5e. Glimpses of Objective Consciousness

217   6. Objective Knowledge, Myths and Symbols of the Mysteries
221   7. The Enneagram

VII /

226   **The ray of creation**
& the Alchemy of Soul

227   1. The Ladder of Jacob
229   Law of Three
231   Law of Seven & the Octave

234   2. Cosmic Octaves & Hydrogens

234   2a. The Big Cosmic Octave
238   2b. Three Octaves, Shocks & Organic Life on Earth
240   2c. The Hydrogen Diagrams

242   3. Foods for the Soul: The Accumulation of Fine Hydrogens
247   4. On Lunacy & Feeding the Moon
251   5. Planetary Influences, Essence and Types & the Causes of War
253   6. Towards Immortality: On the Cosmology of a Human's Possible Evolution
258   7. Beelzebub's Tales

258   7a. The Sacred Rascooarnos, the 'Okipkhalevnian-exchange' & Purgatory
263   7b. A Particle of all that Exists

266   8. Remembering, Forgetting & the Inevitability of Death

268   **The Author**

270   **Bibliography**

274   **ZP Publications**

Preface

In *Boyhood with Gurdjieff*, Fritz Peters recalls experiences he had growing up in association with the teacher and master G. I. Gurdjieff. In the 1920's, Gurdjieff had established the *Institute for the Harmonious Development of Man* at a chateau outside of Paris, France. Peters was a young boy of eleven and served as a houseboy to this enigmatic man.

On one occasion, Gurdjieff asked Fritz to look out of the window, where there was an oak tree and to tell him how many acorns there were on the tree. Peters responded that there were thousands. Gurdjieff then inquired as to how many of those acorns were likely to become oak trees. The boy guessed that perhaps five or six, or maybe not even that many. Gurdjieff then explained the essential nature of his teaching by comparing it to the possibilities that Nature provides:

> "Perhaps only one, perhaps not even one. Must learn from Nature. Man is also organism. Nature makes many acorns, but possibility to become tree exist for only few acorns. Same with man—many men born, but only few grow. People think this waste, think Nature waste. Not so. Rest become fertilizer, go back into earth and create possibility for more acorns, more men, once in while more tree—more real man. Nature always give—but only give possibility. To become real oak, or real man, must make effort. You understand this, my work, this Institute, not for fertilizer. For real man, only. But must also understand fertilizer necessary to Nature. ..."

> "In west—your world—is belief that man have soul, given by God. Not so. Nothing given by God, only Nature give. And Nature only give possibility for soul, not give soul. Must acquire soul through work. ... Even your religion—western religion—have this phrase 'Know thyself.' This phrase most important in all religions. When begin know self already begin have possibility become genuine man. So first thing must learn is know self ... . If not do this, then will be like acorn that not become tree—fertilizer. Fertilizer which go back in ground and become possibility for future man." (1964, pp.42-3)

This work is dedicated to G. I. Gurdjieff and his student P. D. Ouspensky. These individuals have left a profound teaching for the modern world. The *fourth way* deals with the possibilities for the awakening of human consciousness and the evolution of the individual through the 'acquisition' of a soul. Nature has given humans the possibility for attaining real "I" and a soul, but this self transformation is dependent upon attaining self-knowledge, the refinement of the essence and the formation of the *higher being-bodies*. To attain real I, we must seek after truth and come to know ourselves. What these things entail are deep mysteries and there are many psychological illusions—layers of confusion and misunderstanding—which limit humans' grasp of these profound possibilities.

Thirty years ago or so, when I first began the study of these objective fourth way teachings, I could not in my wildest imagination have conceived such possibilities about human nature as explicated by master Gurdjieff. Western psychology has lacked any investigation into the nature of the human soul or the possibilities for states of higher consciousness. By contrast, Gurdjieff provides an ancient science of the soul and a shocking portrayal of the sad life of humankind—governed by their psychological illusions and the common psychopathology of man.

According to Beelzebub, the central character in Gurdjieff's *Beelzebub's Tales to his Grandson*, the three-brained beings on planet Earth are microcosmoses, or *"similitudes of the Whole."* As such, they have the possibility of not only serving local cosmic purposes—feeding the earth and moon as part of organic life on earth—but also of attaining varied levels of *Objective Reason* and individuality, and even of *"blending again with the infinite."* (1950, p. 945) As a microcosm of the macrocosm, a human being can potentially coat higher being-bodies for the life of the soul, instinctually sense cosmic truths and phenomena, and maintain existence within the subtle realms of being after death, achieving different levels of immortality. Unfortunately, humankind came to exist only in waking sleep states of automated consciousness, perceiving reality topsy-turvy, conditioned by pleasure, desires and self love, and wasteful of their sacred substances. Human beings no longer realize their deeper cosmic purposes and possibilities, or attain real "I."

The Gurdjieff fourth way teachings offer a profound analysis of human psychology and a deep metaphysics and cosmology of consciousness. It is a remarkable and coherent system of esoteric teachings about the miraculous possibilities existing for the evolution of the individual human being and about the terror of the situation for humankind asleep.

This book is also dedicated to those *nuts* who sincerely wish to become *oak trees*—among whom I
would include myself. Three other particular and special nuts are James Moffatt, Anita Mitra and Karen Hale, who for many years have shared in the processes of realization and insight, living and loving,
and who have contributed in numerous and varied ways to the refinement and development of *Psychological Illusions*.

Lastly, I would like to thank Željka Županić, from Croatia, who came forward at just the right time and on her own initiative set up this work in such a creative and artistic manner.

Christopher P. Holmes,
Ph.D. (Psych), 2010

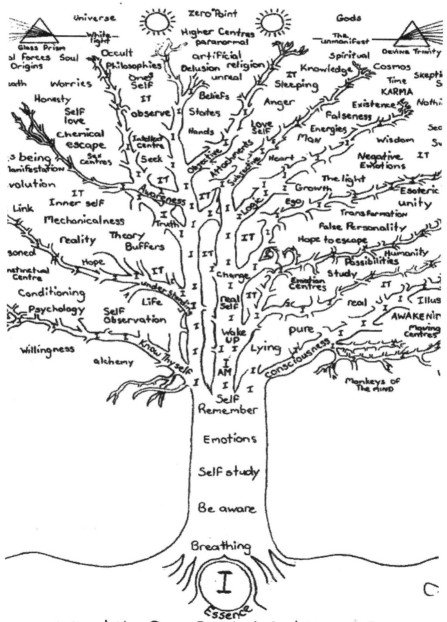

A Seed Has Been Planted And Now I Grow

"So first thing must learn is know self.
... If not do this, then will be like acorn that not become tree ...."

Gurdjieff

I /
Self knowledge
Mystical Teachings and the Fourth Way

1. "Know Self"

According to Gurdjieff and the mystical tradition, the nut can become an oak tree by attaining self knowledge. Human beings can develop and evolve in their consciousness and being, and come to know deeper capacities and dimensions of the self. The fourth way psychology casts a wholly different light upon the nature of human beings and the study of psychology as a practical and theoretical science. Psychology itself must begin with self study, as this is clearly the only way in which to understand the nature of consciousness and to know self.

From the fourth way perspective, modern science is quite mistaken and deluded about the nature of human beings and the universe. We have mistaken ideas about the most basic questions in psychology and about ourselves as individuals. According to the mystics, the possibilities for expanded and heightened states of self realization, spiritual and cosmic consciousness, are latent within human beings. However, until an individual *awakens*, there are different *veils* or covers which limit one's realization of life. Humans, as they are, live in a state of *"waking sleep"* or *"automated consciousness"* and fail to *"instinctually sense reality"* as it is.

In order to evaluate mystical claims and teachings, we have to understand the extent to which people are unconscious. More importantly, we have to come to understand this truth about ourselves. Humans, as they are, exist in a state of *"waking sleep."* As sleepwalkers, peoples' lives consist largely of dreams and imagination, and absorption by the conditioned activities of the mind. Governed by a complex set of psychological illusions, and mistaken incomplete understandings of themselves and life, they live in ignorance of true nature and of self. In the normal waking state of *"automated consciousness"* or *"waking sleep,"* human beings are imprisoned by a thousand and one forces of which they are unaware.

The Gurdjieff teaching reveals the state of sleepwalkers, the hypnosis and conditioning by which they are imprisoned, and can help to liberate us from the illusions which ensnared us. The fourth way provides knowledge and help to those willing to make the necessary efforts to awaken and escape this imprisonment. Gurdjieff's teaching concerns the dissolution of the false consciousness system and the deeper realization that *"I AM."*

To attain self knowledge, the individual has to awaken and overcome the illusions limiting his or her understanding. As it is, people generally think that they already know themselves and it is not apparent how there might be any mysterious secret self-knowledge available to us. To illustrate this point, consider the following article from the *Toronto Sun* in which five weekend shoppers were asked: *"How well do you know yourself?"* The five randomly picked respondents are unanimous in believing that they already know themselves. In fact, they all profess to know themselves either *"pretty well"* or *"very well."* Furthermore, there hardly seems to be anything especially mystical about this knowledge.

The central psychological illusion is that people know themselves pretty well or very well–just as do Jeanine, Gary, Carol, Brian and Anne. They think that they grew up being themselves; that they are pretty level headed and easy-going; that they know their capabilities in food and drink; that they can analyze everything and bring it together–except, of course, why they are always fifteen minutes late.

People think that knowing themselves has to do with being happy with life, experiencing enough pleasure, or having communications which feel good.

Even if we ask these individuals about the universe and the Gods, they would have many attitudes, opinions and beliefs about these things as well. People all tend to have an egocentric attitude; thinking that they are *in the know* and understand themselves, life and the issues of God—at least as well as anyone else might. Unfortunately, most people have no grasp of the profoundly complex nature of life, the self and the cosmos. Instead, they are satisfied to repeat superficial pronouncements and pat explanations, and unconsciously gloss over the awesome mysteries posed by the miraculous nature of existence. Typically, most people have no sense that there is anything mysterious about themselves, the nature of existence, nor any aspect of reality.

Gurdjieff is not referring to ordinary self knowledge when he says *"know self."* This is clear in his explanation of how we must come to realize our "nothingness," as a step in self study and towards awakening:

> To awaken means to realize one's nothingness, that is to realize one's complete and absolute mechanicalness and one's complete and absolute helplessness. ... It is necessary to realize it in clear, simple and concrete facts, in one's own facts. When a man begins to know himself a little he will see in himself many things that are bound to horrify him. So long as a man is not horrified at himself he knows nothing about himself. ... Here he will see his impotence, his helplessness, and his nothingness; or again, when he begins to know himself a man sees that he has nothing that is his own, that is, that all that he regarded as his own, his views, thoughts, convictions, tastes, habits, even faults and vices, all these are not his own, but have been either formed through imitation or borrowed from somewhere ready-made. In feeling this a man may feel his nothingness. And in feeling his nothingness a man should see himself as he really is ...."
> (1949, pp. 218)

Gurdjieff describes three processes involved in attaining *"indivisible I"* – those of awakening, dying and being reborn. Through awakening, a person becomes aware of his or her mechanicalness, conditioning and helplessness. This brings about a dissolution or death of the old self through the realization of one's nothingness. The individual breaks through the false egoism and conditioned personality that dominates the normal state of waking sleep. This dissolution of false personality brings about deeper realizations of the essence of self and possibly leads to real I.

> "... being "born" ... relates to the beginning of a new growth of essence, the beginning of the formation of individuality, the beginning of the appearance of one indivisible I."
> (Ouspensky, 1949, p. 218)

Awakening and attaining real "I" is a long and difficult process. At first, there can be glimpses of such possibilities with new realizations and understandings, and over time this process can evolve into something quite different. However, one's efforts are initially directed towards making false personality less active by observing how one is not properly conscious and by struggling against mechanical conditioning.

When Jeanine, Gary, Carol, Brian and Anne all think that they know themselves "pretty well" or "very well," they are responding only on the basis of what Gurdjieff would describe as the little i's of false personality. They do not *"know self"* and could not even imagine what that entails and what the possession of indivisible I would really mean–in reality rather than in words. It is an awakening to a new world and experiences of the multi-dimensionality of Self.

The mystical claim is that self-knowledge leads to objective knowledge about the nature of the universe and even to divine knowledge of God. Such possibilities rest upon the proposition that there are dimensions to self, which the individual does not realize or at least cannot remember. This type of self knowledge does not mean knowing the ordinary personality with its likes and dislikes, characteristics and peculiarities. In fact, the self or personality which people think they know so well is an illusory self–a persona, mask or veil–which covers the essential self, the real, true, higher or deeper Self, whatever this might be. Mysticism, as a supreme adventure and ultimate science, brings about a transformation within an individual which enables them to realize the supernatural nature of self and its faculties for cosmic knowledge and spiritual realization.

R. Collin (1980), a student of Gurdjieff and Ouspensky, explained that the search for a new state of consciousness is the only way to achieve a unifying understanding of life, and this simply cannot be achieved when individuals themselves are not unified:

> In every age men have tried to assemble all the knowledge and experience of their day into a single whole which would explain their relation to the universe and their possibilities in it. In the ordinary way they could never succeed. For the unity of things is not realizable by the ordinary mind, in an ordinary state of consciousness. The ordinary mind, refracted by the countless and contradictory promptings of different sides of human nature, must reflect the world as manifold and confused as is the man himself. A unity, a pattern, an all-embracing meaning-if it exists-could only be discerned or experienced by a different kind of mind, in a different state of consciousness. It would only be realizable by a mind which had itself become unified.
>
> What unity, for example, could be perceived by even the most brilliant physicist, philosopher or theologian, while he still trips absent-mindedly over a stool, becomes

angry at being short-changed, fails to notice when he irritates his wife, and in general remains subject to the daily trivial blindness of the ordinary mind, working with its customary absence of awareness? Any unity he reaches in such a state can exist only in his imagination.

Thus the attempt to gather all knowledge into a whole has always been connected with the search for a new state of consciousness. And it is meaningless and futile apart from such a search. (p. xi)

In contrast to modern psychology, where the focus of study is always upon other people, groups or organisms, Gurdjieff insists upon the central importance of systematic self-study as the basis for psychology. In order to awaken, an individual must study the parts of their being and the complex processes which are responsible for the lack of consciousness. By studying oneself, *as he or she is*, the individual does so in the context of learning about both the *"psychological illusions"* that limit us and the *"psychology of a human's possible evolution,"* wherein lies our miraculous possibilities. As such, in *Psychological Illusions*, we study humans and ourselves in terms of both normal and supernormal psychology. Doing so, we work not only to free ourselves from illusions, but also, to awaken to the deeper levels of Self and the dormant faculties of our being. Only by overcoming these illusions and misconceptions which govern sleeping humanity can the individual appreciate the profound nature of mystical teachings and realities. Unfortunately, these illusions and misconceptions are also widespread throughout scientific psychology and professional philosophy.

Mysticism is concerned with awakening and knowing self. The fourth way teaching provides a subtle and complex model of what such things entail.

Extract from the *Liber Mutus* of 1718 depicting Angels attempting to awaken sleepwalking humanity. Similarly, esoteric teachings arise from outside of life from higher conscious sources.

2. Mysticism

The Gurdjieff teaching is *mystical* in a number of ways. Firstly, it addresses the fundamental *mysteries* of life. These concern the nature of human consciousness, the nature of "I" within us, and whether or not human beings possess a soul and what this is. The fourth way elaborates upon these fundamental mysteries of human psychology and upon the possible evolution of individual consciousness and being. Gurdjieff also provides a most provocative approach to understanding the nature of creation—the worlds around and within us, and the principles which generate and sustain life. As such, the cosmology and metaphysics of the fourth way teaching establish ways of understanding life which synthesize mystical and scientific perspectives. The Gurdjieff teaching touches upon all such questions—exploring the mysteries of life and death, human evolution, the issues of origins and the underlying metaphysical nature of reality.

Unfortunately, the terms *mystical* and *mysticism* are broadly misunderstood. People have little idea of the aims, methods and claims of mystics, and of the hidden or esoteric teachings. Within modern science and psychology, references to mysticism are almost always negative and pejorative. Scientists and psychologists invoke the terms mysticism and the mystical in order to dismiss what they regard as irrational or unsubstantiated experiences and speculations. Dr. Charles Tart (1975), in an article on the assumptions of western psychology, neatly characterizes the scientist's dislike of such things as mysticism and mystics:

> If a person is a good, competent scientist, the orthodox, Western assumption is that he cannot be a mystic, doing "weird" things inside his head at the same time. A great gulf is considered to exist between the types of mentalities necessary for these two roles ... being a mystic is considered pathological by most orthodox psychologists .... One of the most deprecating remarks you could make about a scientist's work is to say that it shows signs of being "mystical." (p. 111)

In this view, mysticism is at best nothing more than a pseudo-science; at worst, it is complete lunacy. Certainly, a supposedly real scientist in search of truth would not expect to find anything of value in the irrationality and subjectivity of mystical knowledge.

However, within standard dictionaries, the primary meaning of the term *mysticism* certainly suggests extraordinary possibilities for human self knowledge and consciousness:

> mysticism 1: the experience of mystical union or direct communion with ultimate reality reported by mystics 2: the belief that direct knowledge of God or of spiritual truth can be achieved by personal insight and inspiration 3: a vague guessing or speculation; also; a belief without a sound basis: guess. (Time Webster Dictionary)

> mysticism, in its proper meaning, practice of uniting oneself with the Deity or other unifying principle of life, linked with religion; in a more popular sense any sort of non-rational belief. (Columbia Viking Desk Dictionary)

Whereas the scientists might view mysticism as weird and pathological, the true definition of the term suggests a form of ultimate science, which can reveal deeper realities, spiritual truths and even God! There is certainly a great gap between the common deprecating view of mysticism as a *pseudo-science* and the ancient meaning of mysticism as a way of experiencing ineffable knowledge and states of spiritual and divine union. Mysticism is primarily a science of consciousness and concerned with the experience of unified states and the deeper dimensions of Self, reality and even God.

The idea of attaining true self-knowledge is basic to mystical claims and belief. This is evident in Socrates' famous dictum *"Know Thyself,"* from the sixth century B. C.. A variation of this dictum, also from the Greek mystery schools, declares: *"Know thyself, and thou wilt know the universe and the Gods."* Unfortunately, most people have no understanding of the mystical dimensions to these apparently simple aphorisms. In this view, an individual can experience deeper forms of self knowledge, spiritual realization, objective knowledge of the universe and God realization.
These potentials are inherent within the individual psyche, soul and spirit, but must be brought out or realized through experience and transformation. Mysticism is most unusual in what it suggests about the nature of things–all things, from the microcosm to the macrocosm, above and below.
At the deepest levels, knowledge of self enables the individual to experience life in the realm of the miraculous.

The Gnostic Gospels of early Christianity elaborated upon the claims of such hidden self knowledge:

> ... the gnostic gospels... claim to offer traditions about Jesus that are secret, hidden
> from "the many" .... The Greek word *gnosis* (is) usually translated as "knowledge." For
> as those who claim to know nothing about ultimate reality are called agnostic (literally,
> "not-knowing,") the person who does claim to know such things is called gnostic
> (knowing). ... As the gnostics use the term, we could translate it as "insight," for *gnosis*
> involves an intuitive process of knowing oneself. And to know oneself, they claimed, is
> to know human nature and human destiny. ... to know oneself, at the deepest level, is
> simultaneously to know God; this is the secret of *gnosis.* (Pagels, 1981, pp. xviii-xix)

Early sects of the Gnostic Christians taught that to know oneself at the deepest level was simultaneously to know God, or the Father, as the source of the divine, spiritual and soul life within oneself. This is evident when one examines the Gospels of the *Nag Hammadi Library*–manuscripts discovered in Egypt in 1945–which provide a rich source of esoteric Christian teachings. In the *Gospel of Truth*, Christ encourages the disciples to gain the light which is within them, instead of living in outer darkness and to *"proclaim the things that are in the heart of the Father in order to teach those who will receive teaching."* Each person must receive *"his (or her) own name"* and hence become one of the *"sons of interior knowledge:"*

> ... you of interior knowledge ... Say, then, from the heart that you are the perfect day
> and in you dwells the light that does not fail. ... They are the ones who appear in truth
> since they exist in true and eternal life and speak of the light which is perfect and filled
> with the seed of the Father, and which is in his heart and in the pleroma, while his Spirit
> rejoices in it and glorifies the one in whom it existed .... (Robinson, 1981, p. 44 & 49)

The roots of the Self are within the heart, the Father and the pleroma. Those "sons of interior knowledge" have realized their spiritual nature and know of the perfect light within the heart and the nature of the pleroma. The term pleroma, like that of the divine plenum, refers to the fullness of things or the infinite potential latent within God. The *Gospel of Thomas* states:

> ... the Kingdom is inside of you, and it is outside of you. When you come to know yourselves, then you will be known, and you will realize that you are the sons of the living Father. But if you will not know yourselves, then you dwell in poverty, and it is you who *are* that poverty. (Pagels, 1981, p. 154)

In this view, humans ordinarily live in a state of dreams, ignorance and illusion. However, a mysterious, secret self-knowledge can be attained which would liberate us from these delusions and the state of waking sleep, thus enlightening us to such *interior knowledge*.

Various maxims of the mystical traditions express this idea that the individual can come to know the objective nature of the universe and the Gods through self-knowledge. A human is said to be made *"in the image of God,"* and *"a microcosm of the macrocosm."* In a standard dictionary, these terms are defined:

microcosm - a little-world; especially man or human nature that is an epitome of the
world or the universe;

macrocosm - the great world: UNIVERSE ... a complex that is a large scale reproduction of
one of its constituents.

In this view, a human in the full sense of this word, embodies the laws and nature of the larger universe: *"As above, so Below."*

What then is mysticism? Is it the supreme adventure and ultimate science of consciousness or the supreme and ultimate pseudo-science? These are most interesting questions for inquiring minds and it is most worthwhile to explore the teachings, ideas, claims and evidences of the mystical traditions and the Gurdjieff work in particular. This is worthwhile from the vantage point of attempting to attain scientific knowledge about the nature of reality and the nature of human consciousness. It is even more worthwhile to the individual in search of self-knowledge and an understanding of life and its illusions.

3. The Fourth Way

At the turn of the century, G. I. Gurdjieff (1872-1949) and a group of individuals, who called themselves the *"seekers after truth,"* attempted to piece together a system of ancient esoteric knowledge about the origins, nature and purpose of life on Earth. As a result of his search, Gurdjieff came into contact with the fourth way, an esoteric teaching which he dates to *pre-Egyptian times*. Gurdjieff once responded to a student's inquiry concerning the origins of the fourth way, by stating that: *"if you like, this is esoteric Christianity."* (1949, p. 102) However, Gurdjieff maintained that Christian forms of worship and teachings were themselves borrowed from earlier pre-Egyptian times: *"... only not from the Egypt that we know but from one which we do not know. This Egypt was in the same place as the other but it existed much earlier. Only small bits of it survived in historical times, and these bits have been preserved in secret and so well that we do not even know where they have been preserved."* (1949, p. 302)[1]

When introducing the *enneagram*, the mystical symbol unique to the fourth way, Gurdjieff claimed that: *"The teaching whose theory is being here set out is completely self-supporting and independent of other lines and it has been completely unknown up to the present time."* (1949) Gurdjieff claimed that the fourth way had appeared and disappeared several times in the course of human history. As its latest emissary, his mission appears to have been that of introducing this extraordinary system of ideas, practices and disciplines to the western world. Although the fourth way contains elements similar to other esoteric traditions, it stands on its own as a unique teaching. As a system of psychological, mystical, metaphysical and cosmological knowledge, it offers an integrative perspective on the nature of humanity, our psychological possibilities and deep relationships to the larger Universe, and of the mysteries of creation. The fourth way is an ancient and lost teaching–of largely unknown origins, although varied hints are given within *The Tales* as to the unknown history of humanity. There are many enigmas and mysteries surrounding Mr. Gurdjieff, and his masterpiece story of *Beelzebub's Tales to His Grandson*.

The teaching is called *the fourth way* in order to distinguish it from the three traditional esoteric paths of self-development: the way of the *fakir*, the way of the *monk* and the way of the *yogi*. The way of the fakir approaches self-transformation through work on one's physical being and can result in the attainment of will with respect to the body. The monk's way is a path of devotion, whereby its adherents develop emotionally by overcoming personal feelings and awakening the higher faculties of faith, love and religious devotion. Finally, the way of the *yogi* emphasizes the transformation of the mind, which leads to discriminative knowledge of the nature of self. According to Mr. Gurdjieff, each of these approaches can lead to the development of higher faculties and states of consciousness. However, because these paths focus on developing one center of intelligence-the body, emotions or mind- each is limited. In contrast, the fourth way is premised on the necessity of developing the body, emotions and minds simultaneously, while awakening consciousness. By doing so, Gurdjieff says, this path is more efficient and can lead to a more complete and coherent realization of the individual's higher faculties of consciousness and being. Furthermore, the fourth way is unlike the other traditional

---

[1] A recent news item reported by The Associated Press announced "Archeologists discover 2,500-year-old lost cities." The report states that archaeologists had found "an intact city" submerged in water only six to nine metres deep, off the northern coast of Egypt. ... The secretary general of the Supreme Council of Antiquities, Egypt's top archaeology body, describes the find as "the most exciting find in the history of marine archaeology." (Ottawa Citizen, 2001)

paths in that those pursuing it do not have to retreat from the world. It is a path for those who, as the Sufis say, remain *"in the world but not of it."*

Georges Ivanovitch Gurdjieff was an extraordinarily complex, enigmatic, charismatic, outrageous and profound human being. He was described in *Time* magazine (1952) as *"a remarkable blend of P.T. Barnum, Rasputin, Freud, Groucho Marx and everybody's grandfather."* On a superficial level, that description captures something of Gurdjieff's unique and colorful presence. However, everything about Gurdjieff's outward appearance and observable behavior was a part that he was playing as a conscious actor. If he was outrageous or eccentric or behaved in ways that shocked others, he did so to assist in transforming the recipient and for purposes of furthering his teaching. Because no one ever really seemed to have come to grips with what Gurdjieff was doing–even those who were closest to him and his most senior pupils–there was always an air of great mystery surrounding this remarkable man. Therefore, while an outline of Gurdjieff's life provides some useful information about his formative experiences and influences, that which remains unknown about him is likely much more significant than that which we do know.

Gurdjieff was born in the 1870's in the city of Alexandropol in the Caucasus region of Asia Minor, since annexed by Russia and now part of Armenia. His father was of Greek origin and his mother Armenian. Growing up in the town of Kars, he was recognized as being an especially precocious youngster. Consequently, his father and the dean of the local Russian military academy paid him special attention, tutoring him in the study of science, medicine and philosophy. As a boy, Gurdjieff witnessed several unusual psychic and paranormal phenomena. However, when he sought explanations for these strange occurrences, the answers that adults offered were clearly lacking in substance. Rather than simply accepting the existence of the unexplained, such experiences whetted Gurdjieff's appetite for knowledge. He questioned the completeness of the scientific theories and set about searching for esoteric or hidden knowledge about human nature and the deeper purposes of life on earth. Gurdjieff describes these youthful influences as forming in him:

> ... an "irrepressible striving" to understand clearly the precise significance, in general, of the life process on earth of all the outward forms of breathing creatures and, in particular, of the aim of human life in the light of this interpretation. (1933, p.13)

Joining forces with other like-minded individuals, *"the seekers after truth,"* Gurdjieff traveled widely for over twenty years throughout the near and far East, living in monasteries and religious communities, and studying various religious and mystical ideas, disciplines and practices. Speeth and Friedlander (1980) describe his travels:

> His search had taken him to the huts of shamans and the lamaseries of Tibetan Rinpoches, to the ruins of Babylon and Crete, to the libraries and mosques and monasteries of Asia, and to the great religious centers of Echmiadzin, Jerusalem and Mecca. Alone or with companions he had hiked, rafted, ridden horseback, sailed on rivers and oceans, taken trains and camel caravans, crisscrossing an area of thousands of square miles to gather, by whatever means, everything that tasted of deep wisdom. (pp. 13-4)

As a result of his quest, Gurdjieff came in contact with the fourth way teaching.
By 1915, Gurdjieff was established in Moscow where he worked with small groups of select students. Foremost amongst these Russian pupils was P. D. Ouspensky (1878-1947), a noted

journalist, mathematician and scholar of esotericism and mysticism. Like Gurdjieff, Ouspensky had traveled through the East in search of ancient knowledge. However, until he met Gurdjieff in Russia, Ouspensky had been frustrated by his failure to find a genuine esoteric teaching or to come under the influence of a true master. Once he began to study with Gurdjieff, Ouspensky became convinced that "G." was a real teacher and that the fourth way embodied a profound ancient knowledge of humankind and the universe.[2]

Although Gurdjieff had planned to establish his work in Moscow and St. Petersburg, the outbreak of the Russian revolution in 1917 forced him to alter his plans. Amidst the chaos wrought by the revolution, he managed to move a small band of students and their families through Russia and the Caucasus to locate first in Tiflis, then Constantinople and Germany, before eventually settling in France. On the outskirts of Paris, at Fontainebleau, Gurdjieff established the *"Institute for the Harmonious Development of Man"* in 1922. Over the next years, he accepted an assorted group of artists, intellectuals, writers, dancers, musicians and adventurers as students at the Institute.

At Fontainebleau, Gurdjieff brought all of his teachings and techniques together as the Institute's program. Students participated in a highly intense and demanding daily round of practical and physical labor, psychological exercises, sacred dances, lectures, methods of self-study and self-observation, music and meditation. The common aim of these types of work was to reveal to the student the patterns of conditioning and the sources of sleep by which he or she was imprisoned. By challenging the pupil to make the effort necessary to break free of these bonds, Gurdjieff attempted to reveal the forces which form *"false personality"* and a *"false consciousness system."* Life at the institute involved numerous *"shocks"* to awaken the sleepwalkers and forms of work and struggle designed to bring about a transformation within those serious individuals drawn to *"The Work."*[3]

While the intellectual and emotional aspects of Gurdjieff's teaching were extraordinary, his work on a physical level was no less remarkable. Although he referred to himself occasionally as being nothing more than a *"teacher of dancing,"* Mr. G. was an acknowledged expert on the sacred dances of the East. The movements comprising such dances are taught in esoteric schools in order to develop control of attention and of the physical body, and to experience heightened states of emotion and levels of awareness. The sacred dances require exacting discipline and effort, and bring about refined states of presence. The performance of such *"sacred gymnastics"* evokes precise feelings and states of consciousness in both the performers and audience. At Gurdjieff's Institute, training in movement and physical awareness was an essential part of the program, and an area in which his unique presence and highly developed level of being was most obvious.

During the 1920's, Mr. Gurdjieff and his students visited America on several occasions to stage demonstrations of the sacred dances and movements. Many of those who attended those extraordinary performances described them as comprising an art of an entirely unique and objective quality. Such testimony and the commentaries of Gurdjieff's pupils, regarding his instructions in posture, movement, breathing and physical work, are evidence of his sophisticated knowledge of the physical body's functioning and possibilities, and of human psychology.

---

[2] In his writings, Ouspensky consistently refers to Gurdjieff as "G." For the sake of variety and brevity, I will sometimes use that abbreviation or "Mr. G.."

[3] Students of the fourth way often use "The Work" as a term to designate the collective undertaking of this esoteric path. Within the teaching, every effort to awaken is said to be made for three purposes–for oneself, for others and for the Work.

After suffering a nearly fatal automobile accident in 1924, Gurdjieff significantly reduced his efforts in directing the Institute's program and turned his attention to writing. For the next seven years, this was the primary focus of his work. The result of his efforts was the highly unusual and thoroughly misunderstood masterpiece *Beelzebub's Tales to His Grandson* (1950). Written in an extremely strange and challenging fashion, the book is truly remarkable. Its setting is extraterrestrial as the story is told from a cosmic perspective, as befits a work of such otherworldly aspirations and dimensions. The central figure and narrator, Beelzebub, is traveling through the cosmos on the spaceship Karnak. To pass the time and to fulfill his *"being obligations"* to his grandson Hassein, Beelzebub takes the opportunity to educate him concerning the laws of the cosmos by recounting his experiences visiting the planet Earth. In particular, Beelzebub portrays the abnormalities of its inhabitants, those strange *"three-brained beings on planet earth."* Beelzebub describes in great detail the peculiarities of the human psyche and the history of their solar system *"Ors."*

The resulting allegorical and epic tale, which Beelzebub relates, provides a most unusual view of the life of humanity and our role within the larger cosmic drama. An indication of just how far it stands apart from popular literature is found in Gurdjieff's statement of the aim of his first series of writing:

> ... to destroy in people everything which, in their false representations, as it were, exists in reality, or in other words "to corrode without mercy all the rubbish accumulated during the ages in human mentation." (1959, p. 1184)

The extent to which Gurdjieff realizes this grandiose aim testifies to how much *Beelzebub's Tales* is unlike any other popular works of fiction or non-fiction. Gurdjieff purposely makes *Beelzebub's Tales* difficult to understand in order to make the reader work consciously at uncovering the meanings. According to Mr. G., contemporary literature has degenerated into *"word prostitution."* People write books unconsciously and mechanically, and people read books mechanically and unconsciously. Hence, rather than presenting his *Tales* in a fluid and easily accessible fashion, which he refers to derisively as the *"bon ton"* literary approach, Gurdjieff adopts a highly unconventional style. By doing so, he disrupts the reader's usual mechanical associations-disorienting and bewildering him—thereby forcing one to consciously work at making sense of what the author is intending to portray.

Those willing and able to make the special effort necessary to decipher *Beelzebub's Tales* are rewarded with one of the most provocative and astonishing commentaries on the human condition ever penned. Gurdjieff's account of humanity's strange history and his analysis of the unique psychopathology which afflicts these *"three-brained beings"* is both merciless and wonderfully insightful. With an objectivity that only an alien intelligence is capable of providing, Beelzebub paints a searing portrait of life on planet Earth. He portrays all those follies and foibles which beset human beings and which keep them throughout the ages in a state of terrifying unconsciousness. Gurdjieff's assault on the three-brained beings' vanity and self-love, presented with great comic effect, is so thoroughly deflating as to leave any intelligent reader with an entirely different feeling about what it means to be called "man," or what Mr. G. calls *"a man in quotation marks."* *Beelzebub's Tales* clearly stands as one of the most unique works of literature, art and social commentary of modern times. It also contains innumerable deep mystical and cosmic truths about Objective Science and the hidden nature of human beings.

After having completed *The Tales* and closing his Institute in 1933, Gurdjieff moved into a small flat in Paris where he lived through the Second World War, continuing his work in a clandestine fashion with French pupils. After the war, students from England and America again sought out Mr. G. in Paris.

Evening festivities at G's flat involved readings from *Beelzebub's Tales* and memorable discussions and feasts supervised in Gurdjieff's highly idiosyncratic and colorful fashion. He continued to receive and teach pupils until his death on October 22 of 1949.

There are numerous accounts describing people's experiences with this most unusual, enigmatic and inspiring figure. These include works by Ouspensky (1949), Nott (1969, 1962), Popoff (1969), Bennett (1978, 1974), Walker (1969, 1965, 1963), Peters (1974, 1964), Butkovsky-Hewitt (1978), Anderson (1962), Welch (1982), Rehner (1980, 1981) and many more. Taken together, these books form a rich tapestry, depicting this remarkable character, his life and work, and his profound impact upon students.

P.D. Ouspensky is generally acknowledged as the most renowned and eloquent spokesman for the fourth way teaching. Before meeting Gurdjieff, he had written extensively on such subjects as consciousness, the mathematics and philosophy of the fourth dimension, religion, psychology, yoga, ancient symbolism, cosmology and esoteric thought. His early writings include: *Tertium Organum: A Key to the Enigmas of the World* (1922), *A New Model of the Universe* (1969) and a novel *The Strange Life of Ivan Osokin* (1947). Ouspensky was uniquely qualified to comprehend Gurdjieff's highly sophisticated and elaborate psychological and cosmological system of ideas.

In his brilliant book, *In Search of the Miraculous: Fragments of an unknown teaching* (1949), Ouspensky recounts his times with Gurdjieff from 1915 to 1921 and provides verbatim accounts of G.'s lectures on the fourth way teaching. Although he ended his contact with Gurdjieff in 1924 for reasons largely unknown, Ouspensky continued to teach the fourth way system–working with groups of students firstly in England and later in America. His books *The Fourth Way* (1957) and *The Psychology of Man's Possible Evolution* (1950) include his commentaries on the teaching, and question and answer sessions with pupils.

Today there are several hundred books devoted to the fourth way teaching and the lives of Gurdjieff and Ouspensky. These include writings by many accomplished students with backgrounds in psychology, psychiatry, medicine and science, which provide varied and interesting perspectives on the fourth way teaching (Nicoll, 1975; Bennett, 1974, Vaysse, 1979; Speeth, 1976; Walker, 1969, 1963; Foster, 1975; King, 1924). Several prominent psychologists, philosophers and scientists have drawn on the fourth way teaching in exploring the nature of consciousness and altered states (Tart, 1987, 1975; Lilly, 1972; Baba Ram Das, 1972; deRopp, 1979, Leary, 1968). Jacob Needleman and G. Baker (1997) have edited a collection of essays and reflections on Gurdjieff and his teachings.

In addition to a rich written legacy produced by those involved with the Work, Gurdjieff's ideas and influences live on in a myriad of other ways. Throughout the western world, there are groups devoted to the fourth way methods of self-study and inner work developed under the influence of Mr. G.'s students and successors. There are discussion groups on the world wide web at chich@valley.net and FourthWaySystem@yahoogroups.com, and numerous Gurdjieff related groups with web sites and shared resources and events. Thomas de Hartmann, a pianist and composer who was one of Gurdjieff's long-time pupils, recorded many of Gurdjieff's original musical compositions which are available on CD, and popular jazz pianist Keith Jarrett recorded a selection of Gurdjieff's music on his album *Sacred Hymns*. A feature film, *Meetings with Remarkable Men* (1980)[4], follows Gurdjieff's book of the same title–recounting the story of his early search for ancient wisdom.

---

[4] At the film's end, there are demonstrations of the sacred dances which Mr. G. taught and which Jeanne de Salzmann, one of his most trusted pupils, supervised for the production.

However, for the most part, the Gurdjieff teaching is largely unknown within the mainstream of western thought, science and culture–including psychology, philosophy, religion and the natural sciences. This is rather peculiar given that the fourth way provides such an enlightening and integrative view on the nature of human beings and their psychological and cosmological possibilities. The present writing aims to explicate the psychological teachings of the fourth way while illustrating their relevance to the questions and issues of modern psychology. From the perspective of the fourth way, the theories of modern psychology and philosophy are indeed incomplete and confused models of the nature of things. At the same time, Gurdjieff's ideas provide a most useful framework for an integrative analysis of western psychology–particularly of the psychology of consciousness.

The fourth way teaching poses a fundamentally different task for those seriously interested in the study of psychology and self knowledge. This study involves not only the acquisition of a new system of thought or knowledge, but more importantly, an effort to work on one's being. The transformation aimed for within esoteric psychology requires two lines of work: on *knowledge* and *being*. Gurdjieff, Ouspensky and their students have left us a rich legacy of ideas and influences for such a task. The fourth way psychology begins with self-study and intentional efforts to pursue the evolutionary development of consciousness.

Gurdjieff provides a remarkable teaching of what it really means to "know self," a coherent psychological framework for self-study and transformation. In *Psychological Illusions*, this analysis and method of self-study will be the focus of our examination, drawing from Ouspensky's presentations and from Gurdjieff's *Beelzebub's Tales*. In asserting that psychology is a science of *a human's possible evolution*, the fourth way is quite unlike the modern discipline known as psychology. Therefore, a certain willingness to entertain strange and unfamiliar ideas is required of anyone intent on giving this presentation serious consideration.

The fourth way system is quite unlike anything with which we are familiar and it is extremely difficult to really *hear* new ideas. In the preface to *The Psychology of Man's Possible Evolution*, Ouspensky (1950) comments:

> I found that the chief difficulty for most people was to realize that they had really heard *new* things; that is, things that they had never heard before.

> They did not formulate it for themselves, but in fact they always tried to contradict this in their minds and translate what they heard into their habitual language, whatever it happened to be. And this certainly I could not take into account.

> I know that it is not an easy thing to realize that one is hearing *new things*. We are so accustomed to the old tunes, and the old motives, that long ago we ceased to hope and ceased to believe that there might be anything new.

> And when we hear new things, we take them for old, or think that they can be explained and interpreted by the old. It is true that it is a difficult task to realize the possibility and necessity of quite new ideas, and it needs with time a reevaluation of all usual values.

> I cannot guarantee that you will hear new ideas, that is, ideas you never heard before, from the start; but if you are patient you will very soon begin to notice them. And then I wish you not to miss them, and to try not to interpret them in the old way. (pp. xii-xiii)

Certainly, Mr. G. was very aware of the difficulties involved in hearing new ideas. In his book, *In Search Of the Miraculous*, Ouspensky describes how Gurdjieff would offer his pupils the beginnings of ideas and would only provide further elaboration when pupils demonstrated that they had made an active effort to practice and understand what had been explained. To regard these ideas as common fare or to take them in the usual mechanical way is useless. There is nothing familiar or easy in learning esoteric teachings, nor can there be.

Esoteric truths cannot be transmitted whole, here and now. Because people are asleep and under the spell of illusion, they are divided beings who are limited in their capacity to know. Consequently, all knowledge, that these sleepwalkers possess, is fragmented and incomplete. Moreover, it will remain so until there is an awakening of consciousness and the transformation of the individual's being. The evolution of consciousness has to be pursued through the simultaneous work on both *knowledge* and *being*. Only through this metamorphosis can a human being emerge transformed with eyes to see and ears to hear.

Ouspensky described the *devil's mechanics*, which illustrates the notion that *"nothing is done all at once,"* but only little by little:

> Evidently you have no idea what kind of devil's mechanics this is. The whole trick is, that nothing is done all at once; everything is done little by little. ... You never even notice it yourself until everything turns out as it had to turn out. From a distance you can see everything, but when you come close to things you no longer see the whole, you see only separate parts, little details that mean nothing. (1947, p.109)

It is easy to get lost in all the details and never glimpse the larger whole. Understanding the fourth way psychology and its mystical truths is certainly not going to be done all at once. Instead, it has to be done little by little as we attempt to develop along the lines of knowledge and being. Certainly, one is not about to awaken all at once. In that spirit, it is useful to remember that as the saying goes, *"from small acorns, great oak trees grow."*

So to all those "nuts" who would dare to be great oaks, I invite you to attempt to hear new ideas. Gurdjieff's teaching provides a model of human possibilities and human consciousness which is a profound alternative to modern psychology's assumptions and theories. An esoteric perspective reveals that modern thought is rife with delusions, illusions and fundamental errors about what humans are and what they are capable of becoming. At the same time, the fourth way provides a systematic teaching which guides the individual in efforts to escape from the rule of sleep and the mechanical and unconscious state of humanity.

4. The Psychopathological and Sleepwalking State of Humanity

"If a man could understand all the horror of the lives of ordinary people who are turning round in a circle of insignificant interests and insignificant aims, if he could understand what they are losing, he would understand that there can be only one thing that is serious for him–to escape from the general law, to be free. What can be serious for a man in prison who is condemned to death? Only one thing: How to save himself, how to escape: nothing else is serious." (Gurdjieff, in O., 1949, p.364)

An ancient theme of mystical and esoteric teachings is that human beings live under a spell of illusions about themselves and the nature of reality. In the fourth century B.C., Plato depicted humans as prisoners in a cave, chained with their backs to the light and mistakenly believing that the shadows on the wall before them were real. The prisoners live in a state of ignorance and unable to see that these shadows are projections of an unknown source of light behind them. Hypnotized by the play of shadows, they live in darkness and never suspect that there are more fundamental levels of reality. Thus, Plato describes humans as taking the shadows to be truth and as incapable of looking into the true light of existence, even if forced to gaze into the "presence of the sun." To see the light–to awaken–one must *"grow accustomed to the sight of the upper worlds."* (Republic, VII) Plato's analogy of life in the cave is a classic portrayal of humanity's sleepwalking and pathological state. In reality, the masses of humanity are Plato's cave-dwellers. Like marionettes and puppets, people are controlled by invisible strings and the mechanisms by which life's forces act upon us. It is only with great difficulty and struggle that an individual might turn around to see the light and realize the nature of reality.

In the Gnostic *Gospel of Truth*, the nightmare parable provides another harrowing description of humankind's so-called normal waking state:

Thus they were ignorant of the Father, he being the one whom they did not see. Since it was terror and disturbance and instability and doubt and division, there were many illusions at work by means of these, and there were empty fictions, as if they were sunk in sleep and found themselves in disturbing dreams. Either (there is) a place to which they are fleeing, or without strength, they come from having chased after others, or they are involved in striking blows, or they are receiving blows themselves, or they have fallen from high places, or they take off into the air though they do not even have wings. ... When those who are going through all these things wake up, they see nothing, they who were in the midst of all these disturbances, for they are nothing. Such is the way of those who have cast ignorance aside from them like sleep ... they leave them behind like a dream in the night ... . And this is the way he has come to knowledge, as if he had awakened. (Robinson, ed., 1981, p.43)

The *Gnostic Gospels* elaborate the same mystical theme: that humans live in darkness and confusion and that to escape from this spell of illusion, they must wake up, know the Father and recognize the light. People are depicted as *"having no root"* in themselves and as experiencing *"terror and confusion, instability, doubt and division."* This view of the fragmented and fearful state of humanity is quite horrifying. Insecurities, worries, negative emotions and false personality dominate ordinary states of awareness. Further, people do not realize their state, how limited their consciousness is, or how fragmented they are in their being. Humans are lost souls preoccupied by the play of shadows and lived out in states of illusion.

Gurdjieff provides a detailed and sophisticated account of the nature and significance of a human's psychological illusions. While describing normal consciousness as a *"waking sleep,"* he argues that humans do not know themselves or understand the nature of their own consciousness and being. In the waking sleep state, we attribute to ourselves the properties of consciousness, unity of "I," will (or the capacity "to do") and freedom—all of which are illusory. Instead, humans are sleepwalkers in a sleeping world: automatons to whom *"everything happens"* and who are unable to *"do"* anything. Humans do not realize that they exist in a state of semi-sleep, nor do they understand how their low level of consciousness blinds them to the realities of existence. The possibility of freeing oneself from this nightmare requires overcoming one's psychological illusions. Further, in order to overcome these illusions, we must study consciousness within ourselves.

Replying to Ouspensky's protest that scientists, philosophers and psychologists regard consciousness as being indefinable, Gurdjieff dismisses that view as being *"rubbish—the usual scientific sophistry."* He explains that we can only know consciousness in ourselves when and if we have it. Unfortunately, we do not have it very often and when we do, we do not have much of it. Consequently, we do not understand what consciousness is, or how it might be developed or expanded. However, by studying consciousness within ourselves, we can begin to define moments when we are nearer to consciousness and times when we are further from consciousness. This process of self-observation reveals that moments of consciousness are short and are separated by long intervals of unconscious, mechanical working of the machine. People can think, act, speak, work, without being conscious of themselves. In fact, this is usually the case and why Gurdjieff describes the normal waking state as a *"waking sleep"* and a *"relative consciousness."*

Human's primary mistake in thinking about consciousness is to assume that it is always present or that it is never present. In reality, consciousness is continually changing. There are different degrees and levels of consciousness, which can only be understood in oneself by sensation, by taste and inner experience. This is precisely why scientists, philosophers and psychologists fail in their attempts to understand consciousness. They try to define it where it does not exist, equating consciousness with their normal waking state. However, in order to study consciousness properly, we must distinguish consciousness from the possibility of consciousness and intentionally cultivate more developed states. Gurdjieff notes: *"We have only the possibility of consciousness and rare flashes of it. Therefore we cannot define what consciousness is."* (1949, p. 117) It is impossible to define consciousness without grounding that aim in the process of self-observation and systematic self study.

From a fourth way perspective, consciousness is a much more variable and dynamic property than is typically acknowledged. Human awareness is usually embedded and absorbed in the shifting complexes of conditioned thoughts, feelings and actions, which go on in the various minds or parts of a human being. Within these states of absorption and minding activity, there is no "I" present to intentionally act, think and feel. Instead, everything happens mechanically and automatically in terms of conditioning and habits, associative thinking and external influences. In a very real sense, "I" does not exist in most human experience.

"False personality" normally dominates awareness, while what should be the true consciousness, based on the growth of the essence and real "I," passes into the subconscious. As strange and bewildering as these claims may be, it is possible to verify these facts in a concrete and practical way if one systematically observes oneself in day to day, moment to moment activities, over time.

Gurdjieff's practice of "self-remembering" involves making a conscious effort to remember to observe oneself and be more fully aware of one's presence in the here and now. A person can potentially self-remember anywhere at any time in any possible mood or state, activity or situation. Self-remembering is an effort to wake up and be more fully conscious for moments throughout day to day life. The conscious effort put into the practice of self-remembering demonstrates how normally we are not self-aware. Instead, we are continually absorbed in habits of thought, feelings and moods, desires, sensation and action. Indeed, the difficulties that a person encounters in even remembering to practice self-remembering prove beyond doubt the extent of one's unconsciousness.

The idea within the fourth way is that through the practices of self-observation and self-remembering, a person can approach the next state of *"self consciousness"*–a distinct state and experience which is superior to the so-called normal state of *"relative consciousness."* This distinction is critical in understanding the personal and scientific illusions about the nature of consciousness. People have the illusion that they are properly conscious and that they already know the state of self-consciousness. By practicing self-remembering, an individual gains a much deeper and significant appreciation of how the degrees and states of consciousness can vary. We can begin to experience a state of consciousness in which one is more present with a distinct and vivid sense that *"I am here."* The pupil aims to cultivate this state of "self-consciousness" through the practices of self-observation and self-remembering. Of course, this is a gradual process. Unfortunately, people live under the illusion that they are properly conscious, and even that they are normally "self conscious" or could be at will. Just ask anyone on the street, or ask modern thinkers–scientists, psychologists, and philosophers–and they will tell you that humans are self-conscious beings and that it is this property which distinguishes them from other animals.

Another of humans' cherished psychological illusion is the belief that we are unified beings, who know real "I." In reality, a person is fragmented into many little i's, all partial aspects of themselves conditioned to respond to internal and external stimuli. Gurdjieff characterizes the disunity and fragmentation of a human's common sleepwalking state:

"One of man's most important mistakes ... one which must be remembered, is his illusion in regards to his I. ... *Man has no permanent and unchanging I.* Every thought, every mood, every desire, every sensation, says "I." And in each case it seems to be taken for granted that this I belongs to the Whole. In actual fact there is no foundation whatever for this assumption. Man's every thought and desire appears and lives quite separately and independently of the Whole. And the Whole never expresses itself.... Man has no individual I. But there are, instead, hundreds and thousands of separate small I's, very often entirely unknown to one another, never coming into contact, or, on the contrary, hostile to each other, mutually exclusive and incompatible. Each minute, each moment, man is saying or thinking "I." And each time his I is different. ... Man is a plurality. Man's name is legion. (1949, pp. 59)

Gurdjieff paints a devastating portrait of the human condition. Humans are sleepwalkers imprisoned in a sleeping world. Fortunately, he also asserts that it is possible for people to awaken and escape this state. By developing a state of self-consciousness, an individual can acquire those capacities which naturally belong to that level of being—including consciousness, unity (in the form of a real and permanent I) and will (or the capacity to do). Unfortunately, for most people, these aims are meaningless as they believe that they are already self-conscious, unified beings, who possess will or the capacity to do. They already have enough to do, with all of life's problems and woes, without undertaking some fanciful mystical quest to know self. Hence, the masses of humanity are content to lose themselves in circles of insignificant interests and insignificant aims, which Mr. G. describes as comprising the "*horror of the lives of ordinary people.*"

By observing and remembering oneself, the seeker after truth begins to awaken to the reality of their current state of sleep and illusion, illuminating those inner processes which have functioned in darkness. Esoteric self-study comprises a process of "inner alchemy" whereby the light of consciousness transforms the essential nature of one's being. Gurdjieff explains: "*Even a feeble light of consciousness is enough to change completely the character of a process, while it makes many of them altogether impossible. Our inner psychic processes (our inner alchemy) have much in common with those chemical processes in which light changes the character of the process and they are subject to analogous laws.*" (1949, p. 146)

The only hope of escaping the ignorance and darkness of the sleeping world lies in the persistent effort to cultivate self-awareness and the light of consciousness. According to all mystical and esoteric teachings, *consciousness is light*. It is only in the light of consciousness, that humans can realize their ordinary condition of sleep, darkness and ignorance. Maurice Nicoll, one of Gurdjieff's pupils, explains:

> ...what we seek above all things is *Light*–and Light means *consciousness*. We seek to live more consciously and to become more conscious. We live in darkness owing to lack of light–the light of consciousness–and we seek in this work light on ourselves. ... And it is a very strange thing this *light*. It is first to become more conscious of oneself and then more conscious of others. This is a strange experience. I mean by this that the direction in which the work leads you through increasing consciousness, increasing light, is not at all the direction you might imagine as a person asleep, a person who knows only ordinary consciousness... . To become conscious of yourself is a strange experience. To become conscious of others is just as strange and even more strange. The life you yourself lead with passions and jealousies, meanness, dislikes and hatreds, becomes utterly ridiculous. You wonder, in fact, what on earth you have been doing all your life. Have you been insane? you ask yourself. Yes, exactly. In the deep sleep we live in, in the light of the Kingdom of Heaven, we are all utterly insane and do not know what we are doing. (1975, pp. 35-6)

As Nicoll states, the process of becoming conscious is very strange– not at all what was expected as a person asleep.

These are shocking descriptions of the waking sleep condition, which must be *witnessed* within oneself through self-study, self-remembering and the struggle to awaken. Consciousness can be brought to bear within the inner world to dissolve the habitual and sleepwalking state of the nightmare parable. Further, a human being's psychological illusions–their false ideas about themselves and the nature of life—are a first obstacle to awakening. In order to become conscious, a person must realize in a practical way how infrequently and little he or she is conscious and what powerful forces govern the sleepwalking state. Ouspensky explains:

> When we realize that we are asleep we will see that all history is made by people who are asleep. Sleeping people fight, make laws; sleeping people obey or disobey them. The worst of our illusions are the wrong ideas among which we live and which govern our lives. If we could change our attitude towards these wrong ideas and understand what they are, this in itself would be a great change and would immediately change other things. (1950, p. 29)

We do not know real "I" or "Self." This is the fallen state of humanity, those strange three-centered beings on planet earth. In reality, all common knowledge is incomplete but especially people's self knowledge. The process of awakening entails the dissolution of the false personality which obscures the *essence* of our being. As a rich man cannot enter into the Kingdom of Heaven, so also, the individual conditioned by and attached to false ego, cannot enter into the light kingdom and know true existence.

The message of the mystics and spiritual teachers about the sleepwalking and psychopathological state of humanity is most shocking, as are their claims about the hidden and subtle dimensionality of life. Humanity lives in ignorance of the miraculous possibilities inherent within the subtle dimensions of consciousness and being. Consequently, the only aim for a serious man or woman is to awaken and to realize *"I AM"*—to know self and to experience the unifying light of consciousness. This is the way to escape from the underground den and the state of the nightmare parable.

The assumption that normal waking consciousness consists of a single, unified, continuous state is fundamentally mistaken. The study of psychology requires the study of consciousness within oneself through an effort to remember oneself—to remember to be more fully conscious and awake in this moment. The practice of self-remembering introduces the possibility for a transformation in consciousness and of the "I" experience. P. D. Ouspensky explains that we cannot understand supernormal psychology because we do not know enough about ordinary psychology, and self remembering is a method to learn about both.

Mysticism cannot be approached simply on an intellectual basis—but rather requires a transformation of the individual and the awakening of consciousness. This is a basic teaching of the fourth way. These simple ideas are profoundly difficult to understand and are largely hidden in ordinary life. Ouspensky explains that modern thought has completely missed the significance of the extraordinary practice of self-remembering:

> So, at the same time as self-observing, we try to be aware of ourselves by holding the sensation of "I am here"—nothing more. And this is the fact that all Western psychology, without the smallest exception, has missed. Although many people came very near to it, they did not recognize the importance of this fact and did not realize that the state of man as he is can be changed—that man can remember himself, if he tries for a long time. (1957, p. 5)

Western scientists have approached the study of consciousness from a neurological perspective, a biological, philosophical, cultural and experimental perspective. Unfortunately, they have neglected the most obvious and important approach to studying consciousness—through self-study and intentional efforts to awake and to be self-aware! We can only know consciousness within ourselves, and then, only when we have it. Ouspensky argues: "*... psychology begins at this point. ... man does not remember himself but could remember himself if he made sufficient efforts. Without self-remembering there can be no study, no psychology.*" (1957, p. 120) The most destructive illusion in modern science and society is the belief that consciousness can be understood outside of oneself, without self study, self-remembering and a struggle towards awakening.

The mystical quest is to awaken and attain real "I." This entails the emergence of a hidden order of "I," the basis for the mystical declaration that "I AM." As Gurdjieff explains in his final book title, *Life is Real only then, when 'I AM.'*

5. Beelzebub's Tales to His Grandson:

5a. **A New Language**

It is ample testimony to the sleepwalking state of humanity that Gurdjieff's masterpiece story is so largely unknown to modern literary, philosophical and scientific circles. It also testifies to the difficult and otherworldly nature of the *Tales*, that so few interpretive works are available. As an allegorical exposition of an esoteric teaching, *Beelzebub's Tales* contain deep meanings, which are not immediately obvious to the reader, but rather are hidden and encrypted in a unique syntax of language, symbols, myths, tales and sly humour. In its mode of presentation, vision and substance, *Beelzebub's Tales* reveal Gurdjieff to have been a highly enigmatic man of some unusual stature. The *Tales* live up to G.'s stated objective in his writings: *"To destroy, mercilessly ... the beliefs and views, by centuries rooted in him, about everything existing in the world."* Gurdjieff exposes what he labels *"all the rubbish accumulated in human mentation,"* and offers a profoundly alternative cosmic view of the strangeness of the human psyche, the nature of reality and higher faculties of the human soul.

In *Beelzebub's Tales*, Gurdjieff introduces a new language, markedly different from that used in his earlier talks as recorded by Ouspensky and other students. He talks of the Most, Most, Holy Sun Absolute, His Endlessness, the Common Father, Mother Nature and introduces other Angels, Archangels, Sacred Messengers and cosmic characters. There are the Autoegocratic and the Trogoautoegocratic systems, the Sacred Fundamental Cosmic Laws of Triamazikamno and Heptaparaparshinokh, the Foolasnitamnian and Itoklanos principles, and numerous other eccentric and otherworldly terms are used to depict both mundane objects and phenomena and seeming obscure cosmic processes. New twists and turns are provided in Gurdjieff's explanations of the sacred cosmic laws, the issues of origins, the "being foods" and obscure substances —such as Exioehary, Askokin vibrations, the Etherokrilno and the Omnipresent Okidanokh—and descriptions of the various Cosmoses and microcosmoses. Beelzebub reveals secrets about the nature of the higher being-bodies, how these can be coated for the soul and what a soul might attain. He even elaborates on how a human embodies the universe, as a microcosm of the macrocosm, and how it all came about—in the beginning.

With time, patience and effort, the reader begins to learn a new language with very ancient roots and meanings. In fact, Gurdjieff's masterpiece tale can be read many times and always reveals new things full of significance. The reading and study of *The Tales* in fact can serve for individual enlightenment and realization, as a result of impartial mentation and an objective view of the life of those who Beelzebub refers to as *"your favorites,"* those three-brained beings on planet Earth.

5b. About the Strange Psyche of the Three-Brained Beings on Planet Earth

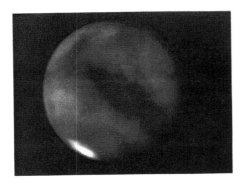

In *Beelzebub's Tales*, Gurdjieff elaborates a highly unusual and provocative story, myth, allegory or tale, about the history of humankind and the *"strange psyches of the three brained-beings breeding on planet Earth."* The story opens in the year 1921 by human calculation, or according to "objective time-calculation," the year 223 after the creation of the World. Beelzebub, his grandson Hassein and other kinsmen and attendants, are travelling through the cosmos on the spaceship *Karnak.* Beelzebub is going to attend a conference being held within the solar system of the Pole Star, after being banished to our solar system for many years. During the course of their travels, Beelzebub takes the opportunity to participate in the education of his grandson Hassein. He elaborates upon the history of the solar system *Ors,* the misfortune which occurred on Earth and how the strangeness of the three brained-beings there came about. All of this is done, as Beelzebub recounts six visits that he made to the earth after being exiled to our solar system. During this time, Beelzebub had set up a telescope and living quarters on Mars. Like a character from another dimension of time, Beelzebub dropped in on the Earth at various periods in human history to study the strange psyche of those *"three brained beings"* and to witness events which were transpiring there. These six visits begin at the time of Atlantis, carry through the times of Ancient Egypt and Babylon, and end in the early twentieth century in Europe, Russia and America. Beelzebub describes the role of various Sacred Individuals and Secret Brotherhoods in the history of humankind, who tried to awaken humankind and to pass on an understanding of Objective Science. The *Tales* include esoteric descriptions of the fundamental cosmic laws, the laws of world-creation and world-maintenance, as well as description of creation processes, the nature of the ethers and the like—all interspersed with the narration.

According to Beelzebub's tales, the cosmic harmony of the solar system "Ors" was disrupted in early history by a cosmic catastrophe. A comet collided with the earth and broke off two fragments which became the moon and a secondary satellite, Anulios, unknown to modern science. This catastrophe threatened to disrupt the broader Cosmic Harmony, until the moons were stabilized in their new orbits. This required that a certain *"sacred vibration," "askokin,"* be produced by the Earth to feed and maintain the moons. Such energies are produced by organic life on earth and by the existence of humankind, the Tetartocosmoses. Beelzebub states *"... by their existence they ... maintain the detached fragments of their planet."* Humanity can and does feed the moon!

Unfortunately, a second unforeseen cosmic misfortune occurred after certain archangels on a Most Holy Commission implanted a special organ called the *Kundabuffer* in humankind at the base of the spine. The purpose of this intervention was to prevent humans from becoming aware of their enslavement to the moon and hence rebelling in order to escape. The properties of this special organ, as described by Beelzebub, are most peculiar in its effects upon humankind. The Kundabuffer causes humans firstly, to *"perceive reality topsy-turvy,"* and secondly, to be conditioned by *"sensations of 'pleasure' and 'enjoyment.'"*

Gurdjieff describes this *"topsy-turvy"* process as taking the *"ephemeral for the real,"* as contemporary three-brained beings have *"mechanized themselves to see nothing real."* One aspect of this peculiarity of the human psyche is the tendency to *"depend exclusively only upon what others say about any) given question"*—that is, the qualities of suggestibility and gullibility. The three-brained beings' knowledge of reality is no longer based upon their own being-experience or the fulfilling of their being obligations, which are called the *"being-Partkdolg-duty,"* nor is it based upon their own *"active deliberations,"* or upon the *"instinctual sensing of reality."* Instead, Beelzebub describes people as ready to believe any old tale, simply recording what is heard, or what one is told or reads, with the formatory mind.[5] People then imagine that they understand themselves and all those things about which they talk and profess. Gurdjieff refers distastefully to *"the scientists of new formation"* and the *"disease of lying."* The three-brained beings breeding on planet earth no longer *"instinctually sense reality"* but came to perceive reality *"topsy-turvy."*

The second major effect of the organ Kundabuffer is also quite odd, as Beelzebub explains, *"that every repeated impression from outside should crystallize in them data which would engender factors for evoking in them sensations of 'pleasure' and 'enjoyment.'"* (p. 88) Thus, the Kundabuffer causes humankind to become conditioned by sense pleasure and enjoyment. Beelzebub consistently describes the laziness of human beings, their self indulgence in imaginary concerns, their vanity and egoism. He further portrays humans as continually misuse their energies, particularly the sexual substances, *"only for the satisfaction of the said impulse"* —of pleasure. Humans do not understand the role that these sacred sexual substances play in the psychology of their possible evolution and the coating of the higher being-bodies.

The Kundabuffer organ was eventually removed from human beings—again by a higher Commission— when the stability of the moons was no longer a threat to the larger cosmic harmony. However, the effects of the Kundabuffer on the human psyche had become crystallized in humans' presences and maintained by the abnormal conditions of being-existence which had become established on Earth. The properties of the Kundabuffer thus passed from generation to generation even in the absence of the organ itself. In various stories to his grandson, Beelzebub provides humorous insights into the peculiarities and deficiencies of the strange human psyches, all explained in reference to this background of cosmic occurrences.

Over time, the strangeness of the human psyches increased and according to Beelzebub, *"the quality of their radiations went steadily from bad to worse."* (p. 106) Great Nature increased the numbers of the three-brained beings on planet earth in order to accommodate the degeneration of the human psyche but other strange phenomena were produced; such as a decreasing age expectancy, from over a thousand years to under a hundred; animal sacrifice and slaughter; and the worst "horror of the situation"—human warfare. These pathological symptoms of the human psyche continue to disrupt the larger cosmic harmony. Beelzebub's tales describe various Sacred Individuals who visited the earth trying to bring sanity back to those disturbed three-brained beings breeding there, mainly through the awakening of various *sacred being-impulses*, especially conscience and the remorse of conscience.

Beelzebub's tales are rich in surreal humour and portray most vividly the horror of the situation and the strangeness of the human psyche evident on that ill-fated planet Earth. Serious undesirable qualities have became crystallized in humans, who are no longer capable of sincere and active mentation but are controlled by the reflexes of the stomach, material interests, sexual itching, self calming and self-love. As Gurdjieff suggests, the only serious thing for a "slug," would be to awaken and overcome the strangeness of their psyche.

---

[5] The formatory apparatus is described by Ouspensky as the mechanical portion of the intellectual center, which simply tape-records or memorizes what is put into it. This is the lowest form of intellectual activity.

5c. **Similitudes of the Whole**

According to Beelzebub, the three-brained beings on planet Earth are microcosmoses, or *"similitudes of the Whole."* As such, they have the possibility of not only serving local cosmic purposes, feeding the earth and moon as part of organic life on earth, but also of attaining various levels of Objective Reason and individuality, and even of *"blending again with the infinite."* (p. 945) As a microcosm of the macrocosm, a human being can potentially coat higher being-bodies for the life of the soul, instinctually sense cosmic truths and phenomena, and maintain his or her existence within the subtle realms of being after death while achieving different levels of immortality. Unfortunately, humans came to perceive reality *topsy-turvy*, to be conditioned by pleasure and self love, and to squander their sacred sexual substances. They no longer remember or realize their deeper cosmic purposes, duties and possibilities.

Gurdjieff describes two principles by which a human can live and die—giving them the unlikely, invented names of *Foolasnitamnian* and *Itoklanos*. In the eccentric and seemingly bizarre language of Beelzebub, the first principle Foolasnitamnian is proper to the existence of all three-brained beings arising on any other planet of the Universe. According to this principle, three-brained beings *" have all possibilities ... for the perfecting in them of both higher-being-bodies."* (p.775) In addition to serving Cosmic purposes, an individual can coat or crystallize higher being-bodies which allow for the continued evolution of the soul.

However, because of a series of cosmic catastrophes, these strange three brained beings formed in ways quite *unbecoming* for such beings:

> "... they began to exist already excessively abnormally, that is to say, quite
> unbecomingly for three-brained beings, and when in consequence of this they had on
> the one hand ceased to emanate the vibrations required by Nature for the maintenance
> of the separated fragments of their planet, and, on the other hand, had begun, owing to
> the chief peculiarity of their strange psyche, to destroy beings of ... their planet ... then
> Nature Herself was compelled gradually to actualize the presences of these three-
> brained beings, according to the second principle, namely the principle "Itoklanoz",
> that is, to actualize them in the same way in which She actualizes one-brained and
> two-brained beings .... (p. 131)

> ... there are transmuted through them the cosmic substances required not for purposes
> of a common-cosmic character, but only for that solar system or even only for that
> planet alone, in which and upon which these one-brained and two-brained beings
> arise. (p. 130)

Beelzebub's Tales describes how human beings became so abnormal in their functioning. They no longer have normal sensations of cosmic phenomena; they are oblivious of the need to fulfill their sacred being-obligations and duties; and their true consciousness is in the subconscious, while a false consciousness system became crystallized in their presences. The terror of the situation is that people *"die like dogs"* according to the Itoklanoz principle and only serve Nature's purposes by becoming nothing more than fertilizer. Beelzebub explains that the majority of contemporary beings *"remain with presences consisting of the planetary body alone, and thus are, for themselves, destroyed forever."* According to Gurdjieff, being a real human is only a possibility—which is generally unrealized. Living in sleep and ignorance, people serve only the purposes of Mother Nature and become fertilizer—that is, food for the earth and moon. However, self knowledge and the struggle to awaken can enable a three-brained being to serve higher and sacred purposes, even to attain real "I" and become *"immortal within the limits of the solar system."* All of these possibilities depend on the chemistry and alchemy of the soul. Although Common Mother Nature provides for the possibility for attaining the soul, this is not guaranteed. It depends upon the individual's conscious efforts to awaken and to fulfill their being obligations and duties. Gurdjieff provides a remarkable teaching for the awakening of humanity–but a dismal view of human psychopathology.

Beelzebub explains to his grandson Hassein that the phrase *"We are the images of God,"* is *"one of the only 'cosmic truths'"* expressed by the three brained beings on planet earth, although they have no understanding of what it truly means. Then, in his humorous and insightful manner, Beelzebub elaborates upon how those *"unfortunates,"* humankind on earth, have taken this deep truth:

> "'Good ... if we are "images of God" ... that means ... means ... "God" is like us and has an appearance also like us ... and that means, our "God" has the same moustache, beard, nose, as we have, and he dresses also as we do. ... almost with a comb sticking out of his left vest pocket ...

> "... those 'learned' beings ... assembled in the city of Babylon ... began to invent various maleficent fictions concerning their 'God,' which were afterward by chance widely spread everywhere on that ill-fated planet. ... it was said ... that that famous 'God' of theirs had, as it were, the appearance of a very old man, just with a heavy beard." (pp. 776-7)

In order to understand how a three brained being embodies the whole of the "Megalocosmos," we will have to consider the creation processes elaborated by Beelzebub, the fundamental principles of world-creation and world-maintenance, and assorted esoteric teachings elaborated throughout the epic *Tales*.

Beelzebub refers to three-brained beings as potentially *"a particle of all that exists."* (p. 163) On another occasion, Beelzebub talks of his efforts to fulfill his being obligations and duties in order to be worthy of *"becoming a particle though an independent one, of everything existing in the Great Universe."* (p. 183) Elsewhere, he describes humans, *"as beings having in their presences every possibility for becoming particles of a part of Divinity ...."* (p. 453)

A soul is not given to a human being but must be acquired. Unfortunately, the cosmic catastrophes which occurred to the earth and the miscalculations regarding the organ Kundabuffer, led to the emergence of a strange breed on that planet. According to Beelzebub, they are willing to believe any old tale and have innumerable other unnatural traits and characteristics formed in their presences. Humans are lulled into sleep, convinced they are eagles and magicians, and that they will never be turned to fertilizer. Humans miss the mark and do not establish their own inner triangle or sevenfold nature, thus completing the inner cosmic octave in order to blend again with the Most Holy Sun Absolute.

Human beings are potentially similitudes of the whole–particles of the Great Universe–with deep hidden roots within vaster dimensions of being and non-being. Behind essence is real I, behind real I, is God, or at least the Most Holy Sun Absolute. Beelzebub's tales to his grandson, Hassein, provide strange and highly provocative insights into the nature of the most peculiar three-brained beings of the planet Earth.

"... the first answer to the question, what is psychology, should be that psychology is the study of the principles, laws, and facts of man's possible evolution."

P. Ouspensky

II /
The Fourth Way
Definitions of psychology

1. The Two Psychologies

In *The Psychology of Being Human*, McNeil and Rubin provide a brief historic overview of developments in modern psychology:

> The term psychology was apparently first used around 1530 by a German scholar Phillip Melanchthon, as a title for some lectures. Its original meaning–from the Greek psyche (or soul) and logos (or study)–was "the study of the soul." Later psyche became translated as "mind" rather than "soul," and in this century, psychology was redefined as the "science of behavior." (1977, p. 4)

Modern psychologists dismiss the idea that human beings have a soul, or some type of spiritual or divine nature. Instead, humans are viewed as simply being biological organisms which have evolved from lower animal forms through physical processes. Their existence is defined in terms of the life and death of the physical body, and neurological processes within the brain are assumed to produce consciousness.

In keeping with this materialist perspective, behaviorism–a theoretical position which focuses exclusively on the study of "external behavior"–has dominated the history of modern psychology. While behaviorism's influence was at its height from the 1920's to the early 1970's, psychologists gradually concluded that the behaviorist definition of the psychology was too restrictive. After some forty years of attempting to deny the relevance of the concepts of *mind* and *consciousness* to the scientific approach, psychologists acknowledged that these terms needed to be readmitted to their discipline! Psychology was then redefined as the science of both observable behavior and the processes of the mind. At the turn of the millennium, psychology is still most frequently defined as *"the science of behavior and mind."*

Ouspensky's (1957, 1950, 1949) elaborations of the fourth way teaching provide an unusual series of *definitions of psychology*, which contrast dramatically with those of modern psychology. Ouspensky began his introductory lectures to the fourth way psychology with these comments:

> I shall speak about the study of psychology, but I must warn you that the psychology about which I speak is very different from anything you may know under this name.
>
> To begin with I must say that practically never in history has psychology stood at so low a level as at the present time. It has lost all touch with its *origin* and its *meaning* so that now it is even difficult to define the term "psychology": that is, to say what psychology is and what it studies. And this is so in spite of the fact that never in history have there been so many psychological theories and so many psychological writings.
>
> Psychology is sometimes called a new science. This is quite wrong. Psychology is, perhaps, the *oldest science*, and, unfortunately, in its most essential features a *forgotten science*. (1950, p. 3)

From a fourth way perspective, modern psychology has lost touch with its origins and is as confused as ever–despite the multiplicity of ideas and theories. For Ouspensky, psychology is an ancient science, although this is not recognized because it has appeared in such diverse forms and under various guises throughout history. Psychology is connected to such things as the ancient religious and mystical traditions of India, the teachings of yoga, Sufism, early Christianity, the schools of the Mysteries in Egypt and Greece, and such subjects as *"astrology, alchemy, magic, and modern Masonry, occultism and Theosophy."* (1950, pp. 5-6)

Ouspensky is talking about a very different tradition of psychology than that within the mainstream of modern academic and clinical psychology. The modern discipline would be described by Gurdjieff, speaking through the persona of his creation–Beelzebub, as simply being the *"wiseacrings"* or *"rubbish"* of the *"scientists of new formation."*

What is this other tradition of psychology and how does it compare with modern thought and science? In P. D. Ouspensky's (1957, 1950, 1949) presentations of the fourth way teaching, he identifies a series of eight *definitions of psychology*. These definitions challenge the modern understanding of psychology and restore its deeper, original meaning–as *the science of soul*. However, the definition of soul, offered within the fourth way itself, is highly unusual and complex, and takes its meaning in terms of the mystical quest to know self. Whereas humans typically think that they either do or do not have a soul, Gurdjieff explains that a human must, in a sense, *"acquire a soul."*

2. The Psychology of
A Human's Possible Evolution

Ouspensky explains that historically there has been two very different forms and definitions of psychology. Firstly, there are those systems which *"study man as they find him, or such as they suppose or imagine him to be."* Ouspensky notes that: *"Modern "scientific" psychology, or what is known under that name, belongs to this category."* Secondly, there are those systems which *"study man not from the point of view of what he is, or what he seems to be, but from the point of view of what he may become; that is, from the point of view of his possible evolution."* For Ouspensky, these latter systems are the original psychologies and only they explain the forgotten meaning of the discipline. Ouspensky concludes:

> When we understand the importance of the study of man from the point of view of *his possible evolution*, we shall understand that the first answer to the question, what is psychology, should be that psychology is the study of the principles, laws, and facts of man's possible evolution (1950, p. 6)

The first systems include modern psychological, philosophical and scientific systems, which study humans as soul-less animals or organisms, while the second systems study humans from the viewpoint of their "possible evolution." Evolution has to do with how an individual might develop and be transformed psychologically–in the inner development of consciousness and being, and in achieving the soul. Nicoll (1975) asserts that: *"Esoteric teaching is about inner evolution."* (p. 246)

For Gurdjieff and other esoteric teachers, the concept of evolution differs radically from that of western science. In psychology, we talk of change, growth and maturation, but not of *evolution*. In the sciences, *"natural evolution"* refers to the development of the diverse forms of organic life on earth from the first molecules, through to complex cells, plants, animals and finally humans. Neo-Darwinian theory describes the metamorphosis of life as being governed by the process of natural selection and adaptation, driven by random mutations in genetic materials. However, Ouspensky rejects all such standard ideas of biological evolution, *"the monkey-to-man business"* as he calls it:

> As regards ordinary modern views on the origin of man and his previous evolution I must say at once that they cannot be accepted. We must realize that we know nothing about the origin of man and we have no proofs of man's physical or mental evolution. ...
>
> Denying previous evolution of man, we must deny any possibility of future *mechanical evolution of man*; that is, evolution happening by itself according to laws of heredity and selection, and without man's conscious efforts and understanding of his possible evolution. (1950, p.7)

Ouspensky bluntly states that we know *nothing* about the origin of humanity, that we have *no proofs* of human's physical or mental evolution, and that there can be no possible future *"mechanical evolution,"* which happens accidentally. Instead, Ouspensky is interested in evolution brought about through the individual's conscious efforts and the struggle to *"know self."* When western scientists or psychologists talk of evolution, they refer to the mechanical evolution of biological forms and not to *"conscious evolution"* or the *"evolution of consciousness."*

This distinction between *mechanical and conscious evolution* is at the heart of the differences between western scientific theories and the fourth way teaching. The fourth way psychology is concerned with the evolution of a human in a psychological, metaphysical and cosmological way, brought about through intentional effort. In modern thought, there is no recognition of the possibility of such conscious evolution–of how an individual might awaken consciousness or realize higher levels of being.

Ouspensky elaborates upon the theme of a human's possible evolution:

> Our fundamental idea shall be that man as we know him *is not a completed being;* that nature develops him only up to a certain point and then leaves him, to develop further, *by his own* efforts and devices, or to live and die such as he was born, or to degenerate and lose capacity for development.
>
> Evolution of man in this case will mean the development of certain *inner* qualities and features which usually remain undeveloped, and *cannot develop by themselves.*
>
> Experience and observation show that this development is possible only in certain definite conditions, with efforts of a certain kind on the part of man himself, and with *sufficient help* from those who began similar work before and have already attained a certain knowledge of methods....

> After this we must understand that in the way of development, man must become a *different being* and we must learn and understand in what sense and in which direction man must become a different being; that is, what a different being means. (1950, p. 8)

Ouspensky elaborates upon this idea of conscious evolution from various angles: what it means to become a different being and which inner qualities and features can be developed or attained. He then describes *"a missing link"* in modern thought:

> There is a missing link in ordinary known theories, even in those ... based on the idea of the possibility of evolution of man.
>
> The truth lies in the fact that before acquiring any *new* faculties or powers which man does not know and does not possess now, he must acquire faculties and powers he *also does not possess*, but which he ascribes to himself; that is, he thinks that he knows them and can use and control them.
>
> This is the missing link and *this is the most important point.*
>
> By way of evolution ... that is, a way based on effort and help, man must acquire qualities which he thinks he already possesses, but about which he deceives himself.
>
> And here we come to at once to a very important fact. *Man does not know himself.*
>
> He does not know his own limitations and his own possibilities. He does not even know to how great an extent he does not know himself. (1950, pp.10-11)

Human evolution involves the development of latent powers and capabilities, which people already believe that they possess. In this way, the psychology of the fourth way deals with the study of a human *"as he is"* and as he is capable of becoming.

Gurdjieff explains that evolution cannot *happen* but requires *conscious effort*, even to acquire capacities which people normally considered themselves to possess—such as consciousness, indivisible I, will and the capacity to do:

> "The evolution of man is the evolution of his consciousness. *And 'consciousness' cannot evolve unconsciously.* The evolution of man is the evolution of his will, and 'will' cannot evolve involuntarily. The evolution of man is the evolution of his power of doing, and 'doing' cannot be the result of things which 'happen.'" (1949, p. 58)

Ouspensky emphasizes the significance of humans' illusions about their existing powers and capabilities, and this defines a starting point of work towards conscious evolution. Human's psychological illusions are deeply ingrained in common ideas about who and what we are. Until we rid ourselves of these misconceptions—that we are conscious, with indivisible I and will—then there is no possibility of becoming in reality, that which we imagine ourselves to already be. Similarly, Gurdjieff explains that because people believe that they already possess a soul, they reject as nonsense the idea of having to attain the soul—or of having to develop *higher being bodies* as vehicles for the soul's existence, within life and for the afterlife.

Gurdjieff provides a radically different perspective on how higher states of consciousness and higher faculties can be approached. However, until we apprehend the nature and significance of human's psychological illusions, then we can little idea of what additional powers and capacities might be acquired. Ouspensky states:

> ... we do not know enough about ordinary psychology; we cannot study super-normal psychology, because we do not know normal psychology. (1957, p. 2)

We must understand ourselves as we are, in order to understand what we might become, and what "a different being" might be. Most importantly, in order to understand the evolution of consciousness, an individual has to realize how little he or she is conscious, and how consciousness can be enhanced through efforts to awaken.

Moments of increased consciousness are attained by overcoming the sleepwalking and conditioned state of ordinary life. The fourth way's depiction of the normal waking state is certainly much more severe than anything modern psychology sets forth. However, its conceptualization of an individual's capacity to experience higher states of consciousness and attain the soul, involves an even more radical departure from the ideas of modern soul-less psychology and the limited materialist understanding of the human condition.

According to the fourth way, humans have the possibility of experiencing four states of consciousness: *sleep*, *waking sleep*, *self-consciousness* and *objective-consciousness*. Ordinarily, humans live in only the first two states–sleep and waking sleep–each of which is highly conditioned and subjective. In contrast, the state of self-consciousness reveals the objective nature of self; and the state of objective consciousness reveals truths about the nature of the cosmos. Ouspensky writes:

> In the third state of consciousness, that is, the state of self-consciousness, we can know the full truth *about ourselves*. In the fourth state of consciousness, that is, in the state of objective consciousness, we are supposed to be able to know the full truth *about everything*; we can study "things in themselves," "the world as it is." (1950, p. 35)

Gurdjieff and Ouspensky approach the idea of a human's evolution from varied psychological perspectives. Firstly, it involves the development of consciousness, will and unity, which people wrongly ascribe to themselves. Secondly, evolution involves attaining the states of self-consciousness and objective consciousness which enable them to know self and the world in an objective manner. Thirdly, G. suggests that there are seven possible levels of human evolution or levels of being. Ordinarily, under the conditions of mechanical life, a human is a man number one, two or three, yet is capable of becoming a human number four, five, six or seven. This evolution involves the formation and crystallization of an individual's *higher being bodies* for the life of the soul. In this case, instead of *"dying like dog"* and becoming fertilizer, the individual might attain other levels of existence and immortality. This evolution of a human being is an alchemical process of accumulating and refining finer matters/energies within the subtle dimensions of being and attaining higher consciousness.

Evolution exists as a possibility for humanity as a whole and for human beings at an individual level. However, Gurdjieff suggests that although the evolution of humankind does occur, it is on such immense time scales that it means little in terms of the life of an individual. The scale of time in which humanity evolves corresponds to that of the evolution of the earth, moon and the planets, involving hundreds of thousands, or millions of years, or, on a scale of *"infinitely prolonged cycles of time."*

(1949, p. 57) From the perspective of an individual's life, there is no apparent evolution of either the planets or humankind. Nicoll writes:

> If a person is told that in, say a thousand million years, all Mankind may possibly be on a higher level of evolution, it cannot interest him in any genuine way or really alter anything for him in his daily life, and his difficulties. (1975, p.245)

For Gurdjieff and Ouspensky, the first definition of psychology involves the study of the principles, laws and facts of the man's possible evolution. However, in order to understand a human's miraculous possibilities, we have to realize the extent of man's unconscious, sleepwalking condition. By doing so, we may begin to understand how acorns might become oak trees, instead of fertilizer, and what inner evolution entails. The fourth way teaching provides a profound psychological, metaphysical and cosmological perspective of the possible evolution of the individual human being.

3. The Study of Language

> " ... we use a special language and ... in order to talk with us, it is necessary to learn this language. It is not worth while talking in ordinary language because, in that language, it is impossible to understand one another. This also, at the moment, seems strange to you." (Gurdjieff, in Ouspensky, 1949, p. 22)

The fourth way psychology introduces a new and more precise language which allows us to come closer to the truth about ourselves, and to communicate more precisely with others who have acquired the same language. This language is actually well attuned to western language usage, although the terms are defined more precisely within a broader framework of ideas. Within Gurdjieff's teaching, such familiar terms—such as consciousness, I, self-consciousness, self-remembering, will, mind, negative emotions, imagination, and so on—are given more precise definitions within a broader model of human nature and man's possible evolution.

Certainly, western psychology is characterized by a great confusion of tongues or *babble*, with many different and inconsistent ways of using even the most basic psychological terms. In contrast, the system of the fourth way provides a precise manner of labeling the complex phenomena of psychology (and cosmology). Ouspensky writes in this regard:

> The study of the methods used in this system by which man can come to a higher consciousness begins with the study of a new language. This language is based on different principles which you do not know yet; but as you go on with your study you will very soon begin to understand them. It is very important to understand the different divisions the system uses, which are part of this language. Man is a very complicated machine and he can be studied in divisions. In ordinary language we do not use these divisions and so people do not understand one another. (1957, P. 78)

Certainly, for an exact science, we need an exact language, and the precision of the fourth way illustrates the confusions existent within known psychological theories.

Ouspensky recalls Gurdjieff's explanation of the problems associated with ordinary language which is *"full of wrong concepts, wrong classifications, wrong associations."* Ordinary thinking is vague and inaccurate, and words take on thousands of different meanings according to the speaker and the complex of associations at work in him at the moment. People do realize how subjective their language is, and how we only vaguely understand each other or even ourselves. G.'s elaborates on the limits of common language usage:

> "The language in which they speak is adapted to practical life only. People can communicate to one another information of a practical character, but as soon as they pass to a slightly more complex sphere they are immediately lost, and they cease to understand one another. ... they imagine that they understand the authors of the books they read and that other people understand them. This also is one of the illusions which people create for themselves and in the midst of which they live. As a matter of fact, no one understands anyone else." (1949, pp. 68-9)

In making this shocking claim that *"no one understands anyone else,"* Gurdjieff refers not only to ordinary people, but to psychologists, philosophers and all those modern thinkers–the *"scientists of new formation"*–who attempt to describe the human psyche. For exact understanding, an exact language is necessary, and so systems of ancient knowledge begin with the study of language.

The fourth way language is elaborated within the context of the system's complex model of man's possible evolution. Although the terms are familiar, they take on distinct and precise meanings when placed within the system's unique framework of ideas, and when elaborated through connections established with other ideas. Words such as "consciousness," "I," "self-consciousness," "self-remembering," "negative emotions," "imagination," and so on, are stripped of their usual associations and assume an exact significance in the dynamics of the fourth way's evolutionary scheme. The fourth way language is more objective and yet provides an approach to understanding the subjective, inner world.

One key to understanding this exact new language lies in grasping the principle of "relativity," on which the language is constructed. Gurdjieff explains:

> "This new language ... *bases the construction of speech upon a new principle, namely, the principle of relativity*; that is to say, it introduces relativity into all concepts and thus makes possible an accurate determination of the angle of thought – for what precisely ordinary language lacks are expressions of relativity."...

> "The fundamental property of the new language is that *all* ideas in it are concentrated round *one* idea, that is, they are taken in their mutual relationship from the point of view of one idea. This idea is the idea of *evolution*. Of course, not evolution in the sense of *mechanical* evolution, because such an evolution does not exist, but in the sense of a conscious and volitional evolution, which alone is possible."

> "The language in which understanding is possible is constructed upon the indication of the relation of the object under examination to the evolution possible for it; upon the indication of its *place* in the evolutionary ladder." (1949, pp. 70-71)

For Gurdjieff, words like "man," "consciousness," and "I," take on very different meanings *relative to* the individual's level of evolution. Take for instance, the word "man." According to G., there are seven classes of human beings corresponding to the categories of possible evolution. The first three types, man number one, two and three, represent three types of sleepwalkers commonly produced by mechanical life. Such men and women "in quotation marks" are not properly conscious, unified or capable of doing. While there are differences in the states of presence which dominate these types, they all live in ignorance of self and of the extent to which everything happens. In contrast, the consciousness and being of human number four is qualitatively distinct. This individual has achieved a balanced development of the mind, emotions and body, attaining a unity of I, and an awakened state of self-consciousness. Consequently, the meaning of terms such as "I", "consciousness," "being" and "self," changes dramatically when speaking of higher types as opposed to the classes of mechanical human beings. Within the fourth way, the meaning of all terms is relative to the evolutionary level of an individual. Thus, the consciousness and I of a sleepwalker is a world away from that of a human number five, which itself is distinctively different from that of humans numbered six or seven.

The richness and precision of the fourth way language develops as one cultivates knowledge and understanding of oneself in terms of the teaching. Self-study reveals the unsuspected complexity involved in knowing oneself as a machine, or organism. One can grasp the extraordinary subtlety and precision of the teaching's language only by developing a sophisticated knowledge of the parts of one's being and about the nature of consciousness. As a consequence of studying oneself in terms of the system and its special language, the confusions of modern psychology and popular speech become most apparent. The scientists of new formation do not know what psychology is, nor consciousness, nor the many different meanings of the word "I," nor the basic parts of a human being.

4. The Study of Oneself

> To *know ourself*–this was the first principle and the first demand of old psychological schools. We still remember these words, but have lost their meaning. We think that to *know ourselves* means to know our peculiarities, our desires, our tastes, our capacities, and our intentions, when in reality it means to know ourselves as machines, that is, to know the *structure* of one's machine, its *parts*, functions of different parts, the conditions governing their work, and so on. (Ouspensky, 1950, p. 46)

At a most basic level, humans can be considered to live in two worlds: an outer world and an inner world.[6] The *outer world* is that which surrounds us externally, with people, rooms, cars, houses, buildings, cities, the country side, the solar system and universe. The outer world is where we live, work and move about. And then, there is another world: our *inner world*. In a sense, "I" exists in the inner world. No one on the outside can experience what goes on within an individual's inner world, as only he or she can observe and experience self. My inner world is invisible to you, as yours is invisible to me, or any outsider. Yet, in a way, one's real life is in the inner world. Each individual lives, thinks, feels and imagines in the inner world. This is the space within which we can be conscious of ourselves and of what goes on within us. We can observe the external behaviour of others, and we can infer their feelings and thoughts, but we cannot directly experience anyone else's inner world of consciousness and experience.

Each person lives in the inner world and in order to study self, one must study this inner world. Just as we can study and observe things in the outer world, so also we can study and observe things in the inner world. For Gurdjieff, any serious form of psychology must focus on studying the inner world. Ouspensky writes:

> Serious study begins in this system ... with the study of oneself, because psychology cannot be studied, as astronomy can, outside oneself. A man has to study himself. When I was told that, I saw at once that we do not have any methods of studying ourselves and already have many wrong ideas about ourselves. So I realized that we must get rid of wrong ideas about ourselves and at the same time find methods for studying ourselves.

> ... So we begin by defining psychology as *study of oneself*. You have to learn certain methods and principles and, according to these principles and using these methods, you will try to see yourselves from a new point of view. (1957, pp. 2-3)

Psychology begins with self study because only the individual has access to the inner world and can study consciousness there, as well as the stream of psychological processes which go on within. Yet a person needs an objective framework of ideas to guide this study of the inner world.

---

[6] Actually, we could also consider a third world underlying, sustaining and unifying both of these, but it is simpler to begin with this dual distinction.

The fourth way psychology provides a framework of ideas for studying ourselves from a new point of view. In order to do this, we have to learn its language, its methods and principles, and apply them in self-study. Ouspensky (1949) recalls Gurdjieff's comments on knowing oneself:

> The next lecture began precisely with the words: "Know thyself."

> "These words," said G., "which are generally ascribed to Socrates, actually lie at the basis of many systems and schools far more ancient than the Socratic. But although modern thought is aware of the existence of this principle it has only a very vague idea of its meaning and significance. The ordinary man of our times, even a man with philosophic or scientific interests, does not realize that the principle 'know thyself' speaks of the necessity of knowing one's machine, the human machine. ... man must study the structure, the functions, and the laws of his organism. In the human machine everything is interconnected, one thing is so dependent upon another, that it is quite impossible to study any one function without studying all the others. In order to know one thing, one must know everything. (pp. 104-5)

Self-study should not be confused with any form of arbitrary self analysis or introspectionist method, as might be fashionable in contemporary psychology. Self study must be based upon objective ideas about the parts of the machine and the nature of consciousness and self. It is necessary to learn the methods of self-study and basic ideas about human nature, and then apply them in self-study.

Information about the dimensions of a human being provides a framework within which to situate self observations. As Ouspensky notes, we need *"help from those who began similar work before and have already attained a certain knowledge of methods."* Any type of self analysis undertaken willy-nilly or in terms of some arbitrary theoretical perspective is useless. In most forms of self-analysis and introspection, one is just another blind man groping in the darkness, taking whatever limited and incomplete information that might be available as representative of the whole. Modern scientific psychology is based on just such arbitrary and partial comprehension of the parts and faculties of a human being.

Further, in order to understand a human's possible evolution, we particularly need to begin with the study of human mechanicalness and the lack of self-consciousness. Gurdjieff remarks:

> we make the study of the mechanicality of contemporary man the groundwork of a correctly conducted self-observation. (1950, p. 1210)

It is not necessary to accept the principles and framework offered by the fourth way teaching on blind faith. In fact, to the contrary, Ouspensky explains:

> There is no question of faith or belief in all this. Quite the opposite, this system teaches people to believe in absolutely nothing. You must verify everything that you see, hear and feel. Only in that way can you come to something. (1957, p. 6)

The fourth way framework must be evaluated through one's own experience: otherwise, it is of no value. The attainment of self knowledge must be based upon systematic self study and direct inner experience and awareness.

5. The Study of the Centers

"We do not realize that there are ... independent beings in us ... independent minds." Ouspensky

Gurdjieff's concept of "the centers" is one of the most unique and important features of his teaching. Understanding the centers is essential in seeking to "know self" and awaken— because it provides part of the framework required for self-study and self-observation. The centers are the parts of the human machine or organism, and each serves different functions within the whole. The functions of each center within the psychological makeup must be understood within self study.

In fact, all things in human life can be related to one of the seven centers:

"Science, philosophy, and all manifestations of man's life and activity can be divided in exactly the same way into seven categories." (Ouspensky, 1949, p. 74) Each of the seven centers is an independent mind responsible for different psychological (or psychic) functions. Five lower centers operate within ordinary states of consciousness and are responsible for a human's normal experience and activities in life; and two higher centers are involved in a human's supernormal faculties and experiences. The five lower centers, as we descend from the head, are:

- the intellectual or thinking center, localized within the head-brain and responsible for the formation of concepts, reasoning and comparison, formulation of thoughts, language faculties, imagination, the stream of thought and mental activity.

- the emotional or feeling center, localized within the "complex of nerves of the sympathetic nervous system," (1950, p. 780) and related to "an independent brain localized in the region of their what is called 'breast' ..." – the heart (1950, p. 779). This center is the basis for feelings and emotions–including happiness, anxiety, anger, sorrow, fear, relaxation, self-satisfaction, love, and other personal and impersonal emotions;

- the moving center, localized within the spinal column and responsible for the performance of learned movement involving muscular control, including the articulation of sounds in speech;

- the sexual center, localized in the sexual organs, glands and substances (hormones) and responsible for sexual arousal, activities and procreation;

- the instinctual center, localized within the spinal column and lower brain structures and primary sensory nuclei, as well as within the stomach and organs, and responsible for the innate or instinctive functions of the body, including metabolic and sensory processes.

Each center is a relatively separate mind or intelligence within the individual–responsible for a particular sphere of life experience and activity. An individual can think, feel, move and sense, and be aroused by sexual desires and impulses. These five centers are responsible for all normal participation and activity in life. Each center has its own forms of knowing, its own speed of operation or time, its own energies and substances. Although each center has a center of gravity or localization, Gurdjieff says that all of the centers can have an influence throughout the body. While each center is responsible for a particular sphere of life experience and activity, they are very intricately inter-connected. Functions and activities in one center are linked with functions and activities within the other centers.

The illustration depicts the seven centers within the three stories of the human organism. The sexual, instinctual and moving centers are depicted in the lowest story, the physical nature, with the emotional center depicted in the middle story, and the intellectual center in the upper story. The two higher centers are represented in the suns.

In contrast to modern conception of human as beings possessing a duality of mind and body, the fourth way provides a more complex model of humans as a three-brained or a three natured being. They function mentally, emotionally and physically. This can be expressed most simply by describing a human being as having a head, heart and hands. However, this three fold nature can be further differentiated into seven centers. The moving, instinctual and sexual centers constitute three aspects of the physical or planetary body, and there are lower and higher emotional and intellectual centers.

The fourth way teaching identifies numerous types of *"wrong work"* within each of the centers as being responsible for the psychopathology which characterizes human's ordinary waking state. Wrong work of the centers includes unnecessary functions like negative emotions, internal considering, inner talking, imagination and daydreaming, bad moods, chronic patterns of muscular tension, insignificant interests and aims, and the misuse and waste of sexual energies. Gurdjieff provides a detailed analysis of these mechanical habits of the centers which dominate the life of humanity. It is necessary to study these various types of wrong work, because it is only by overcoming these processes that the centers can begin to function properly and in harmony with one another. The struggle to awaken begins with the refinement and balancing of the centers' functioning.

Learning to economize the energies produced by the organism, instead of wasting them on useless and unnecessary functions, allows for the accumulation and refinement of more finer matters and energies. Moreover, the accumulation of these finer elements makes it possible for the lower centers to connect with higher centers and, thereby for the individual to experience higher states of consciousness. Essentially, this refinement of energies is an alchemical process!

The base metals of the centers' energies can be transmuted into the gold of the more refined higher centers. By separating the fine from the coarse, as an ancient Hermetic aphorism states, a human is able to evolve consciously by refining the energies needed to coat the higher being bodies for the life of the soul. It is in this accumulation and refinement of subtle energies that the possibility of a human's evolution lies.

Gurdjieff maintains that the higher centers already exist fully developed. However, humans are not ordinarily able to experience them because the lower centers remain undeveloped, dominating the attention and using up the available energies. If the emotional center is harmoniously developed, the increased speed of its functioning brings about a temporary connection with the higher emotional center (the sixth center). Connection with the higher intellectual center is then possible through the higher emotional center. Ouspensky recalls Gurdjieff's comments:

> "...(when) a temporary connection with the higher emotional center takes place ... man experiences new emotions, new impressions hitherto entirely unknown to him, for the description of which he has neither words nor expressions. ...

> "The higher thinking center ... is still further removed from us, still less accessible. Connection with it is possible only through the higher emotional center. It is only from descriptions of mystical experiences, ecstatic states, and so on, that we know cases of such connection ... Our ordinary centers, in transmitting the impressions of the higher centers, may be compared to a blind man speaking of colors, or to a deaf man speaking of music.

> In order to obtain a correct and permanent connection between the lower and the higher centers, it is necessary to regulate and quicken the work of the lower centers. (1949, pp. 194-5)

Psychology, from the viewpoint of the fourth way, must involve self study and the study of the centers– their normal and abnormal functioning. With the elimination or neutralization of the unnecessary activities of the centers, an individual can accumulate more refined substances and make temporary connections with higher centers. This would allow us to realize self and world (cosmos) in supernormal, mystical ways. Gurdjieff suggests that a correct and permanent connection can be made between the lower and higher centers. This is the aim in the psychology of a human's possible evolution.

6. The Study of Consciousness

In order to understand the fourth way approach to the study of consciousness, it is most useful to compare it to western ideas. William James, the 19th century American philosopher, has been one of the most influential figures in the modern study of consciousness and mind. Western psychologists routinely quote James' speculations about consciousness. However, from the fourth way perspective, there are fundamental mistakes evident in James' presentations, which ideas became widespread in contemporary studies of consciousness.

A first issue concerns James' tendency to equate consciousness, in a general way, with the stream of different psychological processes within the mind:

> By states of consciousness are meant such things as sensations, desires, emotions, cognitions, reasonings, decisions, volitions, and the like. (p.15) The first and foremost concrete fact which every one will affirm to belong to his inner experience is the fact that consciousness of some sort goes on. ... we must simply say that thought goes on. (p. 167) ... let us call it the stream of thought, of consciousness, or of subjective life. (p. 173) (1972/1892)

Consciousness is roughly equated with the flow of sensations, desires, emotions, cognition, "and the like," or with the *"stream of thought,"* or the *"stream of subjective life."* James equates consciousness generally with the psychological functions–such as thinking, feeling and sensing.

A second assumption that James makes concerns the localization of consciousness, which he takes to be produced by the brain. In particular, James comments: *"The immediate condition of a state of consciousness is an activity of some sort in the cerebral hemispheres."* (p.18)

A third argument found in James and modern western psychology, is that consciousness is not anything substantive beyond the mind's psychological and neurological processes. Natsoulas (1978), in a more modern review of the consciousness literature, explains:

> James considered consciousness the most mysterious thing in the world. But he was sure it was no actual thing, that it was a non-entity. Those psychologists who would cling to a substantive consciousness were said to be clinging "to a mere echo, the faint rumour left behind by the disappearing 'soul' upon the air of philosophy." (p.906)

The idea of a substantive consciousness is linked to the idea of a soul–an immaterial something connected to the material body/brain. Modern psychology and science has dismissed the idea of humans having a soul or a spiritual nature, and along with this, the idea of a substantive consciousness.

Of course, psychologists and scientists have not proven that consciousness is non-substantive. Nor have they established empirically what brain processes produce consciousness. Consequently, consciousness remains a profound enigma within modern psychology–as William James said, *"the most mysterious thing in the world."* A most recent *Scientific American* (2004) special edition on MIND illustrates these arguments in an article on *The Puzzle of Consciousness*. Nevertheless, traditionally psychologists ignore the many tricky issues involved in the study of consciousness and equate it simply with thinking and other mental processes in the brain.

The fourth way teaching suggests that these ideas from western psychology are seriously misguided. In 1922, Ouspensky commented upon the work of William James and emphasized an important distinction between "psychic functions" and "consciousness," and the importance of considering consciousness as being substantive:

> In conversational language and in every-day psychology, even in psychology purporting to be scientific, the word consciousness is often used as a term for the designation of a complex of all psychic functions in general, or for their separate manifestations. ... to the best of my recollection Prof. William James defined thought as "a moment of consciousness."

> From my standpoint ... it is necessary to regard consciousness as distinct from the commonly understood psychic functions: thought, feeling and sensation. Over and above all this, consciousness has several exactly definable forms or phases, in each one of which thoughts, feelings and sensations can function, giving in each different results. Thus consciousness ... is a background upon which thoughts, feelings and sensations reveal themselves. This background can be more or less bright. But as thoughts, feelings and sensations have their own separate life, and can be regarded independently of this background, so can it be regarded and studied independently of them. ... It is important only to establish the fact that thoughts, feelings and sensations, i.e., psychic functions, are not consciousness. (1968, pp. xiii-xiv)

If the fourth way teaching is correct, the confusion of consciousness with the psychic functions is a profound error in western psychology produced by the manner in which the mind is being used to investigate consciousness. The mind identifies consciousness with its own contents and activities– instead of realizing that it is something else deeper.

What could this something else be? Consciousness is described as a "background" to the psychic functions and thus might be related to ideas about space, within which the psychological process can be experienced. Ouspensky also identifies another important aspect of a substantive consciousness– relating it to *light*:

> (Psychic) functions can be compared to machines working in varying degrees of light. These machines are such that they are able to work better with light than in darkness; every moment there is more light the machines work better. Consciousness is light and machines are functions. (p. 55) ... Energy of consciousness is not recognized by psychology and by scientific schools. ... Consciousness is light, light is the result of a certain energy; if there is no energy there is no light. (1957, p. 68)

Consciousness is associated with *substantive light* energies which illuminate the activities of the centers (or minds). Just as a human can see things in the outer world when there is exterior light illuminating them, so also, there is inner light illuminating the inner world. This inner light of consciousness allows for awareness of the stream of thoughts, feelings, sensations, desires, and so on, which occur within the mind and within other centers.

Nicoll (1975), a student of Ouspensky's, elaborates upon this idea that consciousness is light, and relates it to the practices of self-study. The process of awakening involves an increase in the inner light of consciousness, which illuminates the psychological processes:

> ... consciousness is compared in this system with light. Our inner life is said to be darkness and this is what is meant in the Gospels by the words: 'People who live in darkness.' The idea of Self-Observation is to let a ray of light into this darkness. ... Whereas the ray of a candle illuminates feebly the surroundings, the light of an arc-lamp lights up what were mere shadows before and makes us see everything in an entirely different relation ... (as) sometimes occurs to us in times of trouble and distress when suddenly everything becomes transformed and we see things in an entirely different light. When we are fixed in our negative states, when we are full of self-pity and only conscious of injured self-love, etc., we see everything very darkly. ... But when we have a moment of awakening and are lifted out of that state by the action of the Work, all our thoughts and emotions in that state now seem to be trivial. We cannot understand why we said this thing or thought that thing. This is a moment of illumination, of increased light, and so increased consciousness, in the sense that we are 'knowing together' far more than we do in our contracted state. Everything falls into its right proportion, as it were, in the light of this increased consciousness. ... Quite simply, we rise above ourselves for a moment and see things in a new light. (p. 204)

The light of consciousness illuminates the inner world and allows awareness of our own processes to varying degrees. Illumination, enlightenment and insight are all terms associated with increases in the light of consciousness. Although humans may normally have very little of this substance, consciousness is substantive. We do not appreciate the true nature of consciousness because we are not properly conscious. In fact, there are degrees of consciousness and varied states of consciousness. The states are discrete or discontinuous levels of realization and awareness which come with the evolution of an individual's being.

According to the fourth way, an individual is capable of experiencing or achieving four states of consciousness. Unfortunately, humans' lives are primarily passed in the two lowest levels of sleep and waking sleep. The so-called normal state is one of semi-sleep, which Gurdjieff refers to as relative consciousness or the waking sleep state. However, in this state, people do not realize how they are not self conscious, and what this would mean. The study of psychology must involve the study of consciousness and efforts to develop self-consciousness, the state natural to the individual who is awake, instinctually sensing reality and experiencing higher emotions.

Typically, we assume that humans are properly conscious of themselves during waking periods. Gurdjieff teaches that this is not so, and that instead, people's waking periods are governed by the mechanical, unnecessary wrong work of the centers and the formation of a *"false personality."* Gurdjieff depicts this state:

> "... the first state of consciousness ... is sleep. This is an entirely subjective state of consciousness. ... Then a man wakes up. At first glance this is a quite different state of consciousness. He can move, he can talk with other people, he can make calculations ahead, he can see danger and avoid it, and so on. ... But if we go a little more deeply into things, if we take a look into his inner world, into his thoughts, into the causes of his actions, we shall see that he is in almost the same state as when he is asleep. ...

he does not remember himself. He is a machine, everything with him happens. He cannot stop the flow of his thoughts, he cannot control his imagination, his emotions, his attention. He lives in a subjective world of 'I love,' 'I do not love,' 'I like,' 'I do not like,' 'I want,' 'I do not want,' that is, ... of what he thinks he wants, of what he thinks he does not want. He does not see the real world. The real world is hidden from him by the wall of imagination. He lives in sleep. He is asleep. What is called 'clear consciousness' is sleep and a far more dangerous sleep than sleep at night in bed." (1949, pp. 142-43)

In this view, one can think, feel, act, speak and work, without being conscious of it. In fact, we are lost within the stream of thoughts, imagination, negative emotions and so on. In so-called normal waking consciousness, we do not remember ourselves and are not properly self-conscious.

According to the fourth way, the study of psychology must begin with the study of consciousness and the effort to awaken from this semi-conscious *waking sleep* state. Ouspensky states that our principle error or illusion is to think that we are already properly conscious:

> ... what is called in modern psychology "the subconscious" or "the subconscious mind" ... are simply wrong expressions, wrong terms, which mean nothing and do not refer to any real facts. There is nothing permanently subconscious in us because there is nothing permanently conscious; and there is no "subconscious mind" for the very simple reason that there is no "conscious mind."
> (1950, pp. 32-3)

From the fourth way perspective, modern psychological concepts of the subconscious or unconscious mind are not based in reality. If there is no permanent conscious presence and "I" in the individual, then there is no true consciousness. The familiar concept of "the unconscious" reflects the assumption that people are normally conscious. Gurdjieff stands the entire framework of modern thought on its head by asserting that there is no proper consciousness, but that there could be. Ouspensky (1950) notes:

> ... the first obstacle in the way of the development of self-consciousness in man, is his conviction that he already possesses self-consciousness, or at any rate, that he can have it at any time he likes. It is very difficult to persuade a man that he is not conscious and cannot be conscious at will. (p. 36)

People ordinarily think that they have a conscious mind and that they can be self conscious at will. These are fundamental illusions. Attaining self-consciousness is not simply a matter of reflecting on yourself with the mind, thinking about who you are. Instead, it requires a dissolution of the predominant false personality complex, and awakening within the essence—which is the possible basis for real I.

The four states of consciousness are not simply on a continuum with each other. Instead, the transition from one state to another involves a quantum leap—a discontinuity in the quality and quantity of consciousness. Each state is marked by the appearance of new faculties and capacities, and allows for a greater degree of the realization of the truth of self and the nature of reality. Just as the dream state may be governed by subjective dreams, fears and imaginations, which disappear upon waking, so also, a human can awaken again from the normal waking sleep state and experience moments of true self-consciousness. In the state of self-consciousness, the stream of thoughts, negative

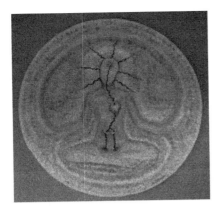

emotions and semi-conscious actions that dominate the waking sleep state are de-automatized and dissipated–allowing for a profoundly deeper and more real experience of "I." Rather than being dominated by "it," one's presence can consist of a coherent three-fold awareness– of head, heart and hands–and a deep experience that "I AM."

It takes time and self study to realize what these distinctions entail and how an individual might experience qualitatively different states of higher consciousness (both self-consciousness and objective consciousness). The difference is partly between being governed by the subjective states and illusions, and the deeper experiences of the true nature of self and the cosmos. The higher states of consciousness allow for new dimensions of experience and knowledge, which are of staggering depth and breadth relative to the so-called waking sleep state.

FOUR STATES OF HUMAN CONSCIOUSNESS

OBJECTIVE CONSCIOUSNESS
awakening of higher intellectual center

SELF CONSCIOUSNESS
awakening of higher emotional center

WAKING SLEEP or RELATIVE CONSCIOUSNESS
level of mechanical humanity

SLEEP
with and without dreams

A final or fifth supreme state of consciousness is also sometimes described within the fourth way tradition. Vaysse (1979) writes:

> The four states of presence possible for man in his life are individual states, however vast and formless they may be. This last state is the supreme Realization (the Buddhist paranirvana, the cosmic mind of Zen, the Yahweh in the Kabbalah, the unconditioned Absolute of metaphysics–beyond all form and all individuality). It is "That" which cannot be named, about which nothing can be said, about which nothing can be known, which can only be spoken about in terms of what it is not, and which is also referred to by such terms as "annihilation," "extinction," "fullness of the Void," "formlessness." ... This is the ultimate end, where a man dissolves in the supreme Realization. (p.66)

The two higher states refer to individualized states existing before supreme realizations of the prime source substances.

In summary: the proper psychological study of consciousness involves an individual's attempts to consciously evolve through a process of self-transformation. This involves overcoming the mechanical functioning of the lower centers in order to awaken and experience directly the higher centers and the higher states of consciousness associated with them. Self-consciousness allows the individual to know the true nature of self, while the fourth state of objective consciousness allows one to know the truth about the nature of the world, or cosmos. Humans can directly experience and know things in themselves, the world as it is. In Beelzebub's terms, humans can *"instinctually sense reality,"* instead of being imprisoned by the usual state of *"automatized consciousness."* The higher states entail possibilities for attaining cosmic and spiritual knowledge and experience. The human venture to attain self knowledge and a unifying knowledge of the whole has to be connected to the experience of such states of heightened consciousness and being.

7. Self-Remembering:
A key, a door, a missing link

Self-remembering is the key to self-study and the ideal method to study consciousness within oneself. Ouspensky states that, when Gurdjieff introduced him to the fourth way teaching, he immediately recognized that this practice is of profound importance. Thus, he argues that:

> ... psychology begins at this point. ... man does not remember himself but could remember himself if he made sufficient efforts. Without self-remembering there can be no study, no psychology. But if a man realizes and bears in mind that he does not remember himself, and that nobody remembers, and yet there is a possibility of self-remembering, then study begins. (1950, p. 120)

Ouspensky adamantly stresses that without self-remembering there is no self-study—no psychology.

Self-remembering involves an effort to awaken by being more present within life situations and under all different kinds of circumstances. Once an individual attempts to do this, they soon realize how impossible this task is for them. There is no central or indivisible I, that has will and the control of attention, and which could 'do' this. Instead, there are one thousand and one little i's which parade out and absorb the attention and engage in the habitual dynamics of the wrong workings of the centers and the concerns of false personality. It is most difficult to maintain awareness of "I am here" for more than a few moments before being distracted and engaged by associative thinking and imagination, by negative emotions and personal concerns—and then slipping back into the unconsciousness of the usual waking sleep. Humans live in a state of forgetfulness, continually absorbed and engaged by everything happening around and within them. Self-remembering requires a conscious effort to wake up and be more fully present amidst the mechanical flow of happenings that condition and enslave us.

Gurdjieff explains how self-remembering is *a method for the study of consciousness—its* appearance and disappearance:

"... you *can know* consciousness only in yourself. Observe that I say you *can know*, for you can know it only when you have it. And when you have not got it, you can know that you have not got it, not at that very moment, but afterwards. I mean that when it comes again you can see that it has been absent a long time, and you can find or remember the moment when it disappeared and when it reappeared. ... by observing in yourself the appearance and the disappearance of consciousness you will inevitably see one fact which you neither see nor acknowledge now, and that is that moments of consciousness are very short and are separated by long intervals of completely unconscious, mechanical working of the machine. You will then see that you can think, feel, act, speak, work, *without being conscious of it*. And if you learn to see in yourselves the moments of consciousness and the long periods of mechanicalness, you will as infallibly see in other people when they are conscious of what they are doing and when they are not.

"Your principal mistake consists in thinking that you *always have consciousness*, and in general, either that consciousness is *always present* or that it is *never present*. In reality consciousness is a property which is continually changing. Now it is present, now it is not present. And there are different degrees and different levels of consciousness. Both consciousness and the different degrees of consciousness must be understood in oneself by sensation, by taste." (1949, pp. 116-117)

Through self-remembering, we study the qualities of consciousness. Usually, we are not conscious of ourselves and the attention is continually absorbed by the turning of the mind, negative emotional states and personal concerns, and everything happening around us. When we remember to be more fully conscious, then we can realize how unconscious we are in the periods before self- remembering. Through self-remembering, we begin to realize how unconscious we normally are, although not at the time, but afterwards when we remember ourselves again. Self-remembering begins to make consciousness as a property more visible to us, by demonstrating the inability to remember self. As a method for the study and enhancement of consciousness, self-remembering reveals the nature of the *waking sleep* state, while at the same time, it begins to de-automatize the usual processes which go on in the state of "automated consciousness."

Despite the importance of self-remembering, defining it is a tricky business. There are many angles from which this practice can be approached and definitions are useful—although only to a point. One must practice self-remembering, learning to define it, as G. says, *"by sensation, by taste,"* in order to gain a true sense of its profound significance. Nevertheless, Ouspensky defines self-remembering quite simply and distinguishes it from the related practice of self-observation:

> Self-remembering is an attempt to be aware of yourself. Self-observation is always directed at some definite function: either you observe your thoughts, or movements, or emotions, or sensations. It must have a definite object which you observe in yourself. Self-remembering does not divide you, you must remember the whole, it is simply the *feeling of 'I,' of your own person*. (Italics added, 1957, p. 107)

Self-observation is directed towards particular contents of experience and the activities of the centers. In contrast, self-remembering is experiencing or feeling/sensing the *whole* of self. Remembering self means being more fully present in such a way that one's experience consists of a deeper sense and feeling that *"I am here."*

On one occasion, Gurdjieff asked a group of his pupils, *"What is the most important thing that we notice during self observation?"* Dissatisfied with their answers, Gurdjieff explained that:

> "Not one of you has noticed the most important thing that I have pointed out to you
> .... That is to say, not one of you has noticed that *you do not remember yourselves*.
> ... You do not feel *yourselves*; you are not conscious of *yourselves*. With you, 'it observes' just as 'it speaks,' 'it thinks,' 'it laughs.' You do not feel: *I* observe, *I* notice, *I* see. Everything still 'is noticed,' 'is seen.'... In order really to observe oneself one must first of all *remember oneself*. ... Try to *remember yourselves* when you observe yourselves and later on tell me the results. Only those results will have any value that are accompanied by self-remembering. Otherwise you yourselves do not exist in your observations. In which case what are all your observations worth?" (1949, pp, 117-8)

At moments of self-observation, we need to remember ourselves and experience being fully present. In this case, there is an enhanced experience of *I*, in addition to the observation of the psychic functions. Ouspensky ascribes major importance to this deceptively simple idea:

> So, at the same time as self-observing, we try to be aware of ourselves by holding the sensation of *'I am here'*–nothing more, And this is the fact that all Western psychology, without the smallest exception, has missed. Although many people came very near to it, they did not recognize the importance of this fact and did not realize that the state of man as he is can be changed-that man can remember himself, if he tries for a long time. (1957, p. 5)

Again, it is impossible to appreciate the significance of this apparently simple practice of self-remembering until one undertakes the study of oneself on that basis. Only then can one begin to understand Ouspensky's claim that the study of psychology has to begin with attempts to remember oneself. Modern psychology has erred in failing to understand the normal state of people. Humans do not remember themselves and are not properly conscious, and have no "conscious self" as such. However, they can study self in the inner world and make intentional efforts to enhance consciousness.

Gurdjieff and Ouspensky refer to the ordinary waking state, the state of forgetfulness, as a state of "relative consciousness" or "waking sleep." Self-observation and self-remembering serve in the development of self-consciousness (and objective consciousness). Ouspensky explains some of the difficulties in understanding consciousness, particularly self-consciousness:

> The third state of consciousness is very strange. If people explain to us what the third state of consciousness is, we begin to think that we have it. The third state can be called *self consciousness*, and most people, if asked, say, 'Certainly we are conscious!' A sufficient time or repeated and frequent efforts of self observation is necessary before we really recognize the fact that we are not conscious; that we are conscious only potentially. If we are asked, we say, 'Yes, I am', and for that moment we are, but the next moment we cease to remember and are not conscious. So in the process of self-observation we realize that we are not in the third state of consciousness, that we live only in two. We live either in sleep or in a waking sleep which, in the system, is called *relative consciousness*. The fourth state, which is called *objective consciousness*, is inaccessible to us because it can only be reached through self-consciousness, that is, by becoming aware of oneself first, so that much later we may manage to reach the objective state of consciousness. (1957, pp.4-5)

Over a period of time, the processes of self-study and self-remembering remove various obstacles to consciousness and allow the emergence of self-consciousness. The basic framework is quite coherent and logical, although it is difficult to realize what lies behind all of the fine words.

To realize what self-remembering is, and is not, is a long and subtle process and various problems arise as people attempt to study and remember themselves. Each person will tend to interpret the term according to their own associations and beliefs. For the time being, it is most useful simply to approach the elusive practice of self-remembering by attempting to do it—anywhere and anytime.

Misunderstandings and misconceptions about self-remembering generate errors and illusions regarding its practice. First and foremost, people are apt to confuse being conscious of self or remembering self with *thinking about ourselves*, or *thinking about self-remembering*. Nothing could be further from the truth. In fact, the continual *turning of the mind*, as it is referred to in Eastern esoteric teachings, is a major obstacle to self-remembering. The associative thinking *happens* mechanically and is *not* something that "I" do, or could even *not do*. Associative thinking and emotional concerns continually engage the attention and prevent people from experiencing the deeper coherence, feeling and sensation that *"I am here."*

Negative emotions, self love and vanity, imagination and internal considering, and the turning of the mind, are all obstacles to self-remembering because each of these processes are based on *identification* and attachment. When a person is in a state of identification, he or she are attached emotionally to anything and everything that captures the attention. In this way, the many little i's are nourished by emotional attachments, sexual desires and instinctual appetites. Gurdjieff depicts the dis-identification process involved in the struggle towards the state of self-consciousness:

> "... a man must die, that is, he must free himself from a thousand petty attachments and identifications which hold him in the position in which he is. He is attached to everything in his life, attached to his imagination, attached to his stupidity, attached even to his suffering, possibly to his sufferings more than to anything else. He must free himself from this attachment. Attachment to things, identification with things, keep alive a thousand useless I's in a man. These I's must die in order that the big I may be born. (1949, p. 218)

It is not possible to self-remember at the same time as being identified. One's awareness is normally identified with or engaged by the thoughts, feelings and concerns of little i's. In contrast, the achieving of self-consciousness involves a change of being, and the emergence of real "I."

A human being in waking sleep (or relative consciousness) is always identified and lost in attachments. When self-remembering, consciousness is centered more in the essence of our being, rather than in imagination and the concerns of false personality. Self-remembering takes considerable time to understand, because we do not know what self is or that "I AM." People know only what Gurdjieff calls the little i's, but not "big I" or "real I."

It is useful to consider the central idea that humans are not properly conscious and it is necessary to remember to be more conscious and aware of self throughout the day, whenever you can remember to do so. Ouspensky (1957) explained:

> When we try to keep all these things in mind and to observe ourselves, we come to the very definite conclusion that in the state of consciousness in which we are, with all this identification, considering, negative emotions and absence of self-remembering, we are really asleep. We only imagine that we are awake. So when we try to remember ourselves it means only one thing—we try to awake. And we do awake for a second but then we fall asleep again. This is our state of being, so actually we are asleep. We can awake only if we correct many things in the machine and if we work very persistently on this idea of awaking, and for a long time. (p. 13)

Self-remembering is both simple and complex—as a practice and as a state. As a practice, it is a missing link in known psychological theories and a key to self-study and the study of psychology and consciousness. As a method, it is a way of attempting to awaken, which begins to demonstrate how we are normally asleep, lived out in an unconscious and mechanical state. When we initially begin to self remember, we cannot do so, because we are always so lost and absorbed by life and everything that happens. However, in time, one begins to understand why the mystical traditions and the fourth way teaching in particular portray humans as living in a state of illusion and forgetfulness. Self-remembering provides a method to overcome this pathological and unnatural condition.

To illustrate the importance of self-remembering, Gurdjieff compares the normal state of sleep and mechanicalness with being imprisoned. Ouspensky wrote:

> G.'s favorite statement was that, if a man in prison was at any time to have a chance of escape, then he must first of all *realize that he is in prison*. So long as he fails to realize this, so long as he thinks he is free, he has no chance whatever. (1949, p. 30)

Self-remembering, combined with self-observation and self-study, provides the means by which a human can realize how he or she is imprisoned. At the same time, it provides the key to escaping this horror and waste. For Ouspensky and Gurdjieff, self-remembering is a necessary method for any meaningful psychology—a form of conscious effort to study consciousness within self.

To awaken, to die, to be reborn—these are the three steps in the process of transformation which Gurdjieff describes. A person has first to wake up—realizing the normal condition of their personal waking sleep and lack of consciousness. Secondly, one has to die to the old, realizing one's nothingness and the lie of false personality. Thirdly, the individual must be reborn within the essence—to realize the higher centers and states of enlightened self-knowledge and objective consciousness. Psychology begins with self-remembering—a key to the process of changing one's being and to the study of consciousness within the inner world.

Gurdjieff depicts the process of self-remembering most succinctly:

> "*I am*; always; *I am*. Never forget. Little by little your "I" shall make a contact with your essence. It is necessary to repeat it many times."
> (Patterson, 2001, p.62)

8. The Psychology of Lying

A seventh definition of psychology drawn from Ouspensky's presentations of the fourth way teaching is perhaps the most odd: Psychology involves the study of *lying*. By lying, Gurdjieff does not mean intentional deception. Instead, he is referring to people's tendency to believe that, when thinking or speaking about things–especially themselves–they do in fact know and understand what they are talking or thinking about. In reality, people have an extraordinarily inflated evaluation of their knowledge and understanding of everything. People regularly speak about all sorts of things that they neither know nor understand in the least. This is what Gurdjieff calls lying.

Ouspensky elaborates on how lying is a fundamental feature of a sleepwalker's mechanical mental attitude:

> Lying fills all our life. People pretend that they know all sorts of things: about God, about the future life, about the universe, about the origin of man, about evolution, about everything; but in reality they do not know anything, even about themselves. And every time they speak about something they do not know *as though they knew it, they lie.* Consequently the study of lying becomes of the first importance in psychology. ...

> Psychology is particularly concerned with the lies a man says and thinks about himself. These lies make the study of man very difficult. Man, as he is, is not a genuine article. He is an imitation of something, and a very bad imitation.

> Imagine a scientist on some remote planet who has received from the earth specimens of artificial flowers, *without knowing anything about real flowers.* It will be extremely difficult for him to define them–to explain their shape, their color, the material from which they are made ... and to classify them in any way.

> Psychology stands in a very similar position in relation to man. It has to study an artificial man, without knowing the real man.

> Obviously, it cannot be easy to study a being such as man, who does not himself know what is real and what is imaginary in him. So psychology must begin with a division between the real and the imaginary in man. (1950, pp. 40-41)

Lies must be understood in relationship to what is real or imaginary within oneself through self study. Lying is an intricate part of a fabric of illusion and deceit. Under the spell of lying, we do not realize that we in fact know nothing–despite all of our fancy words and theories. We are not properly conscious and instinctually sensing reality, but instead are immersed in the lies of the mind, conditioning and false personality. We do not know self and life is thus full of lies–in all of the things that people say and think. Ouspensky elaborates:

> I will try to give some examples of how self-study should begin. We spoke already of lying and I gave a possible definition of psychology as 'the study of lying.' So one

of the first and most important things for you to observe is lying. Very much akin to lying are our illusions, things about which we deceive ourselves, wrong ideas, wrong convictions, wrong views and so on. All these must be studied because until we begin to understand our illusions we can never see truth. In everything we must first separate our illusions from facts. Only then will it be possible to see whether we can really learn something new. (1957, p. 18)

The study of lying applies to knowledge of self, the world and the Gods. From the Gurdjieff-Ouspensky perspective, an artificial man (or woman)—the products of mechanical life and the sleeping world—really knows nothing about the true depths of self or of the nature of reality. Nevertheless, like Jeanine, Gary, Carol, Brian and Anne, we think we know ourselves "pretty well" or "very well." Further, if asked about the origin of humanity, or the nature and purpose of life, or any other subject—even God—we are just as likely to think that we know the answers to these deep mysteries, at least as much as anybody might know.

Of course, lying is not a conscious process. On the contrary, it is precisely because of the fact that we are not properly conscious that we lie. We cannot speak the truth because we do not know the truth—of anything, ourselves or the world. Psychology and self-study begin with a study of what is real or imaginary in what we think we know. Ouspensky explained: *"The most difficult thing is to know, what we do know, and what we do not know."* It is because of the lies that we do not realize all that we do not know. People are governed by illusion and misunderstanding and take the imaginary as the real. Only if we separate the real from the imaginary within ourselves can we come to anything new.

Unfortunately, it is so difficult to really hear new ideas, because we are so full of acquired ideas, beliefs and theories—all lies. Instead, people think that they already possess self knowledge and with this self-consciousness, and knowledge about the world and the issues of the Gods.

The fourth way teaching offers a view of human beings and of the cosmos which violates everything we commonly think that we know, or which the material scientists imagine and assume. Recall Gurdjieff's stated intention in his writings *All and Everything*, "... to destroy in people everything which, *in their false representations, as it were, exists in reality, or in other words "to corrode without mercy all the rubbish accumulated during the ages in human mentation."* (1950, p. 1184) In a very real sense, Gurdjieff's teaching turns all usual knowledge into so much "rubbish"–all lies. These lies are the result of that psychic disease–called the "wiseacring" of *"the scientists of new formation."* This is the terminology used by Beelzebub, explaining to his grandson, Hassein, about those strange three brained beings on planet earth who fail to understand anything of Objective Science. According to *Beelzebub's Tales*, humankind perceives reality *"topsy turvy."*

It takes considerable time however to understand how persuasive lying is—in ourselves, in others, in the arts, culture, the sciences, philosophies and religions. In a way people think that they know everything, whereas in reality, humans asleep know nothing and do not even know that they know nothing. Certainly if life is filled with lies, then we come closer to the truth when we learn what is real and imaginary in ourselves. Without knowing self, how could anyone conceivably know about the cosmos. Self study and psychology demand a study of lying.

9. The Study of A Human and the Cosmos

An eighth definition of psychology is that the study of a human being must proceed in conjunction with the study of the world or cosmos. Esoteric teachings suggest that human beings embody, in the structures of their inner being, the same laws as those operating within the larger cosmos. Accordingly, the individual is said to be a *microcosm* of the *macrocosm*, and to be created *"in the image of God."* Gurdjieff comments:

> "... it is impossible to study man without studying the universe. Man *is* an image of the world. He was created by the same laws which created the whole of the world. By knowing and understanding himself he will know and understand the whole world, all the laws that create and govern the world. And at the same time by studying the world and the laws that govern the world he will learn and understand the laws that govern him. In this connection some laws are understood and assimilated more easily by studying the objective world, while man can only understand other laws by studying himself. The study of the world and the study of man must therefore run parallel, one helping the other." (1949, p. 75)

The study of the cosmos or universe forms no part of modern psychology. A human being is one thing and the physical universe is considered to be quite separate and distinct. Psychology and the social sciences deal with the nature of human beings, while the natural sciences deal with the material world or the universe. Within modern thought, there is no inkling as to how the study of a human being and the universe might proceed together.

However, the fourth way teaching encourages us to *"look at the universe from the same point of view as we look at man and his inner life."* (Collin, 1980, p. xv) The parallel study of a human being and the cosmos provides a very valuable key to approaching the study of cosmic design within the microcosm and the macrocosm. Ouspensky explains that there are certain *"fundamental cosmic laws"* operative within all cosmoses on any order of scale:

> We begin with psychology – the study of oneself, of the human machine, of states of consciousness, methods of correcting things and so on; but at the same time an important part of the system is given to doctrines of the general laws of the world; because we cannot understand even ourselves if we do not know some of the fundamental laws which lie behind all things. Ordinary scientific knowledge is not sufficient for this, because, just as such important points as absence of self-remembering were missing in psychology, so our science either forgot or never knew the fundamental laws on which everything is based.

> As I said, all things in the world, whether big or small, on every scale, are based on two fundamental laws, which in this system are called the Law of Three and the Law of Seven. (1957, p. 16.)

The Laws of Three and Seven provide the foundation for a dramatically different paradigm for understanding the nature of reality and are unlike anything offered within modern science, which has no comparable formulation. These fundamental principles of metaphysics and cosmology have an ancient history and recur throughout mystical and spiritual literature. To compare mystical teachings to modern so-called exact science, we can say that the *"scientists of new formation"* unconsciously *think in twos*–construing everything in terms of dualities; whereas the esoteric and occult teachings articulate the more complex triune and sevenfold nature of things.

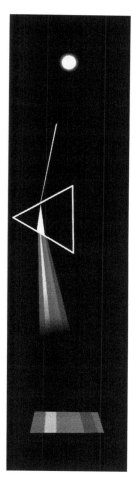

Maurice Nicoll (1975) quotes an ancient esoteric aphorism: *"God ... is first One and then Three and then Seven."* (p. 1386) Esoteric teaching suggest that any cosmos, on any order of scale –from an atom to a cell, a human being, a solar system, or a universe – embodies these principles of design. The simplest demonstration of these principles involves the division of white light by a three sided prism into a spectrum of seven colors. One is divided by three and yields seven. According to the fourth way, these principles of design permeate all cosmic manifestations–on all levels of reality from the microcosm to the macrocosm.

Gurdjieff explains that the *law of three* governs *"the transformation of Unity into Plurality,"* and that it permeates and sustains all cosmic phenomena:

> ... the *fundamental law* that creates all phenomena in all the diversity or unity of all universes. This is the 'Law of Three' or the law of the *three principles* or the *three forces*. It consists of the fact that every phenomenon, on whatever scale and in whatever world it may take place, from molecular to cosmic phenomena, is the result of the combination or the meeting of three different and opposing forces.... According to real, exact knowledge, one force, or two forces, can never produce a phenomenon. The presence of a third force is necessary....

> "Examples of the action of the three forces, and the moments of entry of the third force, may be discovered in all manifestations of our psychic life, in all phenomena of the life of human communities and of humanity as a whole, and in all the phenomena of nature around us. (1949, pp. 77-8)

The universality of the Law of Three means that any phenomenon, on any order of scale, throughout the cosmos and within the individual's inner world, involves a trinity of forces. Pythagoras maintained: *"All things consist in three."* Unfortunately, in the state of relative consciousness or waking sleep, humans perceive only two forces in things and are *"third force blind."* The scientists of new formation consider the opposing positive and negative forces, the active and passive principles, the stimuli and the responses, the mind and the body, or the conscious and the unconscious, but fail to formulate the neutralizing third force which brings the opposites into relationship.

The second fundamental cosmic law in Gurdjieff's cosmology is the *Law of Seven*, or the *Law of the Octave*. Like the law of three, the universality of the law of seven means that it applies everywhere, and so any process in any medium, anywhere, at any time, must be understood in relation to a sevenfold or octave analysis. Once again, this principle has an ancient history and is embodied within different teachings and symbols – including the Genesis myth of creation of the world in six days, with God resting on the seventh, the division of the week into seven days, and the octave patterns in music.

Gurdjieff claims that the Law of Sevenfoldness can be applied to any subject of study within psychology, science and cosmology. As Beelzebub explains to his grandson:

> "... in accordance with this Law, there are in the white ray seven independent colors; in every definite sound there are seven different independent tones; in every state of man, seven independent sensations; further, every definite form can be made up of only seven different dimensions; every weight remains at rest on the Earth only thanks to seven "reciprocal thrusts," and so on. ... the Law of Sevenfoldness will exist on the Earth as long as the Universe exists ..." (1950, p. 461)

The Law of the Octave

Basically, the law of the octave suggests that the development of vibrations of any process can be represented as a scale of seven notes, which is completed in the eighth note.[7] In a musical scale, the notes do, re, mi, fa, sol, la, si, do describe an ascending octave; while the notes do, si, la, sol, fa, mi, re, do depict a descending octave. The ascending octave describes *evolving* processes, in which increasing order, coherence, and unity develop; while the descending octave refers to *involving* processes, in which greater disorder, chaos, interference and division occurs. All of creation involves the manifestation of evolving and involving octaves, in endless permutations and combinations on different scales of being, within different media. Further, just as there are ascending and descending music octaves, so also both types of octaves are present within all scientific and psychological processes.

The law of the octave embodies the principle of the *"discontinuity of vibrations."* Gurdjieff stated that western science in his day assumed the continuity of vibrations. In contrast, the Law of the Octave stipulates that vibrations develop in discontinuous steps or stages or levels. In modern terminology, Law of Seven suggests that all the phenomena of nature are quantized–occurring within discrete quantum levels or steps rather than merely existing as on a continuum. Everything exists in relationship to octave structures, with discontinuities or quantum levels in the development of vibrations.

The verbal formula *God is first One, then Three and then Seven* is applicable to any area of human or scientific inquiry, to any phenomenon of nature, to any aspect of the psychological or soul life, and to any process of creation or destruction, involution or evolution. Gurdjieff explains: *"Different numerical*

---

[7] Within any period or scale, the frequency of vibrations doubles or halves, depending on whether one is ascending or descending the scale. This principle is embodied in the musical octave; the higher do of an octave vibrates at twice the frequency of the lowest do. In fact, Mr. G. states that within ancient esoteric schools the musical octave was devised as a means of representing the law of the octave.

combinations of a few elementary forces create all the seeming variety of phenomena. In order to understand the mechanics of the Universe it is necessary to resolve complex phenomena into these elementary forces." (1949, p. 122)

Examples of the triune and sevenfold/octave nature of things illustrate the basic principles. The first involves the division of white light by a three sided prism into a spectrum of seven colors (indigo, violet, blue, green, yellow, orange and red). The visible spectrum of electromagnetic radiation, or light, comprises such an octave of vibrations. A second example involves the nature of the material world. According to modern chemistry, the material world is composed of atoms (one) composed of protons, electrons and neutrons (three), which combine to form the seven rows of elements on the periodic table. Other octave patterns are also evident within the rows of the periodic table. In addition to these threefold and sevenfold patterns inherent in physical matter, Gurdjieff maintains that they also exist within the subtle planes of matter and being.

Turning to psychology, humans are three brained beings functioning physically, emotionally and mentally, or in the language of Beelzebub, with *"three separate independent spiritualized parts."* (p. 480) Further, these three parts of a human being are composed of seven centers. The pure light of consciousness interacts with and illuminates this system of seven vital centers, each of which has a triune nature as matter, energy and intelligence. Whereas modern scientists almost always talk of a duality of matter and energy, or the mind and the body, esoteric teachings suggest that they are third force blind and fail to recognize the third force embodied in all processes.[8]

Gurdjieff applies the laws of three and seven to elaborate the *"Ray of Creation,"* which involves the creation of the varied *"world orders"* within the larger Cosmos. Somehow, the plurality of life was transformed out of an underlying Unity in the "Absolute;" and the laws of three and seven govern the processes of the involution of cosmic elements and their subsequent evolution. In studying psychology and the possibility of human evolution, we have to understand our place in the Cosmos within the varied world orders–within which we live, move and have our being.

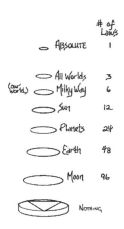

Mr. G.'s cosmic octave, the Ray of Creation, begins from the unified Absolute under 1 law and portrays the generation of successive world orders through the multiplication of the law of three. The first created world order is thus under 3 laws; the second under 6 laws; then 12, and so on–as each world order is subject to the influences of the worlds above, while generating another plane of effects, which become further causes for subsequent effects. This cosmology has seven world-orders arranged hierarchically as they involve from the Absolute. The descent of forces is from divine or spiritual dimensions into increasingly dense material worlds. The top Do of the cosmic octave is the Absolute, the All, and the bottom Do is Nothing. The Ray of Creation is a model of the *matters, forces and intelligence* present everywhere within time/space–a model of the multiple forces permeating the vast sea of space within which we live, move and have our being.

---

[8] In yoga, the triune nature of matter, energy and intelligence are related to the three "modes of nature" (or "gunas") and to a seven fold system of "chakras" or centers connected by three primary nadis or channels (the ida, pingula, and sushumna)–within the subtle anatomy. There are innumerable examples of the triune and sevenfold nature of human beings throughout esoteric and mystical psychology, philosophy, science and religion.

Gurdjieff explains that if we ask, "in what world do we exist," then we realize that we live not in one world, but in many worlds simultaneously. The influences of all the world orders of the cosmic octave interpenetrate all space/time. These worlds are not simply out there in the world around us, or above us, but within the interior dimensions of self and the cosmos of consciousness. The Ray of Creation *involves* from within/without through varied dimensions and world orders:

> The chain of worlds, the links of which are the Absolute, all worlds, all suns, our sun, the planets, the earth, and the moon, forms the 'ray of creation' in which we find ourselves. The ray of creation is for us the 'world' in the widest sense of the term. (1949, p. 80)

Humans live simultaneously in "all worlds" in the universe, within the galaxy of the Milky Way, revolving around the local sun, in relationship to the planetary world, on the earth, with the moon as a satellite to the earth. According to this formulation, the influences of each of these world orders pervade space, one within the other, serving to focus the life of the Absolute into the different realms of cosmic creation. We live within all of these worlds and are subject to the laws and influences of each level of this grand hierarchy of being.

"I" emerges ultimately from within the Absolute and the exists within space/time complex of manifested creation pervaded by this sea of cosmic influences, forces and laws. Mr. G.'s explanations of the cosmic octave provide a profoundly valuable tool for attempting to understand one's position with respect to the many cosmic influences and world orders. According to the fourth way, profound relationships exist between the seemingly outer world of the Cosmos and the inner world of a human being. In fact, all psychological processes are interrelated to larger processes of the cosmic octave.

The teaching of the Ray of Creation illustrates how a human being is a microcosm of the macrocosm and it explains the role played by organic life on earth and humanity within the cosmos. In order for the radiations and influences of the higher worlds to pass onto the earth and moon—the growing tip of the Ray of Creation—something is required to fill the fa-mi interval. Gurdjieff maintains that organic life on earth is based in a side octave, and can provide the necessary *shock* to fill the interval in the larger cosmic octave. Plant, animal and human life on earth thus enables the growth of the Ray of Creation. Humankind as a mass thus serves a cosmic function and is under the influences of the earth and moon, as well as of the planets, the sun and the stars.

Nicoll explains that the primary reason for human creation on earth is the possibility for "individual evolution:"

> Everything depends upon the primary reason for Man's creation on earth—namely, *individual evolution.* Man is created a self-developing organism and if the conditions for his self-development are destroyed, then Mankind, as an experiment, becomes useless. The Sun sows Man on earth primarily as a being capable of a definite inner development and secondarily to serve nature, to serve the necessities of the Ray of Creation. ... Evolution is possible for *a man*; but it is not possible for *Mankind.* (1975, p. 245)

Gurdjieff views humanity as *"an experiment of the Solar Laboratory,"* and the intelligence of the Sun is Divine in relationship to individual human evolution. An individual can come under the higher influences descending from the level of the divine intelligence of the Stars and thus fulfill higher cosmic purposes. The psychology of a human's possible evolution requires the simultaneous study of a human and the cosmos. A human being's hidden potential for the evolution of consciousness is intricately interrelated to the Ray of Creation.

Another feature of the law of octaves is illustrated by the musical scale and the piano keyboard, which consists of seven octaves of notes with white keys as whole notes and black keys as semi-tones (between the whole notes). Observing the keyboard, there are two places in each octave where there are *"missing semi-tones,"* between mi and fa, and between si and do. At these "intervals" there is a retardation in the development of vibration.

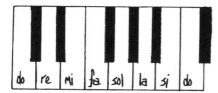

At the points of the missing semi-tones, a *"shock"* is required to further any involving or evolving process. A shock refers to some external force which provides the impetus necessary to overcome the retardation of vibrations and bridge the interval. A retardation of vibrations occurs at the two locations of the missing semi-tones and unless shocks are supplied, the octave's progress will be halted or deviate.

The psychology of a humans' possible evolution is based on the triune and sevenfold nature of things and illustrates the idea of shocks. Gurdjieff suggests that humans under the conditions of ordinary life will be one of three types: man number one, two or three. At this point, the octave of evolution deviates and humans do not develop to the fourth level, or beyond to the fifth, sixth or seventh levels. The nuts or acorns progress so far, do-re-me, but cannot breach the interval. It is necessary then for shocks to be provided from outside of the octave in order to allow the continued evolution of the individual. The shocks necessary for a man's conscious evolution might be provided by esoteric teachings and influences, by efforts to study and remember self, or through direct mystical and spiritual experiences.

Esoteric teachings offer more refined sources of nourishment than found amidst life's normal intellectual ideas and influences. Higher knowledge, schools and teachers, can provide the necessary shocks for the continued evolution of the individual. Human history has been illuminated by the lives of various individuals who have been such higher types. It seems that Gurdjieff had attained the level of being and consciousness of a higher man, although what number he was, we do not know. For those sleepwalkers, living in darkness and ignorant of self, the capacity to imagine, let alone comprehend, the realities in which such individuals exist are profoundly limited. As humans asleep, they do not understand enough about normal (or abnormal) psychology, to begin to approach the realm of the supernormal. For some who come under higher influences, the effect is sufficient to allow their metamorphosis and conscious evolution. However, most frequently, the nuts sound the notes of do, re and mi in the octave of evolution, but then deviate and evolve no further. According to Gurdjieff, the nuts become fertilizer.

By recognizing the law of seven and the principle of the discontinuity of vibrations, we possess a key to many of the mysteries associated with human nature and the study of the cosmos. In this vein, Gurdjieff stated that: "The law of octave explains many phenomena in our lives which are incomprehensible." (1949, p. 129)

This eighth and final definition of the fourth way psychology suggests the most unusual ideas and principles. A human being must be studied in relationship to the cosmos or universe, and in relationship to certain occult (or secret and hidden) principles about the nature of creation. *"God is first One, and then Three, and then Seven."* These profoundly enigmatic principles are well worth personal and scientific consideration. In this view, psychology involves the study of these ancient fundamental cosmic laws and their application to understanding self, human nature and the universe. A human being has hidden relationships to the larger macrocosm of which they are simply ignorant, and the quest for self knowledge must lead to a deeper understanding of the worlds in which we live and move, and have our being.

10. An Overview

Modern psychology has predominantly been defined as a dualistic science of behavior and mind. The *"scientists of new formation"* reject the metaphysical life of the soul or spirit, and along with this, the concept of a substantive consciousness.[9] They focus on the observation of overt behavior, usually that of other people or living organisms, or on some form of introspection or self analysis. In contrast, esoteric and mystical teachings primarily concern the study of a human's inner world. They are premised on the idea that humans in their normal waking state are not properly conscious, but that through self-study and work on oneself, one may awaken and attain higher states of consciousness and being. To do this, we have to study consciousness within ourselves, and struggle to attain the soul and real I.

Unlike western psychology, esoteric psychologies distinguish between the psychological functions and consciousness. Consciousness is something separate from thinking, feeling and sensing. Further, consciousness is substantive and is identified with light and a background of space. Within the inner cosmos of a human being, substantive light energies can illuminate the psychological processes. Most importantly, we can have more or less of this consciousness–this light–which allows for states of self realization and enlightenment–mystical states of union and transcendence.

A materialist world-view and reductionist methodology dominates modern science. By reducing everything to material structures and processes, scientists assume that they can formulate comprehensive explanations of nature and reality. While technological achievements and sophisticated knowledge within the natural sciences attest to the power of this paradigm, it is based on a complex of related but unnecessary assumptions. These assumptions guide and limit the materialists' interpretation of the facts of science.

The assumptions of modern psychology include the beliefs that: a human is the body and brain, and nothing more; humans are conscious beings; consciousness is produced by the activity of the brain; the physical body is the only body which humans have; death is the inevitable end of life; the existence of consciousness terminates with the dissolution of the brain; a "normal adult" possesses a fairly accurate understanding of his or her own personality; reasoning is humankind's highest faculty of intelligence; there are no higher emotions; learning is a matter of accumulating knowledge, and intellectual learning is the highest form; and, being a scientist and being a mystic are incompatible aims and activities. (Tart, 1975) These assumptions underlie the vast majority of modern psychology, philosophy and science. Foremost amongst these assumptions is the belief that neither the soul nor spirit exist, and that consciousness is nothing but the fortunate end-product of the brain's electro-chemical activities.

---

[9] David Chalmers, in a *Scientific American* article, addresses *"The Puzzle of Conscious Experience."* (Dec., 1995) Chalmers describes consciousness as being paradoxically *"the most familiar thing in the world and the most mysterious"* and he notes the *"tangle of diverse and conflicting theories"* existing within the field. Chalmers' solution to this situation is to suggest that consciousness is perhaps a *"fundamental feature of the world"*–irreducible to anything else. He compares this formulation to basic physical concepts such as space-time, mass, charge and so on, which are taken to be fundamental properties of the physical world which cannot be explained in terms of lower order phenomena. In this view, a model of consciousness requires a set of fundamental laws unique to the description of consciousness, analogous to the laws of physics used to describe the physical world. Such possibilities are bringing scientists back to the possibility of a "substantive consciousness" – a consciousness which is "something," whatever that "something" might be.

The fourth way teaching, as a psychology of the *"principles, laws and facts of a human's possible evolution,"* differs most dramatically from conventional thinking on all of these issues of psychology and self knowledge. In Gurdjieff's view: human beings are asleep and not properly conscious; they do not know self; they are ignorant of their essential nature and unaware of their typical mechanical state of existence; consciousness is not produced by the brain, nor exclusively centered there; humans do not exist in only a physical body, but can refine higher being-bodies; learning does not simply involve the rote acquisition of knowledge, and intellectual learning is not the highest mode of knowing; emotions are not all reducible to animal appetites and instincts, and higher emotions reveal more objective truths than normal intellectual functioning; humans do have the potential of attaining real I and a soul. Finally, being a mystic and being a scientist are not incompatible, and in fact, there is no true science without a metaphysical and mystical perspective. On the subject of this last assumption, Ouspensky argues that the supposed antagonism between science and mysticism is a myth. Instead, he argues that:

> ... *science must come to mysticism*, because in mysticism there is a new method – and then to the study of different forms of consciousness, i.e., of forms of receptivity different from our own. Science should throw off almost everything old and should start afresh with a new theory of knowledge. (1922, p. 230)

Whereas the psychologists, philosophers and scientists of modern times, might describe Gurdjieff as a mystic and charlatan, who offers nothing but unsubstantiated and illogical theories, Mr. G. describes *"the scientists of new formation"* as accumulating all the *"rubbish in human mentation,"* while perceiving reality *"topsy turvy."* Of course, what unifying knowledge or understanding of consciousness can be attained by an individual who is not unified or properly self-conscious?

The fourth way embraces Ouspensky's proposed union of mysticism and science. Gurdjieff's presentation of this ancient esoteric teaching recasts it in a form appropriate to humans within the twenty first century. By taking the knowledge of the West and the understanding of the East, he establishes the search for knowledge on a radically different foundation from that of modern thought. As an esoteric psychological system, the fourth way is a means of transmitting conscious influences. It provides a method to assist those who seek to awaken and know themselves through the process of conscious evolution. Real psychology begins with humans as they are and guides them in the effort to know self, the universe and the Gods. Esoteric teachings are sources of higher influence provided to further humans' possible evolution. The light of esoteric influences furnishes shocks by which the octave of a nut's evolution can proceed—sometimes to become an oak tree.

The struggle to escape from prison and the process of awakening begin with a study of ourselves as we are, in our state of automated mechanicalness and semi-consciousness. The fourth way psychology involves learning a new language and a systematic method of self-study. Self-observation involves the study of the centers or parts of oneself and self-remembering as the key to the study of consciousness and experiencing the whole. In this view, it is necessary to overcome the many obstacles to consciousness which exist within the so-called normal life of the individual. Persistent and long term efforts neutralize conditioning and the habits of thinking, feeling and action which dominate human life. With the help of a teacher and the influences of conscious ideas, self-study can bring us to new forms of self knowledge and realization. The psychology of a human's possible evolution begins when he or she makes a systematic effort to study what is imaginary or unreal, and what is real within self and in what we know.

In the light of objective knowledge about human nature and the universe which self transformation uncovers, all of our familiar ideas are revealed to be quite imaginary and based on lies. Humans have a hidden unknown relationship to the deeper nature of the cosmos, to the Common Father, Mother Nature and the Absolute. We do not realize humanity's origins and destiny within the larger Ray of Creation and we do not know self. Gurdjieff provides a profound teaching to help us understand how the microcosm and the macrocosm are interrelated, generated and sustained by the same fundamental cosmic laws. The fourth way places the realities and possibilities of being human in a cosmic context but suggests that only the fully awakened and conscious individual truly exists as a microcosm of the macrocosm.

The content, methods and aims of modern psychology and science are completely at odds with every fundamental aspect of Gurdjieff's teaching. From each perspective, the other is apt to seem most deluded. From a western scientific view, we are likely to dismiss the fourth way teaching as mystical nonsense and vague metaphysical speculations, and deny its relevance to the objective and scientific analysis of human beings. From a fourth way perspective, western psychology is riddled with misunderstanding, misconceptions, inexact language and terminology, and pervasive lying. Everything in its approach to the study and understanding of human consciousness, the mind and self, is fundamentally and irredeemably wrong.

At the very least, the fourth way provides extremely useful and provocative shocks to our beliefs about what we know and do not know—especially about ourselves and about consciousness. The framework of ideas exposes the assumptive basis of modern psychology and science, and suggests miraculous possibilities for human life and the attainment of consciousness. Is humankind really in a semi-conscious sleepwalking state, having only imaginary self-knowledge? If this is so, we can understand what Gurdjieff describes as *"the terror of the situation."* All the nuts turn to fertilizer and do not attain real "I."

"If you understand only a part, it is not understanding. It would be like blind men trying to explain the elephant, one by its tail, another by its trunk, and so on. Understanding means connecting parts with the whole. One can begin from parts, or one can begin from the whole. But whatever one begins from, the more connected things are, the better one understands—if the connections are made rightly and are not merely an illusion."

P. Ouspensky

Enumerating the Whole

1. Enumerating the Whole

In order to understand anything in its entirety, it is necessary to understand the many parts and how these work together to make up the whole. However, in order to understand the parts, it is also necessary to understand their relationship to the whole, because a small part or aspect of something in itself means nothing. Thus, understanding requires simultaneously developing a knowledge of the parts and of the whole, and how these things fit together.

A Sufi story about blind men touching an elephant illustrates this theme:

Beyond Ghor there was a city. All its inhabitants were blind. A king with his entourage arrived nearby; he brought his army and camped in the desert. He had a mighty elephant, which he used in attack and to increase the people's awe.

The populace became anxious to learn about the elephant, and some sightless from among this blind community ran like fools to find it. Since they did not know even the form or shape of the elephant, they groped sightlessly, gathering information by touching some part of it. Each thought that he knew something, because he could feel a part.

When they returned to their fellow-citizens, eager groups clustered around them, anxious, misguidedly, to learn the truth from those who were themselves astray. They asked about the form, the shape, of the elephant, and they listened to all they were told.

The man whose hand had reached an ear said: "It is a large, rough thing, wide and broad, like a rug."

One who had felt the trunk said: "I have the real facts about it. It is like a straight and hollow pipe, awful and destructive."

One who had felt its feet and legs said: "It is mighty and firm, like a pillar."

Each had felt one part out of many. Each had perceived it wrongly. No mind knew all: knowledge is not the companion of the blind. All imagined something, something incorrect. (Ornstein, 1972, pp. 161-2)

Each blind man grasped a part of the elephant and mistakenly assumed that he knew the whole. In the same way, the numerous western psychologies all touch parts of the human being and consider that they grasp the whole. Psychology is awash in divisions and sub-divisions, theories and mini-theories, bits of scientific fact and fantasy. Unfortunately, psychologists lack a view of the whole and do not know how to place knowledge of the parts into a coherent framework. More importantly, we do not understand the basic parts of ourselves.

The Gurdjieff teaching provides an integrative perspective on the parts of human beings and their relationship within the whole; especially in reference to understanding the nature of consciousness, mind and self. The nature of a human's seven centers, the distinction between personality, essence and the body, and discussions of the soul and the higher being bodies, are all parts of a complex framework for understanding the parts of a human being.

The fourth way perspective allows critical insights into the fundamental errors which pervade western psychology. The western discipline is dominated by the tendency to *think in ones* about human beings, regarding them as singular, unified organisms; or, to *think in twos*, regarding humans in simplistic dualistic terms, as simply having a mind and a body, or capable of being conscious or unconscious. Like the blind men, psychologists focus on one part of the elephant and conclude that it comprises the whole; or else they identify their part and then automatically assume that there must another part, a second, which makes things whole.

Gurdjieff explains that dualistic thinking is a product of incomplete understanding, typical of the *scientists of new formation*, who fail to realize third force within all things, and hence are "third force blind." Modern psychology is primarily dominated by dualistic models, whereas mystical psychology elaborates the triune and sevenfold patterns in all things. The fourth way thus offers a more complex and elaborate model of psychology than that within the western study of behaviour and mind.

2. The Dualities of Formatory Mind and Formatory Psychology

One of the most significant and least understood features of modern thought is the extent to which dualities pervade common thinking, as well as modern philosophy, psychology and science. The tendency to think in two's is a *"self-element"* in science: a personal element which people unconsciously introduce into things which they analyze. Understanding such thinking in twos is critical to appreciating the limitations of modern thought and the predominant scientific paradigm. It also prepares us to grasp the deeper idea of thinking in threes and sevens.

P. Ouspensky (1957) describes dualistic thinking as a self-element in science—an example of "formatory thinking:"

> The mechanical part of the intellectual centre has a special name ... called the ... formatory apparatus. Most people use only this part; they never use the better parts of the intellectual centre ... Formatory apparatus has very definite limitations. One of its peculiarities is that it compares only two things, as though in any particular line only two things existed ... Another of its peculiarities is immediately to look for the opposite.... (p. 63)

Formatory thinking is simplistic and dualistic, a lazy mental habit that blinds people to the full spectrum of existence. People look for only two elements, two principles, two alternatives or two parts. Unquestioningly, psychologists have most frequently regarded human beings as having only two parts or existing simply in two states, or under two conditions.

Certainly, life appears to be pervaded by opposites: the males and females, good and bad, positive and negative, up and down, with loves and hates, pains and pleasures, conscious and unconscious, rational and emotional, with a mind and a body, all between life and death. If that is not enough, we have the left brain and the right brain, science and pseudoscience, cause and effect, action and reaction, stimulus and response, input and output, in the binary age of 0 and 1, with subjects and objects, black and white, night and day, hot and cold, in and out, off and on, with good guys and bad guys, in the past and into the future, all made of matter and energy trapped within time and space, between being and non-being, on heaven and on earth, with spirit and matter, God and the Devil. Life is full of opposites or at least this is how people mechanically think about it, although we might wonder is this right or wrong?

A Yin/Yang play of opposing forces seems to dominate our existence—yet this is an illusion which results from our unrecognized patterns of mechanical thinking. Whenever people consider any subject of human discourse or academic science, they tend to uncritically embrace thinking in twos. A serious study of philosophy, psychology and science immediately reveals the pervasiveness of dualistic thinking. In modern psychology, discussions of human nature, consciousness, mind, personality and the self are hopelessly dualistic. The most common tendency is to consider two sides to human nature, two types of consciousness, two types of mind and two dimensions to the self.

The central duality of modern psychology is the view that human beings have primarily two major parts: a mind and a body. Psychology itself is most frequently defined as the science of behavior and mind, and philosophers debate endlessly the mind/body duality. There is the psyche (mind) and the soma (body). Even if theorists ask if there is anything beyond the physical or material body, their considerations are posed in dualistic terms—that is, they speak of the metaphysical or immaterial soul to contrast with the physical and material body.

With reference to consciousness, the most common dualistic distinctions are between the conscious and the unconscious, waking and sleeping, being aware or unaware. Alternatively, other theorists discuss the differences between consciousness and awareness, or between consciousness and self consciousness. At one symposium, the duality was drawn between Consciousness I and Consciousness II, to differentiate the self-consciousness which humans can know from the basic consciousness shared with other living organisms.

These dualities of consciousness are also tied into the dualities of the mind and self. Psychologists almost always think that there are two modes of mental functioning—a conclusion based upon a hundred years of formatory psychological and philosophical inquiry, and decades of split brain research. There are two modes of knowing, two types of intelligence, two types of information processing, two types of mind, and two cerebral hemispheres.

In 1966, Ulrich Neisser, was a major figure in the emergence of cognitive psychology. He commented:

> Historically, psychology has long recognized the existence of two different forms of mental organization. The distinction has been given many names: "rational" vs. "intuitive," "constrained" vs "creative," "logical" vs "pre-logical," "realistic" vs "autistic," "secondary process" vs "primary process." To list them together casually may be misleading ... nevertheless, a common thread runs through all of the dichotomies. (p.297)

The historic tendency to conceptualize mental organization dualistically received a major boost with the modern split brain research. Neurologists since H. Jackson (1864) have taken the left hemisphere to be the center for the faculty of expression required for the analysis of language and speech formation. In contrast, Jackson noted that a patient with a right hemisphere tumor *"did not know objects, persons and places."* Since Jackson, neurophysiologists have confirmed the localization of different mental faculties within the two cerebral hemispheres. The left hemisphere is more dominant in hearing and speaking language; while the right hemisphere is prominent in the perception or cognition of forms and sequences as required in musical abilities, facial recognition, pattern recognition and so on.

In modern split brain research, the corpus callosum–a band of fibers which connects the right and left hemispheres–is surgically severed. This procedure helped to illustrate the varied functions of the two hemispheres, and provided the methodology which has fueled the imagination of three decades of psychologists and consciousness researchers. Based on this research, it seemed that psychologists had hard evidence to support the traditional dualities of the mind. In this vein, Bakan (1978) explained:

> The left hemisphere mode (of thought) is described as symbolic, abstract, linear, rational, focal, conceptual, propositional, secondary process, digital, logical, active, and analytic. The right brain is described as iconic, concrete, diffuse, perceptual, a-propositional, primary process, analogue, passive and holistic. ... The two modes are antagonistic and complementary, suggesting that a unity and struggle of opposites is characteristic of mental functioning. (p. 163)

So many philosophers and psychologists formed their favorite dualities of the mind that it was only a matter of time before all of these dualities were taken to refer to the same fundamental dualistic truth. In 1972, Robert Ornstein published a popular and influential book entitled *The Psychology of Consciousness*, in which he posited the duality of human consciousness and detailed the supposed differences between the right and left hemispheres of the cerebral cortex:

> The recognition that we possess two cerebral hemispheres which are specialized to operate in different modes may allow us to understand much about the fundamental duality of our consciousness. This duality has been reflected in classical as well as modern literature as between reason and passion, or between mind and intuition. Perhaps the most famous of these dichotomies in psychology is that proposed by Sigmund Freud, of the split between the "conscious" mind and the "unconscious." The workings of the "conscious" mind are held to be accessible to language and to rational

discourse and alteration; the "unconscious" is much less accessible to reason or to verbal analysis. ... There are moments in each of our lives when our verbal intellect suggests one course and our "heart" or intuition another. (pp. 74-5)

"Dichotomania" is this unthinking tendency to construe all phenomena in dualistic terms and then to superficially equate these dualities. Dichotomania leads to confusion and Babel. Is the heart really in the right hemisphere along with passion, intuition, and the unconscious? Certainly a long list of philosophers and psychologists have taken a dualistic approach to the mind and to consciousness studies. Unfortunately, this reflects not the dualistic nature of reality but the dualistic thinking of the formatory apparatus of the scientists of new formation.

Gurdjieff explains that one must overcome such tendencies to think in ones and twos:

> Our principle error is that we think we have one mind. We call the functions of this mind 'conscious;' everything that does not enter this mind we call 'unconscious' or 'subconscious.' This is our chief error. Of the conscious and the unconscious we will speak later. At this moment I want to explain to you that the activity of the human machine, that is, of the physical body, is controlled, not by one, but by several minds, entirely independent of each other, having separate functions and separate spheres in which they manifest themselves. This must be understood first of all, because unless this is understood nothing else can be understood. (1949, p. 54)

Mystical and occult teachings provide more complex principles to replace the dualities of formatory thinking and psychology. In particular, the laws of three and seven allow for a more differentiated view of human nature, which includes a heart and soul.

3. The Three, Five & Seven Brained Being

At different times when elaborating the fourth way teaching, Gurdjieff would speak of humans as being composed of a different number of brains or centers. Ouspensky recalls:

> On the first occasion he spoke of three centers, the intellectual, the emotional, and the moving, and tried to make us distinguish these functions, find examples, and so on. Afterwards the instinctual center was added, as an independent and self-supporting machine. Afterwards the sex center.... there are not three centers but five in the ordinary man. ... During the first and subsequent talks on centers G. added something new at almost every talk. As I said in the beginning he spoke first of three centers, then of four, then of five, and afterwards of seven centers. (1949, pp. 55-56)

Within the fourth way psychology, self study and self-observation must be founded upon a knowledge of the centers. Gurdjieff explains that the activities, experiences and functions of the centers constitute the whole of an individual's life:

> "... all manifestations of man's life and activity can be divided in exactly the same way into seven categories." (Ouspensky, 1949, p. 74)

The centers are independent localizations of a human being. Each center adds a dimension to the life of an individual–one's actions, functions and experience. Each center has its own localization–a brain or physical system within the body–as well as its own subjective experienced side; its own intelligence and forms of knowing; its own functions (i.e. activities in the life of the organism for which it is responsible); its own time and speed of functioning; its own forms of memory and imagination; and its own matters and energies, required for activity within the organism. In self-study, the activities of the centers and their subdivisions must be observed and differentiated within oneself.

In *Beelzebub's Tale to his Grandson*, Gurdjieff (1950) most frequently refers to humans as those three-brained or three-centered beings from planet earth:

> "... they, like every other three-brained being of the whole of our Great Universe, have three separately independent spiritualized parts, each of which has, as a central place for the concentration of all its functioning, a localization of its own which they themselves call a 'brain'...." (p. 480)

Humans are three-brained beings and impressions arising from within or without will be perceived independently by these three aspects of a person's presence. Each brain will experience according to the nature of the impressions and independent associations or responses evoked. Gurdjieff refers to these three localizations as: *"thinking center, feeling center and moving-motor center."* (1950, p. 1172) On other occasions, the moving-motor center is referred to as the moving-instinctual center. This triune distinction is most important to understand. Humans experience and function mentally, emotionally and physically–enabling thinking, feeling and sensation/action.

Each center is further divided to include intellectual, emotional and moving (or mechanical) sub-divisions or components. Thus, we could talk of the intellectual part of the moving center, or of the emotional part of the intellectual center, the moving part of the intellectual center, and so on. The portion of a center active in different experiences is related to the type of consciousness and attention involved: (1) Directed attention involves the intellectual divisions of centers; (2) engaged attention involves the emotional portions of centers; and (3) actions with little or no attention involve the moving or mechanical portions of centers.

In the state of waking sleep, human beings are ruled by psychopathological processes and thus live largely in the negative and moving (or mechanical) portions of centers. Everything within a person happens in habitual and mechanical ways, with attention engaged and controlled by inner pushes and outer pulls, or in a semi-conscious manner with little or no attention. The capacity for truly directed and sustained attention depends upon the crystallizing of a conscious subject, or the attainment of real I. Generally, in humans asleep, the mechanical portions of centers dominate and people are unaware of the more conscious portions of these independent minds or spiritualized parts.

Thinking or intellectual center

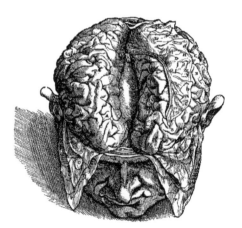

Thinking or intellectual center is responsible for the mental functions, including comparison, classification, judgment, the formation of representations and concepts, reasoning and prediction. The localization of the intellectual center is within the head brain. The thinking center analyzes, compares and associates mentally to impressions. Gurdjieff describes two basic forms of mentation: mentation by thought (involving words) and mentation by form (non-verbal representations). The intellectual center is further divided into three subdivisions, as well as into positive and negative sides.

The intellectual portion of the intellectual center involves directed controlled attention within an area of knowledge in order to formulate a conclusion based upon all available material about a topic of thought and inquiry. It is responsible for the functions of intellectual construction, creative thought and discovery. The emotional portion of the intellectual center consists of intellectual attractions and feelings. These may involves the desire to know and understand, the satisfaction or dissatisfaction of knowing or not knowing, and the pleasures of discovery and insight. The emotional part (and motivational component) of the intellectual center involves engaged attention; i.e., attention attracted and held by the subject matter and the interest aroused.

The moving (or mechanical) aspect of the intellectual center operates with little or no attention and provides the most mechanical responses to incoming impressions. This portion of the intellectual center has a special name: the formatory apparatus. It is responsible for the registration of impressions, memories and associations, and relies upon the simplest repetition of words, phrases and ideas, which are memorized or tape-recorded. The formatory apparatus takes the path of least resistance and effort in responding to impressions, and acts on the basis of past conditioning. It regards things simplistically in terms of opposites and extremes; there are right and wrong, good and bad, likes and dislikes, me and the world, a mind and a body. Formatory thought relies on acquired slogans, catchwords and sayings—all of which are acquired from outside through imitation and rote learning. The process of education and socialization fill the moving portion of the intellectual center with all kinds of words, bits of isolated knowledge and information.

The positive and negative sides to the intellectual center are evident in individual tendencies towards either affirmation or negation; towards saying yes or no to impressions and outside influences. Some people are characteristically negative and respond automatically in a way contrary to new ideas or impressions, if these differ from their acquired beliefs and attitudes. Such people will disagree and look for what is wrong in new thoughts or views. Others are characteristically positive in their outlook and find new ideas and viewpoints agreeable. They will look for relationships and connections with other ideas and for what is true in something, rather than for what is false.

Each tendency, towards the positive or negative alone, creates imbalance—as both sides of the intellectual mind serve complementary purposes. Some people too quickly and habitually react negatively to new impressions, while others too readily find new ideas agreeable and swallow any old tale in a gullible way. In order to develop the capacity for critical thinking and judgment, a balance of negative and positive tendencies, through the cultivation of a neutralizing, third force is necessary.

>
> Vaysse (1979) describes the intellectual center:
>
> At all levels, the function of the intellect is affirmation and negation: yes or no. The intellect receives the data, compares them with what it knows, coordinates, conceptualizes and looks ahead. On the lowest level, it is automatic critical judgment and imagination; on a higher level, it is logical confrontation and foresight. (p. 83)

There are many aspects to consider in studying the thinking center in order to understand it properly. We must also consider it in terms of its relations to the other centers. In fact, most of the time, the intellectual center is controlled by the emotions, sexuality or instinctual centers.

The emotional or feeling center

The emotional or feeling center is the second brain or mind. In *Beelzebub's Tales to His Grandson*, Gurdjieff tells an unusual tale about the fall of those three brained-beings on planet earth, and how the center of their emotional life changed:

> "... in the beginning these three-brained beings of the planet Earth ... had this concentration (the emotional center), similar to us, in the form of an independent brain localized in the region of their what is called 'breast.'

> "But from the time when the process of their ordinary being-existence began particularly sharply to change for the worse, then Nature ... was compelled, without destroying the functioning itself of this brain of theirs, to change the system of its localization.

> "That is to say, she gradually dispersed the localization of this organ, which had its concentration in one place in them, into small localizations over the whole of their common presence, but chiefly in the region of what is called the 'pit of the stomach.' The totality of these small localizations in this region they themselves at the present time call the solar plexus or the 'complex of the nodes of the sympathetic nervous system.'" (1950, pp. 779-780)

The heart can be taken to be the independent brain in the region of the breast. However, this is no longer the center of the emotional life. Instead, the emotional center has been dispersed to the solar plexus (the pit of the stomach) and other nerves of the sympathetic system. Gurdjieff is thus suggesting that ordinarily humans are not properly centered within the heart and that the emotional center has shifted to the solar plexus and 'pit of the stomach,' which became the primary localizations of emotional reactivity.

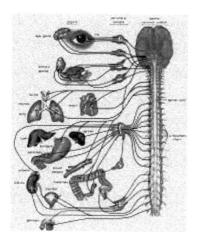

The sympathetic nervous system consists of two nerve tracts that extend from the base of the skull and run parallel to the vertebral column but outside of it. The nerve tracts branch to different plexuses—such as the solar, cardiac and hypogastric plexuses, and then to the different organs of the body—the heart, lungs, stomach and digestive tract, the adrenal glands, spleen, and so on. The accompanying illustration depicts the autonomic nervous system composed of the complementary sympathetic and the para-sympathetic systems. The sympathetic system is active during the "fight or flight" syndrome of arousal, while the para-sympathetic system is dominant during the "relaxation response." The autonomic nervous system exerts a widespread influence on the organs (smooth muscles) and glands of the body, the breath and the heartbeat. The solar plexus is the largest of the nerve plexus and a particularly important center for emotional reactivity—related to the organs of the viscera (i.e., the stomach and intestines) and the adrenal gland. The emotional center is also described as involving the glands of the endocrine system which distribute hormones through the blood, such as the adrenal glands and other glands of secretion, the tear glands and salivatory glands. (Vaysse, 1979)

Beelzebub's descriptions of the centering of emotional reactivity—within the sympathetic nervous system—makes sense when considered from an internal perspective. People experience varied feelings in the solar plexus and the abdominal viscera, as well as within the chest related to the heart and lungs. This is evident in common language. A person can feel anxious and upset, and then sick to the stomach or get butterflies there, or have gut reactions to things, and feel gutless at times. Tension, anxiety and insecurities are experienced and accumulate within the solar plexus and the abdomen. So also, the heart can skip a beat or one can feel the pounding within the chest, the tightness of the chest and rising blood pressure. The chest and abdomen areas are experienced in relationship to varied negative emotional states.[10]

On the other hand, positive emotions, especially love, compassion and empathy, are associated with the heart. This is reflected in common language expressions and in the use of the heart shape as the major symbol of love. People speak of feeling love with their hearts and of feeling sincerity from the bottom of the heart. Some things that we say are heartfelt, like hearty welcomes, if our hearts are really in it. Sometimes hearts are broken or lost or ache with loss and suffering. To have a heart means to show empathy or compassion, as people are sometimes heartless, especially when they commit cruel and violent acts. Many a lost soul is disheartened by the struggles and sufferings in life. Mystical teachings portray humans as *"contracted about the heart,"* absorbed in the false ego and selfishness, and incapable of knowing deeper love or other higher emotions.

Historically, psychologists have ignored the psychology of the heart, although there is growing interest in this area. In fact, psychologist Gary Schwartz suggests: *"If the 20th century has been, so to speak, the Century of the Brain, then the 21st century should be the Century of the Heart."* (Preface, in Pearsall, 1998, p. xiii) The heart is actually the largest source of biophysical energy in the body and is most closely related to the life of the soul.

From a psychological perspective, emotional functions comprise a distinct dimension of life. Vaysse describes this:

> The emotional center "experiences:" each time that an impression reaches it, it likes or dislikes, and experiences a personal approval or disapproval of the impression that is manifested in the form of an emotion. Because of this, each time something touches the person and his emotional functioning, it is automatically accepted or rejected, and at the same time a positive or negative emotion is expressed. This "something" is felt as desirable or undesirable. (1979, pp. 83-4)

The emotional center does not reason and compare in an abstract way. Instead, it defines a given impression by feeling qualities. At more mechanical levels, emotional experience involves liking or disliking, approving or disapproving, finding something pleasant or unpleasant. All experiences are accompanied by emotional reactivity, according to how things affect a person or make them feel.

---

[10] Other feelings can be localized in relation to the cardiac and hypogastric plexuses, and related organs and glands of the chest and pelvic areas. The third largest sympathetic plexus, the hypogastric plexus, is located within the pelvic region and tied to instinctual feelings and states. This plexus is activated in fear and traumatic experience, and in extreme cases can cause a person to urinate or defecate in fright. The tear glands are also innervated by the autonomic nervous system.

The emotional center is subdivided into intellectual, emotional and moving (or mechanical) components. From the perspective of Gurdjieff and his character, Beelzebub, the emotional life of the mass of humanity stands at a low level of development. Beelzebub portrays humans as ruled by negative emotions and patterns of self-love and vanity. This leaves few emotional energies for the experience of objective or higher emotions, derived from the conscious portions of the emotional center. In their state of waking sleep, human beings are too engaged by negative emotions and preoccupied with personal concerns, and the solar plexus becomes the center of emotional reactivity. This wrong work of the emotional center is one of the major woes of humankind.

Throughout a person's learning history, negative emotions–such as anger, anxiety, depression, resentment, boredom, impatience, envy, hostility, irritability, self-love and egotism–are conditioned by life experiences. In addition, emotions are acquired by the imitation of unconscious influences of family, peers, social influences, media and so-called culture. People experience a wide range of unnecessary and useless personal emotions, according to how events impact upon their imaginings and feelings about themselves (their self-love). Negative emotions are experienced when events subtract from the self-love (or vanity) and positive emotions when events reward the self-love (or vanity). The mechanical portion of the emotional center is the basis of human's narcissistic emotional reactivity. Unfortunately, mechanical emotions are the lot of sleeping humanity, who do not know the original center for the emotional life.

Mechanical emotional reactions depend upon the multiplicity of the human being with the many little i's, and leave little energy for the development of true feelings–requiring the presence of real I and the restoration of the original emotional center *"localized in the region of their what is called 'breast',"* the heart. For Gurdjieff, the awakening of the emotional center leads to the experience of conscience and the remorse of conscience. Many of *Beelzebub's Tales* deal with the role which certain cosmic messengers played in the history of humankind through their efforts to awaken conscience within humanity. People's true conscience has passed into the unconscious and a false personality system based on the mental activities of the formatory apparatus and the emotional reactivity of the solar plexus, dominate their lives.

The intellectual portion of the emotional center relates to artistic creation and to the selective evaluation of events in relationship to deeper levels of self. This is also the seat of the magnetic center–associated with the desire to know and understand the nature and purpose of life and of oneself. According to Gurdjieff, the formation of a magnetic center within an individual motivates the search for truth and draws people to more conscious ideas and influences. The magnetic center is not an independent center, but rather the selective intellectual portion of the emotional center. It enables an individual to appreciate the differences between imaginary (or formatory) thought, and more real and conscious influences within life. Those who search for something more significant that lay behind the mysteries of creation are said to have a magnetic center. People with a magnetic center are drawn to teaching such as that of the fourth way, as they are dissatisfied with the usual explanations and incomplete understanding of life. They seek to understand the deeper mysteries of the heart and of self. The emotional part of the emotional center involves feelings such as conscience and remorse of conscience, love and compassion, religious, aesthetic and moral emotions.

Mystical teachings generally stress the importance of finding a path with a heart. A spiritual path or way of knowledge must include the opening the heart within the process of self realization. The sleepwalker has to overcome the heart's contraction–which is expressed in the psychopathology of egoism, self love and self-centered will. The love of God, others and life is associated with the opening and the awakening of the heart. Unfortunately, as Beelzebub explains, instead of the emotional center being localized within an independent mind in the region of the 'breast,' it has been displaced to the complex of the sympathetic nervous system "in the pit of the stomach."

The third "independent spiritualized part" of a human being, which Beelzebub identifies, is actually the "planetary body." However, the physical body or organic nature has three relatively independent aspects. The moving center is distinguished from the instinctual centre and the sexual center is a third distinct aspect of the physical, organic being. Vaysse explains:

> … in ordinary man, the instinctual and moving centers (which take care of the inner and outer work of the machine) are closely connected, and, in addition, are closely related to the organic part of the sex center, forming with it a functionally balanced whole. Thus, it is not too great an approximation, and does not falsify man's nature, to consider him as a being who functions in three ways—organically, emotionally and intellectually—and who is endowed with three brains functioning at three different levels in himself. (1979, pp. 71 - 72)

In self-study, it is useful to consider the simpler three-fold distinction, but also to further subdivide the organic or physical body into the moving, instinctual and sexual centers. Five centers are the foundations for a person's normal functioning in day to day life.

Moving-instinctual center, the third brain, is localized by Gurdjieff within the vertebral column, particularly within the "'brain nodes' of their spinal marrow." (1950, p. 779) This refers to the spinal column and its extension into the brain stem, although this is not the complete story, as each center can have influence over the whole body.

Moving center

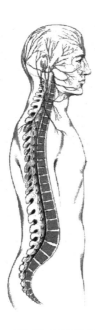

Moving center is responsible for the functions of movement in space, the support and posture of the body, outer behavior and activity. Because we experience the body and its activity through sensation, the moving and instinctual centers are described together as the moving-instinctual center. Sensory nerves from the body enter the spinal cord on one side, while motor nerves exit from the other. The brain stem includes primary sensory nuclei and areas which regulate numerous instinctual bodily processes—such as temperature, breathing, arousal and biochemical balances. The moving center is either active or at rest, with varying degrees of relaxation. This center is responsible for all learned movement including walking, eating, the maintenance of posture, control of the limbs, hands and fingers, and talking. Left to itself, the moving center remains inactive as it has little direction or initiative on its own. It is primarily at the service of other centers which put demands upon it. For instance, although the moving center is responsible for walking (in conjunction with the instinctual center), other centers determine the motives for this activity. Thus, one might walk to a cafeteria, to a friend's residence, to a library or a discotheque—according to the motivations of the instinctual, emotional, intellectual and sexual centers.

Talking provides another important example of how the other centers control the activity of moving functions. Although the moving center is responsible for the articulation of speech, the center in itself has nothing to say but rather expresses the purposes, needs and motives of other centers.

One of the most important ways in which the moving center learns patterns of movement is through direct imitation. The moving center has its own form of intelligence and knowing and can learn through simple observation. With more complex forms of activity, other centers (i.e., the intellectual) are required initially until an activity is learnt, but afterwards the actions can be performed unconsciously, without attention or intellectual control (e.g., driving a car).

The mechanical portion of the moving center is responsible for activity which places no or little demand upon attention. This includes automatic behavior and habits ranging from the simplest habits of fidgeting, to the complicated activities of working, going to the bathroom or driving a car. Even the mechanical portion of the moving center works at a more rapid pace than the intellectual mind. We cannot direct any complex series of movements by thought, except when initially learning activities and performing them at a slow speed. Once learned, the moving center performs at a much faster speed than the intellectual center is capable of maintaining. If a person attempts to drive a car while directing his/her movements by thought, it is immediately apparent how awkward and dangerous this is, like the centipede trying to direct its hundred legs with the mind.

The emotional portion of the moving center provides motivation for activity and movement, and is associated with pleasant or unpleasant sensations. Activities such as games, acting, play, sports and dance are motivated in this way. The intellectual portion of the moving center is required for complicated or new movements which require the control of attention and a degree of self-awareness or self-remembering. Tai Chi and other movement meditations, Gurdjieff's sacred dances, martial arts, intricate handiwork, the invention of mechanical devices and the solution of mechanical problems, all place demands on the intellectual portion of the moving mind, and require the control of attention.

Ouspensky recalls his reaction to Gurdjieff's explanation of the idea of an actual separate moving mind:

> The idea of an independent moving center, which, on the one hand, does not depend upon the mind, does not require the mind, and which is a mind in itself, and which, on the other hand, does not depend upon instinct and has first of all to learn, placed very many problems on entirely new ground. (1949, p. 114)

Most typically within western psychology, movement functions are viewed as one aspect of the mind, dependent upon the sensory-motor strip within the cortex of the brain. In contrast, the fourth way suggests that this might be a control center for moving mind, but that the spinal column is the deeper center of the moving-instinctual brain. To consider the moving center as a separate and independent form of intelligence is a most valuable idea for self-study and self-observation.

The Instinctual center

The Instinctual center is responsible for the internal life of the organism– the unconscious biological and physiological processes, sensory capacities and the pains and pleasures of the body. The instinctual center governs activities such as the growth and maintenance of bodily forms, the regulation of body states, metabolism, breathing, digestion, circulation, hormonal stimulation and sensory processes. Its activities are "instinctive," or innate to the organic body, rather than learned. The instinctual center provides the intelligence that governs the life of the physical body. Somehow the body is able to digest food and water, air and other elements, and to create the energies required for the body and psyche. All of this is done instinctively in accordance with the natural wisdom of the material body and organic nature. Instinctual needs include those for food and drink, for air and light, for safety in situations of danger. Emotions based in the instinctual center include those of pain and pleasure, physical discomfort or feelings of organic well-being. There are some instinctual actions, reflexive in nature, ranging from blinking of the eye, to sneezing and knee jerk reactions.

According to Gurdjieff, the brain of the moving and instinctual mind involves the *"brain nodes of the spinal marrow."* This includes the spinal cord and its extension into the brain stem (including such structures as the medulla, pons and midbrain). The instinctive center includes the capacities for sensory awareness within ourselves and of the surrounding world. These do not have to be learned like moving functions, but are capacities inherent from birth. The sensory realm includes the five capacities of smell, taste, touch, hearing and vision, in addition to internal somatic sensations which arise from the body. These include exteroceptive sensations in the skin which are responsible for the sensations of touch, pressure, heat, cold and pain; proprioceptive sensations, arising from the physical state of the body, from the tensions of the muscles, angulation of the joints, pressure from the body in contact with things, and so on; and visceral sensations from internal organs, including sensations of digestive processes, of inner aches and pains, of heat and blood flow. A human being's awareness of self is anchored in sensory-instinctual awareness of the body. Pain and pleasure derive from instinctual center, and provide powerful human motives and drives.

The process of breathing is carried out instinctively, although it is highly influenced by the other centers and can be brought under conscious control. Gurdjieff advises against artificial use of breathing methods, unless under the guidance of a teacher. However, the study and awareness of breath is an integral part of self-remembering and self-study. Most importantly, self-remembering begins with self-sensing, which anchors awareness in the organic body and within the breath:

> "… at the same time as self-observing, we try to be aware of ourselves by holding the sensation of 'I am here'--nothing more." (1957, p. 5)

Self-sensing and awareness of the breath ground self-remembering in the body, allowing awareness of being here now, and of what is happening within and around us.

In self-study, one needs to identify the varied aspects of one's instinctual center, its processes and their contributions to the overall self experience. Also, one must consider how instinctual processes influence the other centers, and the roles they play in the psychology of life.

Sexual center

Sexual center is the final of the five lower centers. The sexual center is complex and its role within the individual changes according to a person's physical maturation and psycho-spiritual evolution. As a general rule, Gurdjieff states that, in a human asleep, the sexual center enables the process of procreation, while providing various "pleasurings," but it also can play an essential role in the secret processes of refining the "higher being-bodies" for the life of the soul.

From birth, the sexual center gives a particular coloring to the life of the individual according to their masculine or feminine polarities. However, the maturation of the sexual organs and glands occurs later in life after the development of the other centers. Unlike the other centers, the sexual center has no negative side, as sexual sensations are either neutral or positive. Negative sexual experiences are due to the involvement of other centers with negative sides and not inherent to the sexual anatomy. Negative emotions or instinctual bodily reactions (pain or discomfort) can make sexual experience unpleasant.

The sexual center uses the most refined energies of the five lower centers. Its functioning brings a particular acuity, subtlety and speed to other functions. Unfortunately, the sexual energies are frequently misused by the other centers, leading to numerous excesses and varied forms of human psychopathology. Gurdjieff describes the misuse of sexual energy as the principle motive force underlying all forms of human mechanicalness. It is not sex in itself which is destructive, but rather, the misuse of sexual energies by other centers. Gurdjieff describes this as the *"chief evil"* in the life of humanity.

The sexual center also serves the highest purposes of life and makes possible the psychology of a human's possible evolution. Vaysse (1979) explains:

> "… sexual fulfillment leading to the reproduction of life is the crowning achievement of all the organic activity of the human being, and without this fulfillment all this activity, from the organic and natural point of view, is so to speak cut short. But this does not exclude the possibility, from the point of view of higher development of the human being, that this same sexual energy, the finest and most active of the energies which are available to man, should serve not for the reproduction of organic life but for the realization of a higher order of life (a new birth, the opening of another level of life) which can only come about starting from energy of this quality …." (p. 89)

The transformation of sexual energies is linked to the rebirth of the inner being. This involves the awakening of higher centers and to spiritual rebirth. According to Gurdjieff, the accumulation and refinement of the potent sexual energies brings about the "crystallization" of the higher being-bodies, including the astral body and mental bodies—for the life of the soul.

Within the fourth way, students aim to achieve a permanent center of gravity, and this depends upon the proper functioning of the sexual center:

"The role of the sex center in creating a general equilibrium and a permanent center of gravity can be very big. … if it uses its own energy, the sex center stands on a level with the higher emotional center. And all the other centers are subordinate to it. Therefore, it would be a great thing if it worked with its own energy. This alone would indicate a comparatively very high level of being. And in this case … all other centers could work correctly in their places and with their own energies." (Ouspensky, 1949, p. 259)

Understanding sexual energies–their misuse and proper use–provides a key to understanding the psychopathology of humankind and the possibility of a human beings' evolution.

The five lower centers have been considered from the perspective of their neuro-physiological basis or localization, and their functions and qualities–in terms of what work they perform in the organism. Each provides components of the inner "stream of consciousness." Each center contributes a dimension to life, a sphere of existence and life activity, a sphere of mentality, intelligence, energies and substances. Ouspensky comments along this line: *"This system gives a real anatomy of our brain and generally of our whole mentality."* (1957, p. 66) To know self requires the study of the parts of the individual–the human machine–and that includes the study of the centers and their functions. It would also require that the centers be integrated into a whole, and unfortunately, most individuals seldom act with such a unified presence of head, heart and hands.

One of the distinctive aspects of the Gurdjieff teaching is this view that these centers compose distinct, independent parts of the whole. Each center is a living sphere of intelligence and mentality. Ouspensky explains:

> Each function has its own profession, its own specialty. They must be studied separately and their differences clearly understood, remembering that they are controlled by different centers or minds. It is very useful to think about our different functions or centers and realize that they are quite independent. We do not realize that there are … independent beings in us … independent minds. We always try to reduce everything to one mind. Instinctual center can exist quite apart from other centers, moving and emotional centers can exist without the intellectual. We can imagine four people living in us. The one we call instinctive is a physical man. The moving man is also a physical man, but with different inclinations. Then there is the sentimental or emotional man, and the theoretical or intellectual man. If we look at ourselves from this point of view, it is easier to see where we make the chief mistake about ourselves, because we take ourselves as one, as always the same. (1957, p. 54)

This system of five centers forms a basis for self-study and self-observation. Each observation of inner experience or activity can be situated within a framework which enumerates the parts of the whole. However, in studying the centers, it is not enough to simply know their activities intellectually–they must also be understood through inner taste, sensation and experience. The centers account for all the psychological or psychic functions of normal and abnormal psychology.

The psychology of a human's possible evolution provides a highly systematic and articulate view of the human machine, and the processes by which evolution could come about. Gurdjieff summarized some of these principles:

> "… a man has five centers: the thinking, the emotional, the moving, the instinctual, and the sex. The predominant development of any one center at the expense of the others produces an extremely one-sided type of man, incapable of further development. But if a man brings the work of the five centers within himself into harmonious accord, he then 'locks the pentagram within him' and becomes a finished type of the physically perfect man. The full and proper functioning of five centers bring them into union with the higher centers which introduce the missing principle and put man into direct and permanent connection with objective consciousness and objective knowledge." (Ouspensky, 1949, p. 282)

The process of physical self perfection thus involves "locking the pentagram" within the individual– through the integration of the five lower centers. This opens up to a human being the possibility for direct connections with the higher centers, and the possibility for higher consciousness.

The seven centers can be portrayed in an octave pattern in the manner shown below (which corresponds to the system of chakras in yoga). The real "I" might then be taken as the top do. Ascending up the octave is an evolutionary process and leads to the awakening to the higher centers.

Do ◯   "I"

      Shock
Si ◯   Higher Intellectual Center
Fa ◯   Higher Emotional Center
Sol ◯   Intellectual Center
Fa ◯   Emotional Center
      Shock
Mi ◯   Moving Center
Re ◯   Sexual Center
Do ◯   Instinctual Center

Higher Emotional and higher Intellectual centers

Higher Emotional and higher Intellectual centers are the sixth and seventh centers. These centers lie within the realm of supernormal, rather than normal psychology. The higher and more refined spiritual and soul centers are latent within the essence of a human being.

From Gurdjieff's perspective, it is the lower centers which are underdeveloped in humankind and not the higher ones. If the activities of the lower centers were regulated and quickened, then connection is made with the higher centers. The higher centers are present all the time but people fail to realize this because of the low state of normal consciousness and the continual absorption in the centers' mechanical activities. If more energies are refined and accumulated through the practices of self-remembering and self-observation, and the struggle with mechanical habits, then a individual begins to gain glimpses of the deeper levels of self and reality.

The state of self-consciousness involves connection with the higher emotional center. Steps toward awakening involve the refinement of the emotional life and the eventual opening of the higher emotional center–associated with the heart, the original center of the emotional life. Higher emotions are different from the personal emotions which dominate mechanical life, and which are solely the expressions of partial feelings inherent to little i's. In contrast, higher emotions are *"all-inclusive feelings inherent in the total presence of a really established inner I."* (Vaysse, 1979, p. 84) Objective feelings belong to the real being, to a refined and matured essence.

The higher emotional center is the basis for experiences of self-consciousness. In this state, the individual is said to know *"the full truth about himself."* Vaysse elaborates on the nature of higher emotions and objective feelings:

> The feeling of self which accompanies awakening to oneself is the first real feeling that a man can have; further evolution of the emotional center, going hand in hand with the attainment of a real I, approaches progressively the level of refinement of the higher emotional center, makes contact with it and finally merges with it. Not until this level is reached do the great "objective" feelings of Faith, Hope and Love become possible for man. (1979, p. 84)

Beyond self-consciousness, the state of objective-consciousness can be realized by awakening to the higher intellectual center. This fourth state of consciousness is said to reveal the *"full truth about everything,"* "things in themselves" and *"the world as it is."* (Ouspensky, 1950, p.35) In this state, Beelzebub says that the individual *"instinctually senses reality"* and *"instinctually senses cosmic truths."* Such states involve conscious experience within the subtle dimensions of being, the more illumined and formless realms which interpenetrate and sustain life.

Occasionally, people glimpse such higher realms but do not normally attain these levels of being. Experiences gleamed through accidental contacts with the higher centers cannot generally be assimilated by people who have not undergone preparation for such states. Gurdjieff explains:

> "... from descriptions of mystical experiences, ecstatic states, and so on, we know cases of such connections (with the higher centers). ... In most cases where accidental contact with the higher thinking center takes place a man becomes unconscious.

> The mind refuses to take in the flood of thoughts, emotions, images, and ideas which suddenly burst into it. ... But even these moments are so full of unusual shades and colors that there is nothing with which to compare them among the ordinary sensations of life. ... so-called 'mystical' and 'ecstatic' experiences ... represent a temporary connection with a higher center. Only very seldom does it happen that a mind which has been better prepared succeeds in grasping and remembering something of what was felt and understood at the moment of ecstacy. ... Our ordinary centers, in transmitting the impressions of the higher centers, may be compared to a blind man speaking of colors, or a deaf man speaking of music." (Ouspensky, 1949, p. 195)

Myths, symbols and verbal formulas are all used by those who possess objective knowledge to convey something of what is experienced in higher states of unity and realization. In particular, *"'Myths' were destined for the higher emotional center; 'symbols' for the higher thinking center."* (Ouspensky, 1949, p. 279) Gurdjieff assigned an important role to the study of symbols as an important part of the preparation for assimilating objective knowledge; and Gurdjieff's own masterpiece of *Beelzebub's Tales* illustrates the mythic dimensions of human life.

From the viewpoint of a human's possible evolution, the aim is to awaken to the higher centers and to abide in them through the crystallization of the higher being bodies—the astral, mental and causal bodies. This awakening to the higher centers involves an alchemical process of refining the activities of the lower centers and through the growth or formation of the subtle being-bodies, all for the life of the soul and to attain "real I."

In summary: A human being has a threefold nature—functioning mentally, emotionally and physically— and a sevenfold nature in terms of the centers. Of the seven centers, three are based in the physical realm (the instinctual, moving and sexual), two in the emotional nature (emotional and higher emotional), and two in the intellectual or mental realm (the intellectual and higher intellectual). The higher emotional center can be related to the soul life, and the higher intellectual, to the spiritual life. Self-study requires us to make the necessary mental effort to learn the divisions of the centers and use these discriminations as a framework for situating self-observations. The seven centers provide a diagram of a human's *"overall mentality."* Unfortunately, humans hardly know the higher parts of the lower centers, yet alone conceive of the mysteries revealed by the higher centers and states.

4. Essence, Personality & the Organic Body

Another important distinction which Gurdjieff uses in enumerating the parts of a human being involves the distinction between personality and essence. The organic or physical body is taken as a third component, while *"I"* is something else again. Ouspensky recalls Gurdjieff explanation of the essence and personality distinction:

> "It must be understood that man consists of two parts: *essence* and *personality*. Essence in man is what is *his own*. Personality in man is what is 'not his own.' 'Not his own' means what has come from outside, what he has learned, or reflects, all traces of exterior impressions left in the memory and in the sensations, all words and movements that have been learned, all feelings created by imitation—all this is 'not his own,' all this is personality.

> "From the point of view of ordinary psychology the division of man into personality and essence is hardly comprehensible. It is more exact to say that such a division does not exist in psychology at all.

> "A small child has no personality as yet. He is what he really is. He is essence. His desires, tastes, likes, dislikes, express his being such as it is.

> "But as soon as so-called 'education' begins personality begins to grow. Personality is created partly by the intentional influences of other people, that is, by 'education,' and partly by involuntary imitation of them by the child itself. In the creation of personality a great part is also played by 'resistance' to people around him and by attempts to conceal from them something that is 'his own' or 'real.'

> "Essence is the truth in man; personality is the false. But in proportion as personality grows, essence manifests itself more and more rarely and more and more feebly and it very often happens that essence stops in its growth at a very early age and grows no further.

> "Culture creates personality and is at the same time the product and the result of personality. We do not realize that the whole of our life, all we call civilization, all we call science, philosophy, art, and politics, is created by people's personality, that is, by what is 'not their own' in them." (Ouspensky, 1949, pp. 161-2)

Essence is what we are in the subtle dimensions and structures of our being. Various scientists of new formation have imagined this to be a *tabla rasa*, a blank slate, an amorphous mass or a black box in behaviorism. However, these are simply errors. Instead, the essence is the formation of a human beings' centers or being-locations. Vaysse (1979) explains:

> A man's presence ... has seven centers, each of which has a brain as its chief support. Each of these centers has specific qualities, which together constitute what is innate in every man-his own essence. (p. 48)

The essence is composed of finer or more subtle matters than the physical body, even though each center has its physical counterparts. However, the physical body is distinguished from both the essence and personality as being a third factor in the individual's constitution. The physical basis for the centers is within the body, as each center has a brain or *"being-localization"* for its support and manifestation. Yet the essence is not the body, although it is related to it and manifests through it. Vaysse (1979) explains:

> Essence and personality have as their support a third constituent of man: his organic body. This is the instrument through which all the exchanges which make life possible take place. These are the three basic elements given to man. Each of them has its center of gravity in one of the principle centers of man. The center of gravity of the body is the moving center; the center of gravity of essence is the emotional center; and the center of the personality is the intellectual center. ...

> His threefold constitution makes this individuality possible for man ... but since his three parts are independent of each other by nature, individuality is not given to man at birth. It can only be attained as a result of a long work on himself. Knowledge of the body, essence and personality is needed to accomplish this work. (p. 112-113)

Whereas essence is the true nature of the individual, what is *his own*, personality is *not his own,* but rather is that which is acquired from without–from parents and peers, from culture and civilization, from the media and current events, from education. Essence is relatively stable and unchanging relative to false personality, but requires opportunity for growth and expression. The essence is what could grow and evolve, and be the basis for attaining *real I.* In contrast, personality is always changing in response to the influences of external situations and conditioning, as many i's.

Gurdjieff depicts personality as an *"accidental thing,"* as it depends so much on the chance conditions of life and one's contemporary influences, rather than upon what is inherent to the essence of the individual:

> Essence is I–it is our heredity, type, character, nature. Personality is an accidental thing–upbringing, education, points of view–everything external. It is like the clothes you wear, your artificial mask, the result of your upbringing, of the influence of your surroundings, opinions consisting of information and knowledge which change daily, one annulling the other. (1975, p. 143)

A child comes to acquire many things, such as fears, tastes, likes and dislikes, attitudes, opinions and beliefs, ways of controlling the environment and manipulating other people, ideas, traits and characteristics. Early life experiences condition the child along a certain line, as do models within a child's upbringing and social interactions. A child learns false patterns of negative emotions, self-love or self-feeling as modeled and reinforced by others. In later years of childhood, after a child meets more peers and adults and is *educated*, then new worlds of people and influences are available for modeling and imitation. There are innumerable religious, moral and cultural influences, education and media. Impressions from all of these sources combine to make personality all the more elaborate and complicated, and to stuff the individual full of ephemeral knowledge or behaviors. However, personality is always acquired from the external conditions of the child's life and does not originate from within self.

In childhood, impressions from outside interact with the essence. Some impressions will blend with it, while others will be contrary to its feelings and well-being. With time, essence plays an increasingly small role within the life of the child and acquired traits form which have less and less to do with the child's true nature. He or she becomes conditioned by all kinds of unnatural interests, attachments and identifications–all learnt through imitation, suggestion and conditioning.

Under the conditions of mechanical life, a child continually absorbs the unconscious influences of parents, peers, educators and culture, and essence is unable to develop in a natural way. The individual identifies with what is *not their own* and takes personality, with its many interests, attitudes, opinions, beliefs, habits and so on, to be *the self*. In this way, an individual loses touch with the deeper levels of Self and is no longer centered in what is real within their essence. Personality is sometimes all that people know of themselves, beginning with their acquired names and addresses, and other impermanent things. Personality is a broad entity making up much of what people consider themselves to be. Personality and false personality also form to protect the child's essence, especially when he or she is subject to abuse, neglect and disturbed family life. The child has to protect his inner self and deeper feelings.

As a result of socialization, education and culture, personality becomes the more active aspect of the human being and dominates the life of essence. Essence can thus remain at a very immature level of development even in a so-called educated and cultured man or woman. Gurdjieff comments: *"It happens very often that the essence of a grown-up man, even that of a very intellectual and, in the accepted meaning of the word, highly 'educated' man, stops on the level of a child of five or six."* (Ouspensky, 1949, p. 162)

Whereas essence is embodied within the structures of the seven centers, personality is formed from the contents of particular life experiences. The child forms habits or patterns of behavior, feeling and thinking, related to diverse life situations. Over time, these patterns are repeated and become increasing mechanical. Personality is defined, even within western psychology, as the *patterns of thinking, feeling and action which characterize an individual's adjustment to the conditions of their life*. Habit structures form separate personages, or little 'i's, which are controlled by external stimuli, influences and situations. The child comes to act less and less from its real being and more from the patterns of conditioning and imitation.

Gurdjieff views personality in a totally deterministic way. A human being is a machine and the basis of this mechanicalness is the formation and strength of personality:

> "... his actions, thoughts, feelings and words are the result of external influences and ...
> nothing comes from himself. ... he is in fact an automation acting under the influences
> of external stimuli. He will feel his complete mechanicalness. Everything 'happens,' he
> cannot 'do' anything. He is a machine controlled by accidental shocks from outside.
> Each shock calls to the surface one of his I's. A new shock and that I disappears and a
> different one takes its place. Another small change in the environment and again there
> is a new I. ... there is nothing permanent in him from which control could come, not a
> single permanent function, not a single permanent state."
> (Ouspensky, 1949, pp.112-3)

This characterizes the human state of disunity. Humans do not act from the fullness of their being—from a unified state of presence or real I—but rather from habits of thinking, feeling and acting, which are controlled by external stimuli and conditioned by the pleasuring of the body.

According to Gurdjieff, modern life increasingly reinforces the development of false personality at the expense of the essence, with profound implications for the possible evolution of humankind:

> "… in the actual situation of humanity there is nothing that points to evolution proceeding. On the contrary when we compare humanity with a man we quite clearly see a growth of personality at the cost of essence, that is, a growth of the artificial, the unreal, and what is foreign, at the cost of the natural, the real, and what is one's own.

> "Together with this we see a growth of automatism. Contemporary culture requires automatons. And people are undoubtedly losing their acquired habits of independence and turning into automatons, into parts of machines. It is impossible to say where is the end of all this and where the way out..... One thing alone is certain, that man's slavery grows and increases." (Ouspensky, 1949, p. 309)

Despite this dismal view of humankind asleep, individual evolution is a possibility and this depends upon the growth and development of essence and the subsequent attainment of real I. Personality cannot be the basis for this self-transformation—as it is always multi-faceted with separate personages or small 'i's continually replacing each other according to situations, roles and chance happenings.

Beelzebub describes humans' true consciousness as being based in essence, but as having passed into the *subconscious*. A *false consciousness system* then governs the waking sleep state. Work on oneself thus requires learning to make personality *less active* to allow for the growth of essence. It is not easy to distinguish between personality and essence within oneself, or to feel this inner division. Further, one cannot approach the study of essence directly. Only by working to make personality *less dominant*, can impressions impinge upon essence, feeding and nourishing it. Normally, personality reacts quickly to impressions and preempts the experience and action of essence.

Of course, personality is necessary to a human being. A person has to adjust to the conditions of family life, the social realm and external environment, and learn about the world. Gurdjieff stresses the importance of developing the positive aspects of personality and being able to adjust under all of the circumstances which life presents, with many acquired skills and abilities. An individual is considered a more likely candidate for *the Work* if he or she is already a *"good householder"*—that is, one who is capable of dealing with life's normal challenges in a responsible and competent way, and not what Gurdjieff describes as a *"lunatic"* or *"tramp."*

The essence exists initially in a more undifferentiated, crude state and needs to be nourished by life experiences and activities. And although it is the possible basis of *real I*, the development of personality is necessary in order to allow such a refinement to be realized. The critical issue concerns whether or not personality comes to weigh too heavily upon essence and to replace it as the individual's *center of gravity*. Walker explains: *"The personality is a bad master but it may be made into a useful servant."* (1972, p. 109) The task is not to rid oneself of personality but to establish a harmonious balance between personality and essence. Walker explains:

> ... it would be a mistake to take all this too simply and to regard Essence as the ill-treated hero, dominated by the villain of the human drama, Personality, for there was much in man's essence which was primitive, crude and even savage, and a great deal in his personality which was praiseworthy and desirable. ... What is required for man's development is not that his personality should be eliminated, but that it should be rendered much less active than it is. Essence will then be enabled to grow and, as essence is the more genuine part of a man, this is a very necessary preliminary to his development. (1967, p. 87)

The growth and maturation of essence involves a *second education*, whereby personality is made less dominant in a person's psychology. Like the rich man who cannot enter into the kingdom of heaven, so also, the individual rich in personality, self love and false ego, cannot realize the miraculous hidden nature of the essence. People are too identified and attached to the acquired habits which they take to be themselves, but which have been acquired from without. In the false psyche of mechanical humans, artificial aspects of personality become the center of gravity of functioning and experience—all centered in the mind and the formatory center.

From the viewpoint of a human's possible evolution, only the development of essence allows for the attainment of *real I*:

> "... in everything under the care of Mother Nature the possibility is foreseen for beings to acquire the kernel of their essence, that is to say, their own 'I.'"
> (Gurdjieff, 1950, p. 1231)

Real I is based on the development of essence, the opening of higher centers and the attainment of true self-consciousness. Gurdjieff remarks: *"Behind Essence is Real I, and behind Real I is God."*

5. Humans Number One, Two and Three & the Higher Types

People are of three primary types—man number one, two or three—according to which of the physical, emotional and intellectual centers are most dominant within the psyche. Of course, all people function with head, heart and hands (mentally, emotionally and physically), but their *center of gravity*, where consciousness is typically most centered, is primarily within one of these realms.

Man number one, the physical type, is centered predominantly within the moving, instinctual and sexual centers in the organic body. Physical types may work manually in life, perhaps fixing cars, building houses, farming or as an athlete—all moving activities. Others may be more inclined to instinctual appetites, indulging in food and drink, preoccupied with bodily functions, or controlled by the pleasures and pains of the senses. Others will be primarily sexually preoccupied, insecure or indulgent. Man number two is emotionally centered, more preoccupied with relationships, feelings and emotional concerns, sensitivity and self expression. Such types may work with other people, within complex relationships, or be family centered, a care giver, an artist or author of sentimental materials. Man number three is more cerebral and theoretical, centered within the activities of the intellectual mind. Perhaps he or she solves world problems over coffee and donuts, or lectures on history and psychology, keeps accounts or works with computers. This type is most comfortable within the realm of the mind, in the abstract world of ideas and invented theories.

Man numbers one, two and three have primary ways of responding to life situations according to how they are centered. The intellectual will analyze and think about things; the emotional type will be preoccupied with feelings and emotional concerns; and the physical type will be active and labor intensively, or lethargic and do nothing while giving into the inertia of the body. Understanding how different functions or centers are more or less dominant within different people is an important route to understanding individual differences. People's experiences, interests and activities are profoundly affected by the way in which they are typically centered. Gurdjieff explained:

> "... people differ very much in the way they feel their functions.... Some perceive chiefly through their mind, others through their feeling, and others through sensation. It is very difficult, almost impossible for men of different categories and of different modes of perception to understand one another, because they call one and the same thing by different names, and they call different things by the same name. Besides this, various other combinations are possible. One man perceives by thoughts and sensations, another by thoughts and feelings, and so on. ... If two people perceive the same thing differently, let us say that one perceives it through feelings and another through

> sensation–they may argue all their lives and never understand in what consists the
> difference of their attitude to a given object. Actually, one sees one aspect of it, and the
> other a different aspect." (Ouspensky, 1949, p.107)

We have three blind humans touching an elephant, each centered within one of the three primary
divisions of their being. Each emphasizes one part or aspect of the whole to the neglect of the others.
There is a knowledge and being of man number one, two and three. However, Gurdjieff describes
all three as being 'asleep.' *"Man number one, number two, and number three, these are people who
constitute mechanical humanity on the same level on which they are born."* (Ouspensky, 1949, p.71)

Ideally, the three-brained beings would simultaneous develop all three sides of their nature. This is
the route to a more complete knowledge or experience of the world and oneself, and a completed
presence. Gurdjieff explains:

> "... every normal psychic function is a means or an instrument of knowledge. With the
> help of the mind we see one aspect of things and events, with the help of emotions
> another aspect, with the help of sensations a third aspect. The most complete
> knowledge of a given subject possible for us can only be obtained if we examine it
> simultaneously with our mind, feelings, and sensations. Every man who is striving after
> right knowledge must aim at the possibility of attaining such perception."
> (Ouspensky, 1949, pp. 107-108)

Efforts to be more fully aware–intellectually, emotionally and physically–cultivate a new fullness of
one's presence. Of course, the emergence of real "I" involves a much more radical, discontinuous
quantum shift within the individual's inner life.

The process of working on oneself requires work on the physical, emotional and mental levels, and
a simultaneous development of consciousness through self study and self-remembering. These
processes bring about the possibility for an individual's evolution and the attainment of levels four, five,
six or seven. If the primary cord of three notes is harmoniously sounded–the do-re-me–then the octave
of evolution might pass the missing semi-tone in the evolutionary ladder. A *shock* is required to enable
the further evolution of the individual. Such shocks can be associated with mystical experiences and
insights, or with conscious efforts to awaken and self-remember. Most importantly, shocks can derive
from *school influences* and direct contact with the higher emotional life and objective knowledge.

A human number four is a product of school work and cannot develop "accidentally" through life
circumstances or ordinary influences. Gurdjieff describes man number four as having *"balanced the
psychic centers,"* and *"already beginning to know himself"* and his possibilities. A human number
four has not yet attained real "I" but is drawing closer and gaining glimpses of such possibilities. As
a product of school work and *a second education*, such an individual develops *"a permanent center
of gravity which consists in his ideas, in his valuation of the work, and in his relation to the school."*
A human number four is not yet established in the state of self-consciousness or functioning within
the higher emotional center. However, he or she is gaining *a different type of knowledge* closer to
objective truth. Gurdjieff explains:

> "The knowledge of man number four is a very different kind of knowledge. It is
> knowledge which comes from man number five, who in turn receives it from man
> number six, who has received it from man number seven. But, of course, man number

four assimilates of this knowledge only what is possible according to his powers. But, in comparison with man number one, man number two, and man number three, man number four has begun to get free from the subjective elements in his knowledge and to move along the path towards objective knowledge. (1949, p. 73)

Higher influences and esoteric teachings provide a new approach to self knowledge and shocks to further individual refinement and evolution. A man number four has developed and balanced the three sides to his nature, and attaining a new understanding of self, with moments of heightened consciousness and more refined emotional states.

A human number five attains the state of self-consciousness and real "I." Such an individual "knows self," associated with awakening of the higher emotional center. The individual is unified in his or her presence and has attained consciousness and will. Gurdjieff describes a human number five as having *"already been crystallized,"* attaining real "I."

However, the achievement of level five may be the product of right or wrong work. If the individual achieves the fifth level without the transitional level of stage four, subject to school influences, then the crystallization may be distorted or lopsided. The threefold development of mind, emotions and body may not have been properly achieved. This might be the case of a fakir, monk or yogi who attains level five through mastery of only one dimension of their being. In this case, which G. describes as very rare, the human number five can evolve no further to levels six or seven. In order to do so, *"... he must again melt his crystallized essence, must intentionally lose his being of man number five. And this can be achieved only through terrible sufferings."* (1949, p.72)

A human number six begins to experience the faculties of higher intellectual center, while a human number seven has full objective consciousness and the use of the higher intellectual functions. G. describes him as having *"... the objective and completely practical knowledge of All."* As humans asleep, it is impossible to conceive of what such miraculous possibilities might entail.

In terms of enumerating the whole, we have to understand that the meaning of the word "man" is *relative*—having seven levels of meaning. Life influences produce humans number one, two and three, but the evolutionary process deviates or is stalled. The deeper miraculous possibilities for human evolution are only latent and will remain underdeveloped without the necessary shocks and higher influences. All powers and capabilities of the individual are determined by the level of one's being and the states of consciousness achieved. Higher types do exist—although they are very rare and typically unrecognized.

6. The Question of the Soul & the Alchemy of the Higher Being-Bodies

Within *Beelzebub's Tales to His Grandson*, Gurdjieff elaborates upon the issues of the soul and the *"higher being bodies,"* which can be *"coated"* for the life of the soul. One story told by Beelzebub concerns the events surrounding his fifth visit to the earth during the time of Babylon. This tale is recounted in the typical Gurdjieff manner:

"The learned beings collected ... there in the city of Babylon from almost the whole of the planet used often to meet together and of course to discuss among themselves, as it is proper to the learned beings of the planet Earth, questions which were either immeasurably beyond their comprehension, or about which they could never elucidate anything useful whatsoever, either for themselves or for ordinary beings there.

"Well, it was just during these meetings and discussions that there arose among them, as it is in general proper to arise among learned beings there, what is called 'a-burning-question-of-the-day,' a question which in some way or other indeed interested them at that time to, as they say, 'their very marrow.'

"The question which chanced to become the-burning-question-of-the-day so vitally touched the whole being of every one of them, that they even 'climbed down' from their what are called 'pedestals' and began discussing it not only with the learned like themselves, but also here, there and everywhere with anyone they chanced to come across. ...

"It was talked about and discussed by the young and old, by men and women, and even by the Babylonian butchers. Exceedingly anxious were they, particularly the learned, to know about this question.

"Before our arrival there, many of the beings existing in Babylon had ultimately even lost their reason on account of this question, and many were already candidates for losing theirs.

"This burning-question-of-the-day was that both the 'sorry-learned' and also the ordinary beings of the city of Babylon were very anxious to know whether they had a 'soul.'

"Every possible kind of fantastic theory existed in Babylon upon this question; and more and more theories were being freshly cooked up; and every, as it is said there, 'catchy theory' had, of course, its followers.

"Although whole hosts of these various theories existed there, nevertheless they were one and all based upon only two, but two quite opposite assumptions.

"One of these was called the 'atheistic' and the other the 'idealistic' or 'dualistic.'

"All the dualistic theories maintained the existence of the soul, and of course its immortality,' and every possible kind of 'perturbation' to it after the death of the being 'man.'

"And all the atheistic theories maintained just the opposite.

"In short, my boy, when we arrived in the city of Babylon there was then proceeding what is called the 'Building-of-the-Tower-of-Babel.' ...

"And it was precisely these two teachings which began to pass from generation to generation, and to confuse their 'being-sane-mentation' which had already been confused enough without them. ...

"One of these two teachings which then had many adherents in Babylon was just the 'dualistic' and the other, the 'atheistic;' so that in one of them it was proved in beings there is the soul, and in the other, quite the opposite, namely, that they have nothing of the kind." (1950, pp. 329-331, 339)

Gurdjieff writes with a profound sense of humor and cosmic insight, depicting what happened in ancient Babylon when the issue of the soul became the *"burning-question-of-the-day."*

Mr. G. elaborates the dualistic teaching in relationship to the issue of the soul:

"In the dualist or idealist teaching, it was said that within the course body of the being-man, there is a fine and invisible body, which is just the soul. This 'fine body' of man is immortal, that is to say, it is never destroyed.... Every man, already at birth, consists of these two bodies, namely, the physical body and the soul." (1950, p. 389)

G.'s view of the soul is neither atheistic nor dualistic, but something in between. A human can attain a certain immortality of the soul but this is not truly present in the individual unless it is acquired or achieved. The nuts can turn to fertilizer instead of oak trees.

"Yes," replied Beelzebub, "on almost all the planets of that solar system also, three-brained beings dwell, and in almost all of them higher being-bodies can be coated. Higher being-bodies, or as they are called on some planets of that solar system, 'souls' arise in the three-brained beings." (1950, pp. 60-1)

Higher being-bodies need to be coated or crystallized for individual evolution to progress and in order that the soul attain immortality. Gurdjieff provides a fascinating explanation of how such processes occur, what the higher being-bodies are, and how the immortality of the soul might be attained. Bennett (1977) explains:

Gurdjieff intends the doctrine of higher being bodies to be taken literally and with it the immortality of the soul. There is, however, the one all-important distinction from ordinary doctrines of immortality, namely that the soul is not present in man until it is acquired. Moreover, he constantly reiterated that a soul is a rare and most precious possession, to which only those few can attain who are able and willing to pay the price. (p. 107)

Bennett illustrates this teaching with verses from the Gospels: *"For many are called but few are chosen,"* and *"Every tree that bringeth not forth good fruit is hewn down and cast into the fire."* Gurdjieff gives such teaching a twist and suggests that unless they consciously evolve, human beings will *"die like dog."*

The life of the soul is associated with the crystallization and perfection of the *higher being-bodies.* The atheist view of ancient Babylon and modern materialist psychology and science are too simplistic in viewing a human being as having only one body, or simply a body and a mind. So also, the theistic views are dualistic arguing for a body and soul. Mr. G.'s more complex teaching about the higher being-bodies does not fall into either of these formatory and dualistic viewpoints. Instead, he claims that there is an inner hierarchy of subtle bodies which can be crystallized and become vehicles for experience and action for the life of the soul. Furthermore, these different subtle bodies are related to chemical and alchemical processes involving corresponding planes of being within the Ray of Creation.

According to Mr. G., a human being is both a "chemical factory" and an "alchemical factory." We live off certain substances provided in the world and these energies/ substances are refined and assimilated for the functioning and activities of the various centers and bodies. The psyche requires physical energies for moving and instinctual functions, emotional energies, mental and sexual energies. These substances are all produced through the assimilation of three primary "being foods," which include; 1) *food* consumed through the digestive system; 2) the substances in *air*, consumed through breathing and the pores of the skin; and 3) *psychological impressions*, all external and internal sensorial and psychological stimuli. These substances *"feed"* the body, emotions and mind—the three stories or levels in a three-brained being. The human factory receives these three raw materials from the outer world and transforms them into the energies and substances required for life. These same substances can also be accumulated and refined for the crystallization of the higher being-bodies.

In explaining these complex viewpoints, Gurdjieff uses the term *"hydrogens"* in a particular way to refer to varied matters, energies and intelligence which make up the different levels of the world orders.[11] A hydrogen is any substance, element or combination of these, which has definite cosmic properties. In G.'s scheme, we could talk of the hydrogens of wood, of water, of emotional or mental energies, sexual energies, consciousness, of the Sun or Earth, and so on. Hormones and trees, electromagnetism and the forces of nature, all involve substances, energies/matters and intelligence of different degrees of density or vibration. Everything in the Cosmos, from the Absolute to a stone, is composed of "hydrogens" of some density of matter/energy vibration.

The alchemist refers to the four basic *elements* of fire, air, water and earth, and sometimes to a fifth element, the ether. In terms of a human being, the earth represents the material body, water the emotions, air the mind, and fire, the spiritual element and life force. A human is composed of such different elements or substances of different densities and degrees of materiality. Gurdjieff's

---

[11] Whereas scientists generally distinguish matter and energy as dual principles, Gurdjieff's teaching suggests that any hydrogen, or element, has a triune nature as matter/energy and intelligence. Some elements are more in the material mode, others in the energetic mode, and the third in intelligence mode, but all elements have a triune nature..

"hydrogen diagrams" provide a complex way of trying to understand relationships between all of the substances which make up the human psyche, consciousness and the cosmos. There is no comparable framework within modern psychology. The *scientists of new formation* subscribe to a limited conceptualization of materiality and do not deal with the complicated subtle energies and substances of the psyche, or of the spiritual life.

Gurdjieff uses the hydrogen diagrams and the Ray of Creation to elaborate profoundly complex and subtle teachings about the nature of the soul and the higher being-bodies which can be coated to insure "immortality." The immortal soul would be composed of very fine "substances" or "higher hydrogens," relative to those of the material body. Ouspensky (1949) recalls G's explanations of the chemical and alchemy processes involved in the coating of the higher being-bodies:

> "The human organism represents a chemical factory .... transforming one kind of matter into another, namely, the courser matters, in the cosmic sense, into finer ones. The factory receives, as raw material from the outer world, a number of course 'hydrogens' and transforms them into finer hydrogens by means of a whole series of complicated *alchemical* processes. But in the ordinary conditions of life the production by the human factory of the finer 'hydrogens,' in which, from the point of view of the possibility of higher states of consciousness and the work of higher centers, we are particularly interested, is insufficient and they are all wasted on the existence of the factory itself. If we could succeed in bringing the production up to its possible maximum we should then begin to save the fine 'hydrogens.' Then the whole of the body, all the tissues, all the cells, would become saturated with these fine 'hydrogens' which would gradually settle in them, crystallizing in a special way. This crystallization of the fine 'hydrogens' would gradually bring the whole organism onto a higher level, onto a higher plane of being....

> "'Learn to separate the fine from the course'–this principle from the 'Emerald Tablets of Hermes Trismegistus' refers to the work of the human factory, and if a man learns to 'separate the fine from the course,' that is, if he brings the production of the fine 'hydrogens' to its possible maximum, he will by this very fact create for himself the possibility of an inner growth which can be brought about by no other means. Inner growth, the growth of the inner bodies of man, the astral, the mental, and so on, is a material process completely analogous to the growth of the physical body. All the fine substances necessary for the growth and feeding of the higher bodies must be produced within the physical organism, and the physical organism is able to produce them provided the human factory is working properly and economically." (pp. 179-80)

This fascinating passage describes the accumulation and refinement of finer energies or hydrogens. These processes allow for the coating or crystallization of the higher being-bodies, enabling the evolution of consciousness and the soul.

According to Mr. G., a human being can potentially have four bodies: the physical, astral, the mental (or spiritual) and the divine. Each of these is composed of finer hydrogens, more subtle matters/ energies and intelligence, related to different vibration levels of the *"Ray of Creation."* The Ray of Creation is G.'s diagram of the cosmos depicting the involution of different world orders out of the Absolute. As a microcosm of the macrocosm, a human being has levels in his or her makeup which correspond to the levels of the larger Cosmos, within which he or she lives, moves and has their being. A human exists within all levels of the Ray of Creation which interpenetrate each other throughout space/time.

For Gurdjieff, the issues of immortality and life after death depend upon the level of "man" we are talking about. The common fate is not too hopeful:

> "The 'man-machine' with whom everything depends upon external influences, with whom everything happens, who is now one, the next moment another, and the next moment a third, has no future of any kind; he is buried and that is all. *Dust returns to dust*. This applies to him. In order to be able to speak of any kind of future life there must be a certain crystallization, a certain fusion of man's inner qualities, a certain independence of external influences." (1949, p. 31)

A human can "die like dog" and feed the earth, through the decomposition of the physical body, or feed the moon through the dissipation of vital energies.

Alternately, a human *"without quotations marks,"* or a human in the full sense of the word, can achieve immorality. This individual *"possesses four fully developed bodies."* Mr. G. states: *"The fourth room gives man immortality and all religious teachings strive to show the way to it."* (1949, p. 44) When G. discusses death and afterlife possibilities, that possibility is dependent upon the crystallization of the higher being-bodies and their relationship to the Ray of Creation. Ordinary humans, or humans asleep, have only the physical body composed of solid matter which returns to the earth upon death. If an individual has developed the second astral body, consciousness can persist within the astral worlds related to the atmospheres and planetary influences. However, the astral body also is not immortal and after a period of time it also dissipates, undergoing a second death. The third mental or spiritual body is composed of the hydrogens of the Sun and can persist after the death of the astral body. The fourth body is "the divine body:"

> The fourth body is composed of material of the *starry world*, that is, of material that does not belong to the solar system, and therefore, if it has crystallized within the limits of the solar system there is nothing within this system that could destroy it. *This means that a man possessing the fourth body is immortal within the limits of the solar system."* (In Ouspensky, 1949, p.94)

The subtle dimensions of afterlife existence (the astral and mental planes, and so on) exist in relationship to the interpenetrating world orders. A series of deaths or the shedding of bodies occurs within the subtle dimensions. G. uses a unique term, the *"sacred Rascooarnos,"* derived from Russian, to describe the *separation of parts* which occurs during death and afterlife processes. Gurdjieff also suggests that *"what people call 'reincarnation'"* and *"what people call 'existence on the other side'"* are both possibilities for human beings. However, he also states that these possibilities depend upon the existence of the higher being-bodies, which humans may not possess along with their so-called immortal souls. In fact, afterlife conditions *"can be very varied."* (1949, p. 32)

Gurdjieff describes an unusual and awesome possibility of becoming "*immortal within the limits of the solar system.*" The most dismal possibility is that of *"dying like dog,"* if the subtle bodies and essence are not crystallized as vehicles for the life of the soul–to enable consciousness to persist within the more refined world-orders.

Within the fourth way, it is a most serious task to escape from prison, from the general laws of mechanical existence, and to be free. The evolution of consciousness within the subtle realms of the cosmos is the way to liberation and freedom from the mechanical laws which bind consciousness within the lower realms of material existence. The Ray of Creation provides a fascinating perspective on how the subtle dimensions of the inner cosmos of consciousness are interconnected to the hierarchically world order within the larger cosmos and how immortality might be attained but seldom is.

In summary, we have reviewed the major ways in which the fourth way psychology enumerates the parts of a human being–the parts of the machine and those of the higher being-bodies. We began with the study of the seven centers, then the distinction between the personality, essence and the body, and lastly, the possibility for the refinement of the higher being-bodies for the life of the soul. Certainly these are complex views of a human being with many sides to consider beyond the simple dualistic or atheistic views of modern Babylon. Imagine dying like a dog or becoming immortal within the limits of the solar system, or something in between. Do the nuts really have the opportunity to become oak trees, attaining a fourth body and achieving immortality? Unfortunately, all of these miraculous possibilities are denied to humans asleep, who know only two states of consciousness.

THE FOUR BODIES AND THE RAY OF CREATION

ABSOLUTE	
ALL WORLDS	**3 Laws**
ALL SUNS	**6 Laws**
OUR SUN	**12 Laws**
ALL PLANETS	**24 Laws**
EARTH	**48 Laws**
MOON	**96 Laws**

FOURTH BODY
**Divine or Causal Body, I,
Consciousness, Will**

THIRD BODY
**Mental or Spiritual
Body and Mind**

SECOND BODY
**Astral Body or Body Kesdjan,
Feelings, Desires**

FIRST BODY
Physical or Carnal Body

"... they began to exist already
excessively abnormally,
that is to say, quite unbecoming
for three-brained beings."

G. I. Gurdjieff, *Beelzebub's Tales to His Grandson*

Gurdjieff

IV /
The Psychopathology of Humanity

1. A Portrait of "Man" in Quotation Marks

For Gurdjieff, a real man or woman has attained "real I." A man in quotation marks is a sleepwalker, governed by a multiplicity of i's, lost in self-love and vanity, and ruled by negative emotions and imagination. A man in quotation marks is always lost in the world, unaware of what he senses, does, thinks and feels. He is lived out by life in a state of passive awareness and mechanical reactions, controlled by external influences, false personality and conditioning. A human asleep knows only pseudo-i and does not know the real world. In contrast, a real human can "instinctually sense cosmic truths" and "know self." Gurdjieff explains: *"... the difference between a real man and a pseudo man ... is ... between one who has his own "I" and one who has not ...."* (1950, p. 1192)

In his concluding remarks to *Beelzebub's Tales to His Grandson*, Gurdjieff draws a portrait of a man in quotation marks. From the outside, this person seems to embody the virtues of life and success, but if we see into his inner life, we realize that he is essentially asleep, conditioned by the pushes and pulls of external and inner stimuli. Gurdjieff's portrait of a person's inner world is both entertaining and horrifying. He begins by depicting the outward appearances of the person and then he portrays the hidden inner dynamics:

> "You have plenty of money, luxurious conditions of existence, and universal esteem and respect. At the head of your well-established concerns are people absolutely reliable and devoted to you; in a word, your life is a bed of roses.

> "You dispose of your time as you please, you are a patron of the arts, you settle world questions over a cup of coffee, and you are even interested in the development of the latent spiritual forces of man. You are not unfamiliar with the needs of the spirit, and are well versed in philosophical matters. You are well educated and widely read. Having a great deal of learning on all kinds of questions, you are reputed to be a clever man, being at home in a variety of fields. You are a model of culture.

> "All who know you regard you as a man of great will and most of them even attribute all your advantages to the results of the manifestation of this will of yours.

> "In short, from every point of view, you are fully deserving of imitation, and a man to be envied." (1950, pp. 1024-5)

We certainly seem to have an intelligent and cultured "man" in our midst. From the outside, this person presents as clever and successful, even interested in the spiritual nature of humanity. Gurdjieff then goes on to portray a typical morning of this gentleman and the processes of his inner life–that which the man himself does not see nor those around him. Gurdjieff provides a humorous peek into the inner world of a man in quotation marks:

> "In the morning you wake up under the impression of some oppressive dream.
> "Your slightly depressed state, that dispersed on awakening, has nevertheless left its mark.

"A certain languidness and hesitancy in your movements.

"You go to the mirror to comb your hair and carelessly drop the brush; you have only just picked it up, when you drop it again. You then pick it up with a shade of impatience, and, in consequence, you drop it a third time; you try to catch it as it is falling, but . . . from an unlucky blow of your hand, the brush makes for the mirror; in vain you rush to save it, crack . . . there is a star of cracks on that antique mirror of which you were so proud.

"Damn! Devil take it! And you experience a need to vent your fresh annoyance on some one or other, and not finding the newspaper beside your morning coffee, the servant having forgotten to put it there, the cup of your patience overflows and you decide that you cannot stand the fellow any longer in the house.

"It is time for you to go out. The weather being pleasant, and not having far to go, you decide to walk. Behind you glides your new automobile of the latest model.

"The bright sunshine somewhat calms you, and a crowd which has collected at the corner attracts your attention.

"You go nearer, and in the middle of the crowd you see a man lying unconscious on the pavement. A policeman, with the help of some of the, as they are called, 'idlers' who have collected, puts the man into a 'taxi' to take him to the hospital.

"Thanks merely to the likeness, which has just struck you, between the face of the chauffeur and the face of the drunkard you bumped into last year when you were returning somewhat tipsy yourself from a rowdy birthday party, you notice that the accident on the street-corner is unaccountably connected in your associations with a meringue you ate at that party.

"Ah, what a meringue that was!

"That servant of yours, forgetting your newspaper today, spoiled your morning coffee. Why not make up for it at once?

"Here is a fashionable café where you sometimes go with your friends.

"But why did you recall the servant? Had you not almost entirely forgotten the morning's annoyances? But now ... how very good this meringue tastes with the coffee.

"Look! There are two ladies at the next table. What a charming blonde!

"You hear her whispering to her companion, glancing at you: 'Now he is the sort of man I like!'

"Do you deny that from these words about you, accidentally overheard and perhaps intentionally said aloud, the whole of you, as is said, 'inwardly rejoices'?

"Suppose that at this moment you were asked whether it had been worth while getting fussed and losing your temper over the morning's annoyances, you would of course answer in the negative and promise yourself that nothing of the kind should ever occur again.

"Need you be told how your mood has transformed while you were making the acquaintance of the blonde in whom you were interested and who was interested in you, and its state during all the time you spent with her?

"You return home humming some air, and even the sight of the broken mirror only elicits a smile from you. But how about the business on which you had gone out this morning. ... You only just remembered it. Clever . . . well, never mind, you can telephone.

"You go to the phone and the girl connects you with the wrong number.

"You ring again, and get the same number. Some man informs you that you are bothering him, you tell him it is not your fault, and what with one word and another, you learn to your surprise that you are a scoundrel and an idiot and that if you ring him up again... then...

"A rug slipping under your feet provides a storm of indignation, and you should hear the tone of voice in which you rebuke the servant who is handing you a letter.

"The letter is from a man you esteem and whose good opinion you value highly.

"The contents of the letter are so flattering to you, that as you read, your irritation gradually passes and changes to the 'pleasant embarrassment' of a man listening to a eulogy of himself. You finish reading the letter in the happiest of moods.

"I could continue this picture of your day—you free man!

"Perhaps you think I am overdoing?

"No, it is a photographically exact snapshot from nature." (1950, pp.1204-7)

This portrait of a man in quotation marks depicts the inner world of a well respected, cultured and spiritual man about town. There is certainly a great gulf between the superficial outer appearances and the underlying reality. On the one hand, there is that which we imagine ourselves to be, clever and talented men and women about town, capable of solving life's mysteries over coffee and cigarettes. And then there is the inner man or woman, angry when we cannot find our slippers or when our self love or vanity is offended, or who is controlled by negative emotions, the intestines and sex organs. A person is absorbed, moment to moment, by every little thing that happens in the world, each turn of events bringing about different i's. There is a great gap between what we imagine "man" to be, and what the masses of humanity are—in their being. This is the great lie, how man in quotation marks goes by the name "man." In mechanical life, few people realize the terror of the situation.

In one of his Tales, Beelzebub humorously depicts humans as having *"four sources of action"* or motivation, *"existing there under the names of 'mother-in-law,' 'digestion,' 'John Thomas,' and 'cash'."* (1950, p. 343) In G.'s period, the term "John Thomas" signified the penis. In the portrait of a man in quotation marks, the most significant motives seem to be those of the stomach, sex organs, cash and the ego.

Gurdjieff explains how such men in quotation marks are developed in life:

"A man comes into the world like a clean sheet of paper, which immediately all around him begin vying with each other to dirty and fill up with education, morality, the information we call knowledge, and with all kinds of feelings of duty, honour, conscience, and so on and so forth.

"And each and all claim immutability and infallibility for the methods they employ for grafting these branches onto the main trunk, called man's personality.

"The sheet of paper gradually becomes dirty, and the dirtier it becomes, that is to say, the more a man is stuffed with ephemeral information and those notions of duty, honour, and so on which are dinned into him or suggested to him by others, the 'cleverness' and worthier is he considered by those around him.

"And seeing that people look upon his 'dirt' as a merit, he himself inevitably comes to regard this same dirtied sheet of paper in the same light.

"And so you have a model of what we call a man, to which frequently are added such words as 'talent' and 'genius.'

"And the temper of our 'talent' when it wakes up in the morning, is spoiled for the whole day if it does not find its slippers beside the bed.

"The ordinary man is not free in his manifestations, in his life, in his moods.

"He cannot be what he would like to be; and what he considers himself to be, he is not that.

"Man–how mighty it sounds! The very name 'man' means 'the acme of Creation;' but... how does his title fit contemporary man?" (p. 1208)

Gurdjieff draws a dismal view of a human asleep.

The psychology of a human's possible evolution begins with the study of one self as a machine, as a mechanical being controlled by negative emotions, imagination, habits and conditioning. One has to explore the inner world and witness the inner contradictions, the stream of i's, the moods, judgments and negative emotions, the fantasies and self-love, the lying and defences, the principle motive forces behind one's actions. The study of psychology begins with a study of oneself, the personality and false personality, and how these are maintained by the wrong work of centers. In mechanical humans, everything happens, one thing follows another and it all happens in the only way it could happen. It all happens in sleep–waking sleep–and all the while people think that they are properly conscious, that they know themselves, that they can choose and do, that they know what love is and what they are. Would the man in quotation marks, depicted in Gurdjieff's vignette, not state that he knows himself pretty well, or very well? Of course, he would. He would also think that he has a soul and that a place in heaven is already waiting for him.

2. The Wrong Work of Centers

The wrong work of the centers is part of the psychopathology of humankind and a primary focus of initial work to study and observe oneself. This wrong work includes mechanical habits within each of the centers—of thinking, feeling and action—which characterize a person within different areas of life. The wrong work underlies all kinds of negativity, unhappiness and anxiety, violence and addictions, conflicts and emotional issues. The wrong work of centers limits life and self-awareness, and keeps a human being imprisoned by the past and destructive forces in life. If the individual can lessen the controlling influence of these processes, he or she can retain the energies usually wasted in unnecessary and mechanical reactivity, and cultivate a heightened state of being present to the fulness of the moment. The struggle with the habitual side of life is necessary if the individual is to be free from the state of *automated consciousness*, and instead be, *"instinctually sensing reality"* and *"cosmic truths,"*—as described in the language of Beelzebub.

2a. **The Wrong Work of Intellectual or Thinking Center**

The wrong work of the intellectual center includes the turning of the mind, internal considering, the control of the thinking center by other centers, imagination, lying and formatory thinking.

Turning of the mind

A constant turning of the mind goes on in people much of the time. They replay incidents in their mind, talk to people in the inner world, justify different negative emotions, imagine scenarios playing out, anxiously plan the future or rework the past, worry and regret, judge everyone and everything, and consider all kinds of imaginary happenings. The turning of the mind, the continual inner talk and judgment, are wasteful and mechanical patterns, yet highly characteristic of people's unbalanced mental and emotional life. Usually, humans do not even question the nature of their internal states and are unaware of their extensive and convoluted thinking habits. The waking sleep state of automated consciousness is maintained by such inner talk and the continual stream of associative thinking. Furthermore, the activities of the intellectual center are usually controlled by the other emotional, moving-instinctual and sexual centers. One worries away about the mother-in-law, the servant, John Henry, one's injured self love, cash and digestion. More typically, consciousness and attention are absorbed in and engaged by the turning of the mind, and controlled by patterns of personal emotion, pains and pleasures, instinctual needs and sexual interests. Ouspensky states that people seldom use the intellectual center for its natural activity.

Normally, it is impossible for human beings to suspend the inner talk and turning of the mind. The inability to do this demonstrates the mechanical nature of associative thinking. The individual is lost, immersed, engaged and conditioned by the hundreds and thousands of things happening, and the associative thoughts and conditioned emotions.[12] These patterns are beyond control as there is no real I—no true center—from which control might come, or which might manifest real will. The stream of associative thought is a major obstacle to the development of consciousness.

Even attempting to stop the inner stream of thought associations begins with the mind itself, which creates various misunderstandings and problems, as the mind tries to stop itself and gets caught up in various mind games. However, observing the mind and self-remembering serves to de-automatize habitual thought patterns, and by doing so, an individual begins to gain more control over attention. By cultivating a deeper awareness of self, one begins to experience an intensification of consciousness, as the thought stream is deautomatized, diminished or suspended.

Unnecessary talking

Another useless intellectual function is unnecessary talking. People talk too much. Much of our time is passed in talking mechanically about things which have little or no real value. Such talking may give some imagined pleasure or relieve anxiety, or help people socialize, stimulate and titillate, and help to pass the time. People fear being in silence. Again, the aim within the fourth way is to save energies and time by eliminating mechanical and unnecessary talking. We aim to awaken to the reality of each moment. Much of common conversation is unnecessary, draining and wasteful, and binds the energies of attention and life to unimportant attachments, imaginings and insignificant things.

> Gurdjieff explains, in his characteristic broken language, to Fritz Peters:

> "Think necessary talk all time, that learn through mind, through words. Not so. Many things can only learn with feeling, even from sensation. But because man talk all the time—use only formatory center—people not understand this." (1964, p.63)

Self-remembering involves awareness of the fullness of one's presence in the world, in this moment, here and now.

---

[12] These ideas are found throughout mystical teachings. Eastern teachings refer to "the monkeys of the mind," an appropriate label for the inner chatter of associative thinking. Suspending thought is an aspect of gaining control of the attention in the practice of meditation. Yogananda (1972) defines yoga itself as "the science of mind control."

Similarly, Carlos Castaneda's describes the life of a warrior, as taught by his teacher Don Juan, a Native medicine man:

> "For years I have tried to live in accordance with your teachings," I said. "Obviously I have not done well. How can I do better now?"

> "You think and talk too much. You must stop talking to yourself."

> "What do you mean?"

> "You talk to yourself too much. You're not unique at that. Every one of us does that. We carry on an internal talk. Think about it. Whenever you are alone, what do you do?"

> "I talk to myself."…

> "A warrior is aware of this and strives to stop his talking. This is the last point you have to know if you want to live like a warrior." (1971, pp. 262-263)

Internal considering

Internal considering is a term discussed extensively by Ouspensky and Nicoll in their practical explanations of the Gurdjieff psychology. This involves a preoccupation with *our* feelings, wants and desires, thoughts about ourselves, the people in our lives, experiences from the day or from last week and next year. Internal considering may focus on what other people think and feel about us, or on our judgments, thoughts and feelings towards others. We might think that others do not value and appreciate us enough, that they do not care enough, or give us enough attention and thought, that they are idiots and do not understand our special talents, that they are not fair or loving enough. In internal considering, we are preoccupied with what we think and feel that others think or feel, or expect, or want from us; or with what we think, feel, expect and imagine and want from others. We inwardly live before imagined audiences of the other, concerned primarily with ourselves – ME and my self feelings. Internal considering focuses on "i, me, and mine."

Sometimes internal considering takes the form of *account making*. A person feels that others owe them and that they deserve more recognition or reward. We feel cheated, underpaid, unappreciated, misunderstood, put down, inferior or superior, or ... on and on. People imagine and relive past incidents and encounters, feel annoyed or misused, or fantasize what they might have said to the other, or what they might now say, and so on and on. Such matters are a source of endless worry, negative states and imagination.

> Gurdjieff describes internal considering:
>
> "On the most prevalent occasion a man is identified with what others think about him, how they treat him, what attitude they show towards him. He always thinks that people do not value him enough, are not sufficiently polite and courteous. All this torments him, makes him think and suspect and lose an immense amount of energy on guesswork, on suppositions, develops in him a distrustful and hostile attitude towards people. How somebody looked at him, what somebody thought of him, what somebody said of him—all this acquires for him an immense significance."
> (Ouspensky, 1949, p.151)

Internal considering takes various forms. People regard themselves as due special evaluation or consideration for their sufferings and are offended if another talks of hardships or misfortunes. Everyone has their own songs to sing, stories of imagined injustice, sleight and neglect, triumphs and escapades. People are all legends in their own minds.

There are various ways to decrease internal considering. Most importantly, we observe and study what specifically goes on in our thoughts. Imagine videotaping one's stream of associative thought and experience through a day, and then replaying this to oneself or to others! Of course, this would be the most embarrassing and humiliating experience, if anyone could really see into our hidden inner world. The man in quotations marks might be reduced to nothing. In self study, we attempt to do this within ourselves, to observe in an objective and impartial way the contents of internal considering and to be aware of the underlying patterns of motives and concerns.

Awareness or consciousness of something is a pre-condition for gaining control, changing or eliminating it from ourselves. We can learn to observe ourselves in the inner world at more and more points throughout the day and be impartially aware of what is going on within our mind and emotions. At the same time in self-remembering, one makes an effort to be more fully conscious in the moment, bringing attention to the breath, self-sensing and enhancing present awareness. As we are, we do not control our minds but are carried along by the stream of associative thinking, emotional reactions and imagination.

Self study requires cultivating a proper attitude towards oneself and others in life. Internal considering is always based on a certain identification with oneself, or *self-love*. We feel that others do not value us as we should be valued, or as we value ourselves. In internal considering, we forget what we owe—our debts and being obligations. Observing the self-centered, trivial and mean spiritedness of internal considering and the imaginary quality of our concerns helps to engender a correct attitude. We witness internal considering and make an inner separation from "it." By increasing our consciousness of ourselves through self-observation, we reduce the frequency of internal considering in our lives and diminish its force.

The fourth way psychology also encourages external considering—giving attention to the nature, needs and states of others. This practice demands empathy, tact and an adaptation to other's needs and feelings. External considering involves a more practical attitude in life and requires an understanding of people's attitudes, prejudices, likes and dislikes, types and needs. External considering is a form of self-remembering, where one overcomes the attitude of self concern to be more fully present and aware of others.

Imagination

Imagination is another useless function according to Gurdjieff. Each center is capable of imagination, although imagination primarily involves the emotional, instinctive or sexual centers making use of the thinking center. The thinking center is usually at the service of other centers, as daydreaming and imagination coincide with the common inclination to laziness, self-indulgence and inertia. The emotional, moving, instinctual or sex centers attempt to re-live various pleasures previously experienced or imagined. Daydreaming and imagination are automated processes, the opposite of being in touch with the real world and *instinctually sensing reality* in the fullness of the present moment. A popular saying states that we are all legends in our mind. Patterns of imagination create and reinforce such misunderstandings of ourselves and our lives.

Unpleasant daydreams are even more senseless and destructive than pleasant imaginings. Gurdjieff comments on the relationship between daydreaming and psychopathology:

> "Daydreaming of disagreeable, morbid things is very characteristic of the unbalanced state of the human machine. After all, one can understand daydreaming of a pleasant kind and find logical justification for it. Daydreaming of an unpleasant character is an utter absurdity. And yet many people spend nine tenths of their lives in just such painful daydreams about misfortunes which may overtake them or their family, about illnesses they may contact or sufferings they will have to endure. Imagination and daydreaming are instances of the wrong work of the thinking center." (Ouspensky, 1949, p. 111)

Imagination and daydreams vary widely in terms of their contents and serve various desires and attachments. Movies and television present the extremes of morbid and destructive psychological imagination, glorifying negative emotions, hatreds and cruelty. Much of so-called entertainment is of this bent, portraying fantasized tales of destruction, sexual violence and titillation, murder, obsession and psychopathology. These aspects of modern culture—the glorification of violence, imagination and negative states—feeds the formation of false personality and the lunacy of humankind. Other imaginations may be regarded as helping to pass the time and create pleasant sensations or feelings. However, daydreams and imagination become substitutes for action within people's lives. The fantasies become obstacles to awakening to the realities of life. Instead of losing ourselves in such self-indulgences, the aim in *the work* is to attend to real and deeper concerns and matters.[13]

Lying and formatory thinking

Lying and formatory thinking are other forms of the wrong work of the intellectual center. The effects of culture, education, socialization and the media are to create a library of tape recorded ideas, information, concepts, common attitudes and beliefs within the mind. Through imitation, conditioning and education, a person acquires a wide range of thoughts, facts and attitudes about things, which he unthinkingly takes to be his own. In fact, these thoughts and attitudes are acquired from without and are not connected to what a person really knows or to what s/he really is, in his or her essence.

Without knowing ourselves, a human becomes a living lie. We claim to know about all kinds of things; about ourselves, life, God and the universe, the state of humanity, about all and everything. We are full of acquired so-called knowledge which is considered real. People already think that they know the real world, whereas in fact they possess none of the knowledge they imagine themselves to possess. The person has simply been conditioned by others, who in turn were conditioned by the generations before. In a person's essence, he or she really knows little. At the same time, people are full of wrong ideas and lying permeates almost everything said.

This is especially true when it comes to self-knowledge. People think that they know themselves pretty well or very well: knowing their characteristics, their capabilities, aims and values, their failures and virtues, their ambitions, powers and capabilities. Yet these views of ourselves are never put to any form of systematic test or inquiry, and are structured around patterns of false personality and self-love. People see themselves in a favorable light, as being right in their judgments, or somehow more clever and superior—with some imagined quality and supposed self importance. People take their attitudes, opinions and beliefs as always being right, and defend and justify every thought, action or feeling. There are innumerable patterns of attitudes and beliefs which all form part of *the lie* of man in quotations marks. Lying is talking about things and ourselves as if we really know and understand when we do not. We lie because we are not conscious of what we do know and of what we do not know.

Formatory thinking involves the formatory apparatus—the mechanical portion of the intellectual center. The formatory center is like a tape recorder, copying the different ideas, prejudices, attitudes and bits

---

[13] If imagination is used in a controlled way, then it can serve a useful purpose. However, the most common characteristic feature of daydreaming is its uncontrolled and mechanical nature and the self indulgence in personal emotions, pleasurings and unconscious sufferings.

of so-called knowledge to which a person is exposed. Much of education involves filling the formatory apparatus with bits of information, opinions, facts and fantasies, theories and philosophical views. All this comes to be taken as one's own knowledge. Formatory thinking involves the mechanical replaying of the tape recorder and expressing what Gurdjieff describes as *"all the dirt"* that has previously been recorded. Formatory thinking is easy because it involves repeating ready-made phrases and opinions impressed upon memory. Formatory thinking avoids the difficulty or effort required to be fully aware of all of what one does or does not know.

Formatory thinking is characterized by dualistic conceptualizations and formulations—as if there are always only two parts to any whole. There are the good guys and the bad guys, the black and the white, love and hate, me and the other, pleasure and pain. Formatory thinking is also given to extremes, or reflexively parrots clichés, popular sayings and expressions.

Ouspensky distinguishes formatory thinking from the process of *formulation*, which bases conclusions upon awareness of all that one knows and does not know about some subject. Formulation requires attention, effort and a realization of the limits of one's knowledge and understanding. Formatory thinking is subjective, varying according to how a person happens to have been educated and conditioned. In contrast, formulation requires being conscious of all that one really knows, and holding this in awareness in order to arrive at the most informed conclusion.

Gurdjieff labels modern scientists as the *"scientists of new formation."* From a fourth way perspective, modern philosophies, the social and natural sciences, are all based upon a mountain of lies–subjective theories and ideas created by sleeping people. We are full of subjective, personalized theories and viewpoints, all of which are conflicting and incomplete. All the while, this so-called knowledge which people have accumulated within the formatory center is not matched by the development of their being. People think that they know all kinds of things and therefore are never at a loss for an attitude, opinion or belief. In fact, these ideas and theories are not based on people's experiences. Instead, they are nothing but incorrect ideas, which could not be known within their experience, because they are simply invented theories–dirt accumulated in the formatory apparatus. Recall G.'s aim, in *Beelzebub's Tales*, *"... to corrode without mercy all the rubbish accumulated during the ages in human mentation."* (p.1184) Unfortunately, because people are so full of acquired knowledge and psychological illusions, it is particularly difficult for them to really hear anything new.

The antidote to lying and formatory thinking is a deeper awareness of what one does and does not know, and this is a starting point within the fourth way. Along this line, Ouspensky writes: *"The most difficult thing is to know what we do know, and what we do not know"* (1922, p.7). Similarly, Nicoll (1971) writes: *"But if you know you do not know, you are more conscious."* (p.69)

These are major examples of the wrong work of the intellectual or thinking center, the useless functions of the mind that maintain inner disunity, illusion and unreality. Awakening requires the study of the mechanical processes of the thinking center which maintain the state of automated consciousness.

2b. **The Wrong Work of Emotional Center**

Negative Emotions

The fourth way offers a dismal view of the role of negative emotions within the life of humanity. Negative emotions are a central and pervasive feature of human abnormality and pathology. Ouspensky states that there are *"no necessary negative emotions."* Negative emotions are never justified, never useful, never productive, never glorious and noble. Instead, negative emotions are useless and waste the energies of the emotional life as well as the energies of other centers. The fourth way psychology highlights the extent to which negative emotions govern the sleepwalking life of humanity and the horror of this situation.

There are innumerable types of negative states and emotions: anger, hostility, envy, boredom, depression, anxiety and worry, resentments, suspicion, fear, self-pity, annoyance, jealousy, mistrust, emotions of violence, and so on and on. Ouspensky describes negative emotions as a terrible phenomena, which solve nothing, yield no knowledge, make life a burden and result in the great violence and suffering of humankind. Even worse is the fact that people do not realize that negative emotions are something which might be questioned or struggled with in order to eliminate.

People even imagine that they control their negative emotions, manifesting them as they like or as they *choose,* and that negative emotions express their real self. Humans in the state of relative consciousness glorify negative states and take them to be motivating, or as providing catharsis, or as giving oneself life, vitality and purpose. All of these rationalizations are simply wrong ideas which justify weaknesses and stupidity. People do not choose their emotional reactions but are mechanically controlled by them. In fact, as they are, people *cannot stop* the stream of habitual negative emotional reactions and states.

> I want particularly to draw your attention to this idea of negative emotions and the state of negative emotion. ... It is necessary to realize that there is not a single useful negative emotion, useful in any sense. Negative emotions are all a sign of weakness. Next, we must realize that we can struggle with them; they can be conquered and destroyed because there is no real center for them. If they had a real center, like instinctual emotions, there would be no chance; we would remain forever in the power of negative emotions. So it is lucky for us that they have no real center; it is an artificial center that works, and this artificial center can be abolished. When this is done, we will feel much better for it. Even the realization that it is possible is very much, but we have many convictions, prejudices and even 'principles' about negative emotions, so it is very difficult to get rid of the idea that they are necessary. Try to think about it... (1957, pp.69-70)

Negative emotions have an artificial center in the formatory mind and the wrong attitudes and beliefs of the many different little i's which make up false personality. Ouspensky explains:

> ... false personality ... is, so to speak, a special organ for negative emotions, for displaying, enjoying and producing them. You remember that there is no real center for negative emotions. False personality acts as a center for them. (1957, pp. 173-174)

Negative emotions are based upon patterns of conditioning, mistaken ideas and incorrect thinking, negative imagination and states of identification. Typically, we regard negative emotions as being justified reactions to external conditions, caused by someone or something else. In this way, humans misunderstand the essential nature of negative emotions and fail to recognize that they are simply conditioned reactions and patterns of false personality. From this perspective, negative emotions are expressions of our weaknesses, our imaginary concerns and compulsions, our lack of true consciousness.

Modern culture consistently reinforces and glorifies negative emotions; portraying them as being not only appropriate, but justifiable and honorable reactions to any and all situations. Educators, parents, peers and the media suggest that negative emotions can be right or noble, genuine expressions of one real self. Even psychotherapists share this view—believing that anger and worrying are, to a certain extent, natural, useful and appropriate processes. All in all, people cling to negative emotions and even celebrate them. Consequently, they cannot even imagine why they would want to oppose their negative emotions.

Of course, there is only one way to verify the view that negative emotions are unnecessary, wasteful and useless, and that is to study oneself. Unfortunately, the study of negative emotions is very difficult to do in an impartial way and people have little motivation for controlling their manifestations. Nicoll (1975) explains:

> ... we identify with our emotions more than with anything else and so I repeat, we take our emotional state always for granted—not as something that we have to observe and separate from. Everyone has a typical series of constantly recurring emotional states which vary from the greatest excitement and enthusiasms to the most depressed and morbid feelings. But because the force of the emotions is so blinding people remain fixed on the turning wheel of their emotions. In other words, people do not distrust their emotions but take them as if they were genuine and quite real states. They accept their emotions as right at any particular moment. And because emotions are so difficult to observe, owing to our tendency to identify with them, they do not observe them as something to observe and not go with. The starting-point always lies in self-observation ... The effort of internal attention will then begin to separate you from the emotional state and you may be able thereby to disarm it—i.e. not go with it, not believe in it, not take it for granted. (p. 811)

There are various practices which aid the struggle against negative emotions. Firstly, there must be a conscious effort to observe and study negative emotions by becoming aware of them as they arise within one's inner life. Without making an effort to study oneself, a person is simply carried along by negative feelings whenever they occur. People are normally *fused* and *identified* with these states. Negative emotions control and enslave people—yet they have no objective view of how this all happens. In order to begin to free ourselves from the unconscious rule of negative emotions, we must objectively see what they are—what they arise from in us and what value or role they have in life. The first practice is thus self-observation and self-study.

A second aspect to the study of negative emotions involves the struggle with *identification*. Typically, we tend to identify "I" with "it," and lose ourselves in negative emotions, imagination and internal considering, while absorbed in these processes. The Buddhist view of *attachment* as the root cause of all suffering may be likened to the process of identification. We are attached to negative states and absorbed by these sub-identities or little i's. However, by observing and remembering ourselves, one inwardly separates from such negative states and maintains a deeper sense of one's abiding presence within the fullness of the moment. In this case, there is an inward separation between I and *it*–even if only slightly or momentarily before one gets caught up again in the patterns of personal concerns.

Insights into patterns of negative states help to de-automatize these processes, as one loosens the attachment and identification. In doing so, one aims to lessen such destructive patterns formed in false personality. M. Nicoll compares this to tending a garden and getting rid of the weeds which would overtake the vegetables. Similarly, observation and awareness of negative states begins to weaken the continual states of attachment and identification, allowing one to remove the weeds of negative states from one's inner life.

A third practice is forming of the right mental attitudes, or right thinking. Ouspensky notes:

> We have to begin with right understanding, right attitude. As long as we think negative emotions are unavoidable, or even useful for self-expression, or something like that, we can do nothing. A certain mental struggle is necessary to realize that they have no useful function in our life and that at the same time all life is based on them. (1957, p. 70)

It is necessary to prepare the ground for the study of negative emotions by creating right attitudes and understanding. Ouspensky comments: *"... mental work comes first."* (1957, p. 70) One must take the idea that negative emotions are destructive and unnecessary and try to understand these principles through the process of self-study. Negative emotions can be viewed from an impartial perspective: questioning their usefulness and justification; seeing one's indulgences and pleasure in them; and examining them afterwards when one is less identified. Each person has individual work to do in identifying their particular patterns of negative feelings and states.

It is necessary to have the idea of struggling with negative emotions and then to apply this within self-study and inner work. A person can *think rightly* at the times of negative emotions and be aware of what they really involve within oneself and the situation. The origin of negative states must be understood within oneself rather than simply being viewed as caused by others, or situational and accidental occurrences. The light of consciousness and self-remembering begin to illuminate what negative emotions really entail and their useless and unnecessary nature.

A fourth aspect to the study of negative emotions involves the rule of *not expressing* them. In order to understand what negative emotions entail–their mechanicalness and control over the person–it is necessary to struggle with their expression both inwardly and outwardly. One must see through *work i's*, or work ideas, at times of negative emotions. We must come to know how negative emotions move, think, feel, smell and taste, how we justify them, and in what weaknesses or past conditioning they are formed. By self-observing, the individual begins to separate I from "it" through increased consciousness. Moments of non-identification bring about deeper insights, new emotional states and gradually, an increased inner light or illumination.

The study of negative emotions requires a resistance to negative states and reactions and their hold upon oneself. This is not simply to restrict the outward expression of the emotion while feeding it internally with justification, negative imagination and internal considering. Repression or suppression only maintains negative emotions at a deeper subconscious level. One has to find reasons and a viewpoint which demonstrate why negative emotions are unnecessary–understanding what these states involve from different angles and from the perspective of *work ideas*. Most importantly, one needs to self-remember at times of negative emotions to enhance one's consciousness of all that they involve. One comes to view negative emotions as mechanical and automatized reactions of "it," rather than as expressing real I.

Negative emotional patterns are acquired throughout childhood and form patterns of false personality. A child imitates other people and their emotional displays. He or she learns manners of expression, feelings and imagination, which support the identification with negative emotions. A child also learns to control and manipulate others through the display of negative emotions and can maintain a false exterior in order to hide their inner feelings and insecurities. Family, peers, socializing agents and cultural models all provide potential influences for imitation. Children observe other people's negative emotions and are the victims of them. Unfortunately, over time, people come to think that their negative emotions comprise their *real self*. Negative emotions assume control of the thinking center and motivate self-justification and internal considering. To make matters worse, the inclinations of false personality towards laziness and self indulgence provide no basis for a struggle with negative states within oneself.

All of these things need to be studied and verified within oneself, and doing so requires an exertion of *conscious effort* to observe and struggle with these states. This cannot simply be done as an intellectual task–dealing with negative emotions in the abstract. Instead, it is necessary to observe one's particular states; to label and classify them; to recognize their smell, taste, and walk; to realize where they originate. This all needs to be done in a personal way. Ouspensky writes: *"You must find which negative emotions you chiefly have, why they come, what brings them, and so on."* (1957, p.73)

It is useful to study negative emotions within three spheres of life; within oneself by means of self-study and self-observation; in others whose negative states are intertwined with one's own; and within society and the larger world scene. The fourth way teaching suggests that the world is largely governed by negative emotions and the history of humanity provides ample testimony to their pervasive and destructive nature. Little by little, one can begin to understand more objectively what negative emotions entail, of what stuff they are made and how they detract from life. It is necessary to acquire a new perspective, and to bring light to bear within the inner world–to realize how insane you have been.

Negative emotions drain vital life energies, diminish consciousness and disrupt the harmonious development of an individual's essence. They are useless–yet they govern the life of sleepwalking humanity and maintain human lunacy and madness:

> So if one is trying to create consciousness, one must at the same time struggle with negative emotions, for either you keep them or you develop–you cannot have both together. (Ouspensky, 1957, p.75)

The fourth way presents a dismal view of humanity asleep, ruled by negative emotions and self-love. Tragically, from this viewpoint, people know little of the broader positive emotional states that emerge with moments of awakening.

Mr Self-Love and Madame Vanity

There is another side to the psychopathology of the emotional center and to false personality. Gurdjieff claims that people generally have no *real feelings* as such–but only mechanical emotions based upon patterns of *self-love*. Unfortunately, this self that we love is not the real self–the essence–but instead, is the false personality which consists of imaginary ideas and feelings. The phenomena of self-love are very broad and take many forms and endless disguises. For men, Gurdjieff uses the term *Mr. Self-love*, whereas for women, he uses the phrase *Madame Vanity*.

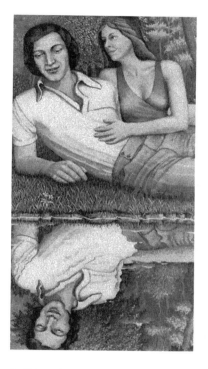

Self-love colors ordinary love to such an extent that people are unable to feel the real existence of others, except as reflections of their own self-love. Self-love demands a favorable reflection of ourselves in others. If we believe that this exists and we get what we want, then we are happy, and if it does not, then this so-called 'love' can turn quickly to dislike, anger, self-pity or hatred.

In children, self-love develops, at least in part, because adults laud the child with a chorus of praises, rebukes, criticism and false adoration. A child comes to do things not for the intrinsic value of activity but for praise or to be noticed, or to achieve some imagined superiority. The child becomes a satellite to others, seeking approval, appreciation or love. As a result, the child becomes centered within the other, rather than within the self –that is, within the essence. Self-love brings about a falsity of action such that the person is concerned not with the activities per se, but rather with how they will be seen or what their actions make them. People are full of false ideas about themselves in relationship to others, and strive for favorable reflections of themselves in the others' eyes.

Self-love does not necessarily involve loving or liking ourselves but includes feelings of worthlessness, self condemnation, self pity, self hatred or guilt. Most generally, self-love involves self-centered thoughts and emotions, which can be positive or negative. Some people love to hate themselves, to feel that they are awful and have nothing to give or offer others, and that their pains, suffering and problems are the worst in the world. People indulge in feelings about their sufferings, inadequacies and misfortunes. Typically, such feelings of inferiority are compensated for by striving for superiority, righteousness and some other inflated sense of ego. Self-love takes many forms. Gurdjieff depicts normal so-called *love* in this passage:

'With ordinary love goes hate. I love this, I hate that. Today I love you, next week, or next hour, or next minute, I hate you. He who can really love can *be*, can *do*, *is*. ... As we are we cannot love. We love because something in ourselves combines with another's emanations; this starts pleasant associations, perhaps because of chemico-physical emanations ... or from feelings–I love you because you love me, or because you don't love me; suggestions of others; sense of superiority; from pity; and for

many other reasons, subjective and egoistic. ... Everything attracts or repels. There is
the love of sex, which is ordinarily known as "love" between men and women–when
this disappears a man and a woman no longer "love" each other. There is love of
feeling, which evokes the opposite and makes people suffer. Later, we will talk about
'conscious love.' (Nott, 1969, pp. 22-23)

Ordinary love is based on self-serving motives, pleasant sensations and feelings, but can change
quickly as the experience passes and other things happen. The succession of different feelings,
desires and states, or i's within the individual involve a shifting complex of loves, hates, judgments,
annoyances, worries, and so on. The ordinary *love* of little 'i's–partial aspects of oneself–is
inconsistent. People love today, resent a minute later and hate tomorrow, and never notice the
inconsistencies within themselves. Thus, Gurdjieff stresses that only the rare individual –who can *be*,
who can *do* and who *is*–is capable of experiencing true love. Real love involves the conscious portions
of the emotional center and the higher emotional center, and the awakening of consciousness. He or
she who can truly love has attained real "I."

In describing the strange psyche of those three-brained beings on planet earth to his grandson
Hassein, Gurdjieff, in the guise of Beelzebub, explains:

> "... in none of the ordinary beings-men here has there ever been, for a long time, any
> sensation of the sacred being-impulse of genuine Love. And without this "taste" they
> cannot even vaguely describe that most beatific sacred being-impulse .... Here, in
> these times, if one of those three-brained beings "loves" somebody or other, then he
> loves him either because the latter always encourages and undeservingly flatters him;
> or because his nose is much like the nose of that female or male, with whom thanks
> to the cosmic law of "polarity" or "type," a relation has been established which has not
> yet been broken; or finally, he loves him only because the latter's uncle is in a big way
> of business and may one day give him a boost, and so on and so forth. But never do
> beings-men here love with genuine, impartial and non-egoistic love."
> 1950, pp. 357-358)

Only sincere and continued self-observation can illuminate the ridiculousness of one's self-love; which
is not even the love of anything real, but of imagined and infatuated views of oneself. Self-love is the
motive force behind imagination, internal considering, lying and negative emotions. It is hard ever to
see self-love as it is so pervasive and colors everything people do. Further, self-love defends itself at
every step, as we typically consider ourselves always right–each a legend in their own mind. Self-
love and self-feeling so thoroughly color life, that people feel and know little of the real world or of the
existence of others.

A person's level of being is directly connected to the quality of his or her emotional life.
Vaysse (1979) explains:

> ... the operations of the emotional center depends entirely on the level of presence;
> in man's ordinary state, only one of his personages is there and so it is only a matter
> of emotions (partial feelings inherent in one single aspect of oneself) and not of real
> feelings (all-inclusive feeling inherent in the total presence of a really established inner
> I). Man in his ordinary state has no true feelings. He has only automatic emotions,
> the emotions of reaction, depending entirely upon which personage is present. The

> personage changes according to circumstances, and its "feeling" changes with it....
> The emotional center becomes capable of real feeling only when a stable presence,
> relatively independent of the surrounding circumstances, has been developed. ...
> True feelings are not negative: they have no negative aspect. ... At the ordinary
> level ... the emotional center agrees or refuses and the emotions which we live
> with can be positive, neutral or negative according to how they (impressions) strike
> the emotionality–that is to say the specific self-love–which animates each of our
> personages. (pp. 84-85)

When somebody *"steps on our corns,"* a Gurdjieff expression, or offends our self-love, then we feel
negative emotions; and when somebody flatters the self-love, or vanity, then we feel so-called positive
emotions. From a fourth way perspective, the emotional life of humans seldom involves anything
more than the simple emotional reactivity of false personality with its many little i's. Moments of
awakening in essence bring deeper emotions–such as the remorse of conscience and the realization
of the *sacred being-impulses* of faith, hope and love. True emotions involve more intense and beatific
feelings and experiences, than the emotional reactions based on attachments and the identification
with personal concerns.

2c. **The Moving and Instinctual Life**

The study of moving center involves the observation of mechanical activities, mannerisms and
postures. Collin provides a vivid image of the typical unconscious moving life of humans:

> ... with large numbers of lazy and sedentary people in modern life ... their lives
> contain almost no intentional movement, they are completely filled with unintentional
> movement, aimless movement. ... Only a man who has already begun to study himself
> will realize what an immense part such pointless movement plays in human life. Not
> only all obvious kinds of fidgeting, restlessness, mechanical gestures of the hands and
> arms, changes of bodily position, stroking the face and chin, tapping with fingers or
> feet ... the mechanical play of the facial muscles ... *they are never still.* ... Almost all the
> waking and sleeping life of many city-dwellers is occupied by involuntary, unrecognized
> and completely aimless motion. ... a very large part of human life is given over to the
> performance of habits ... . (1980, pp.112-113)

There are various things to observe in the study of moving center. First, there are postures, the
static positions that the body assumes from moment to moment. Everyone has a limited number
of fixed postures which are habitually assumed–whether slouching, sitting or standing–and which
are associated with various i's. Secondly, there are gestures and mannerisms that occur frequently
and which typify different people. People have all kinds of mannerisms and habits evident in social
situations or in solitary activity. One can also observe the tone of voice that accompanies words and
reveals their underlying meanings. We can also study movements of body as a whole–as in walking,
running, playing sports and so on.

Observation of muscular tensions is another aspect of the study of moving center. Whenever people
engage in activities, they tense up muscle groups unnecessarily or out of proportion to the effort

required. In addition, people have chronic patterns of muscular armoring built up within the body, which can be discovered through self-study. By self-remembering and working with the breath, muscular tensions and energy blocks within the body can be increasingly identified and reduced.

Work on the moving center also involves learning *to do*–with controlled attention and self-awareness. In order to realize this more conscious state of presence, it is especially important to breathe deeply and to be more consciously centered within the physical sensations of self while experiencing inner dynamics and energies. By doing so, it is possible for the individual to develop awareness of his moving presence and not be continually lived out by mechanical habits operating without attention.

Another line of work on moving center involves engaging in activities which demand conscious movement and self-control–ranging from movement meditations, to building or doing things outside of the usual habitual activities. There are various ways of inhibiting, disrupting, and studying the moving mind and of learning conscious movement and activity.

It is difficult to realize how little awareness people have of their physical being. Chronic patterns of muscular tension, shallow breathing and habitual postures restrict the sensation and experience of the physical realm. The patterns of negative emotion and false personality, the turning of the mind and the imagination, all contribute to the deadening of sensory awareness and absorption by mechanical activity. The patterns of false personality are ingrained within habits of movement, muscular armoring and restrictions of the breath. As a child matures, awareness shifts from the body and essence into the world of the formatory mind and the false personality.

As we are now, we walk, eat, wash ourselves, and sit down, in habitual ways, with little or no awareness and attention. People are not conscious of their postures, gestures, the unnecessary strain and haste, muscular tensions, or of how energies move within the body. Considerable time, energy and life are wasted on unnecessary mechanical actions and habits. In the psychology of a human's possible evolution, it is very important to work towards a more conscious moving presence.

Gurdjieff emphasizes that a person should be careful in interfering with the instinctive life of the organism. However, there is much to learn about what the instinctual life is within us and how instinctual processes interact with other centers. The instinctual life is the body's basic physical nature–which includes the innate processes that control biological functions; the senses which allow for awareness of the physical body and the surrounding world; the appetites and needs of the stomach and digestion; as well as the aches, pains and pleasures of the body.

A person can be controlled by the stomach and continually overeat. This increases the blood flow to the gut and consciousness can actually be centered there. Many people have their consciousness centered in *'the pit of the stomach.'* Alternatively, consciousness can be enhanced to the muscles when one is involved in physical activities; or to the sexual organs, when one is sexually aroused. Again, increased blood flow to each of these areas of the body is related to an enhanced awareness of them and a centering of one's consciousness there. The pleasures and pains associated with the organic body provide motivation for learning and conditioning and can control the attention, emotions and the mind.

By making repeated efforts to self-remember, one is able to sense and experience the world much more vividly and intensely. Normally, the habitual turning of the mind and emotions makes one largely oblivious to the sensory realm and as a result it is reduced to a fraction of its potential. However, by sensing one's physical presence—in the breath, in movement and sensation, in internal sensations and in awareness of the external environment—one remembers onself physically. In this way, the act of *self-sensing* plays an integral part in self-remembering. By grounding one's state of presence in an increased consciousness of his or her physical being, the individual is more fully present to the moment.

Vaysse elaborates the importance of developing a fuller consciousness of the sensory realm:

> What relates us to the body is the sensation we have of it—the inner perception of my physical being, the physical sensation of myself. But sensation has an even greater importance because, if our aim is eventually to develop a stable presence in ourselves, the sensation of our physical being is an inherent part of this. ... This calls for a new relationship to come into existence in me: I —conscious of—my sensation. ... we need to develop a more steady and longer lasting consciousness of our body and its situation. (1979, p. 161)

2d. **The Misuse of Sexual Energy**

The energies of the sexual center consist of extremely refined energies and are highly potent and capable of dominating other activities of the human organism. The dynamics of the sexual center and the use and abuse of sexual energies are profoundly important subjects to understand in order to grasp the idea of the psychology of a human's possible evolution. According to Gurdjieff, sexual energies play a central role within the chemistry and alchemy of the human organism and the misuse of these energies plays a critical role in maintaining the sleepwalking condition of humanity.

Gurdjieff explains that the sexual center has only positive feelings and sensations—unlike the other centers which each have positive and negative, pleasant and unpleasant sides. The sexual center is either aroused and involved, or *"there is nothing, an absence of any sensation, a complete indifference."* Negative sexual experiences arise through the involvement of the negative sides of the emotional and instinctual centers—associated with negative emotions and conflict or with physical pain and discomfort. Different inner defenses, or *"buffers,"* also serve to delimit and distort the healthy expression of sexual energies.

Gurdjieff describes the misuse of sexual energy as a principle motive force underlying many forms of mechanicalness:

> ... sex plays a tremendous role in maintaining the mechanicalness of life. Everything that people do is connected with 'sex': politics, religion, art, the theater, music, is all sex. Do you think people go to the theater or to church to pray or to see some new play? This is only for the sake of appearances. The principle thing, in the theater as well as in church, is that there will be a lot of women or a lot of men. This is the center of gravity of all gatherings. What do you think brings people to cafes, to restaurants, to various fetes? One thing only. *Sex*: it is the principle motive force of all mechanicalness. All sleep, all hypnosis, depends upon it. (1949, p. 254)

Sex, in ten thousand and one disguises, is a primary underlying motive in social life and activity. Of course, others can stay home and watch movies and TV, with their principle sexual flavor and stimulation, listen to popular music, cruise the web, read newspapers and magazines, or follow commercial sports–all with their particular sexual emphases and titillations. Sexual energies can dominate and obsess the mind and emotions, and are the source of endless imagination, fantasy and social activity. Gurdjieff describes sex as the primary center of gravity of social gatherings and states that modern life creates an enormous number of *sexual psychopaths.*

The abuse of sex is not simply the excess of sexual activity. Further, abstinence is not a simple solution, although for some types it may be useful at certain periods in their development. The greater problem is the self-deception involved when volatile sexual energies are borrowed and used by other centers:

> You must understand where lies the chief evil and what makes for slavery. It is not in sex itself but in the *abuse of sex.* ... Sex, in fact, governs all other centers. ... The energy of the sex center in the work of the thinking, emotional, and moving centers can be recognized by a particular 'taste,' by a particular fervor, by a vehemence which the nature of the affair concerned does not call for. The thinking center writes books, but in making use of the energy of the sex center it does not simply occupy itself with philosophy, science, or politics–it is always fighting something, disputing, criticizing, creating new subjective theories. The emotional center preaches Christianity, abstinence, asceticism, or the fear and horror of sin, hell, the torment of sinners, eternal fire, all this with the energy of the sex center. ... Or on the other hand it works up revolutions, robs, burns, kills, again with the same energy. The moving center occupies itself with sport, creates various records, climbs mountains, jumps, fences, wrestles, fights, and so on. In all these instances, ... there is always one general characteristic and this is a certain particular vehemence and, together with it, the *uselessness* of the work in question. Neither the thinking nor the emotional nor the moving centers can ever create anything *useful* with the energy of the sex center. This is an example of the 'abuse of sex.'...
>
> At the same time union with, and the use of its energy by, the thinking center creates far too great an imagination on the subject of sex, and in addition a tendency to be satisfied with this imagination. Union with the emotional center creates sentimentality or, on the contrary, jealousy, cruelty. This is again a picture of the 'abuse of sex.'"
> (1949, pp. 257-9)

The study of sexual center involves recognizing the particular fervor and taste of activities based on the misuse of sexual energies.

In *Beelzebub's Tales to his Grandson*, Gurdjieff (1950) provides additional remarks on the misuse of sexual energies within the life of humanity. Gurdjieff labels sperm as *Exioehary*, and describes it as a sacred substance required for the development of the higher being-bodies for the life of the soul. The transmutation of sexual energies is essential to the inner alchemy by which the astral and mental bodies are crystallized. In the *Tales*, Gurdjieff explains what unfortunately happened on planet earth– as a consequence of cosmic disruptions and the degeneration of the psyche of humankind:

> ... a being impulse began to be formed in them which later became predominant. This impulse is now called 'pleasure'; and in order to satisfy it they had already begun to exist in a way unbecoming to three-centered beings, namely, most of them gradually began to remove this same sacred being-substance from themselves only for the satisfaction of the said impulse. (p. 276)

Sexual energies are used up solely for the experience of pleasure and humans fail to realize the role that these energies play in the psychology of their possible evolution and the coating of the higher being-bodies. This major waste of vital energies serves the further degradation of the human psyche. Gurdjieff also describes onanism, or masturbation, as means of *self calming*, of putting oneself to sleep and maintaining mechanical life.

For Gurdjieff, sexuality is a sacred activity—but conscious sex is very different from unconscious sex. The proper functioning of the sexual center plays a central role in *"creating a general equilibrium and a permanent center of gravity"* within an individual, but its improper functioning plays an equal role in maintaining the psychopathology of humanity.

In summary: understanding the wrong work of centers provides one way of approaching the common psychopathology of human beings. Gurdjieff elaborates a systematic and detailed view of the unbalanced states of people with their many minds, and how these seldom act together in a harmonious and natural way. The wrong work of the centers creates useless functions or activities which limit the possibility of inner change, the accumulation of energies and the evolution of consciousness.

To know self involves a study of the life of the machine. It is not sufficient to simply know these things intellectually; rather it is necessary to understand the wrong working of the centers through the struggle to escape from the domination of these processes. The struggle against habitual activities brings home the realization of one's mechanicalness and the present low level of one's being. As humans are, the centers seldom function harmoniously together and each substitutes its activities for another, borrowing energies and material. Further, humans use primarily the mechanical portions of centers, while the higher emotional and intellectual sides of the centers are undeveloped. Of course, these points all need to be verified within one's experience through prolonged self study. The subject matters of the wrong work of centers provide many things to observe and study, and with which to struggle in order to awaken.

3. False Personality, Buffers & Chief Features

The word *persona* is from the Greek language, and refers to an outer mask worn by actors on a stage. These masks were on sticks and would be held up in front of the face as the actors assumed different personalities. Personality forms as the child adapts to life and is shaped by family and environment. As children grow, they acquire habitual patterns of thinking, feeling and acting which form personality and false personality—the masks they learn within their own personal life dramas.

Aspects of personality are useful and necessary to the life of the individual, such as the acquisition of practical knowledge, language and social skills. Ideally, personality is consistent with the essence of the individual and allows for natural self expression. Unfortunately, the usual conditions in life are often highly unnatural and many artificial habits and emotional patterns are acquired by the child. Irrational and destructive patterns of thought, emotion and action develop as ways of adapting to unnatural conditions, such as enduring abuse and neglect, and to cope in stifling living situations amidst unhappiness, addictions and conflict. As a person grows older, consciousness can become increasingly centred within the false personality and less within the essence. The false personality becomes an outer self system based on conditioning, imitation and learning to cope with negative experiences.

False personality forms to protect the essence and the deeper emotional and soul life of the individual. The essence may need to be defended against aggression and conflict, physical and emotional abuse and dehumanizing experiences. A child can live amongst extremely destructive influences within the family and social life, and have to conceal from others what is their own or real in themselves. Early childhood experiences are immensely important in fostering the development of the essence or giving rise to varied psychopathologies. If conditions are particularly threatening and hostile, an inner split between essence and false personality forms from an early age. This process is portrayed by psychiatrist, Karen Horney:

> How is it possible to lose a self? The treachery, unknown and unthinkable, begins with our secret psychic death in childhood. ... It is a perfect crime in which ... the tiny self

gradually and unwittingly takes part. He has not been accepted for himself, as he is. ... Therefore he must be unacceptable. He himself learns to believe it and at last even takes it for granted. He has truly given himself up. No matter now whether he obeys them, whether he clings, rebels or withdraws—his behaviour, his performance is all that matters. His center of gravity is in 'them,' not in himself. ... And the whole thing is entirely plausible; all invisible, automatic and anonymous! This is the perfect paradox. Everything looks normal; no crime was intended; there is no corpse, no guilt. All we can see is the sun rising and setting as usual. But what has happened? He has been rejected not only by them, but by himself. (He is actually without a self.) What has he lost? Just the one true and vital part of himself; his own yes-feeling, which is his very capacity for growth, his root system. But alas, he is not dead. "Life" goes on, and so must he. From the moment he gives himself up, and to the extent that he does so, all unknowingly he sets about to create and maintain a pseudo-self. But this is just expediency—a self without wishes. This one shall be loved (or feared) where he is despised, strong where he is weak; it shall go through the motions (oh, but they are caricatures!) not for fun or joy but for survival; not simply because it wants to move but because it has to obey. The necessity is not life —not his life—it is a defence mechanism against death. It is also the machine of death. (1949, p.93)

The individual loses touch with the essence and a pseudo-self or false personality comes to act as the center of gravity. The false self has its origins in the child's natural opposition to destructive influences, in the child's suffering at the hands, feelings and mind of others, and exposure to the greater psychopathology within human society. The outer self protects what is real within the child, yet is cut off from the life and vitality of the body and essence. Still everything looks normal from the outside because the split is on the inside and is not realized even by the individual.

False personality is increasingly made over to conform to the demands of the other, or into a self which will defy and act against others. Splitting occurs between the centers, as the child feels one thing, thinks another, and acts quite differently on the outside. The patterns of false personality involve the mechanical wrong work of the centers—unnecessary negative emotions, selfishness, formatory thinking, imagination, internal considering, inner talking, the misuse of sexual energies, and so on. Negative emotions are unnecessary and unreal but have an artificial center in false personality, as they are based on self-love and formatory thinking.

There are common features to false personality. One involves a falsity of action, where the impressions that activities will produce on others (imagined audiences) or on self (to maintain the self-image or personal fictions) become more important than the activity itself. Falsity of action involves doing things for the wrong reasons, to be seen, and thus in the wrong way. Also, false personality cannot adapt as it is inflexible and offers no resistance against automatic responses and reactions. False personality attempts always to maintain its inclinations and to resist changes in habits and routines. It has no interest in going against the current of mechanical conditioning.

Wrong ideas about ourselves serve as a foundation for false personality. Ouspensky writes:

> ... 'false personality' ... is our imaginary picture of ourselves, because we put into it all that we think of ourselves, which is generally imaginary. All study comes down to the study of this imaginary picture and to separating ourselves from it. ... This mechanical part of us is chiefly based on imagination, on wrong views of everything, and above

all on a wrong view of ourselves. We must realize how much we are in the power of this false personality and invented things which have no real existence, and we must separate what we can really depend on from what is not dependable in ourselves. (1957, pp.165 & 167)

Gurdjieff's portrait of *"man in quotation marks"* illustrates the dynamics of false personality. This person does not see his inner inconsistencies, the lack of attention, the unnecessary nature of his negative emotions, his pettiness and self love. Of course, he does not see these things as he is embedded in them, lived out and conditioned by everything around him and by years of unconscious life experience. The man in quotation marks does not see the mechanicalness of his false personality or his own nothingness.

Walker (1963) recounts Madame Ouspensky's comments about the illusory nature of false personality and self-love:

> And what fantastic things these personalities were when we managed to catch sight of them. Madame Ouspensky ... possessed a special gift for seeing below the surface and revealing to us what she had discovered there. She sometimes likened our personalities to large hot-air pies which we were carrying about with us very carefully in the hope that they would be duly admired. Her allegory was a particularly appropriate one, for the crust of a hot-air pie is so thin that the slightest knock from somebody else will cause it to crumble, and thus reveal to the world the emptiness within. Aware of this danger, we are constantly on our guard protecting our personality from all rough handling, insisting always that we are in the right and others in the wrong, and justify our every action, thought and feelings. (p. 95)

False personality is strongly defended and justifies everything–but in reality is quite non-substantive.

Gaining a practical knowledge of yourself involves a study of your particular false personality. False personality maintains the state of *"automated consciousness,"* so that we no longer *"instinctually sense reality."* Although we identify with false personality and take this as ourselves, it is really *not I*. Ouspensky explains:

> False personality is opposed to 'you,' it is your wrong idea of yourself–exactly what you are not. (1957, p.165)

To develop true self-consciousness and awaken within the essence, it is necessary to study false personality. If false personality can be made *less active*, this will allow the enhancement and growth of essence. Ouspensky's comments:

> Work beings with struggle against false personality. Everything one can get one gets only at the expense of false personality. Later, when it is made passive, one may get much at the expense of other things, but for a long time one has to live, so to speak, off false personality. (1957, p. 176)

Work begins with observing and identifying patterns of false personality and struggling to free oneself from these. Whereas essence is full of light, alive and vital, false personality is under the most negative and destructive influences. A lunatic, under the control of the moon, is most dominated by false personality, imagination and violence. False personality imprisons humankind, placing them under a greater number of mechanical and unconscious influences. In Gurdjieff's Ray of Creation, false personality is related to the moon which is under ninety six mechanical laws.

The aim in the fourth way teaching is to take the active momentum away from false personality and particularly destructive i's. The struggle with false personality is against the mechanicalness of ordinary reactions to life. It is necessary to learn *not to do* many things which normally happen. However, false personality is not interested in the work or self remembering, or anything which might disrupt its false security and self importance.

Humans have many defences, or buffers, which prevent them from seeing false personality for what it is. Buffers allow false personality to be maintained by preventing the impact of different selves or i's upon each other. They allow a person to act, think and feel in contradictory and inconsistent ways from moment to moment, day to day, year to year, without being aware of the inner contradictions and fragmentation. Buffers allow all kinds of antagonistic and conflicting i's to live beside each other, quite unaware of each other and the lies of life. They allow false personality to maintain itself as a false consciousness system, apart from the development of essence, without the person being aware of the great inner split in their being or their inner nothingness. Buffers protect the hot-air pies so that they will not receive any sudden jolts or shocks.

Gurdjieff explains:

"We fail to see how contradictory and hostile the different I's of our personality are to one another. If a man were to feel all these contradictions he would feel what *he really is*. He would feel that he is mad. It is not pleasant to anyone to feel that he is mad. Moreover, a thought such as this deprives a man of self-confidence, weakens his energy, deprives him of 'self-respect.' Somehow or other he must master this thought or banish it. He must either destroy contradictions or cease to see and to feel them. A man cannot destroy contradictions. But if 'buffers' are created in him he can cease to feel them and he will not feel the impact from the clash of contradictory views, contradictory emotions, contradictory words.

"'Buffers' are created slowly and gradually. ... A man is surrounded by people who live, speak, think, and feel by means of 'buffers.' Imitating them in their opinions, actions, and words, a man involuntarily creates similar 'buffers' in himself. 'Buffers' make a man's life more easy. It is very hard to live without 'buffers.' But they keep man from the possibility of inner development because 'buffers' are made to lessen shocks and it is only shocks that can lead a man out of the state in which he lives, that is, waken him. 'Buffers' lull a man to sleep, give him the agreeable and peaceful sensation that all will be well, that no contradictions exists and that he can sleep in peace. *'Buffers' are appliances by means of which a man can always be in the right.* 'Buffers' help a man not to feel his conscience. (Ouspensky, 1949, pp. 154-155).

A normal mechanical person would go mad if their buffers were removed all at once and they had to face their inner state and nothingness. To keep one's sleep, humans defend against such a possibility and buffers enable them to maintain the inner blindness. On the other hand, awakening requires the gradual destruction of buffers and the courage to seek out the many inner contradictions, conflicts and falsity.

A particularly important role is assigned by G., in *Beelzebub's Tales to His Grandson*, to the *awakening of conscience* as a route to overcoming the abnormalities established within the strange psyche of those three brained beings on planet Earth. Again, G. provides shocking insights into how mechanical humans deal with what he calls, so humorously, the arising of the *prick* of conscience:

> "... these favourites of yours (humankind), particularly the contemporary ones, become ideally expert in not allowing this inner impulse of theirs, called Remorse-of-Conscience, to linger long in their common presences.

> "No sooner do they begin to sense the beginning, or even only, so to say, the 'prick' of the arising of the functioning in them of such a being-impulse, than they immediately, as it is said 'squash' it, whereupon this impulse, not quite formed in them, at once calms down.

> "For this 'squashing' of the beginning of any Remorse-of-Conscience in themselves, they have even invented some very efficient special means, which now exist there under the names of 'alcoholism,' 'cocainism,' 'morphinism,' 'nicotinism,' 'onanism,' 'monkism,' 'Athenianism,' and others with names also ending in 'ism.' (1950, p. 382)

Gurdjieff's writing is full of subtle and rich humour, portraying so simply the follies, weaknesses and stupidities of humankind. There are many ways of squashing the pricks of conscience, all part of what Beelzebub labels the Evil God of "*self calming.*"

Besides understanding the general features of false personality within oneself, it is necessary also to identify one's own peculiarities, or chief feature. Ouspensky explains:

> Chief feature or chief weakness is in false personality. In some cases it is possible to see definitely one, two or three features or tendencies, often linked together, which come into everything like an axis round which everything turns. This is chief feature. Sometimes it is very clear and apparent, but sometimes it is difficult to describe. Our language has often no words, no forms to describe it and it can only be indicated in a roundabout way. It is interesting that one can hardly ever find one's own chief feature, because *one is in it*, and if one is told, one usually does not believe it. ... a chief feature means constant loss of energy, so we must find this leak and stop it. (1957, p.177)

There are some common chief features. Along this line, Ouspensky comments: "*...imaginary personality, or false personality, is chief feature for everybody.*" (1957, p. 179) Laziness is another common feature, as false personality does what is easiest and corresponds with its inertia and force of habit. People cannot exert conscious effort from false personality as promises and intentions are not followed through and tasks are left incomplete, as feelings and motives change from moment to moment. Another general feature of false personality is its selfishness and the attitude of self love or vanity. As well, Gurdjieff states that another chief feature for humans is that they are asleep and not properly conscious.

Other examples of chief features drawn from G.'s characterizations of some of his students, include such comments as: "*he is never at home,*" "*he did not exist at all,*" "*a tendency always to argue,*" "*he had no conscience,*" or "*no shame.*" (Ouspensky, 1949, pp. 267-8) Other teachers of Gurdjieff's ideas relate chief features to the seven deadly sins-of pride, envy, gluttony, anger, greed, lust and sloth.

It is generally impossible for a person to realize their chief feature on their own, even though other people may recognize some aspects of one's false personality, or character. Nicknames can sometimes capture characteristic features of false personality. In the student/ teacher relationship, the teacher will be able to point out chief feature and show how to struggle against it. This is evident in many stories of Gurdjieff providing shocks to his students and outsiders.

Chief feature is an axis about which everything revolves. We are embedded within chief features and cannot see them as they colour everything, even the way we look for them. Ouspensky writes:

> It is like a special breed of dog. If you do not know it, you cannot speak about it. Even to seek little bits of it is quite enough, for every small part of it is the same colour. If you see this dog once, you will always know it. It barks in a special way, walks in a special way. (1957, p.175)

A practical working knowledge of oneself thus begins with a study of false personality–its features, inclinations, its self-love and imaginary ideas, its smell and walk. We must separate from "it," and take the activities and features of false personality not as what we are, but as what we are not. False personality is the most mechanical aspect of people, the most imaginary and under the greatest number of accidental laws. All of this has to be observed and understood within oneself many times. The study of humanity and oneself begins with a study of the mechanicalness of false personality. Self study brings deep realizations. Gurdjieff explains:

> "The study of the chief fault and the struggle against it constitute, as it were, each man's individual path, but the aim must be the same for all. This aim is the realization of one's nothingness. Only when a man has truly and sincerely arrived at the conviction of his own helplessness and nothingness and only when he feels it constantly, *will he be ready for the next and much more difficult stage of the work*." (1949. p. 226)

To realize one's nothingness is a stage involving the removal of buffers, the witnessing of the inner contradictions and lies, and the breaking down of conditioning and false personality. One must face the inner nothingness and the lie of oneself in order to be reborn in essence and take part in the possible evolution of the inner being. False personality cannot evolve.

4. Lunatics, Tramps and Hasnamuss Individuals

In his talks with Ouspensky and in *Beelzebub's Tales*, Gurdjieff mentions various types of false personality structures which are particularly destructive. These include lunatics, tramps and hasnamuss individuals.

Ouspensky defines a lunatic as *"a man who always runs after false values, who has no right discrimination. He is always formatory."* (1957, p. 299) As the name implies, the lunatic is most under the influence of the moon, of imagination and false values. The lunatic is not necessarily the person who has lost his mind in a psychiatric sense, although he may well qualify. However, Ouspensky explains that the lunatic can also be the statesman or professor, learned people or those occupying important social positions. The defining attribute is the falsity of values and the imaginary nature of their concerns. Gurdjieff describes lunatics as *"doomed to turn eternally in and the same circle ... merely 'food for the moon.'"* (1949, p. 360)

Whereas lunatics have false values, the tramp has no values and is not really interested in anything in life. Nothing is taken seriously or as having value. It is this attitude towards life and not material poverty which defines the tramp. Once again, Ouspensky explains that tramps could be rich or well established, yet still have no real valuation of life and its possibilities. He or she lacks any capacity for self-discipline and an essence evaluation of what is good or bad, and maintains an inflated evaluation of their own self worth. Gurdjieff describes tramps as including, *"... all the so-called 'intelligentsia'– artists, poets, any kind of 'bohemian' in general, who despises the good householder ..."* (1949, p. 363) Both tramps and lunatics are regarded as unsuitable for *the work*.

A third type, Hasnamuss individuals, may also be tramps and lunatics, but are the most dangerous and destructive of the disturbed types. Ouspensky describes the Hasnamuss individual:

> "... he never hesitates to sacrifice people or to create an enormous amount of suffering, just for his own personal ambitions." (1957, p. 300)

Within *Beelzebub's Tales*, various stories are told about the processes of reciprocal destruction, the wars and violence brought about by Hasnamuss individuals, throughout the history of humanity. The Hasnamuss have also destroyed various sacred Messengers, while repressing and obscuring their more conscious teachings which might have changed human history. Hasnamuss individuals have even invented various religions with fantastic fictions, which lead to mass confusion and the further degeneration of "sane mentation" among their followers.

According to Beelzebub, the term Hasnamuss refers to people who *"... for some reason data have not been crystallized for the Divine impulse of 'Objective Conscience'."* (1950, p. 235) Beelzebub describes seven *"Naloo-osnian-spectrum-of-impulses,"* which are primary features of such people. These include:

> (1) Every kind of depravity, conscious as well as unconscious
> (2) The feeling of self-satisfaction from leading others astray

(3) The irresistible inclination to destroy the existence of other breathing creatures
(4) The urge to become free from the necessity of actualizing the being-efforts demanded by Nature
(5) The attempt by every kind of artificiality to conceal from others what in their opinion are one's physical defects
(6) The calm self-contentment in the use of what is not personally deserved
(7) The striving to be not what one is. (1950, p. 406)

Certainly, Beelzebub outlines a charming list of characteristics. Such impulses are formed within the crystallized "egoism," so prominent among the strange psyches of those three brained-beings on planet Earth. The Hasnamuss individual no longer experiences the impulses of *"being-self-shame,"* and the history of humanity testifies to the horrors caused by these *"terrestrial nullities."*

Beelzebub uses the term Hasnamuss to refer in a negative way to certain classes of people whose actions, manifestations and impulses represent the worst psychopathology of humankind, and who cause the worst sufferings, falsity and misunderstanding among the three-brained beings on Earth. A certain definite *"something"* has become formed, or crystallized, in an individual—as a relatively fixed characterological complex which dominates their 'common presence.' The fact that data for the Divine impulse of Objective Conscience are not crystallized in them, suggests that a false consciousness system is in full sway and the real consciousness has passed into the subconscious. Such individual's will be primarily egotistical and care little how much suffering and misfortune they cause others.

Hasnamuss individuals may refer to those consisting of only a planetary body, but includes those who have at least partially coated the higher being bodies. At a later point, we will consider four types of Hasnamuss individuals described by Beelzebub and their afterlife fates—where they face *"'serious-retributive-suffering-consequences'."* (p. 406) Hasnamuss individuals have the most disturbed and crystallized forms of false personality and narcissism. Unfortunately, human history is littered with their names, while modern civilization came almost completely under their influence.

The Hasnamuss are controlled by the three lower motivations of money, sex and power, and do not attain to the awakening of the heart or to the possibilities inherent to the higher life of the soul. They are the product of lunacy and delusion. They feel such self-satisfaction from leading you astray, engaging in every kind of depravity and they indeed have such "irresistible inclinations to destroy the existence of other breathing creatures." Such types came to rule the human race, all part of the new world psychiatric disorder. This is the scum that rose to the top of the waters of life and their crimes are the blood streaks through human history. They represent the lowest three levels of possible human evolution and they do not attain to the awakening of the heart nor attain real 'I.' The pseudo-illuminate are not so illumined but accept the false light of the moon and the lower mind. Their false consciousness system and inner nullity has prevented the human race from attaining to higher consciousness and being-existence, and they have distorted and obscured the messages and teachings of all of the Sacred Messengers as described by Beelzebub.

5. A Human Being as a Chemical Factory

Gurdjieff describes a human as a *three-brained* being and as having *three stories*. Each of these stories has a primary *being food* which is taken in from the outer world and transformed into the energies required for the life activities of the physical body, emotions and mind. These three being foods are those of physical *food*, *air* and *psychological impressions*. Within the individual chemical factory, these three substances are taken in as energies or matters and refined for the use of the centers, for consciousness and for the possible crystallization of the higher being-bodies. Mr. G. offers an intriguing view of humans as chemical and alchemical factories.

A human being absorbs, refines, uses, wastes and accumulates energies provided by the three being foods-of food, air and psychological impressions, which feed three possible bodies-the planetary body, astral and mental bodies. However, although the human chemical factory is designed for the possibility of a very large output, this is seldom achieved under the ordinary conditions of life. Instead, humans continually waste precious energies and do not accumulate the *hydrogens* necessary for coating the higher being-bodies for the life of the soul.[14]

Gurdjieff explains the principle of learning to conserve vital life energies:

> "... in everything we do we are tied and limited by the amount of energy produced by our organism. Every function, every state, every action, every thought, every emotion, requires a certain definite energy, a certain definite substance. ... It is only necessary to learn how to save the greater part of the energy we possess for useful work instead of wasting it unproductively. ... In beginning to struggle with all these habitual sides of his life a man saves an enormous amount of energy, and with the help of this energy he can easily begin the work of self-study and self-perfection." (Ouspensky, 1949, pp.179-80)

Under the conditions of mechanical life, the energies of the centers and of consciousness are continually squandered or misused through unnecessary and unproductive activity and the varied wrong work of centers. Negative emotions are particularly destructive from the point of view of a human's possible evolution. Ouspensky writes:

> Leaks of energy were already spoken about, but the worst of all is expressing negative emotions. If you can stop the expression of negative emotions, you will save energy and never feel the lack of it. We can only hope to become conscious beings if we use in the right way the energy that is now used in the wrong way. The machine can produce enough energy, but you can waste it on being angry or irritated or something like that, and then very little remains. ... These leaks have to be studied, because with some kinds of leaks it is not worth going on until they are stopped, for the more one accumulates energy, the more will leak out. It would be like pouring water into a

---

[14] At a latter point, Gurdjieff's hydrogen and food diagrams will be used to explain these processes in a more detailed way. The concern here is with the pathology of the human psyche in terms of the energy dynamics.

> sieve. Certain negative emotions produce precisely such leaks. In certain situations some people go through a whole range of negative emotions so habitual that they do not even notice them. It may occupy only five minutes or five seconds, but it will be sufficient to spend all the energy their organism produced for twenty-four hours.
> (1957, p.69)

Plugging the leaks of energy from the human chemical factory can very quickly bring results–if one can lessen wastage on negative emotions, the wrong work of centers and the patterns that constitute false personality.

The view of humans as chemical factories is a most valuable aspect of the fourth way psychology. Gurdjieff provides a differentiated perspective on the various energies or substances which compose a human being. In western psychology, questions of the different types of energies responsible for the psychological life of human are largely ignored. When psychologists and philosophers approach this topic, they most frequently speak of simply one form of mental, psychic or instinctual energy, or two. The fourth way teaching is far more complex in the ways it approaches the subject of the energies, matters or substances which compose a human being.

At one point, Ouspensky (1957) distinguishes four types of energy within the life of a human:

> We must distinguish four energies working through us: physical or *mechanical energy*–for instance, moving this table; *life energy* which makes the body absorb food, reconstruct tissue, and so on; *psychic or mental energy*, with which the centers work, and most important of all, *energy of consciousness*.
>
> Energy of consciousness is not recognized by psychology and by scientific schools. Consciousness is regarded as part of psychic functions. Other schools deny consciousness altogether and regard everything as mechanical. Some schools deny the existence of life energy. But life energy is different from mechanical energy, and living matter can be created only from living matter. All growth proceeds with life energy. Psychic energy is the energy with which the centers work. They can work with consciousness or without consciousness, but the results are different.
> (Emphasis added, p. 68)

Mechanical and life energies are required for the planetary body, psychic energies are required for the centers, and then there are the substances or hydrogens of consciousness.

Each center has particular hydrogens with which it works. The sexual, emotional, moving, instinctual and intellectual centers work with matters designated by their hydrogen level. Any hydrogen has some degree of density of substance, energy and intelligence associated with it. All of these hydrogens are wasted under the condition of mechanical life. The sexual center can work with a very high octane and volatile energy H 12, which plays the vital role in procreation and in the possible refinement of an individual's higher being-bodies. This potent sexual energy is usually squandered uselessly or destructively in the misuse of sexual energy. While the emotional center can work with finer energies (also H 12), it seldom does so due to the domination by negative emotions and personal feelings based on denser hydrogens–H 48 or H 96. Intellectual center, particularly the formatory apparatus, is relatively slow in operation and assigned the hydrogen level of H 48. The higher intellectual center works with very fine matters or hydrogens, H6. According to Gurdjieff, each center is designed for particular substances or hydrogens, although they borrow and misplace energies from one center to another. People are controlled by the misuse of energies through the wrong work of centers, especially the emotional and sexual energies which are so vitally important to a human's possible evolution.

People also squander the energies of consciousness. Ouspensky notes that energy is necessary for consciousness:

> If you have no electricity, or if you have a pocket torch with a bad battery, you may have a flash and then nothing. Consciousness is light, light is the result of a certain energy; if there is no energy there is no light. (1957, p. 68)

Just as one can save and accumulate energies for the centers, so also one can save and accumulate the energies of consciousness. By maintaining continual interests, attachments and identifications with insignificant events, things and people, humans constantly waste the force of attention and consciousness. A human being's attention is usually engaged and controlled by everything happening and this passivity depletes the energies of consciousness.

The process of self-study, self-observation and self-remembering can bring about more *light*, more higher hydrogens, for consciousness in the inner world. The light of consciousness has chemical and alchemical effects in terms life dynamics of the individual. Gurdjieff explains:

> "... in observing himself a man notices that self-observation itself brings about certain changes in his inner processes. He begins to understand that self-observation is an instrument of self-change, a means of awakening. By observing himself, he throws, as it were, *a ray of light* onto his inner processes which have hitherto worked in complete darkness. And under the influence of this light the processes themselves begin to change. There are a great many chemical processes that can take place only in the absence of light. Exactly in the same way many psychic processes can take place only in the dark. Even a feeble *light of consciousness* is enough to change completely the character of a process, while it makes many of them altogether impossible. Our inner psychic processes (our inner alchemy) have much in common with those chemical processes in which light changes the character of the process and they are subject to analogous laws." (1949, pp.145-46)

Self-observation brings light to bear upon the wrong work of centers and disrupts the usual automatic processes. Patterns of negative emotions and self-love, formatory thinking and lying, daydreaming and imagination, postures and mannerisms, the falseness of personality, the misuse of sexual energies, can gradually be de-automatized through the increase of consciousness. This serves to further deepen awareness and produce a greater refinement of energies and inner light. The energies of consciousness and the centers can be retained and accumulated.

Gurdjieff explains an essential role that self remembering has in the inner chemistry and alchemy of a human being. By maintaining consciousness and attention at the point of the reception of psychological impressions, these impressions acquire an increased force which alters the chemistry and alchemy of these substances within a human being. Self remembering acts as what Gurdjieff calls the *first conscious shock* to intensify the quality of psychological impressions, which leads to the refinement of more subtle energies. A person asleep has no energies for such conscious efforts of self-remembering and does not even realize that they are lost amidst the activities of the machine and lived out by life. It is possible to accumulating more inner light and higher hydrogens through the processes of self-observation and self-remembering. Unfortunately, humankind asleep knows none of this—of the energies of consciousness, of the centers or of the higher being-bodies.

The aim in the fourth way psychology is to overcome the psychopathological state of oneself and to refine and accumulate more subtle matters or finer hydrogens within one's being. These higher hydrogens permeate levels of denser matter and are the basis upon which the growth of the finer being-bodies depends. Individual transformation involves the accumulation of finer hydrogens which allow for higher states of consciousness, connection with the higher centers and the crystallization of the higher being-bodies. Recall Gurdjieff's explanations:

> "All the fine substances necessary for the growth and feeding of the higher bodies must be produced within the physical organism, and the physical organism is able to produce them provided the human factory is working properly and economically." (1949, p. 180)

The possibilities of awakening and higher states of consciousness require that one study self as a chemical factory with alchemical possibilities.

6. A View on the Sleeping World

> "People have been told almost since the creation of the world that they are asleep and that they must awaken. ... Men take it simply as a form of speech, as an expression, as a metaphor. They completely fail to understand that it must be taken literally. ... So long as a man sleeps profoundly and is wholly immersed in dreams he cannot even think about the fact that he is asleep. If he were to think that he was asleep, he would wake up. ... And men have not the slightest idea what they are losing because of this sleep." (Gurdjieff, in O., 1949, p.144)

Humans' central psychological illusion is that they know themselves. The illusion is that they live a conscious, consistent and willful existence, knowing themselves, conscious of what they are, of what they think, feel, and do, and that they make choices and know how to love. The fourth way teaching instead portrays humankind as not properly conscious, as lacking a permanent and constant state or real I, and as lived out in a mechanical and conditioned fashion by a thousand and one forces of which they are unaware. Humans are sleepwalkers, half asleep or semi-conscious, in a state which Gurdjieff labels as *"automated consciousness"* and *"waking sleep."*

The idea that humans are asleep, living in illusion and ignorance of self is a central theme of mystical psychology. With this idea comes the aim of awakening. Sufi mystics suggests: *"Man, you are asleep, must you die before you awake."* Similarly, an aphorism of Gurdjieff's reads: *"The only thing is to awake."* Ouspensky gives this theme a somewhat different twist: *"All people in life are asleep, but not all are dead - yet."*

The central aim of esoteric psychology is to overcome the sleep walking state of mechanical life, to be reborn in essence and to attain real "I." A human being can be reborn and experience the world with a new completeness, vibrancy and wakefulness. Humans can also possess new powers and capabilities, many of which they mistakenly think they already possesses—such as real I, will, objective knowledge and the capacity for love.

It is very difficult to realize the mechanicalness of everything and of oneself. Without a conscious struggle against the current of mechanical happenings, the subtleties of life never become apparent. If we begin to awaken even momentarily, then gradually we can build on this and come to realize more and more deeply the nature of humankind's sleep state.

K. Walker, a student of Gurdjieff and Ouspensky, recounts his disturbing vision of the sleepwalking state of humanity:

As I drove back to Harley Street (London) that evening, I turned over in my mind, all that Ouspensky had said about sleeping mankind. If it were really true that not only myself, but that everybody else was asleep, what a revolutionary change we should have to make in our view of human life on this planet. A sleeping world! A world of drowsy people drifting about in the streets, closeted in government offices, conducting affairs of State, hurrying into the lobby of the Houses of Parliament to record their votes, dispensing justice from the Bench; people doing a thousand different things and doing them all in a state which approximated to a state of sleep! Yes, Ouspensky had meant us to take his words on the subject, literally. He had pictured a world of somnambulists, a world of men walking about automatically, without their being aware of what they were doing, a world of people behaving entirely mechanically and according to conditioned habits. (1965, pp. 45-46)

Humans are marionettes, characters in a Punch and Judy show, pulled this way and pushed that way, all in sleep. As machines, they are imprisoned by dozens of mechanical laws of which they are unaware. The pomp and nobility of human life is a facade to conceal the realities of the sleeping world. Ouspensky states: *"Sleeping people fight, make laws; sleeping people obey or disobey them. ... all of history is made by people who are asleep."*

Author, D. King (1963) describes his brief alterations in awareness brought about by efforts to self-remember while waiting for a commuter train. His account presents a terrifying vision of the psychopathology of humankind:

... the scene altered unexpectedly and with a startling abruptness, as if one stage set had been substituted instantly for another. ... it was chiefly the other people who held the focus of attention. They looked dead, really dead. One expected to see signs of decay but of course there were none. What one did see was stark unconsciousness, scores of marionettes not self-propelled but moved by some force alien to themselves, proceeding along their automatic trails mechanically and without purpose. Some of the mouths were open and they looked like holes in cardboard boxes. The faces were

> blankly empty; even those upon which otherwise some expression would have been
> noticeable, had been drained of any significance and one saw that those expressions
> were unrelated to the entities that wore them. For the first time the concept of the
> zombie became credible. (p.123)

This was a glimpse of the mechanical, artificial and unconscious state of humanity asleep.
True existence is hidden and the masses do not "instinctually sense reality" or cosmic truths.

Self-remembering illustrates how asleep humans are and the terror of the situation. Ouspensky
recounts his early experiences:

> After this there followed a strange period of time. It lasted about three weeks.
> And during this period from time to time I saw "sleeping people." This requires a
> particular explanation.

> Two or three days after G's departure I was walking along the Troitsky Street and
> suddenly I saw that the man who was walking towards me was *asleep*. There could
> be no doubt whatever about this. Although his eyes were open, he was walking along
> obviously immersed in dreams which ran like clouds across his face. It entered my
> mind that if I could look at him long enough I should see his dreams, that is, I should
> understand what he was seeing in his dreams. But he passed on. After him came
> another also sleeping. A sleeping coachman went by with two sleeping passengers.
> Suddenly I found myself in the position of the prince in the "Sleeping princess."
> Everyone around me was asleep. It was an indubitable and direct sensation. I realized
> what it meant that many things could be *seen* with our eyes which we do not usually
> see. These sensations lasted for several minutes. ... I at once made the discovery
> that *by trying to remember myself* I was able to intensify and prolong these sensations
> for so long as I had energy enough not to be diverted, that is, not to allow things and
> everything around me to attract my attention. When attention was diverted I ceased
> to see "sleeping people" because I had obviously gone to sleep myself. I told only a
> few of our people of these experiments and two of them when they tried to remember
> themselves had similar experiences. (1949, p. 265)

The practice of self-remembering reveals one's unconsciousness and conditioned state, and that of
everyone around. Humans are sleepwalkers living in illusion and ignorance of self. In fact, people have
no idea of the profound sleep in which they live–a sleep perpetuated by the whole of mechanical life,
by man's psychological illusions and even by the moon.

As Gurdjieff states, there is only one thing which is serious and that is to escape from the general law
and to be free. This means overcoming the conditioning and sleepwalking state which governs the
mass of humanity. Self-remembering as a practice helps us to glimpse the reality behind all the fine
words about the sleep state of humankind. People do not know self nor do they realize *"the horror of
the situation."* Gurdjieff explains:

> "A modern man lives in sleep, in sleep he is born and in sleep he dies. . . . *sleep* is the
> chief feature of our being ... . if a man really wants knowledge, he must first of all think
> about how to wake, that is, about how to change his being." (Ouspensky, 1949, p. 66)

The sleep walking state of humankind is a central feature of human psychopathology.

7. Beelzebub's Tales: Human Psychopathology and the Process of Reciprocal Destruction

"... it was possible sometimes to observe very strange manifestations of theirs, that is, from time to time they did something which was never done by three-brained beings on other planets, namely, they would suddenly, without rhyme or reason, begin destroying one another's existence. ... from this horrible process of theirs their numbers rapidly diminished ... ." (Gurdjieff, 1950, p. 91)

In *Beelzebub's Tales*, Gurdjieff elaborates a highly unusual story or tale about the history of humankind and the *"strange psyches of the three brained-beings breeding on planet Earth."* Recall that the cosmic harmony of our solar system *"Ors"* was disrupted by a cosmic catastrophe when a comet collided with the earth and broke off two fragments—the moon and a second unknown satellite. Until the moons were stabilized in their new orbits, a certain *"sacred vibration," "askokin"* was required to be produced by the Earth to feed the moons. Thus, humanity, as part of organic life on earth, came to serve a purpose in maintaining the moon. Further cosmic misfortunes occurred after the organ "Kundabuffer" was implanted in humankind in order to prevent them from becoming aware of their enslavement by the moon. The two primary effects of the organ Kundabuffer described by Beelzebub are to cause humans to *"perceive reality topsy-turvy"* and to be conditioned by *"sensations of 'pleasure' and 'enjoyment.'"*

The first effect of the Kundabuffer was to cause the three-brained beings breeding on planet Earth to perceive reality *"topsy-turvy."* Thus, contemporary three-brained beings have *"mechanized themselves to see nothing real,"* to be dominated by formatory thinking and to have no true knowledge of their nature. Their bob-tailed reason has degenerated so far that they are incapable of their own *"active deliberations,"* or of *"instinctual sensing reality."* Further, humans no longer fulfill their sacred being obligations, or *"being-Partkdolg-duty"* –of conscious labours and intentional suffering.

The second major effect of the Kundabuffer has been that humans became conditioned by the sensations of pleasure and enjoyment–increasingly lazy, indulging in imaginary pleasurings and wasting their sexual substances. The three brained-beings forget about the psychology of their possible evolution and the necessity of coating the higher being-bodies.

Although the Kundabuffer was removed, its effects on the human psyche had become crystallized within humans' presences and maintained by the abnormal conditions of being-existence established on Earth. The consequences of the organ were thus passed from generation to generation. Over time, the strangeness of the human psyches increased and, according to Beelzebub, *"the quality of their radiations went steadily from bad to worse."* (1950, p. 106) In varied stories to his grandson, Beelzebub provides profound insights into the peculiarities and deficiencies of the strange human psyche.

Although Great Nature increased the numbers of the three-brained beings in order to accommodate the degeneration of the human psyche, other strange phenomena were produced–such as decreasing age expectancy, animal sacrifice and slaughter, and the worst *"terror of the situation,"* which is warfare or the process of *reciprocal destruction.*

> "... on that strange planet alone in the whole of the Universe does that horrible process occur among three-brained beings which is called the 'process of reciprocal destruction of each other's existence,' or, as it is called on that ill-fated planet, 'war.'" (1950, p.107)

Gurdjieff views war as the most insane and pathological sign of humans' mechanical and delusional life, the primary symptom of the degeneration of their radiations and strange psyches. Warfare and animal sacrifice disrupt even the larger cosmic harmony by producing a surplus of low quality Askokin vibrations.

On hearing from his grandfather of the horrors of war, Hassein is shocked by how such a *"need for periodically occupying themselves with the destruction of each other's existence"* could run *"like a crimson thread through all your tales."* (pp. 1055-6) Further, Hassein wonders, how would the power possessing beings not be able to eradicate such gross evils? Beelzebub then elaborates upon the causes of war in a unique style by characterizing the psychological development of those *"power possessing beings,"* who might assume such a role in eradicating warfare. In explaining to his grandson, why humans are so unable to work together to eliminate the horrible process of warfare, Beelzebub draws this portrait of the power possessing beings, who are also *"men in quotation marks:"*

> "... I must tell you that thanks to the abnormally established conditions of being-existence there, the 'waking psyche' as it is expressed there, of each one of them gradually becomes from the very beginning of responsible existence such that he can 'think sincerely' and see things in the true light exclusively only if his stomach is so full of the first being-food that it is impossible for what are called 'wandering nerves' in it to move, or, as they themselves say, he is 'stuffed quite full'; and besides, all his needs already inherent in him which are unbecoming to three-brained beings and which had become the dominant factors for the whole of his presence, are fully satisfied, of course, only for that given moment. ...

> "When these three-brained beings of your planet, particularly of the present time, who have the means of gorging to satiety and of fully satisfying all their other needs and who perhaps could do something for the struggle against this phenomenal evil prevailing on their planet, are satiated, and their mentioned needs are satisfied, and they are seated on what are called their 'soft English divans' in order, as is said there, 'to digest it all'–they do not profit, even during this time so suitable for sincere thinking ... but indulge instead in the maleficent self-calming. ...

> "For instance, when after gorging and satisfying themselves these important and power-possessing beings of the Earth are seated on their said divans, the associative thoughts which ought inevitably to flow in them receives shocks from the reflexes of their stomach and sex organs and wander freely in all directions, as they say there, 'to their hearts content,' and so pleasantly free and easy, as if they, that is these thoughts of theirs, were 'strolling of an evening in Paris along the Boulevard des Capucinus.'

"When these power-possessing beings of your planet are seated on their soft divans, subjects like the following a-think in them.

"For instance, how to get his revenge on that acquaintance of his, John Smith, who a few days before looked at a woman he 'liked,' not with his right eye but with his left.

"Or this 'digesting' terrestrial power-possessing or important being thinks: 'Why did not my horse come in first yesterday at the races as I expected, but some other?'

"Or, 'Why do those stocks which are in fact quite worthless, go up every day on the market, higher and higher?'

"Or, finally, he thinks something of this kind: 'If I were in John Smith's shoes who invented a new method of breeding flies for making ivory from their skeletons, then from the profits obtained I would do this, that, and the other, and not as that fool, who, like a dog in the manger, will neither himself eat nor let others eat,' and so on in the same strain.

"Still, it does occasionally happen there, that some power-possessing or important being of the Earth suddenly chances to think not under the influences of the reflexes of his stomach and sex organs, but thinks sincerely and quite seriously about these or other questions, with particular regard to this terrifying terrestrial question.
(1950, pp. 1057-61)

Beelzebub's tales are rich in such surrealistic humour and portray most vividly the horror of the situation and the strangeness of the human psyche evident on that ill-fated planet earth. Serious undesirable qualities have become crystallized in humans, who are no longer capable of sincere and active mentation but are controlled by the reflexes of the stomach, material interests, sexual itching, self calming and self-love.

According to Beelzebub, the three-brained beings on planet Earth are "microcosmoses" or *"similitudes of the Whole."* As such, they have the possibility of not only serving local cosmic purposes, feeding the earth and moon as part of organic life on earth, but also of attaining varied levels of Objective Reason and individuality, and even of *"blending again with the infinite."* (1950, p. 945) As a microcosm of the macrocosm, a human being can potentially coat higher being bodies for the life of the soul, instinctually sense cosmic truths and phenomena, and maintain their existence within the subtle realms of being after death achieving different levels of immortality. Unfortunately, humankind came to perceive reality so topsy-turvy, conditioned by pleasure and self- love, and wasteful of their sacred substances, such that they no longer realize their deeper cosmic purposes and possibilities.

Human came to live and die, not according to the principle *Foolasnitamnian*, which is proper to the existence of all three-brained beings, but according to the principle *"Itoklanoz"* –which governs one and two brained beings, who have no opportunity to coat higher being-bodies. Thus humans can die like dog and serve only local cosmic purposes.

Humans asleep, ruled by the common psychopathology, no longer have normal sensations of cosmic phenomena, are oblivious of the need to fulfill their sacred being obligations, have their true consciousness in the unconscious and are likely to become simply fertilizer, possibly for future human.

Thus, upon death, the majority of contemporary beings *"remain with presences consisting of the planetary body alone, and thus are, for themselves, destroyed forever."*

A real human is only a possibility and one generally unrealized. This is the plight of the lost souls, the acorns or nuts, which could become oak trees. Only through awakening and knowing self can the three brained-beings serve deeper cosmic purposes. Gurdjieff, as Beelzebub, provides a dismal view of the psychopathology of humankind.

"... before man can acquire any new powers and capabilities, he must actually develop in himself those qualities which he thinks he possesses, and about which he has the greatest possible illusions."

P. Ouspensky

V /
The Illusions of Consciousness, Will and Unity

1. The Illusion of Self Knowledge

The central psychological illusion is that people know self. Recall the answers of Jeanine, Gary, Carol, Brian and Anne when asked the question, *"How well do you know yourself?"* Each responded immediately by saying *"I know myself pretty well (or very well)."* They repeatedly use the word I in their descriptions of themselves and in their explanation of why they think that they know themselves. Each speaks as if there were some central and unified I. They identify I with their names and social identities, with various likes and dislikes, attitudes and opinions, life experiences and personal characteristics. Each speaks as if they knew and could speak for the whole of themselves.

Certainly from the point of view of the Gurdjieff teaching, people do not know what real "I" is nor what self knowledge involves. Ouspensky (1950) writes:

> To know oneself–this was the first principle and the first demand of old psychological schools. We still remember these words, but have lost their meaning. We think that to know ourselves means to know our peculiarities, our desires, our tastes, our capacities, and our intentions ... (p. 46)

Jeanine, Gary, Carol, Brian and Anne make the exact mistake mentioned by Ouspensky, identifying self with their peculiarities, desires and tastes, attitudes and opinions, and so on. In the state of waking sleep, people do not strive after self-knowledge in any systematic way or even realize that this might be done. We take ourselves and life for granted and generally think that we know ourselves and what the world is, and even about the issues of the Gods.

Knowing yourself from a fourth way perspective has various levels of meaning. However, Ouspensky explains where it begins:

> ... to know ourselves means ... to know ourselves as machines, that is, to know the structure of one's machine, its parts, functions of different parts, the conditions governing their work, and so on. We realize in a general way that we cannot know any machine without studying it. We must remember this in relation to ourselves and must study our own machines as machines. (1950, p. 46)

The first level of self knowledge focuses on the study of ourselves as we are, the parts of our being and our varied states. One begins by viewing oneself as a machine conditioned by a thousand and one life influences and experiences, and controlled by habits of thinking, feeling and action which characterize false personality. However, the aim is to come eventually to know self at a deeper level– what we are in the roots of being, in the development of the essence and in the possible soul life. To know self ultimately means to know real "I" through the process of awakening and transformation. However, the psychology of a human's possible evolution begins with the study of ourselves as we are, under the conditions of ordinary life, limited by misunderstanding and illusion. We must realize what powers and capabilities humans lack in the usual state of automated consciousness. The next aim is to realize the hidden dimensions of consciousness and being, attaining mystical self knowledge and experience.

The central illusion of humankind is that we "know self." The components of this illusion concern the different powers or capabilities which men and women think that they possess but which in reality they do not. Three primary illusions or misunderstandings concern the human faculties of consciousness, unity of I, and will (or the capacity to do). The fourth way psychology begins with a study of humans as they are in their machine-like nature, lacking true consciousness, will and unity, and then describes evolution in terms of the development of these capacities. Humans can awaken and experience new states of consciousness and awareness; attain a unified "I;" and develop real will. Unfortunately, wrong ideas and convictions about the nature of consciousness, unity and will, are major obstacles to self knowledge. If we can begin to understand these illusions, there is chance of escape, of awakening and evolution.

2. The Illusion of a Unified and Permanent 'I'

"One of man's most important mistakes," he said,

"One which must be remembered, is his illusion in regards to his I."

- Gurdjieff –

We lie when we use the word I. One aspect of ourselves speaks as if it could speak for the whole of ourselves, as if it knew and understood itself and the whole. We continually say I, although we do not really understand what this I is. A most important question to ask if we search beyond naive psychology to inquire more deeply into the nature of things is "what is this I?" In fact, how many selves might there be, if not one? Could we talk of two selves, three, a hierarchy of selves, a legion of selves? Lastly, what self do we have to know in order to know ourselves, the universe and the Gods? The methods of the mystical and spiritual traditions are to enable us to realize what real "I" is, and that "I AM." Ouspensky recalls Gurdjieff's discussions of a man's many little i's:

> "Man such as we know him, the 'man-machine,' the man who cannot 'do,' and with whom and through whom everything 'happens,' cannot have a permanent and single I. His I changes as quickly as his thoughts, feeling, and moods, and he makes a profound mistake in considering himself always one and the same person; in reality he is always a different person, not the one he was a moment ago.

"Man has no permanent and unchanging I. Every thought, every mood, every desire, every sensation, says 'I.' And in each case it seems to be taken for granted that this I belongs to the Whole, to the whole man, and that a thought, a desire, or an aversion is expressed by this Whole. In actual fact there is no foundation whatever for this assumption. Man's every thought and desire appears and lives quite separately and independently of the Whole. And the Whole never expresses itself, for the simple reason that it exists, as such, only psychically as a thing, and in the abstract as a concept. Man has no individual I. But there are, instead, hundreds and thousands of separate small I's, very often entirely unknown to one another, never coming into contact, or, on the contrary, hostile to each other, mutually exclusive and incompatible. Each minute, each moment, man is saying or thinking 'I.' And each time his I is different. ... Man is a plurality. Man's name is legion. ... "Man has no individuality. He has no single, big I. ... "And each separate small I is able to call itself by the name of the Whole ...." (1949, pp. 59-60)

Real "I" is only a possibility. At the level of false personality, there are hundreds or thousands of different i's, associated with different habits and patterns of thought, feeling and sensation elicited by the many people and situations of life. A human's many i's are simply partial aspects corresponding to particular situations. Vaysse (1979) explains:

... in life, instead of manifesting himself with an "individuality" in which the functions always express harmoniously what he is in the depth of his essence, a man manifests differently according to circumstances, behind the mask of diverse personage, multiple little "I's" which give him an acquired exterior, foreign to his true self. The whole of this together forms his "personality." But, without the work of self-observation, properly conducted, man obviously has no knowledge of this state of affairs. (pp. 28)

Ouspensky (1957) simply notes: "*... we do not know what 'I' is.*" (p. 165)

Although we are always talking for ourselves as if we really knew and understood the whole, the only real I we have is in our imagination and lying. We think that we can speak for the whole of ourselves and it is very difficult to persuade someone who is convinced of their personal unity that there are many i's. A human's name is legion, yet we consider ourselves as one.

However, the possibility of awakening and of acquiring real "I" exists and then the whole of life would take on new meanings and appear in a new light. In order to understand the process of awakening, we have to understand our sleep and illusions. This is where the Work begins. J. Cox (1980) expresses these themes:

Without the constant effort and Remembrance to consciously self-observe, a man never sees for himself that he is not a single, unified "I"; he will live out his days foolishly believing that his real self is whatever opinionated and temporary "I" happens to be thinking or speaking. Without the proper methods, a man continues to be a reactionary machine that changes uncontrollably from moment to moment in response to his ever-changing environment. Without a man sincerely taking the ideas of the

> Work and using them as his new mirror to study life, he will continue to think in his old established patterns, and can, thus, never learn anything new or see things in a refreshed light.
>
> Nothing can change what we are, but the liberating truth of the Work is to free a man from his delusions of what he thinks he is. The Work cannot touch or help you until you know what you are not, and this requires great effort and a life of dedicated struggle. (pp. 72-73)

An individual can struggle to awaken. This is the quest for those who would seek the truth about self and search for the miraculous possibilities which lie behind the surface appearances of life. Few oppose what Cox (1980) describes as the "Great Machine" and aim towards awakening.

The possibility of real I depends upon the growth and refinement of the essence and the attainment of self-consciousness. The psychological evolution of the individual produces a new experience of "I," which development does not naturally or mechanically occur. Further, real I is not achieved by fusing the small i's into one big I, as people commonly think. Instead, it involves neutralizing and eliminating the small i's and cultivating the essence and the capacity to be fully present. Finally, there can be the emergence of a new order of the I experience. No number of small i's will ever become a real I. To begin, one must overcome the slavery to mechanicalness and the illusion of having a central or unified "I."

3. The Illusion of Will

The belief that we possess will or the capacity to do is another central psychological illusion. Of course, we think we do things every day from the moment we wake up until we go to sleep. It seems that we are always doing things. We get up, eat, go to work, look after business, attend classes, interact with others, do household chores, and so on and so forth. Of course, we have the capacity to do or so we think.

From the viewpoint of the fourth way, humans can do nothing. Instead, they are automatons controlled by external stimuli and conditioned habits of thinking, feeling and action. We are deluded to think that we make conscious choices and decisions, that we are capable of free and independent actions, and that we can control ourselves and our lives. All of these beliefs are in error, as really "everything happens." Ouspensky explains:

> Everything 'happens.' People can 'do' nothing. From the time we are born to the time we die things happen, happen, happen, and we think we are doing. This is our normal state in life. ...

You must understand that nothing happens at the time it happens; the necessity of it happening was created long ago. Things happen by themselves; whether you do or do not do something may have been decided ten years before ... and that determines what you will do tomorrow—you cannot change it.

We think we can take a certain decision and act accordingly. In reality we are controlled not by internal decisions but by external influences. If the internal decision corresponds to the external influence, we will do it, otherwise we will not. But we can create in ourselves powers to 'do.' Nature has made us machines acting under external influences, but with a possibility to develop our own motor. If there is no inner motor, we will always turn round in the same place. ...you can 'do' nothing, things happen mechanically. One thing comes after another and just happens or does not happen, and you cannot help it.

... we are carried by the current but we think that we carry the current. ... If one is trained to do something one learns to follow a certain trend of happenings, and then these develop, and one runs behind although one thinks one is leading.

'Doing' begins with going against the current-first in yourself, in personal things. (1957, pp. 242-7)

This is a dismal picture indeed. Gurdjieff and Ouspensky view humans under the conditions of ordinary life as completely automatized, mechanical beings lived out by life. A human's little daily wills and wants change as quickly as the little i's, their moods, desires and irritations, the itches of the stomach and the wanderings of the sex organs. Although people think that they make conscious decisions or that they could not do what they do, these are all simply lies or illusions. Really, there is nothing permanent within the individual from which real will might arise—as this would require the presence of real "I."

This is the common psychopathology of humankind. Their position in the world, their identity, is always shifting with situations and external stimuli and people have no inner motor capable of initiating independent thoughts, feelings and movements. Little i's have little self-wills, daily desires and interests, but not conscious will. A partial aspect of a whole cannot do anything. Conscious will requires the awakening of "I" and action originating from a deeper level within the individual. People lack will just as they lack inward unity and self-consciousness.

Fortunately, it is possible to escape this sleepwalking condition and to develop an inner motor. Unfortunately, people do not see the need for this as they think that they already possess will and that they carry the current of everything that happens in their lives. Why expend great effort to acquire something one imagines he already possesses? Once again, man's psychological illusions are a major obstacle to conscious change. It is most difficult to realize how one really runs behind, swept along by the stream of mechanical life, while all long we think we are doing.

Gurdjieff depicts the common state of a human being using an Eastern parable of a horse, carriage, driver and passenger. The horse represents the emotional and desire nature of the individual, the carriage is the body, and the driver is the mind. In a human as he or she is, the horse has not been properly cared for, nor is it controlled by the driver; the carriage has been left unattended and is dilapidated, un-oiled and falling apart; and the driver, has been partying in the local pub and lost control of the reins. The fourth element in the parable is the passenger, whose voice is unheard by the driver. The passenger is real "I" but remains completely passive in relationship to the horse, carriage and driver.

Gurdjieff compares the situation of mechanical humanity with that of an individual who has attained a certain development of consciousness, will and unity:

> "In the first case ... in relation to the functions of a man of physical body only, the automaton depends upon external influences, and the next three functions depend upon the physical body and the external influences it receives. Desires or aversions–'I like,' 'I don't like'–that is, functions occupying the place of the second body, depend upon accidental shocks and influences. Thinking, which corresponds to the functions of the third body, is an entirely mechanical process. 'Will' is absent in ordinary mechanical man, he has desires only; and a greater or lesser permanence of desires and wishes is called a strong or a weak will." (In O., 1949, p.42)

Sensations	Emotions	Thoughts	Little i's
automaton worked by external influences	desires produced by automaton	thoughts proceeding from desires	different and contradictory "wills" created by desires

The direction of causality is from without and control lies within the external situation. Stimuli act upon and control the physical, then the emotional and thirdly the intellectual responses in a mechanical manner. The resultant will is created by the desires evoked by external stimuli and conditioned responses.

A second situation depends upon inner development or evolution, such that the individual attains self consciousness, unity and will. In this case, the direction of the causal movement is reversed and actions originate from a unified presence or real "I."

body obeying desires and emotions subject to intelligence	emotional powers and desires obeying thought and intelligence	thinking functions obeying consciousness and will	I Consciousness Will

"In the second case, that is, in relation to the functions of the four bodies, the automatism of the physical body depends upon the influences of the other bodies. Instead of the discordant and often contradictory activity of different desires, there is *one single I*, whole, indivisible, and permanent; there is *individuality*, dominating the physical body and its desires and able to overcome both its reluctance and its resistance. Instead of the mechanical process of thinking, there is *consciousness*. And there is *will*, that is, a power, not merely composed of various often contradictory desires belonging to different "I's," but issuing from consciousness and governed by individuality or a single and permanent I. Only such a will can be called "free," for it is independent of accident and cannot be altered or directed from without." (pp. 42-3)

Consciousness, will and a single I are capacities which develop together as aspects of the same thing. This evolution of a human's powers moves against the current of mechanical life. Instead of being fragmented, semi-conscious and governed by external stimuli, the individual manifests with a unified presence dependent upon the growth of essence and awakening of real "I." Such a higher type, a man number five in whom the "I" is stable, would be consciously aware of their thoughts, feelings and actions, with a center of gravity in real I. The master would be in communication with the driver, who would rein in the horse and attend to the carriage.

A description of Gurdjieff illustrates such a stable posture:

Gurdjieff manifested himself in ways never elsewhere encountered by the writer, in ways so different from those of others that they constituted a plain and perceptible difference in level of existence upon his part. ... He is the only person ever met by the writer who gave the indubitable impression that all his responses, mental, emotional and practical, were mutually in balance and thus the further impression that everyone else was out of step, but not this man himself. It is just what would be expected, though unpredictable, by a sophisticated Waking person when confronted by someone else in the state of Awakeness. (King, 1963, pp ix-x)

People do not know real will, nor realize how they are normally carried by the current of mechanical happenings.

4. The Illusions of Consciousness

4a. **The Invisibility of Consciousness**

The nature of human consciousness is an extremely deep mystery, which has been widely recognized within science over the past decade. However, scientists and philosophers use the term consciousness in a thousand and one ways, with ten thousand and one meanings and interpretations. Confusion and misunderstandings around the issues of consciousness are deeply embedded within the scientific literature and within popular thought. People do not understand the issues of consciousness—what it is and what it is not.

In his spiritual autobiography, James Moffatt (2002) depicts the mysteries of consciousness with humorous insights, while providing glimpses of the depths of the consciousness issue:

> "Consciousness"—what do i mean when i use that term? What is consciousness? Well, that is the big question. As far as questions go, it's pretty much in a class of its own. It's the World Series, the Stanley Cup, the Superbowl, the Greater Intergalactic Open, and the heavyweight championship of the world of Big Questions all rolled into one. People win Nobel Prizes, receive huge research grants, become knights of the realm, gain international acclaim and celebrity as scholars and thinkers, and much, much more— just for beating around consciousness' bushes or hanging out under its porch light looking for its keys. Mathematicians forge its signature; physicists trace its shadow. Chemists scour its soup pot; biologists listen to its heart beat, draw its blood lines, and chart its pulse. In the most remote ranges of the Himalayas, there are said to be monks who draw closer to consciousness' door simply by chanting its postal code. ...
>
> Ah, consciousness ... the cosmic key that unlocks the doors to eternal mysteries ... the straw that stirs the universal fluids ... the meaning of meaning ... the mirror with which God does His tricks ... but what, pray tell, is it? You can know it—more or less. You can lose it—without missing it—for the longest time. You can focus it, reflect on it, summon it ... elevate, expand, and divide it .... You can refine it, define it ... you can wine & rhyme & divine it ... you can even make space and time for it ... but the one thing you can never do is to know consciousness when you do not have it. Pretty tricky business— trying to think of what consciousness may or may not be. Questions about the nature of consciousness have stymied some major league thinkers, driven others to the intersection of Angst & Despair, and simply worn out the rest. ....

The origin and nature of consciousness are big league questions, and we will have to wine, dine and then divine them.

To begin in a general way, consciousness refers to the inner awareness each of us has within ourselves and within our lives. You cannot see my inner world of experience and I cannot see your inner world. And yet, it is within this inner world, that we, or I, exist. To understand the issues of human consciousness we have to explore the nature of this inner awareness and experience. Understanding consciousness within ourselves is *the key* to unlock the eternal mysteries.

The issues of consciousness are profoundly important from both a scientific and individual perspective. What is this inner consciousness? Where does it come from and what types of experience are possible for human beings–both during life and after death? Few people are seriously interested in trying to understand the nature of consciousness, even their own consciousness. In fact, people do not even realize that this is something that an individual might aim to do. Consciousness as a variable or a quality of the inner life is seldom considered. People are too busy and attached to the dramas of their lives to wonder about such seemingly philosophical issues. Consciousness is simply there, or so it seems, and it is taken for granted.

However, the extent of an individual's conscious development will determine the quality and richness of life. A person's state of consciousness makes life what it is, although we generally have no understanding of this. Normally, people consider themselves asleep at night and awake and conscious during the day and the matter seems to end there. Although people talk of developing consciousness, they usually have little idea of what such a process entails. Consciousness is invisible to us and taken for granted. Our consciousness seems final, the only type of consciousness that there might be, or that we might know. In a sense, people are embedded in their state, like fish in water, and do not recognize consciousness as a something which makes life what it is. We simply assume that somehow consciousness is there.

The study of consciousness is essential to free a human from the illusions under which he or she lives. As it happens, people take themselves to be properly conscious, when they are not. Instead, they are only *relatively conscious*, lost and embedded in states of *waking sleep*. It is necessary to make consciousness visible to oneself, as something which can be studied and increased. Gurdjieff explains that self study is the only way to approach these issues:

> "Your principle mistake consists in thinking that you *always have consciousness*, and in general, either that consciousness is *always present* or that it is *never present*. In reality consciousness is a property which is continually changing. Now it is present, now it is not present. And there are different degrees and different levels of consciousness. Both consciousness and the different degrees of consciousness must be understood in oneself by sensation, by taste. No definitions can help you in this case." (In O., 1949, p.117)

The study of consciousness involves the practices of self-observation and self-remembering. The individual can make intentional or conscious effort to wake up and to be more fully present. By self-remembering at different moments within varied situations of life, at different times throughout the day, we study the appearance and disappearance of consciousness. The practice of self-remembering helps to make consciousness visible to us. It cultivates the inner taste and sensation of consciousness. Through self-remembering, a person can begin to understand how they are normally lived out by life in a mechanical and unconscious manner.

There are many questions about what the philosopher William James, described as the *"most mysterious thing in the world"* –human consciousness. The most obvious obstacle to understanding consciousness is our lack of it. A second major obstacle to understanding consciousness is the wrong ideas within popular thought and within the vast scientific and psychological literature. As scientists trip absent mindedly over their stools, fail to realize when they irritate their wives, when they are not fully satiated and desire to pleasure the sexual organs, or maintain their stock interests–it is easy to philosophize about consciousness without realizing at all what it is. The literature on consciousness produced by the *"scientists of new formation"* is written by people in states of waking sleep who do not know self in the manner described by the mystics. We have to study consciousness by attempting to become more conscious. An individual can cultivate consciousness through the practice of self remembering and this provides a key to awakening.

A most important issue is whether or not consciousness can exist apart from the physical body, either after death or during life, and whether or not a human has a soul or at least the possibility of one. To begin to understand these deep questions, we need to understand how we are so little conscious and what this means in terms of our lives and the broader life of humanity. It is very hard to make consciousness visible to oneself as a something or anything, that makes life what it is. Since we do not know what real "I" is, or that "I AM," it is impossible for us to know what consciousness is.

4b. **Normal States of Consciousness**

According to Gurdjieff, there are four states of individual consciousness possible for human beings. Unfortunately, humankind spend their lives in the two lowest of these, sleep and waking sleep. Occasionally, individuals experience flashes of the third state of self-consciousness, sometimes elicited by unusual or traumatic events or unexpected circumstances. The fourth and highest state of objective consciousness occurs only among individuals who have attained self-consciousness and developed the higher being bodies, and who thus live within the realm of the miraculous.

The differences between the four conscious states cannot be understood as simply on a continuum. The transition from one state to another involves a radical *quantum shift* in awareness and not simply a difference of degree or quantity of consciousness. Each state is marked by the appearance of new faculties and capabilities, and a dramatic shift in the inner taste and sensation of "I." Just as waking sleep state is qualitatively different from that of sleep, so also, a moment of self-consciousness is dramatically different from the usual state of waking sleep. Gurdjieff suggests that the two lowest levels of human consciousness, sleep and waking sleep, are all that most people experience, except at rare moments in their lives.

There are two phases of sleep, *with and without dreams*, each of which involve different processes and serve different functions. In *deep sleep without dreams*, the connections between centers are broken and instinctual processes restore the energies of the centers. According to Gurdjieff, each center has two smaller energy accumulators associated with it and can draw from a larger accumulator. In sleep, the energies of the centers are restored but this depends upon the suspension of the connections between centers. Many people do not experience the deepest levels of sleep.

According to Vaysse (1979), the deep sleep state involves "*... a return to the primordial state of serenity,*" and as *"a return to the state of pure "essentiality," analogous to the embryonic state of the essence, increased by such development of essence as has been attained up until then through life experiences.*" (p.54) Deep sleep allows a return to essence and the merging with deeper life forces which sustain us. Consciousness is centered within the deeper essence and withdraws into the primordial formless realms within the universal essence. All of this occurs in a passive way, with the suspension of personal manifestations and the disconnection of the centers. Deep sleep serves the functions of the organic nature and the essence.

Dreams and sleeplessness are produced when the centers are incompletely disconnected. For instance, a man lies in bed worrying about the day's activities, about his money or his wife, imagining and a-thinking in his head, controlled by the needs of the emotions, the stomach and sex organs. When he begins to dream, these same motivational concerns are imaged in his dream life elaborated with residues from the day's experiences and prior life memories.

Ideally, a person would have no subjective dreams. Vaysse (1979) explains:

> ... in a man whose daily activity is complete, harmonized, and fully "satisfying," the disconnection of the various centers on going to sleep takes place harmoniously, progressively, completely, and apparently without dreams.... (p. 56)

Common dreams reflect a disturbance of the natural functioning and the contents of dreams are determined by the quality of this disturbance (its causes and significance). A first type of *associative or reactive dreams* are mechanically produced by memories of the day's experiences (day residues). A second form of *compensatory dreams* reflect long lasting personal emotions and conflicts, and the unbalanced life of the essence. In compensatory dreams, something is missing in the life of the individual and dreams serve to compensate for this condition. Thirdly, *symbolic dreams* give glimpses into the life of essence through archetypal symbols and deeper experience of the causative realms. Such dreams may involve glimpses of the higher emotional center.[14]

For the most part, dreaming sleep is a subjective and passive state in which a person is surrounded by images, fantasies, vague perceptions and illusions. The psychic functions work without direction or integration and no external results are produced. Dreams are the most subjective of people's manifestations, based upon personal experiences and conflicts, dissatisfactions and wishes. A human being spends one third of life in dreams and sleep. However, the level of dreams does not simply disappear with the light of day.

The second state of consciousness emerges upon waking, and is labeled by Gurdjieff as *waking sleep* or *relative consciousness*. Although a person is now awake, this is far from a real awakening or a clear consciousness. In fact, the waking sleep state is still almost entirely subjective and passive, dominated by daydreams and imagination and controlled by external influences and past conditioning. Further, the dream level of consciousness does not disappear when the person wakes up but remains in the background. Ouspensky compares this to the stars which are not visible during the daytime when the sun is most intense but are still present in the background.

The waking sleep state is dominated by the wrong work of centers, the continual absorption of attention in identifications and attachments, negative emotions and self love, internal considering, lying, imagination and daydreams. The inner life is dominated by mechanical habits and the continual wastage of psychic energies. This is why there is no conscious mind as such, which would require that actions derive from a stable and evolved presence or real I.

---

[14] These three types of dreams are outlined by Vaysse and correspond roughly to the views of Freud, Adler and Jung, as to the nature and function of dreams.

Gurdjieff's view of the waking sleep state is recounted by Ouspensky:

> "... a man wakes up. At first glance this is a quite different state of consciousness.
> He can move, he can talk with other people, he can make calculations ahead, he can
> see danger and avoid it, and so on. ... *And yet he does not remember himself*. He is
> a machine, everything with him *happens*. He cannot stop the flow of his thoughts, he
> cannot control his imagination, his emotions, his attention. He lives in a subjective
> world of 'I love,' 'I do not love,' 'I like,' 'I do not like,' 'I want,' 'I do not want,' that is, of
> what he thinks he likes, of what he thinks he does not like, of what he thinks he wants,
> of what he thinks he does not want. He does not see the real world. The real world is
> hidden from him by the wall of imagination. He *lives in sleep*. He is asleep."
> (In Ouspensky, 1949, pp. 142-143)

During waking sleep, a person has a more critical attitude towards impressions and is capable of
practical activities. However, for the most part, the normal state possesses few of the characteristics
which people and scientists ascribe to it. In the ordinary waking state, the formatory apparatus, the
mechanical part of the intellectual center, acts to co-ordinate impressions and reactions.
The activity of this apparatus is that of automatic reaction based upon conditioned responses,
associative emotional and thought patterns. The automated habit structures provide a sense of
personal continuity.

What is absent within waking sleep is connection to real I as a center of gravity for the psyche.
Mechanical reactions do not originate from the participation of the centers acting as a whole, with a
unitary "I" based in essence. Instead, the essence is in the subconscious and the formatory apparatus
provides an *artificial center of gravity* within the structures of the false personality. The mind is
dominated by the needs of one center and then another, according to the strength of external stimuli,
or internal impulses and itchings. The fragmentary states of little i's change from moment to moment,
situation to situation. What is considered to be normal rational consciousness is neither normal,
rational or conscious—in the true meaning of these terms. This is the lot of those three brained-beings
on planet Earth asleep to their true nature. Still worse, they think they know about themselves, the
universe and the Gods.

Western psychology deals with a duality of the conscious and unconscious, being aware or unaware,
and suggests that there is an integrated ego or self that is the center for this consciousness. From the
Gurdjieff view, a human has no central or permanent I, no real center for an integrated consciousness.
There is then no *conscious mind* as such, but only partial awareness associated with different i's
dominated by habits of thought, feelings and behavior. The so-called conscious mind is itself a form of
unconsciousness, ruled by underlying dreams, protected by buffers and lies, dominated by associative
thinking and preoccupied with stomach reflexes and sexual imagination.

True self-consciousness involves something very different from the personalized, subjective and
accidentally acquired consciousness, which is considered to be *the conscious mind*. Ouspensky
explains: *"There is nothing permanently conscious; and there is no "subconscious mind" for the very
simple reason that there is no "conscious mind."*" (1950, pp. 32-33) Since there is nothing permanently
conscious in a human being, then even the so-called conscious state is itself a semi-conscious or
waking sleep state.

"A man in quotation marks" is not self-consciousness with the presence of real I, awakened and development in essence. Instead, a human in waking sleep is absorbed by the stream of fleeting "i's," elicited according to what stimuli or impressions are received at any moment. Further, the state that people ordinarily regard as self-consciousness is structured about the formation of personality and false personality, and not established within the essence. People do not know real I or the true self-consciousness state.

4c. **Nature's Very Funny Trick**

It is very difficult to realize how we are not properly conscious and what this entails. Ouspensky explains this in terms of *nature's very funny trick*:

> ... the first obstacle in the way of the development of self-consciousness in man, is his conviction that he already possesses self-consciousness, or at any rate, that he can have it at any time he likes. It is very difficult to persuade a man that he is not conscious and cannot be conscious at will. It is particularly difficult because here nature plays a very funny trick.
>
> If you ask a man if he is conscious or if you say to him that he is not conscious, he will answer that he is conscious, and that it is absurd to say that he is not, because he hears and understands you.
>
> *And he will be quite right, although at the same time quite wrong.* This is nature's trick. He will be right because your question or your remark has made him vaguely conscious for a moment. Next moment consciousness will disappear. But he will remember what you said and what he answered, and he will certainly consider himself conscious.
>
> In reality, acquiring self-consciousness means long and hard work. How can a man agree to this work if he thinks that he already possesses the very thing which is promised him as the result of long and hard work? (1950, pp. 36-7)

The basic point of nature's little trick is that if you question somebody's consciousness, the inquiry itself elicits a tendency towards self-observation and increased consciousness. The person then becomes more conscious for a moment and assumes that they are always conscious of themselves in this manner. Because of nature's trick, people take themselves to be normally aware of themselves. In contrast, the practice of self-remembering illustrates how one is normally lost in the activities of the centers and in a state of forgetfulness.

J. Jaynes (1976) recognizes the point illustrated by nature's little trick and uses a most apt metaphor to compare consciousness to light:

> When asked the question, what is consciousness? we become conscious of consciousness. And most of us take this consciousness of consciousness to be

what consciousness is. This is not true. ... Consciousness is a much smaller part of our mental life than we are conscious of, because we cannot be conscious of what we are not conscious of. How simple that is to say; how difficult to appreciate! It is like asking a flashlight in a dark room to search around for something that does not have any light shining upon it. The flashlight, since there is light in whatever direction it turns, would have to conclude that there is light everywhere. And so consciousness can seem to pervade all mentality when actually it does not. (pp. 21-23)

This illustrates the problem in how western psychologists and philosophers approach the study of consciousness. What we think about consciousness comes from trying to be conscious of it, and then it is no longer the normal consciousness which we set out to examine. It is now more conscious of itself. Investigators of consciousness have been blind to the psychology of the methodology, and often consider normal consciousness to include self-consciousness.

Gurdjieff's approach to the study of consciousness is novel in the recognition given to these paradoxes:

"... you *can know* consciousness only in yourself. Observe that I say you *can know*, for you can know it only when you have it. And when you have not got it, you can know that you have not got it, not at that very moment; but afterwards. I mean that when it comes again you can see that it has been absent a long time, and you can find or remember the moment when it disappeared and when it reappeared. You can also define the moments when you are nearer to consciousness and further away from consciousness. But by observing in yourself the appearance and the disappearance of consciousness you will inevitably see one fact which you neither see nor acknowledge now, and that is that moments of consciousness are very short and are separated by long intervals of completely unconscious, mechanical working of the machine. You will then see that you can think, feel, act, speak, work, *without being conscious of it.*" (Ouspensky, 1949, p.116)

The quality of normal consciousness cannot be grasped when the person is actually embedded in the state. However, at moments of remembering self, we can realize how we were not previously conscious. In fact, we do all kinds of things without being aware of what we are doing, and most of life is lived out in this manner.

Nature has tricked various psychologists and philosophers who attempt to study normal consciousness by trying to be aware of it. Of course, the normal consciousness is no longer normal consciousness, but instead, involves at least self observation, vaguely closer to self-consciousness. Nature's little trick is actually quite simple, although at the same time incredibly subtle and complex. It can be illustrated by considering the remarks of various authors exploring consciousness.

Sartre (1969) is tricked in just this manner, as is evident in his comments:

... if my consciousness were not consciousness of being consciousness of that table, it would then be consciousness of that table without consciousness of being so. In other words, it would be a consciousness ignorant of itself, an unconscious–which is absurd. (p.lii)

Sartre suggests that when a person is conscious of something, he is simultaneously *conscious of being conscious* of that thing. Otherwise, as Sartre notes, we would have *a consciousness ignorant of itself*, which would be a form of *unconsciousness*. Sartre regards this possibility of a consciousness ignorant of itself as absurd. However, this is a most appropriate description of relative consciousness or the waking sleep state described by Gurdjieff. This is absurd and that is why human beings lead such absurd lives as sleepwalkers. Normally, consciousness is ignorant of itself and hence is a form of unconsciousness.

Sartre fails to realize that when he sets out to examine the nature of consciousness, then indeed, that consciousness is made conscious of itself, as this is exactly what he has set about to do: i.e., to become conscious of consciousness. However, consciousness cannot become conscious of itself and remain simply consciousness. Instead, there is an increase of consciousness through the very act of inner attention and self-observation. Sartre wakes up from his relatively conscious state, becomes conscious of his consciousness, and then thinks that this consciousness, conscious of itself, is always there. The properties of a self-conscious state are then ascribed to normal consciousness. Meanwhile, Sartre's usual relatively conscious state escaped him and he was unknowingly closer to self-consciousness, although by no means in the fully developed self-conscious state of real I.

Varied theorists approach the study of normal consciousness by trying to be conscious of it, while overlooking how the observation process itself alters what one finds. W. James (1972) falls prey to the illusory feature of nature's little trick. He starts out by describing his methodology:

> The order of our study (of the stream of consciousness) must be analytic. We are now prepared to begin the introspective study of the adult consciousness itself. (p.166)

James concludes that consciousness always involves an awareness of oneself (of one's personal existence):

> Whatever I may be thinking of, I am always at the same time more or less aware of *myself*, of my *personal existence*. At the same time it is I who am aware; so that the total self of me, being as it were duplex, partly known and partly knower, partly object and partly subject, must have two aspects discriminated in it ... the *Me* and ... *the I*. (1972, p.189)

James introspects upon the nature of consciousness and finds that it involves two discernable aspects–an I and a Me. What he fails to recognize is that the act of introspection changes the nature of the consciousness and introduces the distinction of the I and the me. James's description of consciousness masks the fact that the I and the me are not usually differentiated, but instead, the "I" is normally entirely passive.

Tart's (1968) comments also illustrate the methodological confusions generated by nature's little trick, when we try to understand consciousness:

> After discussing some of the philosophical and semantic difficulties in defining states of consciousness, I always ask whether anyone has the slightest doubt that he is awake, that is, in a "normal" state of consciousness at that moment; I have never found anyone who had difficulty in making this distinction. (p. l)

Very few people realize the elusiveness of normal consciousness. When a person is asked if they are conscious of themselves, they become conscious of themselves and think that this type of consciousness is typically present. They do not realize how the question or remark has prompted an alteration and increase in awareness. Nature is indeed very tricky.

Most central to the process of waking up is separating the "I" from me, from the machine. However, true self-consciousness is not simply acquired by moments of increased self awareness, but is rather based on the longer term development of the essence and the attaining of real "I." The usual self reflection only elicits intellectual and personality processes centered in the formatory apparatus, which are mistakenly taken as self-consciousness.

4d. **The Tricks of Thought & Self-Analysis**

> First and foremost amongst psychologists' errors is their conviction that they can know consciousness by thinking about it. Believing that they can generate the right ideas to understand it, psychologists have thought about consciousness and concluded that it is essentially equivalent to thinking. More correctly, psychologists tend to equate consciousness with the contents of awareness, but they think of thought as being, by far the most important of them. ... To psychologists—indeed, to all scientists—all of this is most reasonable. Thought is their currency, and ideas comprise the capital with which they invest their efforts and stake their claims and aims. (Moffatt, 2002)

In order to understand what self-consciousness is, it is useful for us to consider what it is not. The tendency among psychologists, philosophers and other thinkers has been to identify consciousness with thought, and self-consciousness with thinking about ourselves. From the perspective of the fourth way, these obvious errors are pervasive within modern thought.

William James (1892) was highly influential in western psychology in defining consciousness as equivalent to the psychological functions, particularly the stream of thinking. Recall James' comments: *"A "river" or a "stream" are the metaphors by which it (consciousness) is most naturally described. In talking of it hereafter, let us call it the stream of thought, of consciousness, or of subjective life."* (p. 173) James's remarks created confusion and babble and made no contribution to exact language. Consciousness was also equated roughly with "states of mind," "the stream of thought," or of "subjective life." From a fourth way perspective, consciousness must be distinguished from thought and the activities of the centers.

In modern psychology, Ey (1978) outlined what he viewed as "common knowledge" among psychologists; namely, that consciousness is essentially verbal in nature:

> It is common knowledge (psychologists have all noted and it is not an original
> discovery to repeat it) that to be conscious is to know one's experience, and that all
> experience insofar as it is "known" by the subject is discursive. ... Consciousness's
> proper manner of being, its proper language, lies in the verbalization of the phenomena
> which unfold in consciousness. ... to be conscious is to be capable of grasping one's
> knowledge in the categories of verbal communication. ... language is thus a structural
> quality of consciousness. (p.16)

From the perspective of the fourth way teaching, consciousness exists in relationship to the psychic
functions but is of a fundamentally different nature. Consciousness is viewed as illuminating the
thoughts, feelings and actions, or as providing a spatial background for such. Certainly, language is
not a "structural quality of consciousness."

Thinking that consciousness is thinking arises as a confusion when an individual thinks about
consciousness, and then identifies it with the thinking process. Vaysse (1979) makes these points in
his critical account of modern psychology:

> Self-analysis or introspection is the usual method applied in modern psychology
> ...(A) very bad effect of this analytical method is that it makes for arbitrary divisions
> of the functions of the man who studies himself in this way; whichever function is
> predominant (almost always the intellectual) stands apart from all the other functions
> and looks at them in its own way, and often evaluates or judges all of them as though it
> understood them. Such an attitude can but increase the predominance of one function
> over the other ... No observation has any real value for self-knowledge unless it is
> looked at in relation to the whole structure of the observer ... (pp. 19-20)

Consciousness is not thought and in fact the stream of thought is an obstacle to the development of
consciousness. K. Walker recounts Ouspensky's comments:

> "Self-remembering is not thinking about ourselves or about anything else" he said, "It is
> consciousness, or awareness of ourselves. 'Thinking' is one thing and 'consciousness'
> is an entirely different thing. We can think about the subject of 'consciousness' and in
> doing this we lose all awareness of what we are trying to do –to remember ourselves.
> There can be thinking without any awareness of thinking, and still more important,
> there can be consciousness devoid of any thought. The latter is what happens in
> higher states of consciousness. You will find, if you persevere in your efforts of self-
> remembering, that the associative thinking, which goes on all the time by itself, is the
> chief obstacle to our attainment of any higher level of consciousness. (1965, p. 45)

Self-observation and self-remembering serve to disentangle self from such inner talking and associative
thinking. In practice, the differences between consciousness and thinking are not easily understood,
because the thinking process so routinely engages the attention. Furthermore, people commonly
confuse thinking about oneself with self-consciousness–an even worse mistake which leads them to
think that they already possess self-consciousness. However, the latter is really a very distinctive state
and experience, which only emerges with the longer term development of the essence.

The tricks of thought and the intellect have resulted in western psychologists and philosophers
mistakenly identifying consciousness with language, self-analysis and other cognitive faculties. They

have been bewitched by the mind which asks the question "What is consciousness?" and then thinks about it. This confusion is evident even in the famous dictum of Descartes, *"I think, therefore I am,"* which only justifies the western scientists' association of "I" with thinking and the mind.

The development of consciousness and self-consciousness requires a stilling of the mind and the suspension of associative thought. This theme is reflected in a wide range of Eastern and Western mystical teachings and is the basis of meditation practices. Yogananda (1972) defined yoga as the *"science of mental control,"* and explained that the attainment of higher consciousness requires a suspension or neutralization of the incessant waves of thoughts and emotions that arise and subside in consciousness (pp. 261-2). It is necessary for the usual "turning of the mind" to be suspended in order to become more conscious.

The mistaken tendency to identify consciousness with thought is a product of failing to understand the nature of the observer (or thinker). The tricks of thought are similar to nature's little trick. In order to understand consciousness, we must understand the psychology of our methodology and approach such study in a different manner through the practices of self-remembering.

4e. **The Centering of Consciousness**

Most psychologists and scientists think that consciousness is centered in 'the mind' within the head brain. Scientists such as Carl Sagan, Roger Sperry and Francis Crick, all relate consciousness either to the cerebral cortex responsible for complex mental functions, or to the reticular activating system and brain stem which moderate states of sleeping, waking and arousal. Alternatively, other theorists suggest that there are two modes of consciousness related to the right and left hemispheres of the brain, or three levels of the mind–the reptilian complex, the limbic system and the neocortex distinction of Paul MacLean. Others, more progressive, consider that consciousness has to do with more widespread holographic patterns occurring along neural networks. However, even in modern holographic viewpoints, consciousness is still assumed to be located within the head brain.

Of course, to locate consciousness, one must first ask what it is. Western psychology locates consciousness within the mind and the brain because it is identified with thought and mental processes. However, within western psychology, a great diversity of views has arisen over the past twenty five years of consciousness studies. K. Pellitier (1978) notes:

> Our present science and common sense support the concept that awareness resides predominantly at a point behind the eyes, between the ears, and above the neck. In contrast to this naive belief stands a vast array of information, ranging from Vedantic texts to laboratory research results, that supports the concept that the entire body is an instrument of consciousness. One particular component of awareness resides in the brain, while other physiological systems of the body seem more attuned to other aspects of awareness. Thus, our language is laden with expressions indicating that the seat of the emotions lies within the heart and cardiovascular system. ... That aspects of consciousness are distributed in the body musculature, cardiovascular system, internal organs, and brain has been recognized in all meditative systems and has been the cornerstone of a wide range of body oriented therapies ... Recognition of the inter-

connections between states of consciousness and variations in neurophysiological activity supports an expanded concept of awareness that contends that the entire organism is an expression of consciousness and various components of an individual's total consciousness are located throughout the body. (pp. 22-3)

Pellitier's views are consistent with the fourth way psychology which states that consciousness exists in relationship to the various centers. In this vein, consciousness can be located in relationship to the head-brain and the thinking center, or the emotional brain and the complex of the sympathetic nerve nodes, or in relationship to the body with its moving, instinctual and sexual functions. Ideally, from a fourth way perspective, consciousness would exist simultaneously in relationship to the thinking, emotional and physical centers. Consciousness would then involve the simultaneous awareness of the head, heart and hands; or of the mind, feelings and sensations. Each center is an instrument of knowledge and experience, and so, to know something completely, consciousness would exist simultaneously in relationship to all of the centers.

The formation of false personality tends to center consciousness within the head-brain, in the formatory apparatus of the intellectual center. This apparatus serves as the basis for the usual patterns of thinking, self concern and imagination. Chronic muscular contractions and restricted breathing further limit consciousness of the lower body and reduce awareness of emotional, sensory and sexual experience. In learning to self-sense and self-remember, the person must be more fully conscious mentally, emotionally, and physically simultaneously, and not embedded in the stream of associative thought. Breath awareness is a vital aspect of such present centeredness. Perhaps Descartes might reason, "I breath, therefore I can think." Breath awareness is within the present moment and intimately tied into the process of self study and self-remembering.

However, within the Gurdjieff framework, the issue of the centering of consciousness is highly complex, as it is also relative to the evolution of the individual. We need to understand the centers, states of consciousness, the anatomy of the higher being-bodies and the nature of the soul, in order to sound the postal code of the mysteries of human consciousness. The state of self-consciousness and real "I" are associated with the higher emotional center—and an organ in the region of "the breast" —and with hydrogens or substances of different subtle cosmic levels.

The manner in which consciousness is centered is then relative to what type of human we are talking about, whether one who will die like dog or one who will attain immortality within the limits of the solar system. One person may have consciousness centered in their thoughts and mind, while another has crystallized higher being bodies and can maintain consciousness within more subtle hydrogen levels. The issues of the centering of consciousness are related to deeper issues concerning human evolution and the possible alchemy of the blood and soul.[15]

---

[15] Dr. Holmes' writings on Within-Without from Zero Points (2007) focuses primarily upon the enigmas of human consciousness and provides extensive explorations of modern scientific views and mystical/spiritual perspectives. Book I, The Heart Doctrine: Mystical Views of the Origin and Nature of Human Consciousness, argues that consciousness actually originates from within the heart center and that consciousness within the mind is only secondary to this..

5. The Study of Consciousness

5a. **Self-Observation & Self-Consciousness**

Normally, people are absorbed by or embedded within the stream of experience and action, and there is little awareness of self maintained in relationship to the flow of the inner subjective life. We do not know together the I and the me, and instead are fused or merged with the world. Ouspensky writes:

> In this state, man has no separate awareness. He is lost in whatever he happens to be doing, feeling, thinking. Because he is lost, immersed, not present to himself, this condition is known ... as a state of waking sleep. (1957)

The opposite of being fused with the world involves maintaining an awareness of self in relationship to the ongoing stream of experience and activity. Walker (1967) explains:

> Self-observation soon confirmed for me the truth of Ouspensky's statement that we did everything without our being aware of ourselves whilst we were doing it, our attention being entirely taken up with the activity, so that none was left over for simultaneous consciousness of ourselves. It was only by deliberately *dividing* the attention and by directing a portion of it backwards on to ourselves that awareness of ourselves could be maintained, and I realized that this artificial division of attention was the gist of self-remembering and also of self observation. When we made this division the backward-glancing part of our attention took note of our own thoughts, feelings and movements, and became what we now called the 'observing I' and what the Hindu philosopher calls 'the Witness.' (pp. 43-44)

The difference between relative consciousness and self consciousness can be portrayed pictorially using arrows to represent the direction of attention. In a relatively conscious state, attention is absorbed by the objects of awareness, either external sensations or internal processes (such as feelings and thoughts):

I ⟶ **Observed stimuli**

In this instance, awareness is solely of the content of experience and there is no simultaneous awareness of self as present.

In contrast, in self observation there is bi-directional attention and awareness. There is the observing and the observed, the I and the me, connected by attention:

I ⟷ **Observed stimuli**

A distinction between ordinary consciousness (relative consciousness) and self-consciousness is made by various authors in Eastern and Western traditions. However, the manner in which the scientists of new formation describe self consciousness is not at all what is intended by Gurdjieff in his use of the term, but is closer to self-observation. For example, Pribram (1976) describes self-consciousness as a distinct conscious state:

> ...self-consciousness can be clearly distinguished from other forms of consciousness. Self-consciousness is said to occur when an observer is able to describe both the observed and the observing. (p.52)

Unfortunately, psychologists and philosophers most frequently think that humans normally possess self-consciousness or that one can acquire it through a simple shift in attention and self observation.

Rollo May's (1964) provides a valuable discussion of the distinction between consciousness and awareness, which helps us to understand self consciousness:

> Consciousness ... from the Latin verb conscire, refers to knowledge which is felt inwardly, that is, to knowing with, not only with others but with oneself in the sense of consciousness of the fact that I am the being who has a world. I can be aware of this desk on which I write simply by touching it. But consciousness refers rather to the fact that I can be aware that I am the being who has this desk. Consciousness is a term that must not be lost. It refers to the central ontological characteristic that constitutes the self in its existence as a self ... (p. 96)

> Awareness is a capacity we share with animals and much of nature. ... It is possible ... to be aware without being conscious. ... Consciousness is the distinctively human form of awareness–the particularly human capability not only to know something but to know that I know it, that is, to experience myself as subject in relation to an object or as I in relation to Thou. (pp. 124-125)

May correctly regards consciousness (or self consciousness) as a *central ontological characteristic that constitutes the self*. Consciousness is somehow inherent to the nature of self. However, May's views differ from the fourth way in that he implies that humans generally possess self consciousness. For Gurdjieff too, consciousness is a characteristic of the self but a human being asleep does not realize this fundamental capacity. One can acquire real "I" and self-consciousness only through efforts towards awakening. Self-consciousness is much more than simply momentary self awareness produced by reflection upon oneself. Instead, it is dependent upon the longer term refinement of the essence and the attaining of real I. True self consciousness is a distinct stage of awakening and self realization.

Psychologist Charles Tart (1975, 1974) differentiates basic awareness from the contents of awareness and then describes consciousness as a combination of these two elements. The particular contents of awareness are the product of the mind's varied psychological structures and together with attention-awareness determine one's conscious experience:

> *Conscio*usness, as we ordinarily know it in the West, is not pure awareness but rather awareness embodied in the psychological structure of the mind or the brain. Ordinary

experience is of neither pure awareness nor pure psychological structure, but of awareness embedded in and modified by the structure of the mind/brain ... (1975, pp. 258-259)

Tart then differentiates "self awareness" from simple "consciousness:"

Another basic theoretical and experiential given is the existence, at times, of an awareness of being aware, self-awareness. The degree of self-awareness varies from moment to moment. At one extreme, I can be very aware that at this moment I am looking at the plant in front of me. At the other extreme, I may be totally immersed in the sight of the plant, but I may not be aware of being aware of it. That is, there is an experiential continuum, at the one end of which attention/awareness and the particular content of awareness are essentially merged, while at the other end of the continuum there is awareness of being aware in addition to the particular content of awareness. ... The lower end of the self awareness continuum, relatively total absorption, is probably where we spend most of our lives, even though we like to credit ourselves with high self-awareness. The higher end comes to us more rarely, although it may be sought deliberately in certain kinds of meditative practices.... (1974, pp. 92-93)

The capacity for self awareness results from the attention/awareness energy backing off from the psychological structures and remaining as a pure awareness. Tart explains the profound importance of these distinctions:

"The ultimate degree of separation of attention/ awareness from contents–allowing for self-awareness–that is possible in any final sense varies with one's theoretical position about the ultimate nature of the mind. If one adopts the conventional view that mental activity is controlled by the electrical-structural activity of brain functioning, there is a definite limit as to how far awareness can "back off" from particular contents, since that awareness is a product of the structure and contents of the individual brain....

A more radical view, common to the spiritual psychologies, is that basic awareness is not just a property of the brain but is at least partially something from "outside" the workings of the brain. Insofar as this is true, it is conceivable that most or all content associated with brain processes could potentially be "stood back" from so that the degree of separation between content and attention/awareness, the degree of self-awareness, is much higher than in the conservative view.

Whichever ultimate view one takes, what is psychologically important for studying consciousness is that the degree of separation of attention/awareness from content, the degree of self-awareness, varies considerably from moment to moment. (1974, pp.93-94)

One can be more or less self-conscious but typically attention and awareness is embedded within the activities of the mind. Humans pass their lives at the low end of the awareness continuum, only partially conscious, partially awake. A variety of Western theorists distinguish between relative consciousness and self conscious states, but unfortunately regard self-consciousness as common to people or at least easily attainable. The scientists of new formation do not begin to grasp the profound significance that these distinctions have for human development and the possible evolution of consciousness.

Within the Zen tradition, the most immediate aim is the cultivation of mindfulness. Powells (1961), in *Zen and Reality,* explains:

> The process of mindfulness could perhaps most aptly be designated by the term 'objectification', i.e., the depersonalization of the experience of the 'I,' the subjective experience, and making it objective. This entails drawing an ever wider circle around the 'I' and observing it in its relationships. (p.47)

This description of mindfulness is similar to that of self-observation, with the dividing of attention and maintenance of I in relationship to me, or it.

It is hard to realize what all of this means, if you have not approached the practical studies suggested in this work. It is hard to appreciate the types of structures and interrelationships which become evident in developing even a basic understanding of the machine, and of one's personality dynamics and psychopathology. Unfortunately, we do not know real I, and must free ourselves from many attachments in order to draw closer to a deeper knowledge and experience of self.

5b. **Identification and Attachment**

In order to understand what is meant by self-observation and self-consciousness, we must consider the term *identification*. People often observe themselves in a state of identification but seldom *without identification*. Within the Gurdjieff teaching, only observation accompanied by dis-identification has value in leading to self-consciousness. When we identify, each transitory thought, negative emotion, fantasy and reaction is taken as I. We identify I with the me or it. To observe without identification means to regard these same thoughts, feelings, and reactions as not-I. Real self-observation means standing apart from habits of thought, feeling and action, and realizing how mechanically everything happens within oneself and in life. It thinks, it feels, it daydreams, just as it makes love and fights wars, goes to church, or does not go, and so on. In fact, there is no permanent or stable I which could prevent anything from happening. It all happens in sleep as humans are almost always attached and identified.

Self observation is an active means of self change, but it can only function in this way if it is accompanied by non-identification. As people are, they are always identified and herein lies their slavery and prison. Nicoll explains, "... *whatever we identify with at once has power over us, and the more often we identify with something, the more we are slaves to it."* (1975, p.23) Identification is a central feature of waking sleep. People are always lost or immersed within life, fused with whatever is happening. Even when they think that they are observing or conscious of themselves, they still do not overcome the attitude of identification. In fact, self consciousness is the opposite of identification. Nicoll (1975) writes:

> You cannot become conscious of anything in yourself as long as you identify with it. To become really conscious of anything in yourself is to be no longer identified with it,

> no longer it. If I become conscious of my mechanical forms of suffering and internal
> account-making and my negative states, they are no longer me. I detach myself from
> them, I let them go, as it were, I no longer feel myself by means of them. As a result,
> my feelings of myself will change. This act allows transformation to work. (pp. 897-898)

Western psychology has quite missed this aspect of self-consciousness. Any form of self-observation, even with identification, is taken to be self-consciousness.

Eastern psychologies similarly recognize the phenomena of dis-identification. Buddhists talk of attachment and the necessity for the individual to give up attachments, which are the root of suffering. Unnecessary suffering is maintained by the individual's thousand and one attachments to the transient and impermanent objects of thought, desire, sense and imagination. Through the inner separation from the objects of attachment, an individual can come to be in the world but not of the world.

In the *Tales*, Beelzebub talks of the struggle between the planetary body and the higher being-bodies. These levels of functioning are *"always sensed by us either as "desires" or as "nondesires."* (p. 373) The desires are attachments and identifications based within the body and personality formation, whereas the non-desires involve the cultivation of awareness and the higher being-bodies. Beelzebub places this process in a cosmic perspective:

> "And so, only he, who consciously assists the process of this inner struggle and
> consciously assists the "non-desires" to predominate over the desires, behaves just in
> accordance with the essence of our COMMON FATHER CREATOR HIMSELF; whereas
> he who with his consciousness assists the contrary, only increases HIS sorrow."
> (1950, p. 373)

The separation of I from attachments and desires brings about a second stage of transformation involving the realization of one's nothingness:

> "'To awake,' 'to die,' 'to be born.' These are three successive stages. ... a man must
> die, that is, he must free himself from a thousand petty attachments and identifications
> which hold him in the position in which he is. He is attached to everything in his life,
> attached to his imagination, attached to his stupidity, attached even to his sufferings,
> possibly to his sufferings more than to anything else. He must free himself from this
> attachment. Attachment to things, identification with things, keep alive a thousand
> useless I's in a man. These I's must die in order that the big I may be born. But how
> can they be made to die? They do not want to die. It is at this point that the possibility
> of awakening comes to the rescue. To awaken means to realize one's nothingness,
> that is to realize one's complete and absolute mechanicalness and one's complete and
> absolute helplessness. And it is not sufficient to realize it philosophically in words. It is
> necessary to realize it in clear, simple, and concrete facts, in one's own facts. When a
> man begins to know himself a little he will see in himself many things that are bound to
> horrify him. So long as a man is not horrified at himself he knows nothing about himself.
> (1949, pp.217-8)

If the individual begins to awaken, they die to the old identifications, attachments and desires—and realize their helplessness and nothingness. The third stage, to be reborn, refers then to a new growth of the essence, the coating of the higher being-bodies and the appearance of real I.

5c. **Self-Observation & Self-Remembering**

Self study involves self-observation and self-remembering. These are *keys* to the study of psychology and hopefully to the development of consciousness within ourselves. The aim is to attain self-consciousness and glimpses of objective consciousness. As it happens, most people think that they are already properly conscious and that self-observation is nothing new to them. These attitudes make it difficult to learn the methods of self-observation and self-remembering, which must be understood in relationship to many other things about the parts of one's being, the nature of consciousness and so on.

In *relative consciousness*, the person is one with the world, fused or merged with it, absorbed in everything that happens. Self-observation then divides oneself in two. The attention of self-observation enhances awareness of what is happening in the fullness of the present moment. When we self-observe, we try also to be as *fully present* as possible, aware simultaneously of what is going on within and about us. The quality of the I which observes must be enhanced through the simultaneous process of self-remembering. Self-remembering involves a special *conscious effort* to double the quality of attention within the moment. Ouspensky (1957) explains that self-observation is *"always directed at some definite function,"* whereas self-remembering involves being aware of the whole, while enhancing the feeling of 'I.'

Self-observation is of the activities of the centres or definite psychological and personality dynamics. Self-observation begins to separate self from the machine creating inner division. In contrast, self-remembering creates a feeling of wholeness, of being fully present mentally, emotionally and physically. Whereas self-observation is being aware of the parts, self remembering is a deeper simultaneous awareness of the whole. The quality of "I" has to be enhanced during self-observation for it to merge into self-remembering.

Ouspensky recalls Gurdjieff's explanation that the most important thing we notice through self observation is that:

> ""*you do not remember yourselves*." ... "You do not feel yourselves; you are not conscious of yourselves. With you, 'it observes' just as 'it speaks,' 'it thinks,' 'it laughs.' You do not feel: I observe, I notice, I see. Everything still 'is noticed,' 'is seen.'... In order really to observe oneself one must first of all *remember oneself*."... Only those results will have any value that are accompanied by self-remembering. Otherwise you yourselves do not exist in your observations. In which case what are all of your observations worth?" (1949, pp 117-8)

Instead of simply observing with small i's of personality, it is necessary to enhance the experience of being present and the quality of "I." *It* cannot observe, *I* must.

Self-remembering enhances self-observation, as the I sensation is more present allowing for a broader experience of knowing together what is happening within one and around one in the environment. Self-remembering and self-observation proceed together as one takes more into the sphere of attention and awareness. The aim is to know together the *"sum total of all the current responses, sensory, emotional and mental and their integrations"* and *"what these constitute in reality."* (King, 1963, p. 115) What is being described can obviously not be done all at once, just like that, now in this moment. Vaysse (1979) explains:

> Real self-observation, as we understand it, is only possible if the one who observes
> –"I"–is present while the observation is going on; the integration of what is observed
> will be the more valid and complete the more the one who observes is present, that
> is, able to take account, in the field of attention directed towards himself, of a greater
> number of elements. This presupposes that he already recognizes these elements and
> is able to keep them together with some stability, which can be called keeping oneself
> in a state of being present to oneself. This state is not a natural one for us but it too can
> be developed by the work of self-study, and each time it arises in us we recognize it by
> a special inner consciousness, a special inner sense of self which, once it has been
> experienced, is unmistakable. (p.37)

The more one is present, then the greater the number of elements which are held together within
the sphere of attention. This allows for an increasingly rich awareness of the complete integration
of mental, emotional and sensory processes, all existing in relationship to an active source of
consciousness. This brings us closer to real I, which Vaysse describes as giving a *"special inner
consciousness"* and a *"special inner sense of self."* One can know far more together within the
fullness of the moment with increases in the illumination of consciousness and the presence of real "I."
Consciousness, light and knowing together are intimately linked, and all are increased through self-
remembering and the enhancement of the presence of I.

Hanh (1974) recounts this vignette in *Zen Keys* to illustrate the practice of mindfulness, which is
comparable in part to that of self-remembering:

> I remember a short conversation between Buddha and a philosopher of his time.
> "I have heard tell of Buddhism as a doctrine of enlightenment. What is its method? In
> other words, what do you do every day?
> "We walk, we eat, we wash ourselves, we sit down ...
> "What is there special in those actions? Everyone walks, eats, washes himself,
> sits down...?
> "–Sir, there is a difference. When we walk, we are aware of the fact that we walk; when
> we eat, we are aware of the fact that we eat, and so on. When others walk, eat, wash
> themselves or sit down, they are not aware of what they do." (p.21)

The mindful individual is aware of what they do and not simply embedded in the flow of experience.

> A student, Kathryn Hulme recalls Gurdjieff's description of being more fully present:

> "When you do a thing," he said once, "do it with the whole self. *One thing at a time.* Now
> I sit here and I eat. For me nothing exists in the world except this food, this table. I eat
> with the whole attention. So you must do–in everything. When you write a letter, do not
> at the same time think what will be the cost of laundering that shirt; when you compute
> laundering cost, do not think about the letter you must write. Everything has its time.
> To be able to do one thing at a time ... this is a property of Man, not man in quotation
> marks." (1966, p. 91)

A human, as a machine, is not capable of maintaining such a presence. Indeed, there is usually no
conscious subject behind consciousness. There is no self-consciousness and no essential centre of
gravity in real I. The consciousness of essence has become part of the subconscious and there is no
conscious mind as such. The most important implication is that human are asleep in a sleepwalker's

world and do not know real I. Consider the title of Gurdjieff's last book, *Life is Real only Then, When "I AM."* If there is no "I AM," then we have a *"consciousness ignorant of itself,"* as Sartre expresses it—which is absurd. It is absurd to wake up and glimpse a world of sleepwalkers.

5d. **Self-Remembering & the Illusions of Self-Knowledge**

The central psychological illusion of humans is that they "know self." Of course, when people claim that they know themselves, they are thinking of their personal identity, their likes and dislikes, their hobbies and talents, and so on. Most people do not think that they know themselves in terms of understanding the anatomy of the centers, or knowing the issues of consciousness, or knowing the mystical dimensions of self. In fact, most people do not even realize that there are mysteries in these questions— as they have so little experience of what they really are in the depths of being.

From the perspective of the fourth way and of esoteric teachings, people live in ignorance of their true nature. Instead, people are conditioned by everything around them, their histories, their educations, their upbringing, and so on, and they do not realize the profound enigmas of their existence and awareness. The fourth way offers a dismal view of humankind asleep, the men and women in quotations marks, whose daily moods are governed by circumstance, whether or not their slippers are beside their beds and how satiated they are. In this view, the only serious thing is to escape from the imprisonment of mechanical life.

The practice of self-remembering begins to reveal the truth about ourselves—one's conditioned state and the illusory nature of one's consciousness, will and unity of I. If a person sets the intention of self-remembering, they soon realize how impossible a task this is. *We cannot remember ourselves,* except with a change in our being It is only little i's which want to remember, i's which form part of *"work personality."* But these i's are soon lost in the flow of experience and people are continually re-absorbed by the usual patterns of associative thought, personal emotions, and mechanical habits which govern their lives. And while they are so absorbed, they have again forgotten themselves.

A person cannot remember self because they are so conditioned and do not know real I or have real will. Instead, they have little daily wills and wants, the little i's of false personality. The conditioned patterns of life continually absorb attention. If a person knew real I, they would be in the state of self-consciousness or self-remembering. Instead, they wish one moment to remember and a moment later something else happens, and they forget themselves and their intentions. People are carried along with the current of mechanical happening, while all the while they think that they are properly conscious, know real I and have will. In fact, they possess none of these qualities and cannot even imagine the miraculous possibilities which would arise if in fact they did. The attempt to self-remember begins to illustrate to a person how asleep they ordinarily are and how they lack true consciousness, will and unity of I.

The practice of self-remembering begins to reveal one's unconscious and conditioned state, and that of everyone around. Humans are sleepwalkers, living in illusion and in ignorance of self. In fact, people have no idea of the profound sleep in which they live, a sleep perpetuated by the whole of mechanical life, by the moon and by their psychological illusions. As Gurdjieff states, there is only one thing which is serious and that is to escape from the sleepwalking state which governs the mass of humanity.

6. The Dual Consciousness

It is remarkable how Gurdjieff presents his teachings within *Beelzebub's Tales* in an almost totally new language and format than that used in his earlier more formal lectures recorded by Ouspensky and other students. It is unfortunate that many of the Gurdjieff study groups focus primarily upon Ouspensky's presentations rather than upon the more obscure and difficult *Tales*.

With reference to consciousness, Beelzebub explains that the *"genuine being-consciousness"* of those strange three-brained beings on planet Earth has passed into their *"subconscious."* In consequence, a *"fictitious consciousness"* has become dominant. The distinction between the "genuine being-consciousness" and the false consciousness system is between consciousness rooted within the essence and one structured around false personality.

While elaborating upon the phenomenon of hypnosis, Beelzebub explains to his grandson, how a *"two-system-Zoostat"* or *"two independent consciousnesses"* formed within the strange psyches of those three centered beings. Beelzebub emphasizes the destructive roles of education and socialization in forming this false consciousness system:

> "... ensuing from the abnormal conditions of the being-existence of your favourites ... from the beginning of the arising of their offspring, they intentionally try by every kind of means, for the purpose of making them respond to these abnormal conditions round them, to fix in their 'logicnestarian-localizations' as many impressions as possible obtained again due to the results of their abnormal existence—which maleficent action of theirs towards their offspring they call 'education'—then the totality of all such artificial perceptions gradually segregates itself in their common presences and acquires its own independent functioning, connected only as much with the functioning of their planetary body as is necessary merely for its automatic manifestation, and the totality of these artificial perceptions is then perceived by them, owing to their naiveté, as their real 'consciousness.'" (1950, p. 565)

This description is of the effects of education and socialization in impressing upon the centers (or the logicnestarian-localizations) all of the "artificial perceptions" which come to constitute the false personality. This system is based upon the formation of habit structures which allow for the automatic functioning of the individual. This artificial, fictitious or "false" consciousness is then unknowingly taken to be the real consciousness of the individual.

This fictitious consciousness is formed from the perception of accidental and mechanical impressions and the sounds of words which are described as "empty," or as having meanings not connected to genuine being data or direct experience. Mr. G. describes the formation of this false consciousness:

> "... when these children grow up and become responsible beings, they already automatically produce their manifestations and their acts; just as during their formation they were 'taught,' just as they were 'suggested to,' and just as they were 'wound up;' in a word, just as they were 'educated.'" (1950, p. 378)

Beelzebub explains what happens to the consciousness based on essence, which should be the predominant system:

> "But as for the sacred data for genuine being-consciousness put into them by Great Nature—which consciousness ought to be possessed by them from the very beginning of their preparation for responsible existence together with the properties inherent in them which engender in them the genuine sacred being-impulses of 'faith,' 'hope,' 'love,' and 'conscience'—these data, becoming gradually also isolated and being left to themselves, evolve independently of the intentions of the responsible beings, and of course also independently of the bearers of them themselves, and come to be regarded as what is called the 'subconsciousness.'" (1950, p. 565)

Hence all the "sacred data" inherent within humans which could allow for responsible life become isolated from their general functioning and remain in a primitive state, while the "false consciousness" predominates in their automatic functioning.

This is how Beelzebub explains to Hassein the formation of the strange psyches of those three-brained beings breeding on planet Earth, who perceive reality topsy-turvy and are so conditioned by egotism, the impulses of pleasure, the sense organs and sexual organs.

In recounting his work as a hypnotist while visiting the Earth, Beelzebub explains that the functioning of these two consciousness systems is related to differences in the blood flow within the human organism. In particular, he explains that the *"centre-of-gravity-of-the-blood-pressure"* in their presences will sometimes predominate within one part of the general system of blood vessels, and at other times within another part of the blood vessels. These differences are related to differences between the waking and sleeping states and used to explain the phenomena of hypnosis. Beelzebub functioned as a hypnotist putting humans into a state by altering the particularities of their blood flow—primarily through the use of his own Handbledzoin (or blood of the Kesdjan, or astral body), which he also labels as "animal magnetism" in accord with the terminology used in Mesmer's day. However, Beelzebub explains that even the ordinary waking existence of humans flows under the influence of such a hypnotic state.

Humans subsequently no longer instinctually sense reality and cosmic truths, nor acquire genuine being-Reason as is proper to three-centered beings, nor experience the sacred being-impulses. A false "egoism" has been formed and is the root of all those other peculiar being impulses which Beelzebub describes as *"existing under the names of 'cunning,' 'envy,' 'hate,' 'hypocrisy,' 'contempt,' 'haughtiness,' 'servility,' 'slyness,' 'ambition,' 'double-facedness,' and so on and so forth."* (p. 379)

The true consciousness, now in the subconscious, requires for its growth, the fulfilment of individual *"partkdolg duty"*—conscious labours and intentional suffering, which would help accumulate data for the development of the faculties of genuine being-Reason. Beelzebub describes the activities of various sacred individuals or messengers, who visited the Earth attempting to awaken the genuine being impulses within humankind still latent within the so-called "subconscious." Particularly, Beelzebub emphasizes the importance of the awakening of objective conscience, which from a person's early life, has been *"driven-back-within."*

The lot of humankind on that ill-fated planet Earth has been to become crystallized within a false consciousness system and one of the few sources of hope for humanity still lies in the awakening to the deeper dimensions of self latent within the subconscious in the deeper emotional nature. In the Ouspensky version, the only hope is the dissolution of the false personality, the attainment of true self-consciousness based upon the growth of the essence, and the awakening to the higher emotional center.

7. Illusions of Freedom, Souls & Immortality

Within *the Work*, there is only one thing which is serious and that is to escape–to escape from the general law and to be free. Unfortunately, humans are willing slaves and even proud of their chains. Gurdjieff compared the position of human beings to that of being imprisoned:

> G.'s ... favourite statement was that, if a man in prison, was at any time to have a chance of escape, then he must first of all *realize that he is in prison*. So long as he fails to realize this, so long as he thinks he is free, he has no chance whatever. No one can help or liberate him by force, against his will, in opposition to his wishes. If liberation is possible, it is possible only as a result of great labor and great efforts, and, above all, of conscious effort, towards a definite aim. (1949, p. 30)

Humans do not realize their situation and how they are imprisoned, and so do not make conscious effort towards the definite aim of awakening, attaining the soul and achieving real I.

Gurdjieff emphasizes that to escape from the prison of mechanical life, the control of false personality and the moon, one must have the help of those who have escaped before and who can help to show the way: *"Only they can say in what way escape is possible...."* (1949, p. 30) The role of the fourth way and of esoteric teaching is to light the way and provide the influences, guidance and shocks, to enable individuals to escape. However, this is a long and difficult venture and human beings have complex psychological illusions which obscure the way and maintain their sleep to the realities of the situation.

Another story told by Mr. G.'s was about *"a very rich magician who had a great many sheep,"* and this also depicts the sad situation of human beings. According to this story, the magician did not want to have to hire shepherds or build fences to protect his flock, to prevent the sheep from falling into ravines, wandering into the forest, or running away. However, the sheep knew that the magician wanted their skins and flesh, and feared for their fates:

> "At last the magician found a remedy. He *hypnotized* his sheep and suggested to them first of all that they were immortal and that no harm was being done to them when they were skinned, that, on the contrary, it would be very good for them and even pleasant; secondly he suggested that the magician was a *good master* who loved his flock so much that he was ready to do anything in the world for them; and in the third place he suggested to them that if anything at all were going to happen to them it was not going to happen just then, at any rate not that day, and *therefore* they had no need to think about it. Further the magician suggested to his sheep that they were not sheep at all; to some of them he suggested that they were *lions*, to others that they were *eagles*, to others that they were *men*, and to others that they were *magicians*. "And after this all his cares and worries about the sheep came to an end. They never ran away again but quietly awaited the time when the magician would require their flesh and skins.

> "This tale is a very good illustration of man's position." (Ouspensky, 1949, p.219)

The sheep think that they have souls, that they are immortal and will live happily ever after, and that they have good masters who will look after them. All the while, they are kept for the shearing, hypnotized by the disease of tomorrow, imagining that they are eagles and magicians. For Gurdjieff, there is urgency in terms of the individual awakening and attaining real I, to escape the fate of being skinned. All of the magician's false promises and arguments only create a web of illusion to keep the sheep asleep and hypnotized.

"'To awake,' 'to die,'
'to be born.' These are three
successive stages."

"... owing to faith alone does
there appear in a being,
the intensity of being-self-
consciousness necessary
for every being, and also the
valuation of personal Being
as a particle of Everything
Existing in the Universe."

G. I. Gurdjieff, *Beelzebub's Tales to His Grandson*

VI /
Towards awakening
Objective Knowledge & Higher States

1. The Inner Work: Order in the Household

The Work, the esoteric fourth way teaching, aims to bring about a transformation within an individual–a *metanoia* or change of mind. Humans as they are have missed the mark and need a new form of education. J. Cox (1980), in the guise of Mr. G., writes:

> The Work in all of its many and varied forms can be said to be an unnatural, second education of man; an education to teach him the "truth," to show him the reality of life. … The truth which shall set a man free is the truth about himself…. (pp. 70-71)

The processes of awakening, dying and being reborn are complex with many levels of realization, illumination and attainment. Mechanical life and the abnormal conditions of human being-existence engender traits quite unbecoming to three-brained beings. Gurdjieff explains that what should be the dominant consciousness has passed into the subconscious and a false consciousness system now predominates. Humans perceive reality topsy-turvy, are conditioned by the impulses of pleasure and sexuality, and governed by such characteristics described by Beelzebub as numerous forms of egoism, including *"… self-love, vanity, pride, swagger, imagination, bragging, arrogance, and so on."* *(p.356)* As such, the strangeness of the psyche of the three-brained beings breeding on planet earth is that they do not *"instinctually sense reality,"* or *"instinctually sense cosmic truths,"* or experience *"the Divine Sacred Being-impulses,"* or attain higher gradients of *"Divine Reason"*–all of which faculties are described by Beelzebub as inherent possibilities within human nature.

Individual human evolution is not required by nature and the evolution of humanity is over far greater time periods than that of a human lifetime–on the scale of the evolution of the planets and solar system. Humans can die according to the principle governing one and two-brained beings and serve only local cosmic purposes, and are not guaranteed endless life in heaven or over the longer term development of the solar system. Humans can die like dog and feed the earth and moon.

According to Gurdjieff, human evolution involves the evolution of consciousness, unity and will, the refinement of the higher being-bodies, experience within the realms of higher emotions and higher intelligence, and attaining real I. To awaken requires the dissolution of the false personality and automated consciousness, and the rebirth and growth of essence which is the basis upon which real "I" is attained. Beelzebub talks of the ultimate possibility of *"becoming a particle, though an independent one, of everything existing in the Great Universe."* (1950, p. 183) This is the quest or search for the miraculous. The individual can become what Beelzebub describes as *"a genuine son of our COMMON FATHER CREATOR of all that exists."* (p. 368)

There is a great gap existing between the ordinary waking sleep state and the state of awakened self-consciousness. An individual must learn of this gap and how to breach it. J. Cox (1980) describes transformation in terms of three postures–beginning with the person asleep in the *shifting posture*, then making conscious effort to awaken through the *transitional posture* and thirdly, attaining a *stable posture*–the establishment of a unified and permanent I. Cox explains the first stage:

> The Posture of an ordinary man is always shifting. Where and how he stands is
> inseparably connected to the ever-changing shift of the life-of-life. His internal states
> are not his own; they have been formulated within him by past circumstances and they
> are thus forever tied to this source. (1980, pp. 78)

As humans are, they have a shifting, changing posture. Attention is always held captive by the impact
of impressions and the identity shifts from one moment to the next as different i's are elicited. Past
conditioning and false personality provide the many i's. This is where a person begins when they
seek a second education. At this point, false personality calls itself I and humans are men in quotation
marks. This is described by Nicoll:

> ... everything outside effects or has power over us. We are continually distracted,
> just as a dog is distracted by everything he sees, hears, or smells. The tumult of
> sense-impressions, the riot of thoughts, the surging of emotions and imagination, the
> thronging of desires, having nothing central between them to steady them. Between
> that which is pouring in from the outside through the senses, and that which is going on
> within, nothing permanent intervenes to subject all those random activities to order, to
> bring them into alignment and produce a point of consciousness between inner
> and outer. (1975)

A work aphorism suggests that at first a person is one, then two and then One. Initially, before
encountering *the Work*, a person is fused or embedded in life and unable to separate from life's
effects upon them. They are always lost to themselves and everything that happens. In the second
transitional phase, a person divides him or herself in two—through self-observation, self-study and self-
remembering. This begins to enhance the separation of I from the false personality.
Nicoll (1975) explains:

> We then begin to see ourselves, as it were, on the stage in front of us. We begin to
> see all sorts of different 'I's in us, saying this and thinking that, and behaving like
> that and holding forth like that, as something unreal, something that is not oneself,
> something that has nothing to do with Real 'I.' In other words, we begin to see our
> mechanicalness. All this is a very great step to take and once a person has taken it he
> or she can never be the same person again. (p.900)

Self-observation involves witnessing the many i's as *it*, rather than as I. It divides a person in two, in
that they are less fused with the world. Jan Cox describes the transitional process:

> ... the ultimate Aim of all Work is to produce a man of solidity and oneness, but first
> he must be made to see his present unstable condition. So one first studies himself in
> pieces, bit by bit, and atom by atom. ... you are simply struggling to become familiar
> with yourself and your position in an objective, impartial manner, and what you begin
> to see is that internally you are already such a fragmented, dissected being. ... no one
> can comprehend the message of the Work unless he personally understands his own,
> personal Posture in the total scheme-of-things in an objective fashion. ... (p. 76) The
> transitional Posture to which I refer is the multi-faceted mental, emotional and physical
> struggle to study and become familiar with oneself in a new, nonsubjective manner.
> (1980, p. 100)

Whereas the transitional posture is the journey, the stable posture is the goal and it depends upon the refinement of the essence and the attainment of true self-consciousness.

At the same time as energy is withdrawn from one level of ourselves, the individual begins to accumulate more subtle energies related to the deeper levels of being—related to the essence and the life of the soul. Nicoll (1975) writes:

> The soul in man can be related to a lower or a higher level. A man must lose his soul in regards to a lower level of himself in order to find it at a higher level.

A person cannot remain as they are and simply add something new on top of the old. Instead, we have to die to one level of ourselves in order to be born to another. Jan Cox expresses these themes with a unique insightfulness:

> "Those unlucky enough to discover one such as me at first think that what they want is a psychic tailor to adjust their acquired uniform to a proper fit. What they want is the impossible—to wake-up personality. Ignoring the Carpenter's words, they want me to help construct the new house of Essence on the swamp of personality: they want to gold plate a shithouse. But it cannot be done, and only the Church will tell you otherwise and maybe a politician or two." (1976, p.54)

It is necessary to separate in a radical way from the false consciousness system. This takes inner work, conscious effort and struggle. Unfortunately, few people glimpse why such work and effort is worthwhile. They 'love' themselves too much—their attitudes, opinions, moods, their fictitious self-images, cunning and lying, their negative emotions and imagination. People would not want to give these up except to achieve a better fit. There is no real "I" in the strange psyche of those three-brained beings breading on planet earth.

Gurdjieff provided another more complex approach to depicting the phases of *the inner work*. He recounts an Eastern allegory comparing a person with a household of different servants (i's):

> There is a very good Eastern allegory which deals with the creation of 'I.' Man is compared to a house full of servants, without a master or steward to look after them. So the servants do what they like; none of them does his own work. The house is in a state of complete chaos, because all the servants try to do someone else's work which they are not competent to do. ... The only possibility for things to improve is if a certain number of servants decide to elect one of themselves as a deputy steward and in this way make him control the other servants. He can do only one thing: he puts each servant where he belongs and so they begin to do their right work. When this is done, there is the possibility of the real steward coming to replace the deputy steward and to prepare the house for the master. ... This allegory helps us to understand the beginning of the possibility of creating a permanent 'I.' (Ouspensky, 1957, p. 33)

The allegory begins with the household in complete chaos and the servants doing as they please; as corresponds to the *shifting posture* of a person dominated by changing i's. In the second phase, a *deputy steward* is appointed to bring order into the household. A deputy steward involves a more conscious nucleus of i's within a person which introduces more conscious ideas and influences into the household.[16] The Work can be introduced into all areas of life, as light into the inner world, while cultivating a deepening sense of I. The deputy steward is a more unified group of *work i's* which bring order into the chaotic scenes of the shifting i's. The deputy steward weeds out destructive or wasteful i's, limiting the wrong work of centers and the expressions of false personality. The deputy steward is connected to the practices of self study and self-remembering. The inner work initially lives off false personality and making it less active–thereby saving and accumulating the vital energies otherwise wasted. The deputy steward prepares the household for a real steward, which could ultimately yield to a master–"real I."

Permanent I is a source of real will and control in relation to the intellectual, emotional and physical life. Here the individual is unified and can abide in the state of self-consciousness. Gurdjieff would regard one who has attained permanent I as a man without quotation marks. Such an individual would think, feel and act consciously, while aware in a much expanded way of the objective nature of themselves, others, the world and cosmos.

In some ways, the term *permanent I* is misleading. Ouspensky (1957) explains:

> The name 'permanent I' is not very successful because it is not permanent for a long time; it only comes and stays when it is necessary, and when it is not necessary it may go away again. So it is better to say 'real I.' When this 'I' comes, it controls all other 'I's. It can control everything in a way that no existing 'I's can, so it is quite new in a sense. But when this one 'I' comes, it does not mean that it will stay. First it may not be necessary for it to be there, because smaller 'I's must also learn to act in the right way.
>
> Secondly it needs very intensive work, and if work slackens it cannot stay. So there are many conditions for its presence, but if you experience the taste of it being there once, you will know many things and you will be sure of many things which now you can only surmise. (p.182)

Real I is capable of a great intensity of work and is not always required–just as a master is not always necessary within a household. The experience of permanent I is highly distinct from the usual self-feelings and reveals deeper truths about the multi-dimensional nature of the self and the world. Ordinary life is spent in passing time, one little i following another, always shifting and carried along by the current of mechanical happenings. Amidst this kaleidoscope of i's exists the possibility of permanent I.

---

[16] Initially, work i's are related to the magnetic center, the intellectual part of the emotional center. The magnetic center involves the emotional desire to know and understand the nature and purpose of life and oneself. According to Gurdjieff, people with a magnetic center seek the deeper truths and are more readily drawn to esoteric or school influences. These individuals have more conscious feelings that something larger lay behind the ordinary appearances of reality and so they seek for the miraculous–as did Gurdjieff and Ouspensky and many others before and since. The magnetic center involves "... 'special interests', 'ideals', 'ideas' or something like that." (Ouspensky, 1957, p. 182).

2. Being-Partkdolg-Duty

In *Beelzebub's Tales to His Grandson*, Gurdjieff places particular emphasis on the necessity for an individual to fulfill their *being-partkdolg-duty*. Such duties consist of *"conscious labours"* and *"intentional suffering."* These activities are described as *"the sole possible means for the assimilation of the cosmic substances required for the coating and perfecting of the higher being-bodies...."* (p.792) Unfortunately, the three-brained beings on earth established such *"abnormal conditions of external ordinary being-existence"* that they no longer fulfill their *being-Partkdolg-duty.* Much of strangeness of the human psyche is attributed to this failure of *"your favourites"* and the role that this plays in the *involution* or *evolution* of the sacred sexual substances.

It is not easy to define exactly what such *being-partkdolg-duty* involves and the different meanings of this term as intended by Beelzebub–or Gurdjieff. One approach is to consider Beelzebub's life and visits to the earth–as a character in a life drama. Beelzebub exemplifies what conscious labours and intentional suffering might involve. Beelzebub undertakes varied tasks on earth under conditions foreign to his nature and plays a role in the service of our Endlessness. At the end of the book, Beelzebub, because of his meritorious work, acquires additional forks in his horns–signifying his attainment of higher levels of Divine Reason and the coating of the higher being-bodies. Beelzebub's stories also describe other sacred messengers and individuals actualized from above who undertook such conscious labours and intentional suffering through their efforts on earth to help humankind and to restore cosmic harmony. Gurdjieff himself throughout his life similarly undertook such conscious labours and intentional suffering–in his searches, through his efforts to awaken, in his work with and for others and humankind.

Conscious labours include efforts to observe and remember oneself, making conscious efforts in the inner struggle towards self perfection and self-remembering. Conscious labours can also be in relationship to others in the work, in service to humankind, or as required by nature or in service of our Endlessness. With reference to *intentional suffering*, Beelzebub explains that Lord Buddha taught *"... the greatest intentional-suffering can be obtained in your presences if you compel yourself to be able to endure the displeasing-manifestations-of-others-towards-yourselves."* (pp. 241-2) Such an attitude towards others is in dramatic contrast to what Beelzebub describes as the property of *your favourites* *"to always grow indignant at the defects of others around them."*

At one point, Hassein asks his grandfather Beelzebub to explain why those three-brained beings *"take the 'ephemeral' for the Real,"* and why in humans' reason *"fantasy may be perceived as reality."* Beelzebub then explains that *"this particularity in their psyche"* arose because their *"predominant part"* allowed the other parts of their presence to *"perceive every new impression without ... 'being-Partkdolg-duty' but just merely as, in general, such impressions are perceived by the separate independent localizations."* This describes the predominant part–false personality based in the formatory mind–functioning separately from the other centers. The three separate brains then associate quite independently and give rise to three quite different *"being-impulses."* Humans are described as then no longer capable of *"conscious active manifestation."*

One of the effects of this is that the *"subjective being-convictions"* formed in people are not based upon their own *"logical deliberations"* and life experiences, but only upon *"what others say about the given question."* (p. 104) Beelzebub depicts this:

> "In general, any new understanding is crystallized in the presence of these strange beings only if Smith speaks of somebody or something in a certain way; and then if Brown says the same, the hearer is quite convinced it is just so and couldn't possibly be otherwise. ... This strange trait of their general psyche, namely, of being satisfied with just what Smith or Brown says, without trying to know more, became rooted in them already long ago and now they no longer strive at all to know anything cognizable by their own active deliberations alone." (p. 104)

People do not form their *"own subjective being-convictions"* based on their logical and active deliberations. Instead, the formatory apparatus simply records things heard and repeats them as one's own. The faculties for sane and logical deliberation thus atrophied.

Beelzebub also discusses conscious labours and intentional suffering in terms of the struggle within an individual between the processes of the planetary body and those of the higher being-bodies within the planetary body. The struggle between these two natures concerns the predominance of "desires" or "non-desires." Beelzebub explains:

> "... only he, who consciously assists the process of this inner struggle and consciously assists the "non-desires" to predominate over the desires, behaves just in accordance with the essence of our COMMON FATHER CREATOR HIMSELF; whereas he who with his consciousness assists the contrary, only increases HIS sorrow." (p. 373)

This struggle is particularly relevant in terms of the involution or evolution of the sexual substances within the individual.

According to Beelzebub, three main substances or being-foods are taken in and refined within the human organism. One product of the evolution of the food octaves is sperm in men and other comparable sexual substances in the ovaries of women. Beelzebub explains to Hassein that the three-brained beings know of the *"being-Exioehary,"* which they call sperm, but they perform all kinds of *"manipulations"* with it–wasting and squandering it whenever possible. Beelzebub describes such misuse of sexual energies as the *"chief vice of contemporary three-brained beings"*–and relates this back to Roman times with orgies and other such vices. Further, because *your favourites* do not actualize their 'being-Partkdolg-duty,' these substances begin to *"involve back ... towards those crystallisations from which their evolution began."* This involution of the sexual substances tends to *"'deperfect' their previously established essence-individuality,"* leading to innumerable "illnesses" and diminishing the *"thirst for Being."* (pp. 793-794) And so, the strange three brained beings on planet earth do not use the substances of the 'being-Exiohary' for their own self-perfection–to coat and perfect the higher being-bodies or even to *consciously reproduce* themselves. Without such an inner alchemy, the beings are described as *"strongly sensing the emptiness of their existence."*

Beelzebub explains that the knowledge of the origin and significance of the *"being-Exioehary'* was known among some of the inhabitants of Atlantis and afterwards among various groups of genuine initiates. However, after periods of war and other catastrophes, this ancient knowledge was lost. Fragments of such a knowledge survived but without any precise understanding of what was involved.

This led some of the three-brained beings to strive for self-perfection by *"abstaining from the ejection from oneself in the customary manner of these substances formed in them called sperm ...."* (p. 807) Unfortunately, these beings did not understand the necessity of the fulfilling of their being-Partkdolg-duty in order for this abstinence have its desired effect—in terms of quenching the thirst for being. Instead, they began *"to imitate"* the practices of the genuine initiates and began to organize themselves in various groups and sects putting this abstinence into effect. Thus, *"monasteries"* were established and various *"monks"* began to refrain from the ejection of sperm but little was ever achieved as the brothers did not understand the importance of fulfilling one's being obligations, or of *"intentionally absorbing"* the second and third being-foods.

Beelzebub explains that the Exioehary can:

> "... transform completely into new higher substances and in order to acquire vibrations corresponding to the vibrations of the next higher vivifyingness ... it requires just that foreign help which is actualized only in the presences of the three-brained beings exclusively owing to those factors mentioned by me more than once and which are manifested in the 'being-Partkdolg-duty,' ... which factors until now serve as the sole possible means for the assimilation of the cosmic substances required for the coating and perfecting of the higher being-bodies and which we at the present time call 'conscious labours' and 'intentional suffering.'" (p. 792)

Unfortunately, those strange three-brained beings strive only for their own welfare and the *"free gratification of the multitudinous vices and multiform vices fixed in their essences."* (p. 794) Thus, the sexual substances within the body are not refined so as to produce the substances required for the higher being-bodies, but are instead squandered in the multiform sexual vices and the desires predominate over the non-desires.

3. Consciousness, Light and Knowing Together

Western psychology has treated consciousness as non-substantive—as nothing apart from the activities of the mind and the functions of knowing. This was noted by Natsoulas (1978) who predicted that *"psychology will not again define consciousness as a substance or entity again."*

> ... (the behaviourist upheaval ... was) due to fear, on the part of psychologists who aspired to be true scientists, that the study of consciousness was nothing less, after all, than the (disguised) pseudoscience of the soul that was to have been forestalled: Consequently the psychology without a soul ... is now attacked on behalf of a psychology without a consciousness, on the ground that the latter standpoint alone can give assurance against entangling alliances between psychology and metaphysics. (1978, p.906)

A view of a substantive consciousness links the study of consciousness to metaphysics and the human soul. Of the many issues in the literature on consciousness, the question of the substance of consciousness is one of the most mysterious and fundamental. The scientists of new formation, as described by Beelzebub, assume that there is no soul life and have strong prejudices, ignorance and fears of entangling materialist views with metaphysics or objective science.

Within mystical and esoteric teachings the substance of consciousness is most frequently equated with light. This equation is not simply a metaphor but coveys deep truths about the nature of consciousness. Consciousness illuminates the inner world—the varied activities of the minds or centers. Just as external light illuminates the outer world for human perception, so also there is an inner light which allows for illumination and awareness within the inner world. The counterpart of light is darkness, which corresponds with notions of the unconscious or subconscious where there is a lack of the light of awareness. Humans asleep live in relative darkness and do not realize the inner light and how this light might be increased.

Ouspensky (1957) provides a number of statements relating consciousness to light and to the illumination of the inner world:

> (Psychic) functions can be compared to machines working in varying degrees of light. ... Consciousness is light and machines are functions. (p. 55) ... Consciousness is light, light is the result of a certain energy; if there is no energy there is no light. (p.68) ... Attention acts like a light, and imagination is like a chemical process that can only go on in the dark and stops with light. (p. 371)

> This sensation of light ... is experienced at the moment of the expansion of consciousness.... (Ouspensky, 1922, p.233)

From a psychological point of view, consciousness is light which illuminates the psychological functions. The aim within the Work is to increase consciousness bringing greater light into the darkness of ourselves. This light allows insight, internal sight, realizations, illumination and enlightenment. Increases in consciousness have chemical and alchemical effects within the inner life of human beings.

Maurice Nicoll (1975), psychologist and student of Gurdjieff and Ouspensky, provides profound commentaries on the equation of consciousness with light, and on the manner in which the work acts within the inner world:

> ... in this system ... what we seek above all things is Light—and Light means consciousness. We seek to live more consciously and to become more conscious. We live in darkness owing to lack of light—the light of consciousness—and we seek in this work light on ourselves. Everything this system says about work on oneself—about self-remembering, about struggling with negative emotions, about internal considering, about self justification, and so on, has as its supreme aim to make a man more conscious—to let light dawn in him. And it is a very strange thing, this light. It is first to become more conscious of oneself and then more conscious of others. This is a strange experience. I mean by this that the direction in which the work leads you through increasing consciousness, increasing light, is not at all the direction you might imagine as a person asleep, a person who knows only ordinary consciousness—that

is, the first two states of consciousness in which humanity lives. To become more conscious of yourself is a strange experience. To become conscious of others is just as strange and even more strange. The life you yourself lead with passions and jealousies, meannesses, dislikes and hatreds, becomes utterly ridiculous, You wonder, in fact, what on earth you have been doing all your life. Have you been insane? you ask yourself. Yes, exactly. In the deep sleep we live in, in the light of the Kingdom of Heaven, we are all utterly insane and do not know what we are doing. The work begins to teach you what to do. To awaken—that is the object of this work. (pp. 35-6)

The influences of esoteric teachings and the fourth way are to bring light into the inner world. Through self-observing and self-remembering, and dis-identifying from automatized personality structures which typically engage awareness, the individual can enhance this light for experiences of expanded states of self-consciousness and objective consciousness.

Consciousness, light and knowing together are intimately linked. Nicoll (1976) comments:

> ...Consciousness means, literally, 'knowing together.' A development of consciousness would therefore mean knowing 'more together,' and so it would bring about a new relationship to everything previously known. For to know more always means to see things differently. ... An increase of consciousness is likened to an increase of light. But we shall see eventually that an increase of consciousness does not mean only that we see with greater clarity what was formerly obscure. The quality is changed. For the moment, the man who experiences it himself is changed. It is not merely the quantity of consciousness that is altered, but its very nature. (pp. 22-3)

As the individual sees in a new light, the usual difficulties, concerns and associative processes can disappear as if unreal and the stuff of dreams.

In moments of illumination, there is an increase in light as one simultaneously knows together far more than is usually experienced with a narrow focus of attention conditioned by personal concerns and identifications. Nicoll writes:

> We must imagine that to be conscious in a higher Hydrogen or by means of a higher Hydrogen is similar to having a greatly increased light shed on everything. Whereas the ray of a candle illuminates feebly the surroundings, the light of an arc-lamp lights up what were mere shadows before and makes us see everything in an entirely different relation; ... seeing new relations sometimes occurs to us in times of trouble and distress when suddenly everything becomes transformed and we see things in an entirely different light. ... This is a moment of illumination, of increased light, and so increased consciousness, in the sense that we are 'knowing together' far more than we do in our contracted state. Everything falls into its right proportion, as it were, in the light of this increased consciousness, so we can say that at that moment we were conscious in a higher Hydrogen. Actually, at such a moment we are conscious at a higher point in the universe regarded as a scale of qualities represented by Hydrogens. Quite simply, we rise above ourselves for a moment and see things in a new light. (1975, p.204)

As personality and false personality complexes are dissipated, energies are released allowing for expanded states of knowing together, of insight and illumination. The light of consciousness can be accumulated and increased, or wasted and depleted. Activities within the various minds can occur within consciousness or in the absence of consciousness and the absence of light. Mystical teachings and the fourth way help to bring light into the hearts and minds of human beings. This light is a very strange thing and of different qualities. These are basic dynamics underlying the dissolution of false personality, the development of self-consciousness and the approach to real "I." Increases in consciousness are associated with light and with the accumulation of higher hydrogens, which have chemical and alchemical effects within the inner life of a human being. Self-remembering and self-observation enhance the presence of light within the inner world. This is similar to the Gnostic Christian practice of light-gaining and living in the light. The gospel of Matthew states: *"The light of the body is the eye: if therefore thine eye be single, thy whole body shall be full of light."* (6, 22) If a human's eye, or "I" be single, then s/he shall be filled with light!

The topics of consciousness, light and metaphysics are of profound importance to explorations of the nature of human beings. The modern scientific theories about consciousness, that most mysterious thing in the world, amount to what Beelzebub describes as so much rubbish and twaddle. The equation of consciousness, light and knowing together provides important insights into the nature of the inner world and the process of awakening. Humans can experience greater light within the inner world and be conscious within higher hydrogen levels. The process of awakening involves the increase of light and higher hydrogens within the mind, heart and the higher being bodies, as the individual approaches real "I."

4. The Awakening of Conscience: the Sacred and Divine Being Impulse in the Subconscious

In his story to Fritz Peters about the acorns and oak trees, Gurdjieff explained that a human's soul is given by Mother Nature but only as a possibility for growth. Just as the acorns might become oak trees or fertilizer, so also, human beings might become real men and women, or just fertilizer. The awakening of conscience is ascribed a central role in determining a human's fate:

"Nature only give possibility for soul, not give soul. Must acquire soul through work. But, unlike tree, man have many possibilities. As man now exist he have also possibility grow by accident–grow wrong way. Man can become many things, not just fertilizer, not just real man: can become what you call 'good' or 'evil,' not proper things for man. Real man not good or evil–real man only conscious, only wish acquire soul for proper development."

... "Think of good and evil like right hand and left hand. Man always have two hands—two sides of self—good and evil. One can destroy other. Must have aim to make both hands work together, must acquire third thing: thing that make peace between two hands, between impulse for good and impulse for evil. Man who all 'good' or man who all 'bad' is not whole man, is one-sided. Third thing is conscience; possibility to acquire conscience is already in man when born; this possibility given-free-by Nature. But is only possibility. Real conscience can only be acquired by work, by learning to understand self first. ... (Peters, 1964, pp.42-3)

The influence of the Work is intended to awaken the objective feelings of the remorse of conscience, which is closely tied to the dissolution of the false consciousness system. Unfortunately, people have many defences or buffers which prevent the impact of different i's upon each other, and which allow false personality and the state of automated consciousness to be maintained. Buffers allow a person to act, think, and feel in contradictory ways from moment to moment, day in and day out, without being aware of it, without seeing the meanness and negativity, the egoism and imagination. Buffers allow antagonistic and contradictory i's to be maintain along side of each other; and they allow false personality to maintain itself apart from the essence, without people being aware of the pathology of their inner state. Buffers prevent humans from experiencing the great inner gulf between what they think they are in their minds and what they are in their hearts and being. An individual in the Work must seek out these inner contradictions and lies.

Gurdjieff explains the nature of conscience, its relationship to consciousness, and its role in the Work:

"In ordinary life the concept 'conscience' is taken too simply. As if we had a conscience. Actually the concept 'conscience' in the sphere of the emotions is equivalent to the concept 'consciousness' in the sphere of the intellect. And as we have no consciousness we have no conscience.

"Consciousness is a state in which a man knows all at once everything that he in general knows .... "Conscience is a state in which a man feels all at once everything that he in general feels, or can feel. And as everyone has within him thousands of contradictory feelings which vary from a deeply hidden realization of his own nothingness and fears of all kinds to the most stupid kind of self-conceit, self-confidence, self-satisfaction, and self-praise, to feel all this together would not only be painful but literally unbearable.

"If a man whose entire inner world is composed of contradictions were suddenly to feel all these contradictions simultaneously within himself, if he were to feel all at once that he loves everything that he hates and hates everything that he loves; that he lies when he tells the truth and that he tells the truth when he lies; and if he could feel the shame and horror of it all, this would be the state which is called 'conscience.' A man cannot live in this state; he must either destroy contradictions or destroy conscience. He cannot destroy conscience, but if he cannot destroy it he can put it to sleep....

"But fortunately for man, that is, for his peace and for his sleep, this state of conscience is very rare. ... for him, there is no danger whatever of a sudden awakening. Awakening is possible only for those who seek it and want it, for those who are ready to struggle with themselves and work on themselves for a very long time and very persistently in

order to attain it. For this it is necessary to destroy 'buffers,' that is, to go out to meet all
those inner sufferings which are connected with the sensations of contradictions. ... the
result of his work will be every possible discomfort and suffering from the awakening of
his conscience.

"But conscience is the fire which alone can fuse all the powders in the glass retort
which was mentioned before and create the unity which a man lacks in that state in
which he begins to study himself. (1949, pp.155-6)

Gurdjieff assigns a central role to the awakening to conscience in the alchemy of transformation.
Conscience is a state in which a human *"feels all at once everything that he in general feels and can
feel."* This form of feeling together serves to unify an individual's presence thus overcoming inner
inconsistencies and contradictions.

The awakening of consciousness destroys buffers and awakens conscience from the prior
subconscious. Ouspensky explains (1957): *"... buffers do not like light. When buffers begin to
disappear and become less strong, conscience begins to manifest itself."* (p.154) This requires an
expansion of consciousness and the dissolution of false personality maintained by buffers, particularly
the Kundabuffer. The awakening of conscience involves remembering oneself in time, observing the
many contradictory i's and overcoming the state of automated consciousness crystallized around
egoism, self-love and vanity.

Conscience also brings other feelings as the individual is reborn, and attains a clearer and more
unified state. Ouspensky recalls Gurdjieff's explanations:

"... if these moments of conscience became longer and if a man does not fear them but
on the contrary, co-operates with them and tries to keep and prolong them, an element
of very subtle joy, a foretaste of the future 'clear consciousness' will gradually enter into
these moments." (1949, p.156)

Within *Beelzebub's Tales to His Grandson*, Gurdjieff's elaborates upon the nature of conscience
and the awakening of conscience, and this theme is tied into the history of humanity and to the
catastrophes that occurred on of that ill-fated planet Earth. Beelzebub's explanations of the unknown
history of humanity and the planet are intertwined with stories about his visits to earth and the roles of
various Sacred Messengers and Divine Teachers–such as Saint Buddha, Jesus Christ, Mohammad,
and particularly Ashiata Shiemash. These Sacred Messengers have intervened in attempts to
normalize the strange psyches of those peculiar three-brained beings breeding on planet earth, whose
actions threaten the larger common cosmic purposes and harmony.

In *The Tales*, Gurdjieff describes conscience as a *"fundamental Divine impulse."* Unfortunately, he
explains that there is *"... a total absence of the participation of the impulse of sacred conscience in
their waking-consciousness."* Humankind came to *"strive to arrange their welfare during the process
of their ordinary existence, exclusively for themselves,"* and because of this egoism and the evil god
"self-calming" used to squash any prick of conscience—and manifest in such "isms" as nicotinism,
alcoholism, cocainism, and the like—the sacred being impulse of conscience passed into the
subconscious. However, this sacred being impulse did not simply disappear. Beelzebub explains:

> ... in that consciousness of theirs, which they call their subconsciousness, even in the beings of the present time, the said data for the acquisition in their presences of this fundamental Divine impulse conscience does indeed still continue to be crystallized and, hence, to be present during the whole of their existence. (1950, p. 381)

According to Beelzebub, the awakening of conscience is one of the few avenues remaining to change the sorry state of those unfortunate, three-brained beings. The data necessary for the awakening of the sacred being impulse conscience have not undergone the more complete *"degeneration to which all the other sacred being-impulses were subject"*–those sacred impulses of Faith, Love and Hope. The need for the awakening of conscience is a primary theme of *Beelzebub's Tales*, especially given the horrors of the situation with humankind engaging in the processes of reciprocal destruction, war and animal slaughter, and producing an increasingly inferior quality of Askokin vibrations. Whereas human beings asleep are governed by the push and pulls of the good and bad, *"real man only conscious,"* and he has acquired conscience. Gurdjieff states that this real conscience has to be acquired by work and the fulfilling of one's being duties and obligations.

The awakening of conscience brings about a form of conscious suffering, compared to the unconscious sufferings based on the desires and attachments of the planetary body. Beelzebub provides a cosmic perspective of the origins of the sacred being- impulse of conscience:

> "The factors for the being-impulse conscience arise in the presences of the three-brained beings from the localization of the particles of the "emanations-of-the-sorrow" of our OMNI-LOVING AND LONG-SUFFERING-ENDLESS-CREATOR; that is why the source of the manifestation of genuine conscience in three-centered beings is sometimes called the REPRESENTATIVE OF THE CREATOR. (1950, p. 372)

Beelzebub explains that human beings can assume a role in bearing the *"Sorrow of our Endlessness."*

Morality, as humans commonly understand it, is very different from the moral sense awakened with conscience and the awakening of consciousness. Ordinary *"subjective morality"* is an accidental thing based on conditioning, imitation and rote learning, indoctrination, education, external rewards and punishment. Subjective morality differs from one individual, time and country to another. In contrast, *"objective morality"* is the same everywhere and involves an increased consciousness of the objective nature of self and the realities of life and the cosmos. Objective morality and conscience are based upon a deeper consciousness than people ordinarily know and the "instinctual sensing of reality" and cosmic truths.

Gurdjieff (1950) explains that humans can work in order to have the Divine function of conscience in their consciousness, by *"transubstantiating"* in themselves five *"being -obligolnian-strivings,"* being obligations or duties. These being obligations are elements of an objective morality:

> "The first striving: to have in their ordinary being-existence everything satisfying and really necessary for their planetary body.

> "The second striving: to have a constant and unflagging instinctive need for self-perfection in the sense of being.

"The third: the conscious striving to know ever more and more concerning the laws of World-creation and World-maintenance.

"The fourth: the striving from the beginning of their existence to pay for their arising and their individuality as quickly as possible, in order afterwards to be free to lighten as much as possible the Sorrow of our COMMON FATHER.

"And the fifth: the striving always to assist the most rapid perfecting of other beings, both those similar to oneself and those of other forms, up to the degree of the sacred 'Martfotai,' that is, up to the degree of self-individuality. (p.386)

The first being obligation refers to maintaining the physical body and not being overly indulgent and conditioned by physical desires, the stomach and sex organs. The second involves striving for one's self-perfection, the attainment of real "I," one's individuality. The third involves seeking after truth about self and the nature of the world–striving to understand the fundamental cosmic laws which create and sustain life. The fourth involves paying for our arising in order to help lighten the Sorrow of our Common Father, overcoming egoism and striving to lessen the suffering and unhappiness within the world. The final striving, or being obligation, is to help others towards their self-perfection, to attaining their real "I."

Beelzebub, in *The Tales*, explains that if it were not for the cosmic catastrophes which occurred, it would be natural for humankind as three centered beings to strive in these directions. Humans would engage in "conscious labours" and "intentional suffering" in order to fulfill their "being-Partkdolg-duty." Such conscious labours are efforts to observe and remember oneself, and struggle towards one's self perfection. Intentional or voluntary suffering involves bearing consciously the unpleasant manifestations of others. The degradation of humankind has led humans to forget their being-Partkdolg-duty and sacred being obligations, and strive instead only for their own welfare, pleasuring, egoism, self-love and vanity, all through insincerity and cunning. The sacred being obligations form a part of "objective morality" and serve to connect humans to deeper cosmic processes, the sacred and divine.

Gurdjieff describes humans *"as beings bearing in themselves particles of the emanation of the Sorrow of our COMMON FATHER CREATOR."* (1950, p. 385) The awakening of conscience is thus a profoundly important stage in the transformation of the emotional life leading to the awakening of higher emotional center and connection with the emotional life of the Common Father.

The possibility for remorse of conscience also prevents the "final degradation" in humankind of the other sacred being impulses of *"Faith, Love, and Hope."* The experience of remorse and of the sorrow of the Common Father are steps to awakening and transformation. Fortunately, the data are still present within human beings for such "sacred being impulses," although they have passed into the subconscious, while humans invent ever new mean for self-calming. The nature of true conscience has to be understood in terms of much deeper cosmic processes.

5. Glimpses of Mystical States

5a. **Science #4 & Supernormal Psychology**

> "... the whole of knowledge is contained in the soul of man, and mysticism is the way to this knowledge and the way to God." (Ouspensky, 1969, p.19)

The term *mysticism* is typically used in highly varied and subjective ways to refer to all kinds of theories and beliefs about the soul, life after death, spirits and the hidden forces in nature. Often it is regarded as the antithesis of objective science or exact knowledge. The worst thing which might be said of a scientist's work is that it is *mystical*–suggesting that it is pseudo-scientific, vague or misty.

However, Ouspensky defines mysticism, in a psychological way as involving *"... special states of consciousness, and ideas and conceptions of the world directly resulting from these states."* (1969, p.18) In this view, mysticism is the way to deeper knowledge of the soul and God, and the nature of reality. Thus, Ouspensky suggests that science must come to mysticism and to the study of mystical states which can reveal new orders of truth, meaning and interrelatedness.

Of course, it is natural that deeper knowledge of the nature of life and the unity of creation could only be revealed in deeper states of consciousness. Recall Collin's description of the usual approach to unified knowledge based upon humans' normal states of disunity and unconsciousness. Collin questions what unity can be realized by even the most brilliant scientist or philosopher if he or she *"remains subject to the daily trivial blindness of the ordinary mind."* The usual state of waking sleep and the lack of development of human beings imposes definite limitations to their knowledge. The search for *unifying knowledge* must obviously entail also a search for more unified state of consciousness and more highly developed states of being. Collin explains: *"... the unity of things is not realisable by the ordinary mind in an ordinary state of consciousness. ... A unity, a pattern, an all-embracing meaning-if it exist-could only be discerned or experienced by a different kind of mind, in a different state of consciousness. ... Thus the attempt to gather all knowledge into a whole has always been connected with the search for a new state of consciousness. And it is meaningless and futile apart from such a search."* (1980, p. xi)

The fourth way teaching defines the higher states of consciousness in terms of the *cognition of truth*. The state of self-consciousness reveals the full truth about ourselves and the fourth state of objective consciousness reveals the full truth about everything, the world, the laws of nature, the origins of reality. Ouspensky states: *"We can study "things in themselves," "the world as it is."* (p.35) These states of higher consciousness involve the awakening to the higher emotional and intellectual centers, and the development of the higher being-bodies. Higher states introduce new dimensions to life, new states of objective emotions and direct super-sensual forms of knowledge and experience.

Ouspensky (1957) states that science must come to mysticism, because it provides a new theory of knowledge based upon the study of consciousness. At one point, Ouspensky explains this in relationship to the idea of man number one, two and three, and the necessity of a science number four:

> Certainly science No. 1, 2 and 3 is all we know. It uses man's present state of
> consciousness and present functions as an instrument for getting certain results.
> Science No. 4 will begin with improvement of instruments. If you have to work in any
> particular branch of science, you have a certain instrument for this work and get certain
> results. But suppose you can have a better instrument; you will immediately get better
> results. Science No. 4 involves improving the instrument of knowing—man's functions
> and state of consciousness. (pp. 40-1)

It is extremely difficult to realize how this is so and what it could mean. R. Collin (1984) explains
the relationship between humans' ordinary state of relative consciousness and expanded states of
knowing together:

> The characteristic of the ordinary logical mind by whose speed is measured the life
> of the physical body is that *one thing is known or experienced after another*. When
> logical mind passes on to the next experience it is unable to retain the experience or
> knowledge that went before. ...
>
> It is not that man's life does not contain enough experience or knowledge for him to
> become wise or illuminated. But relying on the perception of logical mind, he only
> experiences one thing at a time, and forgets this as soon as he passes on to the next.
> If all that he knows at one time or another could be compressed into shorter time, so
> that less was forgotten, innumerable connections of cause and effect, and patterns of
> cosmic influence would appear, which would render him wise beyond imagination.
> (pp. 18-9)

When people are confined by the limitations of formatory mind and personal emotions, they end up,
in the terms of Beelzebub, perceiving reality topsy-turvy and no longer *"instinctually sensing reality"* or
"instinctually sensing cosmic truths."

Methods of self-study and the awakening of consciousness provide a new approach to science
through the development of the higher faculties. Humans can know directly the larger wholes and
attain higher gradients of Divine Reason, if and only if they develop in their being. The light of
consciousness and connection with the higher centres can reveal innumerable connections of cause
and effect, even of cosmic influence. The one who is present, the "I," must be active and thus allowing
us to "know together" in experiences of insight and illumination.

Plato's ideas about *noetic knowledge* depict the possibilities inherent in states of deeper
consciousness and knowing together. Nicoll writes:

> If we could see all the relations and affinities that an object has, *simultaneously*,
> instead of as a confused collection of separately noticed properties ... we would be on
> the *noetic* level of conscious experience. ... The separate sensible properties of the
> object would be merged into its *total significance*. It would be seen as an expression
> of the universe, so that while nothing that our senses told us of it would be lost sight of
> or wrong, it would be invested with a meaning that transcended all sensible perception
> and would become a manifestation of 'intelligible form' or *idea*. At this noetic level the
> world would be experienced in a new way, i.e., as regards the interconnection, relation,
> meaning and significance of everything that we perceive. (1971, p.52)

Self-remembering develops the capacity to know together and a new light is introduced into the inner world, illuminating the psychic functions and enabling tastes of higher states. The methods for light gaining and for knowing together with a unified presence are the only means of perceiving into the subtle underlying realms which create and sustain the phenomena of life. Real understanding can only emerge with real "I." Then, when "I AM," the world is real.

Thus far, the primary focus of *Psychological Illusions* has been on the domain of normal psychology and humans asleep, living in illusion and delusion. A discussion of higher states of consciousness leads to a far broader range of ideas and considerations and must be approached from various angles. Certainly, there is an immensely varied literature on psychiatric, psychic, mystical, cosmic and spiritual experiences, and it is not easy to illustrate all the kinds of experiences and distinctions which need to be considered. As in other areas of psychological study, there is little agreement in modern psychology about what higher states are possible for humans, or how to classify and understand them. This study is bound then to be incomplete and yet it can serve to point towards the miraculous possibilities available to human beings.

States of higher consciousness bring a quality and intensity of experience quite unknown to normal waking sleep state. We cannot expect descriptions of such experiences to ever capture the nature of such expanded states of emotion, knowledge, illumination and realization. Language is an inadequate vehicle for even usual experiences, yet alone for the description of new states of consciousness. All words must necessarily fail to convey the qualities of impressions and feelings experienced. Ouspensky (1969) notes:

> The unknown is unlike anything that we can suppose about it. The complete unexpectedness of everything that is met with in these experiences, from great to small, makes the description of them difficult. First of all, everything is unified, everything is linked together, everything is explained by something else and in its turn explains another thing. There is nothing separate, that is, nothing that can be named or described separately. In order to describe the first impression, the first sensations, it is necessary to describe all at once. The new world with which one comes into contact has no sides so that it is impossible to describe first one side and then the other. All of it is visible at once at every point; but how in fact to describe anything in these conditions—that question I could not answer. I understand why all descriptions of mystical experiences are so poor. (p.27)

Mystical/spiritual experiences transcend the usual patterns of analytic thought and personal emotions. Language must necessarily fail and each author in his understandings will tend to describe such experiences in terms of familiar concepts and labels.

Further, higher states admit of various levels of attainment and may be more or less coloured by an individual's makeup. Spontaneous experiences of higher states are usually simple glimpses or moments of awakening and tend to be abnormal variations of these states, compared with what might be experienced by a man number four, five, six and seven. In these higher types of men, or women, the miraculous faculties are developed more fully and are more stabilized with an abiding experience of I AM. These points are noted by King (1965), a psychologist and student of the fourth way teaching, in his critical account of the so-called *"cosmic consciousness"* experiences reported by Bucke in the classic work *Cosmic Consciousness* (1972).

> We (must) distinguish between the correct or *paradic* state of Objective Consciousness
> and its abnormal counterpart, which goes under the modern name of Cosmic
> Consciousness. Many books have been written about the latter by those who claim to
> have experienced it but the descriptions that are given are not very intelligible. ... all
> this comes about because the subjective entity involved in these experiences is the 'I'-
> entity ... characteristic of the Waking state. When the highest degree of consciousness
> is entered directly from the Waking state, therefore, the vagueness and obscurity of the
> preceding condition is carried over to the succeeding one and the realizations of those
> who have recovered from a spell of Cosmic Consciousness and attempt to tell us of
> it, are scarcely intelligible at all. ... Cosmic Consciousness, entered from the Waking
> state, is basically a pathological condition and generates many kinds of delusions. ...
> According to Bucke's description of it Cosmic Consciousness is a somewhat peculiar
> condition, to say the least of it. (pp. 131-2)

Glimpses of awakened states are coloured by people's personality makeup and by the usual obscurity
of consciousness. As King notes *"Cosmic Consciousness, entered from the Waking state, is basically
a pathological condition ..."* Ouspensky recalls similar comments made by Gurdjieff:

> "If we could connect the centers of our ordinary consciousness with the higher thinking
> center deliberately and at will, it would be of no use to us whatever in our present
> general state. In most cases where accidental contact with the higher thinking center
> takes place a man becomes unconscious. The mind refuses to take in the flood of
> thoughts, emotions, images, and ideas which suddenly burst into it. ... But even these
> moments are so full of unusual shades and colours that there is nothing with which to
> compare them among the ordinary sensations of life. This is usually all that remains
> from so-called 'mystical' and 'ecstatic' experiences, which represent a temporary
> connection with a higher center. Only very seldom does it happen that a mind which
> has been better prepared succeeds in grasping and remembering something of what
> was felt and understood at the moment of ecstasy." (1949, p. 195)

Accounts of cosmic and mystical experiences are generally of an abnormal nature and do not illustrate
well the true forms of self-consciousness or objective consciousness. The aim within a *school* is the
preparation of an individual so as to allow such experiences to be maintained in relationship to real I.

Despite these difficulties and cautionary notes, accounts of mystical experiences are most interesting
and suggestive. Furthermore, descriptions of such states from widely divergent peoples and religions
are surprisingly similar, although the languages and understanding vary. Most importantly,
Ouspensky comments:

> Mystical experiences are intelligible only in mystical states. All that we can get from
> an intellectual study of mystical states will be merely an approximation to, a hint of, a
> certain understanding. (1969, p. 18)

If the intellectual study of such states can give us even approximations and hints, then this is obviously
a profoundly important area of study and investigation. If the whole of knowledge might somehow be
inherent in the nature of the soul of a human being, then indeed scientists and individuals must come
to the study of mysticism and the search for higher states and realizations.

5b. **Glimpses of Self-Consciousness**

Self-consciousness involves awakening within the essence and the emergence of a new feeling of I. The emergence of self-consciousness may create the feeling of emerging from a cloud, haze or dream state, to a new quality and intensity of experience. Self-consciousness is rooted in a fuller awareness of one's being and presence, and of the existence of the world around and within. At the same time that one is more objectively aware of their own existence, there is an expanded awareness of one's interrelatedness with life (others, nature and the world). The world takes on a new immediacy and vibrancy of quality. When Mr. G. was asked what it would be like to be *"conscious in essence,"* he replied simply, *"Everything more vivid."* (Patterson, 1998, p.77)

Various events produced in life can provide the "shocks" necessary to produce moments of expanded self-awareness within people normally in the waking sleep state. Crises can act as a catalyst, or shock, as well as new and unfamiliar situations or places, the loss of life's usual relationships and supports, or shocks produced by death, injuries or near death experiences. Psychotic episodes and psychedelic drugs may also break down automated personality processes, and lead to new and strange experiences. The breakdown of personality and false personality may bring an individual closer to the essence, although often in pathological forms when the essence has remained underdeveloped or has been distorted or crystallized in a pathological manner.

Various events or forces can give rise to a wide variety of psychic, mystical and spiritual experiences. In attaining the state of self-consciousness there is an awakening and rebirth within essence, and a more objective form of knowing. Beelzebub mentions the capacity of *"instinctually sensing reality,"* and *"instinctually sensing cosmic truths."* Life is certainly *more vivid*, and can bring what Ouspensky describes as, *"the first real feelings a man will experience."* (1957)

A first account of the breakdown of automated consciousness and glimpses of self-conscious experience is from the writings of the existentialist philosopher, J. P. Sartre (1964), who came face to face with the bare reality of life:

> So I was in the park just now. The roots of a chestnut tree were sunk in the ground just under my bench. I couldn't remember it was a root any more. The words had vanished and with them the significance of things, their methods of use, and the feeble points of reference which men have traced on their surface. I was sitting, stooped forward, head bowed, alone in front of this black, knotty mass, entirely beastly, which frightened me. Then I had this vision.

> It left me breathless. Never, until these last few days, had I understood the meaning of "existence." I was like all the others, like the ones walking along the seashore, all

dressed in their spring finery. I said, like them, "The ocean is green; that white speck up there is a seagull," but I didn't feel that it existed or that the seagull was an "existing seagull;" usually existence hides itself. It is there, around us, in us, it is us, you can't say two words without mentioning it, but you can never touch it. ... And then all of a sudden, there it is, clear as day; existence had unveiled itself. It had lost the harmless look of an abstract category: it was the very paste of things, the root was kneaded into existence. (pp. 126-7)

Normally, the *bare existence* of things hides from us behind veils of thoughts and personal concerns. In Sartre's account, *"the words had vanished"* along with his usual mental and ego processes which bind awareness. He then encounters this far deeper realm *"kneaded into existence."* Sartre is frightened by these revelations as he has no preparation or understanding, and he experiences depersonalization and *nausea* (related to the activation of the solar plexus.) In his moments of existential awareness, Sartre witnesses the sleepwalking nature of those strolling along the seashore absorbed in their usual mundane realities and asleep to the bare facts of existence.

Another glimpse of self-consciousness accompanied by dread and feelings of unreality is reported in *Autobiography of a Schizophrenic Girl*:

I remember very well the day it happened. We were staying in the country and I had gone for a walk alone as I did now and then. Suddenly, as I was passing the school, I heard a German song; the children were having a singing lesson. I stopped to listen, and at that instant a strange feeling came over me, a feeling hard to analyze but akin to something I was to know too well later—a disturbing sense of unreality. It seemed to me that I no longer recognized the school, it had become as large as a barracks; the singing children were prisoners, compelled to sing. It was as though the school and the children's song were set apart from the rest of the world. At the same time my eye encountered a field of wheat whose limits I could not see. The yellow vastness, dazzling in the sun, bound up with the song of the children imprisoned in the smooth stone school-barracks, filled me with such anxiety that I broke into sobs. I ran home to our garden and began to play "to make things seem as they usually were," that is, to return to reality. It was the first appearance of those elements which were always present in later sensations of unreality; illimitable vastness, brilliant light, and the gloss and smoothness of material things. (Sechehaye, 1951, p.19)

The experience of unreality brought on by the breakdown of this girl's personality brought vivid sensations and impressions—revealing a world quite foreign and frightening. The girl is overwhelmed by her vision and the vastness of things, and she wants to recover her usual sense of reality. Her experiences suggest the strangeness of increased self-consciousness to one insufficiently prepared and dominated by unconscious fears and dreams, and lacking the healthy development of essence. Similar episodes, with feelings of unreality and depersonalization, are characteristic of the onset of acute psychotic episodes. It appears, as Gurdjieff suggests, that if a person has their buffers removed, they can go quite mad. They do not understand what is happening and are overwhelmed by fright, engulfed by the strangeness and otherness of reality.

As moments of self-consciousness are less colored by personality distortions, new realms of feelings and life awareness emerge. The world appears as dynamically vibrant, vital and seething with life:

"I felt that every element of the landscape was alive, the light, air, ground and trees. *All were inter-related, living the same life* ... The forms of things were only the particular expressions of an energy or a substance which they all shared in common."
(In Crookall, 1969, pp.18-9)

"All became alive—the trees, the houses, the very stones ... became vibrant with the life within them ... And not only that, *but everything seemed to be connected with everything else* ... Every common and ordinary thing of which we are conscious, including our bodies, are but parts of one intensely radiant activity."
(ibid, p.22)

Life becomes transfigured and reveals a beauty unspeakable. Individuals feel themselves an integral part of this larger life:

"... the consciousness of God's nearness came to me sometimes. I say God to describe what is indescribable. A presence, I might say, yet that is too suggestive of personality, and the moments of which I speak did not hold the consciousness of a personality, but something in myself made me feel myself ... one with the grass, the trees, birds, insects—everything in nature. I exulted in the mere fact of existence....
(James, 1958, pp. 303-4)

"I suddenly feel the extraordinary value and importance of everybody I meet and almost anything I see ... I see the essential glory and beauty of all the people I meet ... In the flicker of sunlight on a blank wall, or a reach of muddy pavement, or smoke from an engine at night, there is a sudden significance and importance and inspiration that makes the breath stop ... It's like being in love ... The excitement and music of the birds, the delicious madness of the air, the blue haze of the distance, the straining of the hedges, the green mist of shoots about the trees—oh it wasn't these details—it was beyond and around them." (Crockall, 1969, p. 24)

Moments of self-consciousness can bring a new radiance and brilliance to sight, and feelings of enchantment, awe, joy, bliss, rapture and love, and of the unity of life within some Greater Being. Nature is alive, radiant and seething with existence. It stands out, it breaths. There is no question of value, meaning or importance.

Carl Jung (1963) describes his awakening to an integrated inner source of presence and consciousness:

> I was taking the long road to school ... when suddenly for a single moment I had the overwhelming impression of having just emerged from a dense cloud. I knew all at once: now I am *myself*! It was as if a wall of mist were at my back, and behind that wall there was not yet an "I." But at this moment I *came upon myself*. Previously I had existed, too, but everything had merely happened to me. ... Now I knew: I am myself now, now I exist. Previously I had been willed to do this and that: now I willed. This experience seemed to me tremendously important and new: there was "authority" in me. (pp. 32-3)

Jung experiences awakening as if formerly he had been embedded in a cloud or dream. Now, he was fully conscious of himself, with will and able to act with a new feeling of "I."

H. Hesse (1957) depicts the awakening of Siddhartha, the Buddha, and his experience of the unity of life and nature:

> He looked around him as if seeing the world for the first time. The world was beautiful, strange and mysterious. Here was blue, here was yellow, here was green, sky and river, woods and mountains, all beautiful, all mysterious and enchanting, and in the midst of it, he, Siddhartha, the awakened one, on the way to himself. .. Meaning and reality were not hidden somewhere behind things, they were in them, in all of them. ... the world was transformed and he was enthralled. ... He saw trees, stars, animals, clouds, rainbows, rocks, weeds, flowers, brook and river, the sparkle of dew on bushes ... All this, coloured and in a thousand different forms, had always been there. ... he saw and recognized the visible and sought his place in this world. He did not seek reality; his goal was not on any other side. The world was beautiful when looked at in this way—without any seeking, so simple, so childlike. ... It was beautiful and pleasant to go through the world like that, so childlike, so awakened, so concerned with the immediate, without any distrust. ... All this had always been and he had never seen it; he was never present. Now he was present and belonged to it. (pp. 39 & 46)

The existence of the world is revealed to Siddhartha, beautiful and full of meaning, experienced in a childlike and immediate way. Nature shows herself as streaming with life, filled with radiance and colour, beauty and magic.

Nott (1969), a student of Gurdjieff and Ouspensky, describes his experience of awakening to self-consciousness:

> It was during this summer that I had the first deep and vivid experience of higher consciousness. The three previous experiences of this unexpected impact of higher forces were a taste of real consciousness of self. The present one was different. One hot day I was walking from the house across the fields to bathe in the Wisconsin river. About half way a strange and wonderful force began to enter into me and permeate my whole being, and filled me with light and power. I stopped and stood still and let the force flow. Although I was aware of my surroundings—the forest and fields and the hot sun, they were only a background to the inner experience; all anxieties and cares of ordinary life dropped away; at the same time I saw myself and my relations with people quite clearly; I saw the patterns of my life, my organism moving as it were along its appointed path. There was time no longer, and an understanding of the whole of life

seemed possible for me. It was as if for a few moment I had entered into my real life; and the outer life, which had seemed so important and took up all my time, was not the real life but something ephemeral, a sort of cinema film with which I was identified. Only the inner something was eternal–I, the real self of me. I AM. (p.154)

Whereas moments of self-consciousness can occur spontaneously in life, the effect of conscious work upon oneself enhances and deepens such states, enabling one to abide in them. Experiences involve the transformation of the sense of time, illumination of the patterns of one's life, realization of one's interconnectedness to nature and the larger cosmos, and experiences of objective emotions and the sacred being-impulses. The experience of self-consciousness involves a quantum shift in the experience of I and awakening to one's nature as a particle of the whole.

Sri Ramana Maharshi recounts his early experience of self-realization, which was brought about after he was overcome with the fear of death and he pursued an inquiry into self, until he made this breakthrough:

But with the death of this body, am "I" dead? Is the body "I"? This body is silent and inert. But I feel the full force of my personality and even the sound "I" within myself, –apart from the body. So "I" am a spirit, a thing transcending the body. The material body dies, but the spirit transcending it cannot be touched by death. ... All this was not a mere intellectual process, but flashed before me vividly as living truth, something which I perceived immediately, without any argument almost. 'I' was something very real, the only real thing in that state and all the conscious activity that was connected with my body was centered on that. The 'I' or my 'self' was holding the focus of attention by a powerful fascination from that time forwards. Fear of death had vanished at once and forever. Absorption in the self has continued from that moment right up to this time. Other thoughts may come and go like the various notes of a musician, but the 'I' continues like the basic or fundamental *sruti* note which accompanies and blends with all other notes. Whether the body was engaged in talking, reading or anything else, I was still centered on 'I.' Previous to that crisis I had no clear perception of myself and was not consciously attracted to it. ..." (Narasimha, 1976, pp. 21-2)

Sri Ramana had attained his "I" and no longer was a "man in quotation marks." In this case, he attained the level of a higher type, always centered on "I."

5c. **From Personal to Impersonal Emotions & Sacred Being-Impulses**

Higher emotions do not come about through the refinement or intensification of typical personal emotions. Real emotions require overcoming patterns of self love and self-feeling, attachments and identifications. Such personal emotions are based on the complex of nerve nodes within the sympathetic system, particularly in the "pit of the stomach" or solar plexus, and not within the original center of emotions, related by Gurdjieff to an organ in the area of "the breast." All mystical paths teach the importance of transcending personal elements in the emotional life.

Ouspensky (1968) discusses the nature of personal and impersonal emotions as means of attaining knowledge:

> ... *religious emotions* serve knowledge. ... In reality in the soul of man nothing exists save emotions. ... The sign of the growth of the emotions is the liberation of them from the *personal* element, and their sublimation on the higher planes. ... Thus the cognitive power of the emotions is greater in proportion as there is less of *self-elements* in a given emotion ... there are emotions which are unitive, harmonizing, making man feel himself to be a part of some great whole; such are love, sympathy, friendship, compassion, love of country, love of nature, love of humanity. These emotions lead man out of the material world and show him the truth of the world of the wondrous. (pp. 195-200)

Many of the irritations and animosities which normally separate us from each other and from the deeper self are the result of attention to the superficial incidents of thought and behaviour. Humans can reach deeper within themselves, into the soul life of things, and a new realm of objective emotions emerges.

Nicoll (1975) points out how in a way, remembering yourself means forgetting yourself –transcending the usual focus on personal concerns:

> ... all real self-remembering is simply forgetting yourself, your ordinary self, your ordinary negative "I's," your ordinary forms of internal considering, and all the rest of it; and feeling certain that some further state of yourself exists above all this personal uproar that takes place all day dong in each one of you, with which you keep on identifying; and when the Work says that we have Real "I" above us you must understand that this act, so to speak, of separating from False Personality, deliberately at some moment every day, is designed to make it possible for us to come in contact with the first traces of Real "I" which is always there and which is our real goal.

Remembering ourselves de-automatizes or neutralizes the usual closed patterns of identifications. Over time this serves the awakening of higher emotions which unify and harmonize, and give tastes of the ecstasies of the soul. Higher emotions allow the individual to feel and know the miraculous.

With higher emotions and self-consciousness, the individual experiences the life of things as all interrelated and part of some deeper whole. Higher emotions are of a unitive nature illustrating the deep interconnectedness of the cosmos and self within a living Presence. Descriptions of states of awakening portray overwhelming feelings of love, joy, bliss, and ecstasy arising from the experience of awakened "I:"

> In the Divine Mind an unchanging perception of bliss is ever-present. ... Suddenly I became filled with a deep sense of joy. I looked around in wonderment. The car in which I was sitting was filled with joy. ... A telegraph-pole immediately in front of me was filled with joy. The trees were filled with joy. Thoughts such as the following drifted through my mind-God is joy. God is bliss. God is love. Only God is real. Spend your days in seeking Me. Love, joy, peace, bliss. This, this only, hold on to this. For more than two hours I sat in the Brahmic bliss, at one with God, immersed in joy. Some of this joy rubbed of on to me, making a permanent change in personality. I now go about with a deep, abiding sense of peace—"The peace of God which passeth all understanding." (Wilson, in Crookall, 1969, p.159)

> Barriers were down; my aloneness had gone; I was at one with every living creature and thing. I knew that underneath were the Everlasting Arms. ... I realized that the rocks, trees, etc., were I; I, they are all brothers. Because of the experience I know that everything involved in this process is God, is Love, is Light, is Bliss, that everything is in migration towards the Great Awakening to That which, in essence, everything is. (Johnson, in Crookall, p.65)

The state of self-consciousness and connection with the higher emotional center bring about an awakening and realization of the deeper nature of things within a living Presence. The individual instinctually senses reality and cosmic truths:

> "This was no earthly beauty. There was a 'light' on things, and a 'light' in them, so that everything proclaimed itself a vivid part of life. Grass, trees and flowers were so lighted inwardly by their own beauty that the Soul grasped at the miracle of a being so perfect. From all these glorious living things there streamed a 'light' of their own. ... The air itself had a 'light' within it, a sense of being life in itself ... Each thing glowed with its own 'light'.... (Scott, in Crookall, 1969, p.72)

> I felt one with everything and everybody. ... There is no such thing as separateness —no such thing as a world apart from me. The unity of all life, of all existence, was spread before me. There is absolute unity in all creation and one motive power. There is no time and no space. (Johnson, in Crookall, p.59)

Similarly, Ouspensky (1969) writes of his adventures in experimental mysticism:

> "Everything is alive," I said to myself in the midst of these observations; "there is nothing dead, it is only we who are dead. If we became alive for a moment, we shall feel that everything is alive, that all things live, think, feel and can speak to us." (p.290)

The objective feelings of love, compassion, awe, peace, joyfulness and bliss, as well as remorse of conscience and objective moral perceptions, are attendant upon the awakening to higher emotional center. This center is in fact already present but existing at a more subtle hydrogen level.

Impressions taken in during a state of self-remembering become emotional. Even the simplest things can become interesting and beautiful as they reflect meanings never before perceived. In order to experience this, one has only to forget the usual selves and the turning of personal emotions which colour and distort impressions.

Objective higher emotions reveal that love permeates the universe and is a divine and cosmic phenomenon. Gurdjieff mentions the Divine Love of the Common Creator and the commandment to *"Love everything that breathes."* Faith, Hope and Love are the three primary *sacred being-impulses* described by Beelzebub as having atrophied in those strange three-brained beings on Earth. The Sacred Being Impulses can bring a human into touch with the Common Father and Mother Nature. This is an essential theme and truth of religious teachings, of mystical experience and of Beelzebub's tales.

Love is an element of the universe, a spiritual or divine energy which pervades everywhere. In union with all or the larger reality of life, one experiences this directly:

> "God is present by love alone ... By love alone He liveth and feeleth in other persons ... By love alone He enjoyeth all the creatures . . The Soul is shriveled up and buried in a grave that does not love." (Traherne, in Crookall, 1969, p.48)

> "... the great truth (is) that God is love, and that all who love really and truly are in God and He in them ... Everything you love is a step towards Heaven. Everything you dislike so as to make you incapable of loving anyone, takes you down the steps away from Him. ... to be out of love is to be out of the very Being of God. (Stead, in Crookall, 1969, p. 81)

> I will show you the immensity of love. You all live in this ocean of love, sympathy, of understanding. Whatever befalls you, love is underneath, around, and above you, suffering with you, carrying the burden and sharing the joy. So linked are we that, of a great truth, all that you experience reflects on and finds response instantly in Me. (Anon, In Crookall, 1969, p. 85)

Clearly, these descriptions are of a religious nature as a supreme being, identified with God, is taken as the source of transcendental love. God is love, a familiar motto, which can be experienced directly in glimpses and states of higher emotions.

Higher states of consciousness bring the individual to a deeper emotional realization of I AM and a faith that somehow the individual is interrelated to That, which pervades all life. Beelzebub explains the sacred being impulse of faith:

> "... owing to faith alone does there appear in a being, the intensity of being-self-consciousness necessary for every being, and also the valuation of personal Being as a particle of Everything Existing in the Universe." (1950, pp. 191-2)

These descriptions of mystical experiences illustrate how the intensification of being self-consciousness brings about an awareness of self as a particle of everything existing, and a faith in God, the Endlessness, or some ultimate life source.

5d. **Ouspensky on Great Beings & Higher Mind**

Within a human being, there exists an ordering of levels of being or intelligences, that reflects the larger cosmic or universal structures. Objective knowledge suggests that any phenomenal material entity of the four dimensional space-time exists also in interior dimensions, within matters/energies and intelligence of less dense natures. The existence of these interpenetrating planes and higher dimensions unites all things ultimately into the greater whole, the One.

To illustrate the idea of different dimensions take the analogy of a being who lives on a two dimensional space--say perhaps on a sheet of paper. If some larger three-dimensional being were to put a hand onto this plane, the fingers would give five separate points of intersection with the two dimensional plane. The two dimensional being in its travels within its world would encounter five separate objects, or sections of fingers, separated in time and space. Unable to perceive within the third dimension, the two dimensional being would naturally assume that all five points were separate and distinct phenomena, although of the same class or nature. This being would surely be surprised to hear the claim that these separate and distinct objects were really part of one larger being within higher dimensions.

Normally we consider humans as existing in a three-dimensional space, with a fourth dimension of time. All of this exists in relationship to the observer. It is possible then that those objects which appear in the phenomenal world as separated in time and space might appear within deeper and more penetrating state of consciousness to be unified as parts of other great beings within higher or subtle dimensions. Ouspensky (1968) depicts such dynamics:

> When we say *that table*, we picture the table to ourselves in space and time; but when we say *an object made of wood*, not meaning any definite thing, but speaking generally, it will relate to all things made of wood throughout the world, and in all ages. An imaginative person could conceive that we are referring to some great thing made of wood, composed of all objects whenever and wherever *wooden* things existed, these forming its constituent *atoms*, as it were. (p.12)

Concepts and mental functions allow us to conceive of things outside of the conditions of time and space. Higher mental functions might further allow for the apprehension of the thought-forms, ideas or great beings, embodied within objects and processes. In his writings on experimental mysticism, Ouspensky describes direct experiences of such dynamics:

> I remember once being struck by an ordinary cab-horse in the Nevsky, by its head, its face. It expressed the whole being of the horse. Looking at the horse's face I understood all that could be understood about a horse. All the traits of horse nature, all of which a horse is capable, all of which it is incapable, all that it can do, all that it cannot do; all this was expressed in the lines and features of the horse's face. A dog once gave me a similar sensation. At the same time the horse and the dog were not simply horse and dog; they were "atoms," conscious, moving "atoms" of great beings –"the great horse" and "the great dog." I understand then that we also are atoms of a great being, "the great man." Each thing is an atom of a "great thing." A glass is an atom of a "great glass." A fork is an atom of a "great fork." (1969, p.287)

Objects which appear as separate and distinct entities, within ordinary three dimensional space, might in higher dimensions be particles or atoms of underlying great beings or thought-forms. Plato held that the phenomenal world or the world of appearance was the outward expression of the underlying nomenal realm of "Ideas" or "Forms." All things might be atoms of great things, great beings—including humans.

Glimpses of higher intellectual functions suggest such experiences, ideas and possibilities. Humankind is a great being and individual men, women and children are all atoms of this larger humanity—particles of the whole:

> "All humanity is in spirit joined together, forming one body." (Mulford, In Crookall, 1969, p.24)

> "It bound us together in a deep unity of being. I lost all sense of personal identity ... We were no longer separate individuals." (Johnson, in Crookall, 1969, p.24)

> "The proclivities that separate man from man are on the surface, while the real human qualities that tend to unity are deeper and more enduring ... Deeper than all the forces and tendencies that would separate man from his fellows abides the true Inward (Eternal) Self of each; and there, in these silent depths of our personalities, we are one ... . (Jupp, in Crookall, 1969, p.25)

> "All minds may perhaps ultimately be unified at some common source, this forming the common spiritual 'Soul of humanity.' Thus: just as every tree of the forest is undoubtedly a separate living entity, yet their roots are planted in a common soil, unifying them in mother earth, so it is possible that humanity may be in some manner unified in some larger spiritual world, from which we draw our mental sustenance and from which we emerge as seemingly separate beings ... In this vaster Cosmic Mind, all knowledge, all wisdom, may be contained, and the individual human being has only to induce within himself, consciously or unconsciously, the proper mental attitude, in order to open the doors of his inner vision, and receive this influx of knowledge and power." (Carrington, in Crookall, 1969, p.74)

When attention is focussed on the surface features of life, the illusions of separateness arise. If we penetrate to deeper levels of reality, then one's unity with fellow humans can be realized with an expansion of consciousness, knowledge and feeling. This awareness can lead further to the experience of the unified Presence within which we live, move and have our being.

Ouspensky (1968) elaborates:

> From this standpoint every separate life is as it were the manifestation in our sphere of a part of one of the rational entities of another sphere. These rationalities look in upon us, as it were, in these lives which we see. When a man dies, *one eye of the Universe closes* ... Every separate human life is a moment of the life of some *great being*, which lives *in us*. The life of every separate tree is a moment of the life of a being, "species" or "family." The rationalities of these *higher* beings do not exist independently of these lower lives. ...

> To us, life and the psyche are different and separate from each other, because we are inept at seeing, inept at looking at things. And this in turn depends upon the fact that it is very difficult for us to step outside the frames of our *divisions*. We see the life of a tree, of *this tree*; and if we are told that the life of a tree is a manifestation of some psychic life, then we understand it in such a way that the life of *this tree* is the manifestation of the psychic life of *this tree*. But this is of course an absurdity resulting from "three-dimensional thinking" ... The life of this tree is a manifestation of the *psychic life of the species*, or family, or perhaps of the psychic life of the *entire vegetable kingdom*.
>
> In exactly the same way, our separate *lives* are manifestations of some great rational entity. (p.194)

Ouspensky provides an enigmatic view on the nature of things but it is not hard to imagine ourselves as I's, eyes or atoms of great beings. Accounts of mystical experiences capture the flavour of such unusual possibilities.

The idea of great beings leads to the concept of an animistic universe wherein all forms of life, both animate and inanimate, are part of larger intelligences and psyches. Imagine a world-soul, a being whose physical manifestation is the visible world. Alternatively, nature might be some great whole–the body of God:

> ... Nature is the living visible garment of God. - Goethe
>
> ... all are but parts of one stupendous Whole, Whose body nature is, and God the Soul. - Alexander Pope

The Platonic view is that a realm of higher ideas or forms underlies phenomenal manifestations. In this way, all entities have mental or spiritual dimensions underlying them and are ensouled by these underlying principles.

King (1963) discusses such dynamics in relationship to various cosmic forces and entities, particularly in reference to the Sun:

> From the viewpoint of Objective Consciousness we are told that the sun, imprimis, is a creature possessing consciousness, sentience and decision. It is a center and organizer of other very large creatures, the planets, the source of their energies which it radiates to them and the director of their complicated courses. ... the Egyptian priesthood understood the nature of so prominent a god as Re. He was not supposed, in Greekish fashion, to be "the god of the sun," but instead he was the Sun, as we should put it with a capital S.... This is a necessary consequence of the fact that the sun was taken as a being in its own right, a very different sort of being than a human one but nevertheless, like all the semi-independent parts of the universe, an entity possessing its own essential life, sentience and comparable psychic qualities. ... The sun then, was a creature and its attributes as a living being were ... very powerful and superior to those of such an entity as the moon. What has been said of Re will apply also and naturally to all the other entities of this cosmological character, and not only to them but likewise to all such smaller or larger creatures as may in similar fashion constitute semi-independent natural entities. ... But there is another class also

of such gods ... not cosmological formations ... but ... what nowadays we would more customarily designate as cosmic forces. (pp. 143-4)

This quotation is very interesting given the tale from Plato about humankind asleep finally being able to comprehend the light and to *"see the sun in its own proper place."* Esoteric thought regards the Sun as a living, conscious being, whose intelligence gives rise to organic life on earth through the mechanisms of the solar system and the inner cosmos of a human being. The Sun is a Great Being, a High Level of Spiritual Intelligence and Consciousness. Beelzebub talks also of the *Most Holy Sun Absolute*, as the Sun behind the Sun.

From the viewpoint of the scientists of new formation, the personification of cosmic entities and forces seem obviously absurd and is apt to be labelled as superstition, psychoses, primitive or childish animistic thinking. From the vantage point of automated consciousness, scientists imagine a dead universe. The sun, planets, earth, the moon, the seas and the winds, all cosmic forces and entities are regarded as non-conscious, non-sentient entities, dead matter controlled by the blind mechanical forces of nature. In contrast, a mystical view of the universe suggests that it is populated by higher intelligences and beings of various grades—Gods and demigods, angels and archangels, spiritual and divine forces and entities. Such ideas, the stuff of myth, symbol and folklore embody ancient wisdom— which maintains that all things live within deeper great beings.

Generally, we think that as science advances, there is less and less reason to explain the universe with reference to supernatural intelligence, spiritual or divine beings or God. Scientist Carl Sagan illustrates this attitude in arguing that as we know more and more about the laws of nature, then there is less and less reason to believe that any higher conscious, sentient life entities (like the Suns, angels or God) are necessary to account for natural phenomena. From the scientists' perspective, we can explain the opening of the morning glory flower in terms of the effects of the sun upon the hormones and metabolism of the plant, and there is no need to postulate God as micro-intervening in the phenomena of nature.[17]

Of course, if the sun is a conscious, sentient being and the flower an atom of great flower, part of mother nature and ultimately of God, then God would be micro-intervening within the life of the plant, the Sun and the human being. All things are alive and interrelated within higher more subtle dimensions of which most people are unaware.

The famous physicist Eddington once commented that the universe appears to be of a *"mind-stuff."* Similarly, scientist James Jeans argued that the universe looks more like a *"great thought"* than a great machine. If such ideas are considered seriously, then reports of higher states of consciousness and the claims of esoteric teaching take on a new relevance. The universe is indeed of a mind-stuff, the manifestation of higher orders of intelligence within lower orders of materialization. The nomenal world underlies the phenomenal world as the realm of ideas underlies the materialization of form. All entities are part of larger entities, atoms of great being or great thoughts, of spiritual and divine forces.

Science #4 certainly suggests unusual possibilities. Obviously, we think humans to be more conscious and intelligent than the Sun. They can think and make things, grow vegetables, fight and have negative emotions, construct arsenals of weapons for the process of reciprocal destruction, and so much more. The scientists of new formation think that only humans possess consciousness and

---

[17] The Within-Without from Zero Point series provides an extended critical analysis of Dr. Sagan's arguments and those of mechanistic scientists. Sagan writes: "As we learn more and more about the universe, there seems less and less for God to do." (1979)

intelligence, while the Sun is merely a dead material object. Of course, the sun gave rise to organic life on earth, organizes and maintains the solar system, and supplies the light and radiation for the processes of life and evolution; but, the scientists regard the Sun as doing all this in a blind and mechanical way. The significance of cosmic intelligence and sentient life forces has no meaning to the formatory mind in a waking sleep state. To man asleep, there is no appreciation of the interrelatedness of things, and this is just like a three dimensional being trying to apprehend phenomena of higher dimensions.

The usual perception of reality is dictated by the sensible nature of things, rather than through a direct apprehension of their inner nature. Experienced within a mystical state of consciousness, the sun, the moon, the planets, the forces of nature and objects of the material world, all embody consciousness, sentience and intelligence. Through noetic forms of knowledge and higher states of consciousness, one can directly experience the realms of higher intelligence and life forces, which are the foundation for outwardly perceived objects. Thus the experience of instinctually sensing the life and intelligence of the sun arises not from the datum of observation or scientific analysis, but rather, from an expanded state of consciousness which illuminates the deeper, inner structures of existence.

> Each entity, no matter how large or how small is alive and lives within the body of a greater being somewhere along the scale of evolution. (In Crookall, 1969)

To the mystically awakened, outwardly perceived objects are invested with intense significance as expressions of greater beings and ultimately expressions of the universe and the Most Holy Sun Absolute, or God. Ordinarily, humans know only the isolated atoms of great beings and have no idea of the inward dimensions of the cosmic mind stuffs.

5e. **Glimpses of Objective Consciousness**

Objective consciousness is the fourth state of consciousness which an individual might experience— while still maintaining individual identity. Whereas in the state of self-consciousness, an individual knows the truth about self, states of objective consciousness reveal the *"truth about the world."* Objective consciousness reveals the world as it is and things in themselves. This involves more penetrating, expansive and objective states than that of self-consciousness and the direct apprehension of realms of nature, spirit and the cosmos. This state involves connection with the higher intellectual center and the development of the third body—the mental or spiritual body. Vaysse (1979) explains that objective consciousness *"... includes a state of universal presence, objective Knowledge, and a feeling of universal being—and the powers for their manifestation, a level of consciousness, attention and creative will—of which the ordinary man can have no conception."* (p.65)

Once again, there are varying degrees of objective consciousness which might also be of a more or less abnormal nature. Accounts of such states are certainly not widespread but are depicted within literature and autobiographies, as well as depicted in symbolic forms in esoteric teaching, poetry and the arts. It is important to distinguish between abnormal glimpses of objective consciousness and the truer forms of such states as might be attained by a higher type of human, number six or seven. Accounts of spontaneous experiences are glimpses of the elevated realms available to consciousness. The individual experiences vastly expanded states of knowing together, insight and illumination.

Gurdjieff states that the most central idea of objective knowledge is the direct experience of the unity of everything—of life and creation. Normally, humans perceive only the fragmentation of life and reality, the bits and pieces, and not the realms of existence which underlie and sustain outward appearances. Although the idea of such a unity can exist within the ordinary intellectual mind, the awareness or direct experience of this unity can only be attained in states of objective consciousness. It is then revealed that the manifold forms of life all express the One and that all things are created from within/without through a hierarchy of planes of being within one living source. These are ancient ideas central to religious and metaphysical perspectives.

> Suddenly I knew somehow they were true, that Brahman ... was all about me, and through me, and in me. The knowledge did not come from without, unmistakably it came from within. ... The trees, meadows and hedges were all part of me, and I of them, and all were in a great unity which was God. Everything was a whole. I knew with complete, unshakable conviction that I had been in touch with reality. (Crookall, 1969)

> It was as though a spiritual vision communicated itself to me, a feeling of extension and conscious connection with all things–union with the All–of omni-identity, if the word may be passed. (Crookall, 1969)

> ... he looked at a piece of quartz ... and suddenly an intense illumination engulfed him. He saw millions of little stars with rainbow rings streaming from them in place of the piece of quartz, and he felt his consciousness enter into every particle belonging to an infinite whole, while his being was buoyant with intense delight, for he knew that he had looked into God. And then, in a flash, it was gone.

These descriptions all refer to the presence of God or Universal Spirit–an underlying source of intelligence and creation, which gives rise to the manifold of appearances and which interpenetrates and sustains all things.

Ordinary objects or scenes can be experienced within a nomenal mode, with consciousness interpenetrating the objects perceived. Mystical states involve a clarity seldom experienced and the apprehension of life as elements of some far deeper underlying unity. This unity is not simply known intellectually but is instead directly apprehended. A description by the physicist F. Capra (1975) illustrates these differences:

> Five years ago, I had a beautiful experience which set me on a road that has led to the writing of this book (*The Tao of Physics*). I was sitting by the ocean one late summer afternoon, watching the waves rolling in and feeling the rhythm of my breathing, when I suddenly became aware of my whole environment as being engaged in a gigantic cosmic dance. Being a physicist, I knew that the sand, rocks, water and air around me were made of vibrating molecules and atoms, and that these consisted of particles which interacted with one another by creating and destroying other particles. I knew also that the Earth's atmosphere was continually bombarded by showers of 'cosmic ray,' particles of high energy undergoing multiple collisions as they penetrated the air. All this was familiar to me from my research in high-energy physics, but until that moment I had only experienced it through graphs, diagrams and mathematical theories. As I sat on that beach my former experiences came to life; I 'saw' cascades

of energy coming down from outer space, in which particles were created and destroyed in rhythmic pulses; I 'saw' the atoms of the elements and those of my body participating in this cosmic dance of energy; I felt its rhythm and I 'heard' its sound, and at that moment I knew that this was the Dance of Shiva, the Lord of Dancers worshiped by the Hindus. (p.9)

Capra directly experienced the cosmic phenomena which he had ordinarily known only intellectually through his studies of science. In these moments of illumination and higher intellectual functioning, he directly experienced these cosmic rhythms and processes.

A similar experience is recalled by Ouspensky which occurred during his travels aboard a ship when his consciousness merged on a deeper level with the surrounding environment:

"The waves were drawing my soul to themselves. Suddenly I felt it going to them. It was only a moment, maybe less than a moment. But I entered the waves and, with them, with a roar, attacked the ship. And at that moment I became all. The waves–they were myself. The clouds, hurrying from the north, the rain–were myself. The violet mountains in the distance–they were myself. The wind–it was myself. The clouds, hurrying from the north, the rain–were myself. The huge ship, rolling indomitably forward–was myself. I felt that huge iron body is my body, all its movements, waverings, rollings and shudderings, the fire, the pressure of steam, the engine–all this was inside me." (Patterson, 1998, p. 10)

In the year 1899, Dr. Richard Bucke had glimpses of higher consciousness, which lead to his investigation of mystical states and the writing of *Cosmic Consciousness* (1972). Bucke recalls his experience while speaking in the third person:

All at once, without warning of any kind, he found himself wrapped around as it were by a flame coloured cloud. For an instant he thought of fire ... the next he knew that the light was within himself. Directly afterwards came upon him a sense of exultation, of immense joyousness accompanied or immediately followed by an intellectual illumination quite impossible to describe. Into his brain streamed one momentary lighting-flash of the Brahmic Splendor which has ever since lightened his life; upon his heart fell one drop of Brahmic Bliss, leaving thenceforward for always an after taste of heaven. Among other things he did not come to believe, he saw and knew that the Cosmos is not dead matter but a living Presence, that the soul of man is immortal, that the universe is so built and ordered that without any preadventure all things work together for the good of each and all, that the foundation principle of the world is what we call love ... He claims that he learned more within the few seconds during which the illumination lasted than in previous months or even years of study, and that he learned much that no study could ever have taught. (pp. 8-9)

Bucke experienced an illumination of the mind and an awakening of the heart, gaining deep and varied insights into the nature of things. He realized that the Cosmos is a living Presence, that Love is an element of the universe and that the soul principle is immortal. Bucke was filled with feelings of wonder and awe and grasped the basic idea of objective knowledge–the unity of life.

Higher intellectual functions allow the individual to know things in a far more penetrating and dynamic way, apprehending the inner nature and workings:

"I need a kind of understanding ... when, instead of standing outside the things I am
knowing, I become the thing itself and so can know it fully. ... It is as though the Ego,
which is a universal substance, has the capacity to become one with the Universe; not
to know about it, as though the knower and known were two things, but to be loosed
from the individual and set free into the universal mode of experiencing. ... whenever
consciousness can be lifted to this degree of being it opens out on the Universe and
makes you one with whatever is, for the moment, within your power to apprehend. ...
the reality is enacted as though it is within the self, and not without it. ... it is a setting
free of the Ego into its own proper sphere of the universal spirit (from which it has,
apparently, been 'exiled' by partial immersion in the physical body.)"
(E.K., in Crookall, 1969, p.69)

Human consciousness can be set free into universal modes of being and divine mind. Instead of
simply being an attribute of an organic form, consciousness can interpenetrate objects or realms
of existence, knowing things inwardly within higher hydrogen levels, within both spiritual and divine
dimensions. Consciousness can be maintained within realms of universal mind or cosmic intelligence
and dimensions of subtle being:

"In all mystical experiences the sense of separateness, of individuality, is to a great
degree lost. In the state of illumination, that which is known seems to merge with the
knower, so that there is an intimate unity between them. In the profounder mystical
experiences this results in a sense of unity with the All."
(Johnson, In Crookall, 1969, pp.51-2)

"If you inhibit thoughts and persevere, you come at length to a region of consciousness
behind (or within) thought, and different from ordinary thought in its character–a
consciousness of quasi-universal quality, and a realization of an altogether vaster
Self than that to which you are accustomed ... It is to die in the ordinary sense, but
in another sense it is to wake up and find that the 'I,' one's most real and intimate
Self, pervades the Universe and all other beings–that the mountains and the sea and
the stars are parts of one's body and that one's Soul is in touch with the souls of all
creatures. ... I regard the discovery of this experience ... as the most fundamental and
important fact hitherto of human knowledge." (Carpenter, in Crookall, 1969, p.43)

"There is one mind common to all individual men. Every man is an inlet to the same
and to all of the same. He that is once admitted to the right of reason is made a
freeman of the whole estate. What Plato has thought, he may think; what a saint has
felt, he may feel; what at any time has befallen any man, he can understand. Who
hath access to this Universal Mind is a party to all that is or can be done ..." (Emerson,
Essays, in Crookall, p.32)

Deeper levels within self exist within the larger universe, the Common Father or supersoul.
Consciousness within the inner dimensions of the individual can bring about awareness of the unified
nature of self and cosmos. Such experiences involve an awareness of God, or a supreme intelligence
or Presence, within which humans live and move and have their being.

In a paper on experimental mysticism, Ouspensky depicts another form taken within glimpses of
objective consciousness. Ouspensky first describes passing a threshold into experiences of the astral

realms and then passing a second threshold into experiences of the mental world:

> I passed the second threshold ... beyond which a new world began. ... I then found myself in the world of mathematical relations, in which there was nothing at all resembling what occurs in life. ... Everything moved, changed, was transformed and became something else. Sometimes I suddenly saw all mathematical relations disappear one after another into infinity. Infinity swallowed everything, filled everything, all distinctions were effaced. And I felt that one moment more and I myself should disappear into infinity. ... Infinity was not infinite continuation in one direction, but infinite variation at one point. ...

> A characteristic feature of the world in which I found myself was ... its mathematical structure and the complete absence of anything that could be expressed in the language of ordinary concepts. ... I was in the mental world ... but ... only this world "Arupa" really existed. All the rest was the creation of imagination. The real world was a "world without forms."... "mathematical relations" were continually changing round me and within me, sometimes taking the form of sounds, of music, of sometimes the form of a design, sometimes the form of light filling the whole of space, of a kind of visible vibration of light rays, crossing, interweaving with one another, pervading everything. ...

> The number "three" played a very important part in the world in which I found myself. In a way quite incomprehensible to our mathematics it entered into all the relations of magnitude, created them and originated from them. All taken together, that is, the entire universe, sometimes appeared in the form of a "triad," composing one whole, and looking like some great trefoil. Each part of the "triad," by some inner process, was again transformed into a "triad," and the process continued until all was filled with "triads," which were transformed into music, or light, or designs. ... it is absolutely impossible to describe what happened ... there was nothing separate ... All things were connected with one another, and not accidentally, but by incomprehensible chains of causes and effects. ... Everything was living ... . (1969, pp. 285-7)

Ouspensky's glimpses of objective consciousness are of the mental formless realms which underlie, generate and sustain all things. He directly experienced the reality suggested by the law of three and the dynamic mathematical principles underlying and generating manifest phenomena. Infinity was realized not as infinite extension in outward space, but as infinite variability *at a point*.

The mystics and saints of all ages claim that the self, the microcosm, embodies the macrocosm. As a microcosm of the macrocosm, the individual self is intimately related to the larger world and universe. In this way, one might know thy Self, the universe and the Gods. Various Upanishads suggest this possibility:

> As large as the universe outside, even so large is the universe within the lotus of the heart. Within it are heaven and earth, the sun, the moon, the lightening, and all the stars. What is in the macrocosm is in this microcosm ... All things that exist ... are in the city of Brahman. Chandogya Upanishad

Mysticism involves realizing the presence of the living God within Self and in nature; as all are manifestations of one intelligent, living and conscious whole. It is only humans who are asleep to the life and presence of the deeper spiritual and divine realities. Mysticism is the attempt to realize the immanence of the eternal within the temporal, the higher intelligences and life forces, the void and plenum, which underlie and sustain the manifest world. This supreme adventure and ultimate science requires the individual attain to the levels of the spiritual and divine bodies.

In the *Tales*, Beelzebub describes a particular apparatus to his grandson Hassein, which allows for experiences of objective consciousness, and for those involved to:

> "... become again a particle of all that exists ... (and) eyewitnesses of certain of these World-laws, which for ordinary uninitiated three-centered beings are what they call "great-inscrutable-mysteries-of-nature" ..." (1950, p. 162)

In life, individuals sometimes have glimpses into the deeper realities which create and inform life, and realize themselves as particles of all that exists. Gurdjieff maintains that the higher types of humans with crystallized higher being-bodies can attain varied gradients of Divine Reason and function within the subtle dimensions of the Cosmos. Of course, such are only possibilities and dependent upon the possibility of a human's evolution and the crystallization of the higher being-bodies for the life of the soul.

The realm of objective consciousness is accessible to humans number six and seven. In a human number six, the faculties of will and perception within such states are more limited and inconsistent. Glimpses into what life might be like within such levels of objective consciousness are provided by a Mr. Gold (1978), in a book entitled *"Secret Talks with Mr. G.:"*

> "It later became possible for me to influence the forms of the world in a real way and to call upon some beings which I now understand to be spiritualized and crystallized higher beings of certain individuals who have completed themselves to the level of the solar system. I also mastered all sorts of odd skills usually thought of as occult, such as time and space travel in the sense of visiting through images—on many levels of being from the first throes of suffering of the primordial being to the reading of true history of the planet earth as well as many non-terrestrial histories, simultaneous tuning to objective thoughts proceeding through space and time, popularly called telepathy, making thought-forms, reading auras and other such phenomenal results of proceedings in higher cosmoses which appear unusual to ordinary senses and understanding." (p. 6)

> I found that I could at will see either the astral, causal or material reality as real, automatically adjusting the other two realities to inventions of higher thoughts. ... I perceived directly now that everything in the universe was directly connected, and that moreover these forms were all connected just because they were all one and the same, repeated to provide the illusion of complexity.

> I knew during these times objectively without a single doubt that these experiences were real, and that the usual reality in which I lived from day to day was false. I resolved to remember myself, and to know always and in every situation, that compared to that reality, ordinary reality is a dream. (pp. 12-3)

If this is indeed the case, that it is possible for a human being to experience and function in this way within the subtle dimensions of life, then indeed humankind is asleep to the deep levels of nature, Self and the Cosmos.[18]

---

[18] In the Within-Without from Zero Point series, Dr. Holmes provides more extended discussions of mystical states, levels of Samadhi and enlightenment, and cosmic consciousness.

6. Objective Knowledge:
Myths and Symbols of the Mysteries

Gurdjieff refers to people's usual knowledge of life as subjective. It is acquired through the accidental external influences of upbringing, education, culture, lies and formatory thinking. It is based on ordinary methods of observation and the limitations imposed by the state of waking sleep and the lack of true self knowledge. Scientific knowledge is centered primarily within the intellectual mind, little bits of scientific fact, fantasy and philosophy, about all the little parts of humans, life and the world. Meanwhile, we trip absentmindedly over a stool or are under the thumb of the mother-in-law, or involved in big business for plenty of bucks, or sitting on the divan after satisfying the itching of the stomach. Subjective knowledge has no existence in objective reality but is simply part of humans' misunderstanding–imaginary ideas and psychological illusions. It is always incomplete, distorted or imaginary--studing only the fingers of a human being taken out of relationship to the whole of life.

In *Beelzebub's Tales*, Gurdjieff depicts humans as having the potential to *"instinctual sense reality,"* *"instinctual sense cosmic truths"* and to attain different degrees of *"Divine Reason."* Whereas subjective knowledge is centered within one of the three moving-instinctual, emotional or intellectual being-brains, objective knowledge requires the experiencing of the higher centers in the corresponding states of consciousness. This is linked to the crystallization of the higher being-bodies as vehicles for the life of the soul and the attaining of real I—as Gurdjieff suggests by his last book title *Life is Real only Then, When I AM.* Objective knowledge requires the evolution of the human faculties of knowledge and being and the awakening of consciousness. Of course, the intellectual mind can have intellectual knowledge of higher knowledge, but it is only the immediate experiencing of such that is intended by the phrase objective knowledge.

Ouspensky recalls other meanings ascribed by Gurdjieff to the term objective knowledge. These included:

> Knowledge based upon ancient methods and principles of observation, knowledge of things in themselves, knowledge accompanying "an objective state of consciousness," knowledge of the All ... (1949, p. 278)

Ouspensky recalls Gurdjieff's comments verbatim:

> "One of the most central of the ideas of objective knowledge," said G., "is the idea of the unity of everything, of unity in diversity. ... But objective knowledge, the idea of unity included, belongs to objective consciousness. ... With objective consciousness it is possible to see and feel the unity of everything.

> "But for subjective consciousness the world is split up into millions of separate and unconnected phenomena. Attempts to connect these phenomena into some sort of system in a scientific or a philosophical way lead to nothing because man cannot reconstruct the idea of the whole starting from separate facts and they cannot divine the principles of the division of the whole without knowing the laws upon which this division is based. ...

"Realizing the imperfection and weakness of ordinary language the people who have possessed objective knowledge have tried to express the idea of unity in 'myths,' in 'symbols,' and in particular 'verbal formulas' which, having been transmitted without alteration, have carried on the idea from one school to another, often from one epoch to another. ... The aim of 'myths' and 'symbols' was to reach man's higher centers, to transmit to him ideas inaccessible to the intellect and to transmit them in such forms as would exclude the possibility of false interpretations. 'Myths' are destined for the higher emotional center; 'symbols' for the higher thinking center. ... It is always possible to understand anything but only with the appropriate center. But the preparation for receiving ideas belonging to objective knowledge has to proceed by way of the mind ... The symbols that were used to transmit ideas belonging to objective knowledge included diagrams of the fundamental laws of the universe ...." (1949, pp.278-80)

The foremost principle of objective knowledge is the "unity of everything." Secondly, objective knowledge attempts to convey an understanding of how the diversity of life is created and sustained by the unity. Verbal formula, myths, symbols and diagrams of the fundamental laws of the universe depict objective knowledge concerning how the many are generated from the One. Through the cultivation and quickening of the centers, the individual can penetrate more and more deeply the hidden meanings of such formula, myths, symbols and diagrams.

Know thyself is one verbal formula of objective knowledge; so also is the phrase "As above, so below;" and the idea that a human being is a microcosm of the macrocosm. The Law of Three and the Law of the Octave are other verbal formulas, which if properly understood would help one penetrate the world of the miraculous, awakening the faculties of the higher intellectual center. The myths of the *Ladder of Jacob*, Noah's arc, and the Tower of Babel similarly convey ancient secrets. However, the true meanings of these myths, symbols and diagrams can only be grasped with the attaining of higher consciousness, as the false consciousness system will simply obscure the inner meanings.

The study of number symbols, particularly the primary numbers such as One, Three and Seven, is particularly important within the fourth way teaching. The ancient meanings of these primary numbers have to do with understanding the deep generative realms of creation, and how everything emerged out of the nothingness, 0, is unified as a one, 1, with a triune nature of 3, and existing within a sevenfold process 7, completed in the eighth 8, as an octave. The three and seven together add to a ten, 10. The laws of three and seven are the laws by which form is generated out of formlessness, the multiplicity out of the 1 and the 0. Philosophers talk of God as a geometrician and these ancient principles articulate the principles of this inner geometry of being.

Scientists have no comparable idea of how to systematically enumerate the parts of things. Generally, psychology is governed by dualistic thinking and this *"self-element"* is not even realized. If one usually thinks in twos, it requires study and realizations to begin to understand the deep mysteries and objective knowledge embodied in the occult significance of numbers. As G. explains: *"they cannot divine the principles of the division of the whole without knowing the laws upon which this division is based ...."* (Ouspensky, 1949)

The simplest sequence of symbols depicts the levels of evolution of a human being. Gurdjieff begins by representing a human in waking sleep as dual in nature, signified by the two lines:

"Man, in the normal state natural to him, is taken as a duality. He consists entirely of dualities or 'pairs of opposites.' All man's sensations, impressions, feelings, thoughts, are divided into positive and negative, useful and harmful, necessary and unnecessary, good and bad, pleasant and unpleasant. ... This is the duality in which proceeds all the perceptions, all the reactions, the whole life of man." (1949, p. 281)

Mechanical life is controlled by the dualities of human existence, and humanity asleep does not realize the third force or principle in all things. This is the psychology of the mind and behaviour, which has no substantive consciousness, heart, soul or spirit. Formatory thinking is dualistic and mechanical man is lived out by the pains and pleasures of the body, the rights and wrongs of the mind, all between life and death.

Gurdjieff explains that the *"struggle for the realization of consciousness in life"* can lead to the *"Creation of a permanent third principle (which) is for man the transformation of the duality into the trinity."* (p. 282) The trinity is portrayed by the triangle which represents the trinity of creation, of three-brained beings and the triune nature of all things. The triangle depicts the three fold nature of humans' mental, emotional and physical functions. In this case, the emotional center is taken as the neutralizing principle in relationship to the body and mind, enabling transformation to come about to the level of a human number four. The square can represent the four elements of fire, air, water and earth, and the corresponding elements in a human of spirit, mind, emotions and the physical body. In reference to the possible evolution of a human being, this is the *"transformation of the trinity into quaternity,"* and the making of a human number four.

Gurdjieff then relates the pentagram to the human number five, who has harmonized and perfected the five lower centers:

"... if a man brings the work of the five centers within him into harmonious accord, he then 'locks the pentagram within him' and becomes a finished type of the physically perfect man. The full and proper functioning of five centers brings them into union with the higher centers which introduce the missing principle and put man into direct and permanent connection with objective consciousness and objective knowledge.

The six pointed star suggests an even higher type of attainment after that of the pentagram. G. explains:

"And then man becomes the six-pointed star, that is, by becoming locked within a circle of life independent and complete in itself, he becomes isolated from foreign influences or accidental shocks; he embodies in himself the Seal of Solomon.(1949, pp. 282)

The six pointed star, the *Seal of Solomon* or *Star of David*, has deep inner meaning in terms of the completion of life. The figure embodies firstly the triune nature of things, both above and below. The downward turned triangle represents a human's mental, emotional and physical nature embodied in the material world. The upward turned triangle could be taken to represent the astral, mental and causal bodies, or planes of being. The union of the two in perfect symmetry indicates the attainment of the higher being-bodies and permanent self perfection. In terms of creation physics, the *Seal of Solomon* suggests the manner in which all metaphysical and physical laws embody the law of three, above and below, on earth as it is in heaven.

If this sequence is taken to the seventh position, a point might be established within the center of the *Star of David*. This point represents the particle of Divinity, an emanation, which is the ultimate I, embodied below.

The Laws of Three and Seven are profound teachings of the esoteric traditions—verbal formula which have numeric and geometric counterparts. These are the primary principles by which the One generates, sustains and ultimately dissolves the multiplicity of life and creation, the dogs and the cats, the suns and moons, the atoms and quanta. These principles pervade all things in the geometry of form generation from realms of formlessness which underlie all things, as an undifferentiated and perfect unity. The meaning of numbers and *"diagrams of the fundamental laws of the universe"* are profound mystery teachings, which can only be realized in higher states with the awakening to higher centers. Even though such teachings can be found throughout religious doctrines, their inner meanings have been lost.

The law of the octave can be used to depict all involutionary and evolutionary processes within a human being or within nature. According to Gurdjieff, this is another teaching of Objective Science:

> "... the harmonious development of man can be examined from the point of view of the law of octaves. ... every completed process is a transition of the note do through a series of successive tones to the do of the next octave. The seven fundamental tones of the octave express the law of seven. The addition to it of the do of the next octave, that is to say, the crowning of the process, gives the eighth step. The seven fundamental tones together with the two 'intervals' and 'additional shocks' give nine steps. By incorporating in it the do of the next octave we have ten steps. The last, the tenth, step is the end of the preceding and the beginning of the next cycle. In this way, the law of octaves and the process of development it expresses, include the numbers 1 to 10. ... The symbolism of numbers cannot be understood without the law of octaves or without a clear conception of how octaves are expressed in the decimal system and vice versa. ... the key to this unity ... resolves all diversity into the fundamental laws which govern it and which are expressed in the numbers 1 to 10." (1949, p. 282-3)

The key to objective knowledge is the experience of unity within the multiplicity. The study of mystical myths, symbols and numbers can help to cultivate an understanding of the fundamental laws which govern the generation of diversity from the One.

7. The Enneagram

"The enneagram is the fundamental hieroglyph of a universal language which has as many different meanings as there are levels of men. ... The enneagram is a schematic diagram of *perpetual motion*, that is, of a machine of eternal movement. But of course it is necessary to know how to read this diagram. The understanding of this symbol and the ability to make use of it give man very great power. It is ... also the *philosopher's stone* of the alchemists." (Gurdjieff, in Ouspensky, 1949, p. 294)

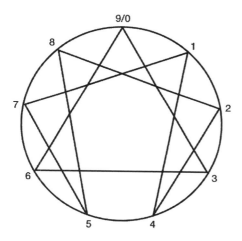

The enneagram is the primary symbol associated with the Gurdjieff teaching. This symbol depicts the laws of three and seven and their interaction in producing any whole. The whole is represented by the circle. Pythagoras suggested: *"The octave formed a circle and gave our noble earth its form."*

The enneagram is a nine pointed figure with three points as part of an equilateral triangle and a six sided interior figure. The triangle depicts the three fold nature of all things, with its points at the numbers 3, 6 and 9, all multiples of three. Six additional points are parts of the second figure connecting the outer points through an internal movement or circulation of energies. These six point have an astonishing quality in that the sequence of these numbers and the inner flow of energies within the enneagram is given by the division of the number one by the number seven: $1/7 = .142857142857....$ This division produces a repeating, non-terminating number which repeats infinitely this sequence of six numbers—142857. Deep inner meanings and teachings are contained within this symbol of objective knowledge.

The enneagram can be used to depict both involutionary and evolutionary octaves, according to how one proceeds around the circle. The notes of the octave and two shock points are represented on the rim of the circle, giving 9 points. The top do is also the bottom do and the symbol as a whole represents a completed octave.

Creation events are an involutionary octave, as from a Unified Absolute, we descend into increasingly dense modes of material creation. In an involutionary octave, the movement is from the top Do of the

---

[19] Actually, it is quite arbitrary how one moves around the circle, as we simply flip the enneagram to reverse the directions of the involving or evolving octaves. Also, we should note that if we take an enneagram to illustrate a completed cosmos, the shock points will be at two of the points of the equilateral triangle, because three octaves are really involved in any one completed octave. If we artificially isolate one octave, we can portray the shock points as in the present diagram but this is somewhat misleading. There are deeper secrets hidden in this issue of where the shock points would be placed in taking the enneagram as representing one octave or a completed process involving three octaves.

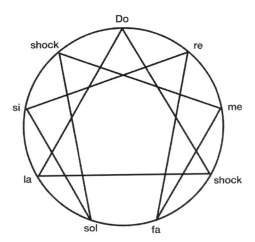

enneagram to the left through the shock point, filled by the Will of the Absolute, to the note Si and around to Do.[19] The Ray of Creation passes between All and Nothing, from the Absolute to the Nothingness, and is depicted by the enneagram— this *"diagram of perpetual motion."*

There are deep mathematical and cosmological secrets within the enneagram which are impossible to simply unravel. It can be related to numbers, to planets, to the anatomy of a human being, to the world of the psyche, to the transformation of the being foods into the higher hydrogens for the higher being-bodies, or to any process embodying the laws of three and seven.

The evolution of a human being can be depicted using the enneagram. In this case, the octave begins from do, representing man number 1, passing to the right on the enneagram to re, man number two, to man number three at mi. At this point, the evolution of the individual comes to a standstill and progresses no further. A "shock" from outside of the system is required to enable the development of the human to the levels of number 4, 5, 6, and 7–passing to fa, sol, la and si. Lastly, in the evolutionary octave, there is a missing semi-tone in the si-do interval. The eighth step is completed in the top do and the dissolution of individual consciousness into the Absolute. Gurdjieff describes Christ as *"a man number eight."* This is the great gap between the level of the Absolute and the individual particles. To breach this shock point means the dissolution of the individualized presence into the Most Holy Sun Absolute.

All processes develop through octaves, with intervals and shocks, with a threefold nature, all within the One. Of course, it is particularly important to study the psychology of a human's possible evolution from this perspective. Mr. G. explains: *"Each completed whole, each cosmos, each organism, each plant, is an enneagram ...."* (1949, p. 293) However, only *completed wholes* have established the *"inner triangle"* and humans as they are, are far from complete. The enneagram is a mystical symbol–a key to the enigmas of creation.[20]

Historically, the search for a means of perpetual motion has been an activity of those at the fringes of science. In modern times, alternative researchers primarily explore what is called the "zero point energy," trying to tap the hidden forces latent within quantum vacuum states and within Space itself. G.'s enneagram depicts the forces latent within Space, which create, maintain and dissolve cosmic phenomena. The Ray of Creation passes from the Absolute to the Nothingness and the Laws of Three and Seven depict the manner in which these processes occur. In this way, the enneagram is a diagram of the perpetual motion latent within the inward dimensions of being.

---

[20] G. also suggested that certain plants having psychotropic effects embody the enneagram with an inner triangle.

[21] [1] In explaining the enneagram, G. comments on the origins of the fourth way and its ancient mystical symbol: "The teaching whose theory is here being set out is completely self-supporting and independent of other lines and it has been completely unknown up to the present time. Like other lines it makes use of the symbolical method and one of its principle symbols is ... the circle divided into nine parts." (1949, p. 286)

[2] Enneagram constructed by Christopher Holmes on the West coast of Vancouver Island and photographed by Miss K, August 2004.

The enneagram is a deep moving image of the dimensions of creation and the passage of laws from one level to another through the processes of involution and evolution.[21] Particularly important areas of study for the enneagram are in terms of the evolution of man, the nature of the alchemical factory, and understanding the Ray of Creation and the hydrogen diagrams. The enneagram is a symbol of the mysteries embodying objective knowledge, although this can only be understood in the corresponding states of higher consciousness. Gurdjieff claims: *"A man may be quite alone in the desert and he can trace the enneagram in the sand and in it read the eternal laws of the universe."* (1949, p.294) Of course, we have to know how to read this ancient symbol and to meditate upon it in order to trans-substantiate its inner meanings in our being.

"... through each of them the
cosmic substances arising
in all seven Stopinders of the
Sacred Heptaparaparshinokh
could be transformed, and
all of them ... besides serving
as apparatuses for the Most
Great Trogoautoegocrat,
could have all possibilities
for absorbing from those
cosmic substances which
are transformed through
them what is corresponding
for the coating and for the
perfecting in each of them
of both higher-being bodies;
because each three-brained

being arisen on this planet of yours represents in himself also, in all respects ... an exact similarity of the whole Megalocosmos."

G. I. Gurdjieff, *Beelzebub's Tales to His Grandson*

Gurdjieff

VII /
The ray of creation
& the Alchemy of Soul

1. The Ladder of Jacob

"Man is an image of the world. He was created by the same laws which created the whole of the world. By knowing and understanding himself he will know and understand the whole world, all the laws that create and govern the world." (Gurdjieff, in Ouspensky, 1949, p. 75)

The microcosm of the individual embodies the same laws and dimensions as embodied within the macrocosm. The inner cosmos of consciousness thus corresponds to the structuring of world orders and dimensions within the larger universe. The hidden dimensions of the microcosm and the macrocosm allow for existence after death, the many phenomena of psychic science, cosmic experiences, higher states of consciousness and ultimately, attaining real I and being a particle of the whole.

G. I. Gurdjieff's metaphysical explanations concerning the origins of the Cosmos and the fundamental cosmic laws comprise a fascinating and provocative alternative to the orthodox materialist viewpoints of modern science. Of particular importance in Gurdjieff's cosmological scheme is the *Ray of Creation*, the hierarchy of successive world orders created and maintained by the fundamental cosmic laws of three and seven. These basic esoteric principles are found throughout the mystical and religious literature of humanity and they provide a way of understanding which is more sophisticated and subtle than anything provided within modern thought, science or philosophy based on a materialist perspective.

M. Reyner, a Gurdjieff student, describes the *Ray of Creation* most simply and eloquently:

Real knowledge ... affirms that the Universe is a living being embodying a succession of levels devolving from a Supreme Intelligence. These succeeding levels form a kind of ladder down which energy is transmitted from the Source, and is returned in modified form in a subsequent ascent.

This is an idea which is implicit in the very word "universe," which means, literally, turning to unity: and is found in many ancient teachings, notably in the legend of Jacob's ladder. ... Jacob dreamed of *"a ladder set up on the earth and the top of it reaches to heaven; and behold the angels of the Lord stood above it."* (Genesis, 28, 12) The rungs of the ladder represent different levels, which while separate and distinct, permit the transference of energies in both directions. ...

The Universe is not some gigantic accident, but a living creation, which is, at all levels, a manifestation of the Deity.

... The unmanifest world is the cause of the happenings in the phenomenal world, and one can apprehend the concept of a succession of intelligences of decreasing order in which every level is responsible for the creation of more detailed behavior of the level beneath.

According to this formulation, the Universe is an ordered structure of world-orders created by the operation of two fundamental principles–the Law of Three and the Law of Seven. (1974, pp. 39-40)

"The Universe is a living being embodying a succession of levels devolving from a Supreme Intelligence." In this view, the laws of nature are the manifestation of higher intelligence and ultimately of the Most Most Holy Sun Absolute. These influences descend holographically through different world orders which interpenetrate and sustain one another. The manifest physical world is simply the outermost expression of underlying dimensions and causative forces. Life did not arise by accident in a universe governed by unconscious and random forces, but is instead the manifestation of higher intelligences emerging within/without from higher dimensions. Life comes from above rather than from below; or from within instead of from without.

The Law of Three and the Law of Seven are fundamental principles which underlie creation, the generation of world orders and all processes of a physical and metaphysical nature. These archaic esoteric principles are found throughout mystical, occult and spiritual literature–articulated by Gurdjieff, Ouspensky and their students, as well as in the Vedic teachings of India, Kabbalah, Madame Blavatsky's Theosophy, mystical Christianity and elsewhere. These deceptively simple laws offer a profound metaphysical teaching.

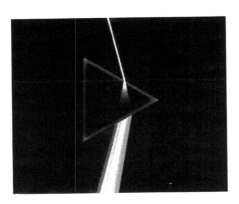

Maurice Nicoll, a student of Gurdjieff and Ouspensky, comments: *"God is ... first One and then Three and then Seven."* (1975, p. 1386) This illustrates the arcane principle of how the Absolute, the 1, manifests a trinity of forces, the 3, and then a seven fold hierarchy of world orders, the 7. This image is illustrated by the division of white light by a three sided prism to produce a spectrum of seven colors: 1-3-7.

Ordinarily, the scientists of new formation and humankind asleep approach existence in terms of dichotomies. The natural sciences deal with the transformations of matter and energy within time and space; while psychology deals with the mind and the body, conscious and unconscious, between life and death. In contrast, mystical schools maintain the triune and sevenfold nature of all things. These Sacred Cosmic Laws, which Beelzebub refers to as *Triamazikamno* and *Heptaparaparshinokh*, depict the manner in which the original Unity of the Most Holy Sun Absolute is transformed and differentiated into a plurality. These principles apply to the movement of inner forces and the crystallization of matter/energy/intelligence within different subtle dimensions of the Cosmos. These laws permeate ourselves and everything which happens in life and in the Cosmos. These principles can be studied within the inner world of consciousness and psychology, and in the outer world, both of which exist in relationship to a third unseen, metaphysical world. These laws are pervasive everywhere, in all phenomena of nature and in all spheres of knowledge.[22]

Law of Three

The Law of Three states that every phenomenon, on whatever scale and in whatever world it may take place, from molecule to cosmic phenomena, is the result of the combination of three different and opposing forces. Contemporary thought realizes the existence of two forces but is *third force blind*. Two forces can never produce a phenomenon and require a third force, which is not directly visible but is *latent within the medium* within which the interaction occurs.

Gurdjieff states:

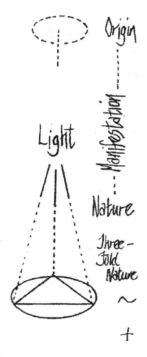

"The teaching of the three forces is at the root of all ancient systems. The first force may be called active or positive; the second, passive or negative; the third, neutralizing. But these are *merely names*, for in reality all three forces are equally active and appear as active, passive, and neutralizing, only at their meeting points, that is to say, *only in relation to one another at a given moment*. The first two forces are more or less comprehensible to man and the third may sometimes be discovered either at the point of application of the forces, or in the 'medium,' or in the 'result.' But, speaking in general, the third force is not easily accessible to direct observation and understanding. The reason for this is to be found in the fundamental limitations of man's ordinary psychological activity.... People cannot perceive and observe the third force directly any more than they can spatially perceive the 'fourth dimension.' ... people cannot observe phenomena as manifestations of three forces because we cannot observe the objective world in our subjective states of consciousness. ... If we could see the manifestation of three forces in every action, we should then see the world as it is (things in themselves). ... The third force is a property of the real world."
(Ouspensky, 1949, pp. 77-8)

The third force is latent within the medium within which the opposing forces operate, acting as the neutralizing or reconciling force which mediates and reconciles the interaction of opposing forces. The third force is latent within the hidden dimensions of space/time. Occult teachings maintain that all things embody such a trinity of forces, which enter into endless combinations and permutations on different planes of creation.

---

[22] It is impossible to fully elaborate the profound metaphysical teachings of Gurdjieff within this work. "The Slugs" focuses on Beelzebub's Tales and its more esoteric side, and explores Beelzebub's metaphysics and cosmology in more detail. Also, the Within/Without from Zero Point series explores relationships existing between the ancient wisdom teachings and the theories of modern physics, astrophysics and cosmology. At this point, the focus is upon Gurdjieff's teaching and cosmological viewpoint, particularly as presented by Ouspensky, but also drawing also from Beelzebub's Tales and other esoteric sources.

The Yin/Yang diagram thought to depict the duality of forces itself contains a tri-unity of forces–the Yin and Yang within the Tao. Matter and energy require a third force of intelligence or information; positive and negative numbers have a third neutralizing principle of 0; human beings function primarily physically, emotionally and mentally, with head, heart and hands. Stimuli and responses require an organism, without which there is neither stimulus nor response. Whenever we specify the existence of a duality, a trinity can be found if we move beyond the superficial construction of formatory thinking and penetrate to the heart of the matter. Third force is hidden to us, unless we could *"instinctually sense cosmic truths,"* as described by Beelzebub.

The Vedic teachings of ancient India describe creation as occurring after the white light of Brahman (God) disrupts the equilibrium of the *three gunas* or the *three modes of nature*. Before creation occurs, the three gunas are in a "seedless" state, perfectly balanced and symmetrical, and hence undifferentiated. The will or light of Brahman breaks this *symmetry* in the modes of nature in the first instant of creation. This symmetry breaking initiates the differentiation of the plurality out of the Unity. The One Brahman first gives rise to a trinity of demigods—Brahma (the creator), Vishnu (the preserver) and Shiva (the destroyer)--Divine Intelligences or demi-Gods which oversee the creation, maintenance and destruction of the universe. Each demigod rules one of the three modes of nature. Dr. R. Mishra (1973) describes the three modes of nature:

Guna means rope. As a rope binds an object and keeps it under control, so *gunas* bind all things from atoms to the sun and keep them under perfect control. Cosmic forces control the multiplicity of the Universe ... they are thus classified...:

1/ *Satoguna*, protonic force, intelligence-stuff
2/ *Rajoguna*, electronic force, energy-stuff
3/ *Tamoguna*, force of inertia, mass stuff

Substances which are self-shining, self-revealing, and which behave as a unit of conscious energy are called *satoguna* (the guna of sattva). Substances which are energetic, which have power of attraction and repulsion, and which behave as units of activity, change, and motion are called *rajoguna* (the guna of rajas). Substance which are units of mass and inertial are called *tamaguna*.

Prakriti (nature, or creation) is a rope made of three strands. ... All things are composed of the three *gunas* and the variety of the world depends on the relative predominance of the different *gunas*. ... (pp. 21-4)

Three forces (intelligence/mind, energy and matter) are proposed as opposed to the familiar duality of matter and energy which dominates modern science. All things are combinations of the three gunas and their numerous generations of causes and effects. Whereas we usually think of causes and effects, actions and reactions, stimuli and responses, the fourth way introduces a more complex form of analysis based on the idea of triune forces within all things.

In *Beelzebub's Tales*, the three aspects of the Sacred Triamazikamno are labeled as the *"Holy-Affirming,"* the *"Holy Denying"* and the *"Holy Reconciling."* The cosmic law is described:

> 'A law which always flows into a consequence and becomes the cause of subsequent consequences, and always functions by three independent and quite opposite characteristic manifestations, latent within it, in properties neither seen nor sensed.' (1950, p. 139)

Within the Absolute, the three forces are unified and constitute one whole. However, as creation proceeds the three forces differentiate and then combine in endless combinations as different worlds and phenomena are manifest. As Pythagoras stated, "all things consists in three."

Law of Seven or the Law of the Octave

The second fundamental cosmic law is the Law of Seven or the Law of the Octave–or the Sacred Heptaparaparshinokh for Beelzebub. This principle is also found throughout the ancient wisdom and mystical teachings. Like the Law of Three, it applies to the creation, maintenance and destruction of all cosmic phenomena on any scale of being, from a supergalactic cluster, to a human being, to a neuron or a quantum. Any realm of science, any phenomena of nature, any aspect of the psyche or soul life, must be understood in relationship to interactions of the laws of three and seven in their endless variations. Gurdjieff comments: "*Different combinations of a few elementary forces create all the seeming variety of phenomena. In order to understand the mechanics of the Universe it is necessary to resolve complex phenomena into these elementary forces.*" (Ouspensky, 1949)

When the Unity becomes a plurality, it embodies these fundamental cosmic laws in the creation of matters and energies, and intelligence upon the seven planes of being. These causes and effects descend from divine and spiritual realms into material forms, as higher intelligences and forces condense into matter. This entails a hierarchy of broken symmetries in higher dimensional space, which precipitates dimensions of being out of apparent non-being.

In terms of creation, Gurdjieff labels the ultimate principle as the "Absolute" and describes the *Ray of Creation* as the materialization of seven hierarchical planes of existence. The Absolute is taken as an eight note, which together with the seven notes of the manifest worlds, gives an octave structure. The eighth note is primary and is the completion of the seven fold scale. In nature, all things exist in relationship to seven interpenetrating dimensions. Ouspensky recalls Gurdjieff's descriptions:

> "The seven worlds of the ray of creation represent seven orders of materiality. ... Thus instead of one concept of matter we have seven kinds of matter ... All these matters belonging to the various orders of the universe are not separated into layers but are intermixed, or, rather, they interpenetrate one another. ... the finer matters permeate the courser ones." (1949, p. 88)

Within the *Ray of Creation*, each level of the Cosmos is permeated by finer, more rarefied matters, energies and intelligence of the higher, more inward dimensions. These matters, energies and intelligence interpenetrate throughout the space/time complex and give rise to outward phenomenon. # [23]

It is essential to differentiate involving and evolving octaves. The descent of divine intelligence and supernal forces into material creation is an involutionary process or devolution. In contrast, the ascent from matter to spirit and the divine, from gross material reality to the subtle planes, is an evolving process. Whereas modern scientists describe all changes of form as evolution, a mystical perspective suggests a more complex arrangement of involution and evolution, and maintenance.

The overall structure of the universe or cosmos has seven planes of existence and humanity has its place within a particular Ray of Creation—considered in relationship to the Sun. The planes of existence are related to the seven centers or dimensions of a human being. People are also of seven types. Men number one, two and three are produced by mechanical life influences, the do, re and me of the octave of human evolution. A man number four is experiencing moments or periods of self-consciousness, although the I is not firmly established; while a man number five, who perfects the lower centers and is established within the higher emotional realm, has attained 'real I.' Man numbers six and seven can function within the higher intellectual center in the state of objective consciousness, realizing the faculties of the spiritual and divine bodies. Ultimately, man number eight represents the full awakened masters, such as Christ, who might declare *"I and the Father are One."* These examples illustrate the law of seven and the idea of evolution.

The ancient Vedic teachings of India articulate the same basic principles. The cosmos is composed of *Prakriti*, the elementary stuff of creation, which is divided into two classes—the Absolute or fundamental, and the relative, of which there are seven grades or subclasses. Mishra (1973) states: *"... prakriti is eight-fold ... with one fundamental and seven relative subclasses."* (p.20) When the universe is withdrawn into Non-Being, during the Nights of Brahma (Brahma means the creator), the fundamental root principle prakriti is in a potential *seed state*. As long as the three modes of nature are balanced and in equilibrium, then Prakriti remains undifferentiated and the universe exists only in a potential state. When the balance of the gunas is disturbed by the Light or Will of Brahman, they enter into enormous varieties of combinations, all of which are asymmetrical, with one guna predominating over the others.[24] Seven world orders emerge when the equilibrium of the three gunas is broken and the three modes of nature interact on successive planes of being through generations of cosmic effects. Vedic teachings articulate the same triune and sevenfold nature of creation, although Gurdjieff's teaching casts a particularly valuable light on the meanings of these sacred principles.

The One is divided by the three modes of nature and produces a spectrum of seven colors or seven degrees of Maya. The Octave or eight-fold pattern in nature includes the seven relative worlds and the one fundamental out of which creation is differentiated. In terms of the light analogy, white light is fundamental and the seven colors of the rainbow are relative. The white light is the One which contains all seven manifest colors within itself.

---

[23] These principles, while outwardly simple, are incredibly complex and subtle when one comes to the application of octave analysis. Firstly, three octaves must be considered together in order to understand any complex phenomena. Further, any note within one octave may comprise another whole octave within itself; and these causes and effects multiply as they pass through varied dimensions.

[24] In terms of modern physics, the process by which creation occurs is described as symmetry breaking in higher dimensional space, which generates different densities of matter/energies and intelligence, and generations of hydrogens. The teachings of Gurdjieff, the Vedas and other esoteric metaphysics are highly relevant to modern concepts, although this is not recognized due to the widespread ignorance and neglect of mystical teachings.

In *Beelzebub's Tales*, the sevenfoldness of all things is described in relationship to the realms of nature—all the way up to the Prime Source. Beelzebub explains:

> ".. 'seven-classes-of-vibrations'" of those cosmic sources, the arising and further action of each of which also arise and depend on seven others, which in their turn arise and depend on seven further ones, and so on right up to the first most holy 'unique-seven-propertied-vibration' issuing from the Most Holy Prime Source ... ." (p. 476)

H. Blavatsky's (1888) *The Secret Doctrine* serves as another source of this ancient wisdom teaching. In *Cosmosgenesis*, Blavatsky states that in relationship to the metaphysical process of creation "*the triune ... emanate the other seven.*" The triune nature inherent within the Absolute emanates the Seven Luminous Lords, the demigods or divine builders who inform and sustain the seven dimensions of the Cosmos. The generation of matter and energy, time and space proceeds as the influences and intelligences descend within/without through higher dimensional space. The triune nature of THAT and the Seven Divine Intelligences create, maintain and destroy all the matters, energies and intelligence embodied within the Cosmos. All things have higher dimensional causes manifesting the Sacred Principles of three and seven out of the One. Blavatsky writes:

> "The Great Water (the Deep or Chaos) is said to be *seven* cubits deep"–"cubits" standing here of course for divisions, zones, and principles. Therein, "in the great mother, all the Gods, and the seven great ones are born." (p. 674)

The Great Water, the Deep, or the Chaos, stand for the primordial root principle of material creation, most similar to the hyperspace and quantum vacuum of the modern physicist.

Gurdjieff and Ouspensky, Blavatsky, the Vedas, the Kabbalists and many other esoteric teachings articulate these ancient principles, symbols of objective knowledge. It is impossible here to fully elaborate these deep mystical laws and to draw their many profound relationships to ideas within modern science and psychology. Scientists generally consider there to be one material world pervaded by dualities, such as those of matter and energy, within time and space, perceived with either the body or the mind. In contrast, a mystical view suggests that a trinity of matter, energy and intelligence manifest within seven discrete interpenetrating dimensions of cosmic space.

The inner cosmos of consciousness embodies the same dimensionality as the inner cosmos of the universe. Further, just as a universe or a human being has a seven fold nature, so also does the Sun, the moon, the planets and the stars. Any cosmos has a sevenfold and triune nature, informed from within/without by the principles latent everywhere in cosmic space. The laws of three and seven are archaic mystery teachings which simply cannot be understood in the usual subjective states of consciousness. Most importantly, the laws of three and seven can be applied to understanding the chemistry and the alchemy of human beings and the cosmos.

Gurdjieff describes the fundamental cosmic laws of three and seven manifesting world orders out of the Absolute, through a hierarchy of causes and effects. This hierarchy forms *the ladder of Jacob* reaching from heaven to earth. As one descends the Ray of Creation, the greater the number of mechanical laws governing life and one's mode of existence, thus limiting the experience of consciousness. A human being, as a microcosm of the macrocosm, is simultaneously composed of hydrogens or substances of all of these interpenetrating planes of being. G. explained: *"... man is indeed a miniature universe; he has in him all the matters which compose the universe."* (Ouspensky, 1949)

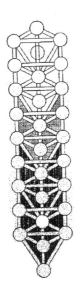

The ancient Kabbalist symbol of the *Ladder of Jacob* is composed of four overlapping *Trees of Life* and it depicts the manner in which creation descends through different dimensions of existence from the Absolute. The laws of three and seven are embodied in myriad of complex ways within the Tree of Life. This glyph is a profound diagram of the fundamental cosmic laws and a symbol of objective knowledge.

2. Cosmic Octaves & Hydrogens

2a. **The Big Cosmic Octave**

"Between *All* and *Nothing* passes the ray of creation."
- G. I. Gurdjieff -

Gurdjieff provides a most interesting cosmology describing seven world-orders arranged hierarchically as they involve from the Absolute. The creation octave is *involutionary* in that it depicts the descent of forces from divine and spiritual dimensions into increasingly dense material worlds. The top Do of the cosmic octave is the Absolute, the All, and the bottom Do is Nothing. Ouspensky recounts G.'s basic outline:

"In the big cosmic octave, which reaches us in the form of the *ray of creation*, we can see the first complete example of the law of octaves. The ray of creation begins with the Absolute. The Absolute is *the All*. *The All*, possessing full unity, full will, and full consciousness, creates worlds within itself, in this way beginning the *descending* world octave. The Absolute is the do of this octave. The worlds which the Absolute creates in itself are si. The 'interval' between do and si in this case is filled by the *will of the Absolute*. ... Si passes into la which for us is our starry world, the *Milky Way*. La passes into sol-our *sun*, the solar system. Sol passes into fa–the planetary world.

And here between the planetary world as a whole and our earth occurs an 'interval.' This means that the planetary radiations carrying various influences to the earth are not able to reach it, or, to speak more correctly, they are not received, the earth reflects them. In order to fill the 'interval' at this point of the ray of creation a special apparatus is created for receiving and transmitting the influences coming from the planets. This apparatus is *organic life on earth*. Organic life transmits to the earth all the influences intended for it and makes possible the further development and growth of the earth, mi of the cosmic octave, and then of the moon or re, after which follows another do— *Nothing*. Between *All* and *Nothing* passes the ray of creation." (1949, p.132)

This is a most profound view of creation. The ray of creation is a model of the forces and intelligence present everywhere within space/time, within the outer and inner cosmos. The ray descends through the cosmic octave differentiating worlds within worlds.

The Absolute is All as it contains all potencies, the sum of all completed octaves. It possesses full unity, will and consciousness, three aspects of one nature under one law. Creation issues from the cosmic Do and the triune creative forces pass through varied states as different forces predominate. This process generates seven discontinuous planes of existence, each of which adds new modifications of the laws governing matter and energy within that realm. Finally, the lower Do is Nothing--which is simultaneously related to the All as the void is to the plenum, as aspects of the Absolute. The Cosmic Octave provides a model of the vast sea of space within which human beings live, move and have their being. We do not live in only one world but in many worlds simultaneously:

> "Our language does not have the idea of worlds contained one within another. And yet the idea that we live in different worlds precisely implies worlds contained one within another to which we stand in different relations." (Ouspensky, 1949, p. 75)

The influences of all the world orders of the cosmic octave interpenetrate all space/time complexes. These worlds are not simply out there in the world around us, but within the interior dimensions of ourselves and the cosmos of consciousness. The Ray of Creation involves from within/without through varied dimensions and world orders.

> "The chain of worlds, the links of which are the Absolute, all worlds, all suns, our sun, the planets, the earth, and the moon, forms the 'ray of creation' in which we find ourselves. The ray of creation is for us the 'world' in the widest sense of the term." (Ouspensky, 1949, p. 80)

Firstly, a human being lives, moves and has their being within the *Absolute*. If God or the Absolute, or the Most Most Holy Sun Absolute described by Beelzebub, is the source of all things, then THAT permeates all worlds. Secondly, we exist within the whole of the Universe, within *All Worlds* which would include all galaxies and super-galaxies. Thirdly, in relationship to the three brained beings on planet earth, the ray of creation passes through a particular galaxy within all worlds, namely the *Milky Way galaxy*. Whereas all worlds include billions of galaxies and other astrophysical systems, humans live in a particular galaxy, the Milky Way, which is *our world*. All worlds and our world exist on different *orders of scale,* one within the other. The Milky Way galaxy is like a grain of sand in the cosmic ocean.

Fourthly, within the Milky Way, our ray of creation is focused through the Sun—one star out of billions within the galaxy. The sun exists on a different order of scale from the Milky Way Galaxy, again as a grain of sand in a vast sea of stars. The sun is the center within the solar system and the planets revolve around the sun creating a sphere of planetary influence and forces. The earth is a planet but because humans live on earth, we stand in a special relationship to it which differentiates it from other planets as far as the ray of creation is concerned. The earth is thus taken as a separate note below the level of the planets. Next, the sphere of the moon is below the earth, as the moon is a satellite to the earth, another generation of effects distant from the unified will of the Absolute. Lastly, the ray of creation extends to *nothing*, which can be taken as space or the Ether, considered in its emptiness. It is the void in relation to the All, or the plenum and fullness of the Absolute. In modern science, this is similar to the concept of the quantum vacuum as a seeming void or emptiness which is simultaneously the plenum, containing all possible forces, particles and laws in an undifferentiated state.[25] Cosmic processes all occur within the apparent emptiness of space—within Mother Nature according to Beelzebub.

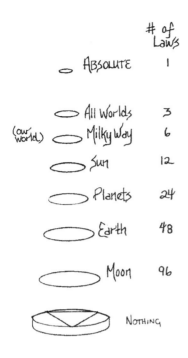

In which world of the ray of creation do humans live? We live within all of these worlds simultaneously. We live within the Absolute, in all worlds, within the galaxy of the milky way, within the sphere of the sun, surrounded by the planetary world system, on earth, with the moon below us, and pervaded everywhere by the nothingness. According to this formulation, the influences of each world order pervade space, one within the other, all serving to focus the life of the Absolute within different realms of creation.

The general design of the cosmic octave depicts the relationships of different world orders to each other and can be used to plot the movements of forces, the multiplication of laws and the processes of involution and evolution. Humankind arises within the space/time complex of the universe and the laws of nature which pervade space/time are everywhere the same. As human beings, we are subject to the laws and influences of each successive level of this inner hierarchy of being. "I" lives within the Absolute and within the space/time complex pervaded by this sea of cosmic influences, forces and laws. Mr. Gurdjieff's explanations of the big cosmic octave provide a profoundly valuable tool for attempting to understand one's own position with respect to the many cosmic influences and world orders.[26]

---

[25] In the Within-Without from Zero Points series, Dr. Holmes provides extended descriptions of these issues of the plenum and void, ranging from esoteric descriptions of creation dynamics to scientific descriptions of the apparent emptiness and fullness of the quantum vacuum.

[26] This concept of Space needs to be considered from a holographic perspective to grasp the significance of these descriptions The influences of higher worlds do not simply come to us from out there in universe, but rather the influences of all worlds pervade space holographically. Interior dimensions create the more detailed behavior and outward forms of the physical world. In this view, the Sun is not simply out there in external space, 92 to 96 million miles away, but it is a level within the self, in the divisions of our atoms.

Gurdjieff explains that each of these world orders is under a different number of laws. The Absolute is under 1 law. In the first created world order, three forces are differentiated and so *all worlds* are under 3 primordial forces. The second world order is subject to six laws, the three laws of the first world order and a second generation of three laws. This same pattern is repeated through the generation of successive world orders—with each world order subject to the laws of the levels above it and then generating three additional forces. The third world order has 3+6+3=12 laws; the fourth world has 3+6+12+3=24 laws; the fifth has 3+6+12+24+3=48; the sixth has 3+6+12+24+48+3=96; and the seventh has 3+6+12+24+48+96+3=192 laws. In this formulation, the greater the number of laws in a given world, then the further that world is removed from the Will of the Absolute and the more it is ruled in an unconscious and mechanical manner. After the first creative impulse, the unity differentiates into a trinity and then generations of pluralities as life becomes increasingly mechanical and law determined.

There are profound similarities and differences between modern scientific views and Gurdjieff's mystical cosmology in terms of the physical and metaphysical views and assumptions. In general, G.'s depiction of the ray of creation is literally true from a scientific perspective. We live in the universe, within a particular galaxy, within a particular solar system, surrounded by planets, on earth, with the moon as a satellite. However, in G.'s account, the cosmos is manifest out of the Absolute, possessing full unity, consciousness and will. In contrast, modern scientists think that the universe manifested out of an unconscious realm of matter and energy and that it was fifteen billion years before intelligent beings and consciousness happened by chance to evolve in the universe.
Occultists suggest that all levels of creation embody spiritual intelligence and supernatural forces, through many generations of causes and effects. The Sun is a living being, as are the Earth, the Moon, and the Planets, all embodying consciousness and intelligence on some order of scale. According to the mystic view, humans live in an intelligent living Cosmos, one ultimately unified and sustained by the Absolute.[27]

The *scientists of new formation* view life as coming from below, as evolving out of unconscious matter through random and accidental effects only after the creation of the varied worlds. For G., life and consciousness come from above and are embodied within the lower material worlds under the influence of higher world orders. The ray of creation is *a living being*, growing and developing, emanating from a supreme source, the Most Most Holy Sun Absolute.

[27] According to Mr. G., the earth may eventually become a sun to the moon, which itself might become a planet, with a further satellite of its own. In this view, the moon is an unborn planet, which may gradually warm and acquire an atmosphere. A new link would then be added to the ray of creation. Similarly, the earth may gradually warm and eventually become a sun to the worlds below it. G. describes this process as evident in the growth of Jupiter, which is becoming a sun for its satellites. These claims are clearly contrary to modern scientific perspectives, although not necessarily to particular evidences.

2b. **Three Octaves, Shocks & Organic Life on Earth**

"These three octaves of radiations ... will enable us to explain the relation of matters and forces of different planes of the world to our own life." (G. in O., 1949, p. 169)

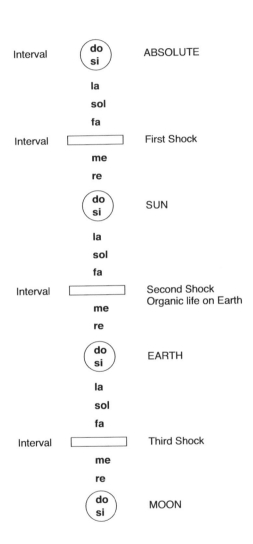

Gurdjieff explains that the *Ray of Creation* can be considered in the form of three octaves of radiation. In this case, the first octave begins in the Absolute and ends in the sun; the second begins in the sun and passes to the earth; and the third passes from the earth to the moon. This produces 22 levels or notes within the Ray of Creation.

In this scheme, there are six shock points to be filled but only three of these need to be filled from outside of the octaves. Gurdjieff explains that the first shock, in the first instant of creation, is filled by the Will of the Absolute. This fills the top do-si interval and provides the impetus necessary to initiate the processes of creation or involution. The other do-si intervals are within the sun and the earth. Gurdjieff explains that the second do-si interval is *"filled by the influence of the sun's mass upon radiations passing through it,"* and that similarly, the third do-si interval is *"filled by the action of the earth's mass upon radiations passing through it."* (1949, p. 169) These do-si shocks involve the influence of the mass of the bodies upon radiations within its space. In modern terms, these effects are consistent with the idea of the gravitational influences of massive bodies producing a curvature of the space/time continuum. The general theory of relativity describes the earth and moon as having such effects, focusing radiations passing through space.

The three intervals between fa and mi need to be filled by *additional shocks.* Gurdjieff says little of two of these but places great importance on understanding the fa-mi interval of the sun-earth octave. Organic life on earth serves a special purpose providing this shock and allowing for the growth of the Ray of Creation. Organic life enters the overall cosmic octave as three notes of a side octave, called *the lateral octave,* which fills the interval within the larger octave. Organic life receives influences from higher sources, the sun and planets, and allows their passage to the earth and the growing tip of the

Ray of Creation, and the moon. According to *Beelzebub's Tales*, organic life produces the sacred Askokin vibrations necessary to feed and maintain the moon.

In the lateral or side octave, the sun is taken as the top do, although it is sol in the main octave. Both the cosmic and lateral octaves share the moon at re, and nothingness as the bottom do. In terms of humankind's place within the lateral octave, the Sun can be taken as a spiritual realm, embodying the intelligence and life which is responsible for creating and maintaining organic life on earth. Nicoll (1974) explains: *"Mankind on earth is an experiment of the Solar Laboratory."* (p. 245)

Gurdjieff describes the role of organic life as twofold: as an *"organ of perception"* and as an *"organ of radiation"*:

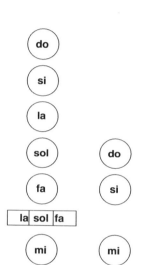

"Organic life represents so to speak the *earth's organ of perception*. Organic life forms something like a sensitive film which covers the whole of the earth's globe and takes in those influences coming from the planetary sphere which otherwise would not be able to reach the earth. The vegetable, animal, and human kingdoms are equally important for the earth in this respect. A field merely covered with grass takes in planetary influences of a definite kind and transmits them to the earth. The same field with a crowd of people on it will take in and transmit other influences. ... All great events in the life of the human masses are caused by planetary influences. They are the result of the taking in of planetary influences. ...

"Organic life is the organ of perception of the earth and it is at the same time an organ of radiation. With the help of organic life each portion of the earth's surface occupying a given area sends every moment certain kinds of rays in the direction of the sun, the planets, and the moon. In connection with this the sun needs one kind of radiations, the planets another kind, and the moon another. Everything that happens on earth creates radiations of this kind. And many things often *happen* just because certain kinds of radiations are required from a certain place on the earth's surface." (Ouspensky, 1949, pp.138)

Humanity is a part of organic life on earth and is influenced by solar, planetary, terrestrial and lunar radiations and influences, just as are all other forms of plants and animals. Humans also radiate or give off influences and energies. In this way, a human or humanity can be regarded as possibly *food* for the moon, or the earth, the planets or the sun. The world order that a human feeds will vary according to what vibrations and energies, or hydrogens, they are made of and by their level of being.

At death, certain energies/matters within a human being, of varying density of materiality, are released into different spheres of the cosmos. Some matters within a human pass to the moon, others feed the earth (the material body), while others feed the planets and sun. R. Collin (1980) writes:

... we know that men's corpses, as complete vertebrate organisms, are eaten by the Earth, and as warehouses of mineral salts by invertebrates, by worms. Further, we have deduced that as magnetic fields they go to feed the moon. What then could it mean that men should be eaten by the Sun? It can only refer to that part of man which distinguishes him from all other vertebrates, that is, his consciousness. The Sun lives on the consciousness of men. Later, we may see better what this enigmatic principle may mean. (p.127)

At physical death and through deaths within the subtle dimensions, the different matters/energies which compose a human being dissipate and return to the world of their arising. These processes are all part of what Beelzebub describes as the *"common-cosmic Trogoautoegocratic-process."* In the *Tales*, Gurdjieff defines this as the system which maintains everything existing in the cosmos through the *"exchange of substances"* and the *"'reciprocal-feeding' of everything that exists."* (1950, pp. 136-7) Beelzebub explains that the fundamental purpose of human life is that the transmutation of cosmic substances necessary for the Trogoautoegocrat process. Everything eats and everything is eaten.

2c. **The Hydrogen Diagrams**

Gurdjieff's use of the hydrogen diagrams is a most remarkable dimension of the fourth way teaching. There is no formulation comparable to this scheme within modern science or psychology. By the term *hydrogen*, Gurdjieff refers to any type of material substance or energy having definite cosmic, psychic or material properties. Hydrogens differ in their "density of vibrations" and "density of matter." The higher the density of vibration then the lower the density of matter--as these qualities stand in inverse relationship to each other. Any hydrogen has a triune nature of material, energetic and intelligence principles, and the degree of intelligence is related to the vividness or intensity of vibration. # [28]

Mr. G. uses the term hydrogen in a generic sense to refer to substances and not simply to refer to the element hydrogen of modern chemistry, even though the terms are related. In science, hydrogen is the basic and simplest element with the atomic number of 1 and its nucleus consists of one proton. From the Gurdjieff perspective, different chemical elements are hydrogens of different densities, substances with different qualities. All compound things are composed of varied hydrogen combinations. In the G. cosmology and metaphysics, each world is composed of hydrogens of different densities of matter-energy-intelligence within the octave arrangements.

Different substances ranging from iron, wood, water, air, electromagnetism, to subtle emotional and mental matters, are all hydrogens of different densities. The term hydrogen is used as a generic term

---

[28] Whereas scientists debate the matter/energy and particle/wave theories in physics in dualistic terms, G. adds a third force of 'intelligence' as an aspect of any cosmic substance or hydrogen. In modern physics, the triune nature of all substances is illustrated by the wave/particle theory where any material particle has a wave motion and any wave motion has a certain material principle, and neither of them completes the whole. A quantum in physics is both a wave and a particle, and something in between.

to refer to any substance with definite cosmic properties. A blood cell involves more subtle hydrogens than a rock, but is more material than the ghostly neutrinos. The hydrogen diagrams provide a scheme by which to consider the various elements or matters which constitute a human being–including the energies of different centers, of consciousness and of the various subtle being-bodies.

In modern science, the periodic table of elements provides a comparable formulation, as it is arranged in seven rows of elements, which rows further embody inner octave patterns. Of course, the periodic tables only consider elements from a material perspective, whereas G's notion of hydrogens is broader and considers the subtle natures of substances. Modern psychology has no comparable formulation for trying to understand the human organism and the varied elements which compose a human from a psychological perspective.

In explaining the three octaves of the Ray of Creation, G. describes the three primary hydrogens, the substances, elements or forces produced by the Absolute as having the densities of 1, 2 and 3. These combine to form the first complex hydrogen of the next generation, which is defined as hydrogen 6 (H6). As creation proceeds, increasingly dense hydrogens are produced by the combination of simpler hydrogens. Using the three octaves of the Ray of Creation, G. derives Hydrogens ranging from H6 to H12288. # [29] G. then explains that H6 and H12 of this scheme are indivisible as far as humans are concerned, and so he reduces the hydrogen number scheme so that it ranges from H1 to H3072. All matters ranging from H6 to H3072 play some role within the human organism.

Gurdjieff provides some examples to illustrate different hydrogens. Iron is related to hydrogen 3072, wood is H 1536, food is H 768, water is H 384, and air-H 192. Each density of hydrogen does not simply refer to one substance but to a cosmic group related by function. Gurdjieff describes the class of hydrogen 96 as bordering on elements studied and hypothesized in science:

> "'Hydrogen' 96 is represented by rarified gases which man cannot breathe, but which play a very important part in his life; and further, this is the matter of animal magnetism, of emanations from the human body, of 'n-rays,' hormones, vitamins, and so on; in other words, with 'hydrogen' 96 ends what is called matter or what is regarded as matter by our physics and chemistry." (1949, p. 175)

G. describes hydrogens 6, 12, 24 and 48 as matters unknown to physics and chemistry, but which include *"matters of our psychic and spiritual life on different levels."*

In relating his scheme to the periodic tables of modern science, Gurdjieff describes modern hydrogen, with the atomic weight of 1, as corresponding to Hydrogen 12. This is interesting given that the level of the Sun, said to be under 12 laws, is composed primarily of the element hydrogen. Other correspondences drawn by Mr. G. include: the association of fluorine, with atomic weight of 19, to Hydrogen 24; chlorine, with atomic weight of 35.5, to Hydrogen 48; bromine, with atomic weight of 80, to Hydrogen 96; and iodine, atomic weight of 127, to Hydrogen 192. These are rough correspondences because modern chemistry does not take into account the psychic and cosmic properties of elements–whereas G.'s scheme considers the material, psychic and metaphysical properties of substances.

---

[29] G.'s detailed explanations of the hydrogens are documented by Ouspensky, particularly in In Search of the Miraculous. (pp. 167-176) I am avoiding some of the complexity of G.'s presentation which is beyond the scope of this work. G. explains the generation of hydrogens by the combination of three prior hydrogens, each conducting one of the active, passive and neutralizing forces—labeled Carbon, Oxygen and Nitrogen. Any hydrogen is a combination of such a Carbon, Oxygen and Nitrogen, and it can serve itself to conduct either of these forces as it is engaged in subsequent interactions.

Gurdjieff states that the hydrogen diagrams provide a way of comparing the intelligence of God to that of a rock, as each can be described as composed of hydrogens of different materiality—whether a H1 or a H3072.

The hydrogen diagrams, in conjunction with an understanding of the cosmic octaves, provide a profoundly valuable way of conceptualizing the interrelationships between cosmic substances within different worlds. They enable us to portray the hierarchies of forces and substances—material, spiritual and divine—which constitute the ladder of Jacob reaching from heaven to earth. As one descends the Ray of Creation into denser and denser hydrogens, a greater number of mechanical laws govern existence and limit the experience of consciousness.

A human being, as a microcosm of the macrocosm, is simultaneously composed of hydrogens or substances of all these interpenetrating planes of being. G. explained: *"... man is indeed a miniature universe; he has in him all the matters which compose the universe."* (1949) In order to understand a human being, we have to study the universe.

3. Foods for the Soul:
The Accumulation of Fine Hydrogens

> "The 'table of hydrogens' makes it possible to examine all substances making up man's organism from the point of view of their relation to different planes of the universe. And as every function of man is a result of the action of definite substances, and as every substance is connected with a definite plane in the universe, this fact enables us to establish the relation between man's functions and the planes of the universe." (Gurdjieff, in O, 1949, p. 176)

The basic ideas of the laws of three and seven combined with the study of the *hydrogen diagrams* provides a way to understand the constitution of the macrocosm of the universe and the microcosm of the inner human being. Each of the seven centers works with hydrogens of corresponding densities, which enables humans' relationship with different hydrogen levels within the Cosmos.

In reference to the psychology of man's possible evolution, a human being is a chemical factory (or alchemical factory), whose every thought, feeling, action and sexual experience uses certain densities of hydrogens. An inner alchemy involves refining more finer hydrogens from coarse materials, like changing base metals into gold. This process allows the inner growth of the essence and the subtle being-bodies—the astral, mental (spiritual) and divine bodies. The accumulation of finer hydrogens is similarly required for contact with the functioning of the higher centers (the higher emotional and higher intellectual) and the attainment of higher states of consciousness (self-consciousness and objective consciousness).

From a psychological point of view, a human's different centers function with hydrogens of different densities. The intellectual center functions with relatively dense hydrogen 48, while the moving, instinctual and emotional centers primarily consume hydrogens 24. The higher emotional center functions only with a finer hydrogen 12 and particular sexual energies at the H12 level are necessary for the refinement of the astral body. The higher intellectual center is on the level of hydrogen 6 within very subtle levels or planes of being. In humans as they are, the lower centers are not connected to the higher centers because of the energy dynamics and it is necessary to "quicken" their functioning to enable such contact.

The hydrogen scheme illustrates the whole idea of alchemy and the transformation of coarse or dense energies/matters into fine energies/matters. A human's level of being depends upon the accumulation of finer or gross hydrogens. The development of the higher being bodies is through the accumulation and crystallization of finer hydrogens within the astral and mental bodies. The processes of self-remembering and working on oneself bring about chemical and alchemical changes in the inner being. Gurdjieff provides an interesting and complex model of how all these things work.

A human being has three essential being foods: Physical *food* which enters the organism through the digestive system into the lowest of the three stories of the human; *air,* which enters into the middle story through breathing and the lungs; and *psychological impressions,* which enter the third story and are processed through the mind and psyche. Human beings take in food (H 768), air (H 192) and psychological impressions (H 48) as life nutrients and somehow, the organism produces the energies and matters for the body, mind and psyche from these three being foods.

Whereas a person might live weeks without physical food (or three days without water), they could only live three minutes without air and only seconds without psychological impressions. Gurdjieff describes psychological impressions as a *"being food:"*

> "Without impressions a man cannot live a single moment. If the flow of impressions were to be stopped in some way or if the organism were deprived of its capacity for receiving impressions, it would immediately die. The flow of impressions coming to us from outside is like a driving belt communicating motion to us. The principle motor for us is nature, the surrounding world. Nature transmits to us through our impressions the energy by which we live and move and have our being." (Ouspensky, 1949, p. 181)

These hydrogens of food, air and psychological impression are transformed into the energies and matters for the body, emotions, mind, sex life and potentially into food for the soul and the higher being-bodies.

Gurdjieff's *"food diagrams"* combined with the hydrogen diagrams portray these subtle and complex processes in a remarkable way. Everything in the Cosmos can be assigned a certain level of materiality/energy/intelligence according to the hydrogen diagrams. Gurdjieff states: *"All psychic processes are material. There is not a single process that does not require the expenditure of a certain substance corresponding to it."* (Ouspensky, 1949, p. 198)

In accordance with the law of seven, Gurdjieff outlines the processes by which the being foods are transformed into the energies required for a human's psychological life. In these diagrams, a critical role is assigned to various shocks which enable the continued development of the food octaves. Firstly, physical *food* enters the lowest story, the stomach, as do 768, where it is refined to re 384, and then mi 192, before it stops at the point of the missing semi-tone. Air enters at this point as do 192 and provides a *"mechanical shock"* to the food octave, which enables it to progress beyond the interval and refine the additional hydrogens of fa 96, sol 48, la 24 and si 12. Si 12 is the vital sexual energies,

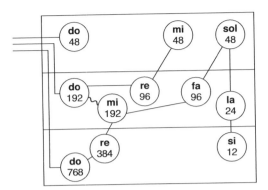

Exiohary, sperm in men. The physical food octave stops at si 12. The second being food, *air,* enters as a do 192 and is automatically refined into re 96 and mi 48, and then progresses no further, stalling at the missing semi-tone interval. The third being food, *psychological impressions* enters as a do 48, but does not have the intensity to provide the necessary shock to the air octave to allow its progression. Normally, psychological impressions are not refined further than do 48. The first food diagram shown below portrays all of the hydrogens produced *mechanically*–with one mechanical shock but no *"conscious shock."*

In the following food diagram, extra hydrogens are refined because of the provision of the *"first conscious shock."* The first conscious shock is the act of self-remembering, the intensification of attention and awareness at the moment of registering psychological impressions, which serves to double their intensity. This shock allows the progression of the air octave so that it passes through the interval mi-fa, to produce the additional hydrogens–fa 24, sol 12, and la 6. The psychological impressions octave also progresses, rather than stalling at do 48, to produce hydrogens re 24 and mi 12. The impact of the first conscious shock thus brings about the refinement of five additional nutrients or hydrogens within the individual: three of the air octave and two of the impressions octave.

Gurdjieff describes the first conscious shock as artificial in that it is not produced by nature or mechanically, but must be produced by *conscious effort* on the part of the individual:

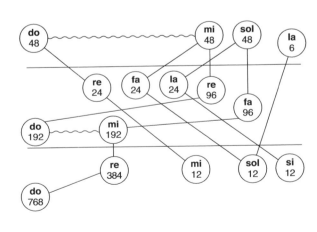

"But what is meant by an 'artificial shock'? It is connected with the moment of the reception of an impression. The note do 48 designates the moment when an impression enters our consciousness. An 'artificial shock' at this point means a certain kind of effort made at the moment of receiving an impression. ... in ordinary conditions of life we do not *remember ourselves* ... that is, we do not feel ourselves, are not aware of ourselves at the moment of a perception, of an emotion, of a thought or of an action. If a man understands this and tries to remember himself, every impression he receives while remembering himself will, so to speak, be doubled..." (1949, p.188)

---

[30] In the Within-Without from Zero Point series, book I, The Heart Doctrine elaborates extensively upon the mysteries of the heart from scientific and mystical perspectives. Whereas the focus of Psychological Illusions has been the psychopathology and sleepwalking state of humankind, The Heart Doctrine elaborates mystical teachings about awakened states of higher consciousness and human enlightenment.

The first conscious shock produces two additional hydrogen 12 in the lowest story associated with the sexual center, two additional H 24 elements related to the emotional center and a first hydrogen 6, related to the higher intellectual center. The first and second diagrams represent the first two stages in the evolution of the human organism. The first stage is a human as created by nature and the second, the individual who creates a first conscious or volitional shock through his or her own efforts.

A *second conscious shock* is also possible and brings about a third stage in the evolution of the human organism as a chemical and alchemical factory. This second conscious shock is not clearly defined because of the difficulty of putting it into words. Gurdjieff suggests that this second volitional shock becomes possible only *"after long practice on the first volitional 'shock',"* and that a man number four is one who achieves the second stage of development and is beginning this third. The second conscious shock involves the transformation of the hydrogens si 12 and mi 12, and is connected with work on the emotional center. Gurdjieff describes it as related to *"the transformation and transmutation of the emotions."* Within the fourth way psychology, this can be related to the breaking through of the false personality structures and the patterns of narcissistic emotions, and awakening to the realm of impersonal or higher emotions. This includes the awakening of conscience and the experience of varied beatific emotions, including the sacred being-impulses of Hope, Faith and Love. Further, as expressed by Beelzebub, the three brained beings might be re-established in the original emotional center, localized within *"an independent brain localized in the region of their what is called 'breast.'"* This organ we will take as the heart.[30]

Attaining the third level of work of the human organism is essential to attaining permanent effects:

> "No serious growth, that is, no growth of higher bodies within the organism, is possible without this transmutation. ... the alchemists spoke of this transmutation in the allegorical forms of the transformation of base metals into precious ones. In reality, however, they meant the transformation of course 'hydrogens' into finer ones in the human organism, chiefly of the transformation of mi 12. If this transformation is attained, a man can be said to have achieved what he was striving for, and it can also be said that, until this transformation is attained, all results attained by a man can be lost because they are not fixed in him in any way ... Real, objective results can be obtained only after the transmutation of mi 12 has begun. ... Right development on the fourth way must begin with the first volitional 'shock' and then pass on to the second 'shock' at mi 12. ... A fairly considerable period of transmutation and crystallization is needed for the transition of man number four to the level of man number five."
> (Ouspensky, 1949, pp. 192-3)

Gurdjieff's hydrogen model is a remarkably subtle scheme with a deep logic and insight. All psychic, intellectual, emotional and psychological processes, even mystical experiences and states, have their own materiality. If the individual is interested in awakening, higher centers or higher consciousness, then they need to accumulate the finer hydrogens corresponding to those functions and states. All of these processes are tied also to the refinement of the higher being-bodies--the astral or Kesdjan, the mental or spiritual, and the divine bodies. Recall Gurdjieff's comments:

> " ... save the fine 'hydrogens.' Then the whole of the body, all the tissue, all the cells, would become saturated with these fine 'hydrogens' which would gradually settle in them, crystallizing in a special way. This crystallization of the fine 'hydrogens' would gradually bring the whole organism onto a higher level, onto a higher plane of being."
> (1949, p. 180)

Separate the fine from the coarse, this ancient alchemical principle refers to the inner work of the human organism and the crystallization of the higher being bodies, enabling a human's possible evolution. The profound teaching of the food diagrams provides a concrete model of such mysterious processes.

In *Beelzebub's Tales*, Gurdjieff provides additional explanations of the food diagrams and the process of the crystallization of the higher being-bodies. The accumulation of sacred sexual substances plays a particularly critical role in these alchemical processes. Beelzebub explains to his grandson:

> This sacred substance which arises in the presences of beings of every kind is almost everywhere called "Exioehary'; but your favorites on the planet Earth call it 'sperm.' ... this sacred substance arises ... chiefly in order that by its means they might, consciously or automatically, fulfill that part of their being-duty which consists in the continuation of their species; but in the presences of three-brained beings it arises also in order that it might be consciously transformed in their common presences for coating their highest being-bodies for their own Being. (1950, pp. 275-6)

Beelzebub explains that the majority of contemporary beings continually waste these sacred sexual substances simply for their own pleasuring—while not realizing how this contributes to the degeneration of their already strange psyches.

Mantak Chia (1984), a Taoist master, similarly explains that the cultivation of male or female sexual energy is essential to the alchemy of the soul. In the preface to Chia's work, Winn explains:

> The Taoist teaching of physical immortality ... means that before (men) die they have the opportunity to cultivate a "solid" or substantial spiritual body, also known as the Immortal Body, the Solar Body, the Crystal Body, and other names. ... The Taoists insist each adept preserve his individual nature within a body (physical or spiritual) so he can oversee the growth of his soul until final union with "wu chi," the nothingness from which the oneness of the Tao emerges. (p. III)

Chia explains that the sperm energy can be mixed with the chi, or vital energy of the organs and refined into shien, or spirit. Thus, the sexual energies link the biological body to the metaphysical identity, the animal nature to the divine.[31]

Also, in *Beelzebub's Tales to his Grandson*, Gurdjieff provides additional commentaries upon the role of various *"bloods"* in the alchemical refinement of the higher being-bodies. He explains that just as physical blood serves to nourish the planetary or organic body, so also, there is *Hanbledzoin* which is the blood of the Kesdjan or astral body; and the sacred *Aiesakhaldan*, which is the being-blood of the highest being-body. Beelzebub explains:

> "It is necessary to tell you that in general the quality of the composition of the blood in three-brained beings and also in the common presences of your favorites depends on the number of the being-bodies already 'completely formed.'" (1950, p.569)

The substances for the various bloods are obtained from the three being foods: physical food serves the organic body; air serves the Kesdjan body and includes elements transformed by the sun and planets within the atmospheres; and, psychological impressions feed the mind body and includes substances formed *"from the direct emanations of our Most Holy Sun Absolute."* (p. 569) The being foods have complex relationships to the larger cosmos, but humans do not absorb or assimilate all the finer hydrogens necessary for the growth of the higher being-bodies. The various bloods of the physical and subtle bodies play a critical role in the chemistry and alchemy of the inner human being.

---

[31] Readers are recommended to Chia's teachings for practical techniques for the cultivation of non-ejaculatory sex, as practiced by the Taoist masters. Chia references Gurdjieff's teachings as supportive of the Taoist philosophies and practices.

3. On Lunacy & Feeding the Moon

"The moon at present *feeds* on organic life, on humanity ... this means that humanity is *food* for the moon. If all men were to become too intelligent they would not want to be eaten by the moon." (Gurdjieff, in Ouspensky, 1949, p. 57)

Humans can feed higher sources or feed lower sources. It is most undesirable to be under the influence of the Moon, a lower order of the cosmic octave, an outpost at the growing tip of the Ray of Creation. Humankind on earth can be subject to different numbers of laws according to their psychological makeup and depending upon what density of hydrogens are most refined in their being.

The idea is to come under the more direct conscious influences associated with the planets, the sun, and the starry world, and out from the mechanical laws and influences of the moon.

According to Mr. G., the moon is a living being, as are the planets, the earth and sun. However, it is a planet in birth, in its early stages of development, capable of eventually attaining the degree of intelligence of the earth. At one time, the sun existed at the level of earth, while the earth was like the moon. As the Ray of Creation evolves, these cosmic bodies attain higher levels of intelligence, although this is not guaranteed. As it is, the moon has no or little atmosphere or rotation, and supports no organic life of its own. However, it maintains important roles in reference to the growth, life and evolution of organic life on earth.

From a scientific perspective, the moon has both gravitational and electromagnetic effects upon the earth and organic life. A relatively strong gravitational pull of the moon is due to the fact that the moon has the largest mass of any satellite in the solar system relative to its parent body. G. explains:

"The moon is the weight on a clock. Organic life is the mechanism of the clock brought into motion by the weight. The gravity of the weight, the pull on the chain on the cogwheel, set in motion the wheels and the hands of the clock. If the weight is removed all movements in the mechanism of the clock will at once stop. The moon is a colossal weight hanging on to organic life and thus setting it in motion. Whatever we may be doing ... depend(s) upon this weight, which is continually exerting its pressure upon us." (1949, p. 95)

Gurdjieff describes the moon's influence as a primary motive force effecting human's mechanical and unconscious actions:

> "All his movements and consequently all his actions are controlled by the moon. If he kills another man, the moon does it; if he sacrifices himself for others, the moon does that also. All evil deeds, all crimes, all self-sacrificing actions, all heroic exploits, as well as the actions of everyday life, are controlled by the moon." (Ouspensky, 1949, p. 85)

Ouspensky's student, Rodney Collin, provides an astonishing and horrifying depiction of how the moon causes common patterns of mechanical movement, gestures and activity among humanity asleep:

> ... with large numbers of lazy and sedentary people in modern life ... their lives contain almost no intentional movement, they are completely filled with unintentional movement, aimless movement, movement *wholly* under the Moon's sway. ... Not only all obvious kinds of fidgeting, restlessness, mechanical gestures of the hands and arms, changes of bodily position, stroking the face and chin, tapping with fingers or feet ... the mechanical play of the facial muscles ... *they are never still*. ... Almost all the waking and sleeping life of many city-dwellers is occupied by involuntary, unrecognized and completely aimless motion. This is what it means to be under the power of the moon. ... Again, we may say that a very large part of human life is given over to the performance of habits; and that all this is under the influence of the Moon. ... Chief weakness is thus built on habit, habit on involuntary action, and involuntary action on pointless movement. And the primary cause of this whole sequence is the apparently innocent influence of the Moon upon liquid matter. (Collin, 1980, pp.112-4)

Collin's suggests possible mechanisms for lunar influences–through effects upon the liquid mass of the planet. Not only are the oceans subject to the tidal effect of the moon but so are liquids incorporated in organic matter. *"Whenever there is liquid there is lunar motion."* (p.111) The moon counters the pull of the earth on organic life and holds organic liquids in suspension. Collin argues that the moon acts upon the lymph system which has no pump of its own (as does the blood circulation powered by the heart and related to the Sun). Thus, the moon maintains the lymph system in suspension which requires movement on the part of person in order to renew lymph circulation. The "lymph itch" demands continual unconscious movement in order to dissipate the irritation that would otherwise build up.

In terms of humans' abnormal psychology, it is not only habits of movement, but all manifestation of false personality with its destructive habits and negative emotions which are under the influence of the ninety-six laws of the moon. The pathological expressions of humanity asleep, especially the process of reciprocal destruction, *"feed the moon,"* all related to the lunacy of humankind and the most mechanical manifestations of the strange human psyche. Ouspensky (1957) explains:

> All our mechanicalness depends on the moon. We are like marionettes moved by wires, but we can be more free of the moon or less free. When we understand that, we will understand the way to become more free is by not identifying, not considering, struggling with negative emotions, and so on. At present we cannot move a step without the energy of the moon ... All sleeping people are under the influence of the moon ... but if a man develops, he can gradually cut some of the wires that are undesirable and can open himself to higher influences. In this way, he can become free from the moon. (Ouspensky, 1957, p.198)

Another major facet of the moon's control over humanity concerns how the moon feeds off the souls of human beings and other organic life forms. Gurdjieff presents a picturesque view: *"The moon is a huge living being feeding upon all that lives and grows on the earth."* (1949, p, 85) Ouspensky explains:

> ...when anything dies–whether man or cockroach–its soul goes to the moon. (p.213) ... The term 'soul' is used is in the system in the sense of life-principle. The soul may be described as a cloud of fine matters or energies connected together and bound to the physical body. As long as it is in the body, the body is alive and body and soul make one thing. When they separate, we say that the body dies. It is this that distinguishes a piece of dead meat from living flesh. (1957, p.180)

The term soul is used here to refer to the fine matter/energies that serve as the vital or animating principle within the body. In a human, the soul may be highly underdeveloped, in which case it has few psychic properties. Gurdjieff portrays the fate of such souls eaten by the moon:

> "The souls that go to the moon, possessing perhaps even a certain amount of consciousness and memory, find themselves there under ninety-six laws, in the conditions of mineral life, or to put it differently, in conditions from which there is no escape apart from a general evolution in immeasurably long planetary cycles. The moon is 'at the extremity,' at the end of the world; it is the 'outer darkness' of the Christian doctrine 'where there will be weeping and gnashing of teeth.'" (1949, p. 85) # [32]

In *Beelzebub's Tales*, G. explains that many of the woes which have befallen humanity relate to an early cosmic catastrophe which occurred when a comet collided with the earth and broke off two fragments, the moon and a secondary moon unknown to us. After this, the *sacred vibrations Askokin* were required to be sent to the moons in order to maintain them. However, as humans developed, the possibility was raised that they might attain *Objective Reason*, as usually occurs among three-brained beings within other solar systems. In this case, they would realize the *"stupendous terror"* of their position–that by their existence, their lives and death, they are simply maintaining the moon. If humans realized the horror of the situation and their slavery to the moon, they might *"be unwilling to continue their existence and would on principle destroy themselves."* (1950, p. 88) It was for this reason, that the accursed organ Kundabuffer was implanted in humans, so that they would *perceive reality topsy-turvy* and be conditioned simply by *sensations of pleasure and enjoyment.*[33]

---

[32] The soul is related by Collin to the magnetic body, or etheric double, matter in the liquid state under the electromagnetic influence of the moon. The etheric body is not a body as such, as are the physical, astral or mental bodies, but rather a form of magnetic field which connects the physical to the astral and mental bodies. Collin (1980) attempts to portray the possible afterlife dynamics of such underdeveloped souls, arguing that: "... the magnetic current released by the death of living creatures flies to the lowest level of the ionosphere, which is now recognized as the level where lunar magnetism takes effect. There it joins the general magnetic current connecting the Earth and the moon. ... In ... minutes that which made the difference between a living and a dead body has flown to the moon which sustained it during life." (p. 122) The dynamics postulated by Collin are not elaborated by Gurdjieff in this way. As a student of Ouspensky, Collin attempted to relate aspects of G.'s cosmology to a study of the solar system and universe, drawing from the scientific views available in the 1940-50 period.

[33] The contemporary heart master, Adi Da (1995) in his autobiography, *The Knee of Listening*, recounts his experiences of the lunar realm: "There were also times when I saw and learned the workings of psychic planes and subtler worlds. I remember once for a period of days I was aware of a world that appeared to survive in our moon. It was a superphysical world or astral world where beings were sent off to birth on the earth or other worlds, and then their bodies were enjoyed cannibalistically by the older generation on the moon, or they were forced to work as physical and mental slaves." (p. 108) Adi Da's remarks are clearly in keeping with Gurdjieff's claims about the lunar world and its feeding off the soul energies released by the death of organic life forms.

Although the organ Kundabuffer was latter removed, its effects on humankind's psyche had become crystallized in their presences, and passed from generation to generation. A number of particularly destructive processes were then observed on planet earth, including increases in the birthrate and the emergence of warfare—the process of reciprocal destruction. Beelzebub describes this horror to his grandson:

> "... it was possible sometimes to observe very strange manifestations of theirs, that is, from time to time they did something which was never done by three-brained beings on other planets, namely, they would suddenly, without rhyme or reason, begin destroying one another's existence. ... from this horrible process of theirs their numbers rapidly diminished ... ." (1950, p. 91)

Wars and animal sacrifice are particularly horrific processes which produce a surplus of the *low quality Askokin* vibrations, threatening not only the evolution of the moon and its atmosphere, but also, the broader cosmic harmony.

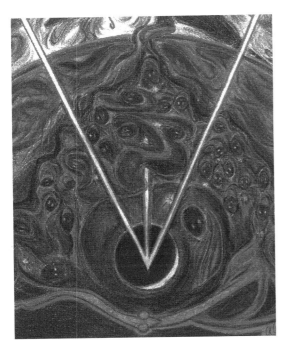

Beelzebub explains that although the moon eventually became stabilised, varied Most High Sacred Individuals then made other cosmic adjustments in order that the Sacred Askokin be produced through other means. In particular, this sacred substance exists in a state blended with two other sacred substances "Abrustdonis" and "Helkdonis," but must be released in order to feed the moon. These substances are in fact those substances by which the Kesdjan (or astral) body and the mental body (or the body of the Soul) are formed and perfected. Unfortunately again, these sacred substances are only separated through an individual's being efforts—*conscious labours* and *intentional sufferings,* or being Partkdolg duties, which are seldom fulfilled given the general degradation of the human psyche and the deterioration of the quality of vibrations given off by humankind.

And so, woe to humanity, through the processes of reciprocal destruction, declining longevity and death, the poor souls produce the vibrations required to maintain the moons. The souls feed the moon and the nuts become fertilizer. The inner cosmos of a human being is intimately connected with the larger cosmos of the solar system and even the universe.

5. Planetary Influence, Essence and Types
& the Causes of War

Ouspensky recounted one of G.'s talks about astrology, essence and types. While on a group walk, a student asked if there was anything of value in astrology. G. explained that there could be if we understood that astrology deals *"with only part of man, with his type, his essence– it does not deal with personality, with acquired qualities."* (1949, p. 366) The group continued to walk along, and suddenly G. dropped his cane. One of the students picked it up and handed it back to him. G. then explained: *"That was astrology. Do you understand? You all saw me drop the stick. Why did one of you pick it up? Let each of you speak for himself."* Each of the five student had a different reaction within the situation according to his type–one who stepped forward and handed back the cane, one who was too distracted, one who did nothing and watched what would happen, and so on. *"This is astrology. In the same situation one man sees and does one thing, another–another thing, a third–a third thing, and so on. And each one acted according to his type."* Gurdjieff had different approaches to what Ouspensky calls *"the science of types"* and he viewed the movements of the planets and other cosmic processes as intimately linked to the subtle nature of human beings.

In *Views from the Real World*, Gurdjieff (1975) describes planetary influence as acting through radiations and emanations to influence the essence of the individual:

> ... all life is coloured by the vibration of the planet nearest to the earth at a given moment. (p. 197) ... All beings born on earth are coloured by the light prevailing at the moment of birth, and keep this color throughout life. ... And indeed planets have a tremendous influence both on the life of mankind in general and on the life of every individual man. It is a great mistake of modern science not to recognize this influence. On the other hand this influence is not so great as modern "astrologers" would have us believe. (p. 257)

Gurdjieff relates levels of human nature to different levels of the Ray of Creation. False personality is under the 96 laws of the level of the moon. The physical body and the personality are under 48 laws related to the level of the earth. The essence is under the 24 laws related to the planets and the 12 laws related to the sun. This includes the astral or Kesdjan body related to the planets and the mental or spiritual body related to the sun. The fourth causal or divine body, real I, is related to the level of all suns—at the level of the galaxy under 6 laws. Behind essence is real I, behind real I, is God. Gurdjieff's views allow us to interconnect psychological processes to varied levels of the cosmic structure, the planes of interpenetrating being.

The Ray of Creation certainly suggests the legitimacy of astrological analysis, although Gurdjieff did not emphasize study along traditional lines. However, an understanding of the elements in magic and astrology provides a way of relating the planets and houses to varied parts of a human essence and the idea of types. The twelve houses of astrology and the varied planets embody the four elements of fire, air, water and earth–four different hydrogens, each embodying different forces. Fire is related to the individuality or spiritual principle and to the realm of the sun. Air is related to the mind and intellect, and the planet Mercury. Water is related to emotions and feelings, and to the planet Venus. The physical body is related to the Earth and to the planet Mars.

The fire signs in the houses of the Zodiac are Aries, Leo, and Sagittarius; the air signs are Gemini, Libra and Aquarius; the water signs are Cancer, Scorpio and Pieces; and the earth signs are Taurus, Virgo and Capricorn. Each of these signs assumes three phases as cardinal, fixed and mutable. Astrological analysis suggests that Cancers and Scorpios will be more emotionally centered, Libras more intellectual, Virgos physically oriented, and Leos, egoistic and I-centered. Of course, astrology is very complex and many relationships must be understood to understand the dominance of different elements within someone's essence. Different planets can be in different signs, as well as in different houses and in different relationships to other planets. Gurdjieff's scheme of the Ray of Creation suggests that a study of astrology could be of value to understanding our essences and types. Astrological influence will be reflected in the relative dominance of different elements and centers within one's nature. We might wonder how when Mr. G. dropped his cane, each of the types might have reacted. Of course, as emphasized by Gurdjieff, personality and false personality can obscure the essence, in which case the individual will not embody their true nature.

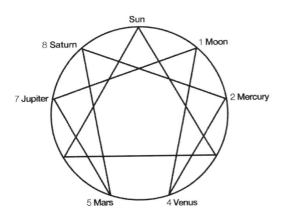

Another approach to astrology associated with some of Gurdjieff's students, particularly Rodney Collin, is to relate the planets to the enneagram. From the Sun there is an outer circulation of light reflected by the different planets and the moon. Each of the points on the inner six sided figure are related to different types—the lunar, mercurial, venusian, martial, jovial and saturnine. Further, just as the number 1 divided by 7 give the repeating non-terminating, number series .142856, so also there is an inner influence and successiveness to one's movement among the types.

The study of astrology can be useful to understanding individual tendencies and proclivities, although this must be based on self study and self-observation.

Gurdjieff also provided provocative statements concerning planetary influence on the masses of humanity, especially in terms of determining larger scale phenomena, such as revolutions, wars and social movements. Ouspensky recalls G.'s remarks to a student who asked "Can war be stopped?"

> "Yes, it can. ... But the whole thing is: how? ... It is necessary to know a great deal in order to understand that. What is war? It is the result of planetary influence. Sometimes up there two or three planets have approached too near to each other, tension results. Have you noticed how, if a man passes quite close to you on a narrow pavement, you become all tense? The same tension takes place between planets. For them it lasts, perhaps, a second or two. But here, on the earth, people begin to slaughter one another, and they go on slaughtering maybe for several years. It seems to them at the time that they hate one another; or perhaps that they have to slaughter each other for some exalted purpose; or that they must defend somebody or something and that is a very noble thing to do; or something else of the same kind. They fail to realize to what an extent they are mere pawns in the game. They think they signify something, they think they can move about as they like; they think they can decide to do this or that.

But in reality all their movements, all their actions, are the result of planetary
influences. And they themselves signify literally nothing. Then the moon plays a big
part in this. But we will speak about the moon separately. Only it must be understood
that neither Emperor Wilhelm, nor generals, nor ministers, nor parliaments, signify
anything or can do anything. Everything that happens on a big scale is governed from
outside and governed either by accidental combinations of influences or by general
cosmic laws." (1949, pp. 23-4)

Gurdjieff regards organic life on earth, including the life of humanity, as representing the *earth's
organ of perception*, taking in planetary influences coming from the planetary sphere and allowing
them to pass on to the earth. Mr. G. states: *"All great events in the life of the human masses are
caused by planetary influences. ... Human society is a sensitive mass for the reception of planetary
influences."* (1949, p. 138) Of course, humankind is asleep to the deeper cosmic mechanism and is
ruled like marionettes.

6. Towards Immortality: On the Cosmology of A Human's Possible Evolution

"In order to be able to speak of any kind of future life there must be a certain
crystallization, a certain fusion of man's inner qualities, a certain independence of
external influences. ... But think for yourselves what there is to withstand physical death
in a man who faints or forgets everything when he cuts his finger? If there is anything
in a man, it may survive; if there is nothing, then there is nothing to survive. But even if
something survives, its future can be very varied." (Gurdjieff, in Ouspensky, 1949, p. 31)

When Gurdjieff is asked whether or not a human being is immortal, he answers *"Both yes and no,"*
and then explains that really *"nothing is immortal"* and that the question has to do with the issue of
existence after death (1949, p. 91). G.'s views on the nature of the soul, the higher being-bodies,
afterlife states and so on, are most complex and presented in fragmentary ways. There are varied
possibilities for a human being to achieve and these involve different levels of immortality. G. explains
that there is definitely *"the possibility of a different 'immortality' for different people."*

Gurdjieff's teachings of the higher being-bodies are explicated in terms of the Ray of Creation. The
inner structure of a human's being-bodies and psychological states reflects the larger structures of
the cosmos. The Ray of Creation allows us *"to see the relation of every action, every thought, every
function to a certain part of the universe governed by its own laws."* (Ouspensky, 1957, p.252) The
varied bodies provide faculties for perceiving and responding to different sources of energy/matter,
radiation and emanations, within the interpenetrating levels of the larger Cosmos.

Within the fourth way, it is a most serious task to escape from prison, from the general laws and to be
free. The evolution of consciousness within the subtle realms of the inner/outer cosmos is the way to

THE FOUR BODIES AND THE RAY OF CREATION

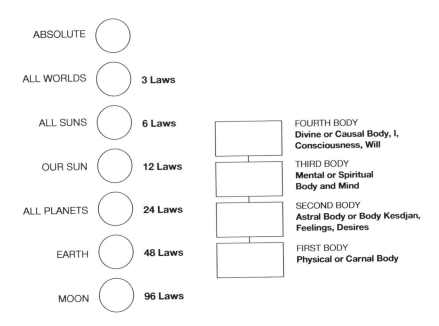

liberation and freedom from the mechanical laws which bind consciousness within the lower realms of material existence—both during life and after death. A position on earth subjects a human to 48 laws, which G. describes: "*We live in a world subject to forty-eight orders of laws, that is to say, very far from the will of the Absolute and in a very remote and dark corner of the universe.*" (Ouspensky, 1949, p. 81) A human can be in a worse position, if they lived on the moon or were under the control of the moon with its 96 mechanical laws, and then capable of evolution only over immense time periods within the larger evolutionary cycle of the moon and planets. From G.'s perspective, the evolution of an individual human being has to do with freeing oneself from mechanical laws. If the individual is free within themselves of the moon's controlling influences and of false personality, then they are under the lesser number of 48 laws associated with the earth, the material body and personality formation. If the individual were further freed of the mechanical laws of the earth and reborn within the essence, then he/she would only be subject to the 24 laws of the planetary world and the 12 laws of the sun. If the individual were further freed of the planetary sphere, he/she would be subject to only the 12 laws at the level of the sun. At the level of real "I," the individual is subject to only 6 laws of all worlds. The idea is to come under the more direct conscious influences associated with the sun, the stars and All Worlds. This is the cosmological basis for a human's possible evolution, as the hydrogen levels of the psyche and inner being are related to the larger cosmic orders. The higher centers and bodies have to be crystallized out of Hydrogens 24, 12 and 6, which allows consciousness to persist within the more subtle planes of being. Each higher being body is under fewer laws and can function within a higher world-order of the Ray of Creation.

[34] Ouspensky's illustration portrays the 'divine body' as the highest being-body. However, within *Beelzebub's Tales*, Gurdjieff refers only to the Kesdjan body (the astral) and the *"highest being-body,"* which is the mental or spiritual body. There is no 'divine body' as such. I tend to interpret the fourth level as being the 'I' itself, the particle of all that exists, the element of Divinity. In this view, it is not a 'body' as such, but the divine element which is embodied in the three planetary, Kesdjan and highest being-bodies. This is more how these distinctions are made within the *Tales*.

Generally, a human's afterlife possibilities are determined by the development and refinement of the higher being bodies within life. Whatever aspect of the human nature, or being-body, is most active in determining the psychological state while the person is alive, determines the afterlife possibilities. For a person whose physical functions predominate, the man-machine, the physical body dies and returns into the earth to the physical elements: *"It is dust and to dust it returns."* (G. In O, 1949, p. 94) Other energies related to the soul, the vitalizing magnetic influences, might pass to the moon, an even more remote corner of the solar system, further removed from the level of the Sun and the Absolute. Other levels of attainment are possible according to whether or not the astral, mental and divine bodies are formed or crystallized through the life of the individual, and most importantly, whether real "I" has been attained.[34]

Whereas varied mystical and religious teachings suggest that humans all have astral and mental bodies and are entitled to every kind of afterlife pleasure, Gurdjieff maintains that this is not so and in fact seldom attained. Although all humans have astral and mental matters, or hydrogens, within their nature, the chemical factory has to save, accumulate, refine and fuse together more of these subtle matters in order to alchemically crystallize and *acquire* the astral and spiritual bodies–as independent vehicles for expanded consciousness and afterlife states.

In explaining these teachings, Gurdjieff drew upon the terminology of Christian doctrines, and differentiates four bodies–the carnal, natural, spiritual and divine bodies; and he borrows from the terminology of theosophists–differentiating the physical, astral, mental and causal bodies. He explains that these other teachings repeat the right divisions regarding a human's inner bodies, but that they have *"forgotten or omitted its most important feature, which is: that man is not born with the finer bodies ...."* (1949, p.40)

None of the higher being bodies are necessary for a person to function within day to day life but are luxuries to be attained only through struggles to awaken. Gurdjieff explains that the physical body is designed so that *"a new independent organism can grow in it,"* (1949, p. 40) and in fact, a series of inner bodies. Within the physical body the astral body can be formed, from which a third mental or spiritual body can be crystallized. Each higher body can acquire control over the lower bodies and realize a new order of knowledge, powers and experience.

Another possibility is that an astral body is formed or crystallized but this crystallization *"takes place on a wrong foundation"* or is incomplete. In this case, the astral body must be *"melted down again,"* which can only be accomplished through suffering, or else the individual remains *"an 'immortal thing.'"* (1949, p. 32) People can generate "friction" and fuse an astral body, but if their development is incomplete or formed around Hasnamussian traits, then this is of no value.

The third mental or spiritual body is composed of the hydrogens of the sun and persists after the death of the astral body. Nicoll explains the deep logic of the Ray of Creation and the potential of humankind:

> In creating the small octave, the Sun is not merely creating on behalf of the Ray itself to fill a missing place, but is also acting for itself. *The Sun wants something* apart from the needs of the Ray of Creation. It is here that the *possibilities* of Man are found. ... *The Intelligence of the Sun wants something for itself in creating Man on Earth* ... It wants Man to ascend from the level of the Earth to the level of the Sun. For this reason it creates Man as something incomplete, as an unfinished being.

Man is created on the Earth as incomplete in order that he may develop up to the level of being represented by the Sun. It is in this sense that Man is said to be a *self-developing organism*. Man is thus an experiment of the Sun, placed on the Earth. He can remain asleep and serve Organic life: or he can awake and serve the Sun. (1975, p.126)

The Sun is the level of spiritual intelligence, H12, and a human is potentially a Son of the Sun.

The attaining of the fourth body is dependent upon the formation of the preceding bodies with all of their *"properties, powers and knowledge,"* but these have yet to be "fixed" or made permanent. Gurdjieff explains the nature of this state: *"The consciousness manifested in the fourth body has full control over the first three bodies and itself."* (1949, p. 40) This is the attaining of real I. This fixing requires *"a special kind of work for all three bodies."* (p. 44) G. explains:

> "The process of fixing these acquired properties corresponds to the process of the formation of the fourth body. And only the man who possesses four fully developed bodies can be called a 'man' in the full sense of the word. This man possesses many properties which ordinary man does not possess. *One of these properties is immortality.* All religions and all ancient teachings contain the idea that, by acquiring the fourth body, man acquires immortality ... When he does learn of this he begins to seek the keys ... especially of the fourth, the most important, room." (1949, p. 44)

The attainment of the fourth body, the divine body or real "I," is related to the level beyond that of the Sun, to the level of the starry world, or the Milky Way galaxy. Gurdjieff explains:

> "The fourth body is composed of material of the *starry world*, that is, of material that does not belong to the solar system, and therefore, if it has crystallized within the limits of the solar system there is nothing within this system that could destroy it. *This means that a man possessing the fourth body is immortal within the limits of the solar system."* (Ouspensky, 1949, p.94)

Certainly, Gurdjieff describes an unusual and awesome possibility of becoming *"immortal within the limits of the solar system."* The more dismal possibility is that of *"dying like dog,"* if the subtle bodies and essence are not crystallized as vehicles for consciousness within the refined world-orders.

In Gurdjieff's teaching, reincarnation, recurrence and varied after life states and processes are possible. The reincarnating and recurring soul lives are needed to further the development of the higher being-bodies in the longer drama of a human's possible evolution:

> "In certain cases of fuller crystallization what people call 'reincarnation' may be possible after death, and, in other cases, what people call 'existence on the other side.' In both cases it is the continuation of life in the 'astral body,' or with the help of the 'astral body.' ... only very few men acquire an 'astral body.' If it is formed it may continue to live after the death of the physical body, and it may be born again in another physical body. This is 'reincarnation.' If it is not re-born, then, in the course of time, it also dies; it is not immortal but it can live long after the death of the physical body." (Gurdjieff , in Ouspensky, 1949, p. 32)

Gurdjieff suggests various dynamics and possibilities for human souls within afterlife states and through recurrent lives.

One of Ouspensky's lifelong interests was in the idea of the possible repetition of lives or eternal recurrence. On one occasion, when Gurdjieff allowed Ouspensky to ask him any question, the issue of recurrence was posed as this was a subject around which Mr. G. was normally evasive, much to Ouspensky's chagrin. However, on that special occasion, Mr. G. explained:

> "This idea of repetition ... is not the full and absolute truth, but it is the nearest possible approximation of the truth. In this case truth cannot be expressed in words. But what you say is very near to it. And if you understand why I do not speak of this, you will be still nearer to it. What is the use of a man knowing about recurrence if he is not conscious of it and if he himself does not change? One can say even that if a man does not change, repetition does not exist for him. If you tell him about repetition, it will only increase his sleep. Why should he make any efforts today when there is so much time and so many possibilities ahead–the whole of eternity? ... Knowledge about the repetition of lives will add nothing to a man if he does not see how everything repeats itself in one life, that is, in this life, and if he does not strive to change himself in order to escape this repetition." (1949, p. 250)

Like the magician who persuades the sheep that they all have souls and need not worry about being skinned, Gurdjieff portrays the ideas of reincarnation and recurrence as potentially acting to put humans to sleep, subject to the *"disease of tomorrow."* He is reluctant to talk of recurrence because unless a human being changes, now in this life and moment, their potentials for evolution will be lost–like the nuts who do not become oak trees but instead fertilizer. Humans are simply too ready to believe in their own immortality and believe any old tale, while neglecting the inner alchemical task of refining the higher being-bodies.

For Mr. G., time is counted and limited, and the illusions of an afterlife and other lives simply detract from the essential messages of awakening and struggle. *"Moreover there is a definite time, a definite term, for everything. Possibilities for everything ... exist only for a definite time."* (G., in O., 1949, p. 251)

7. Beelzebub's Tales

7a. **The Sacred Rascooarnos, the 'Okipkhalevnian-exchange' & Purgatory**

According to Beelzebub, a variety of afterlife fates might await those three-brained beings from planet Earth. Some will die like dog according to the Itoklanoz principle, *"as Nature actualizes one-brained and two-brained beings."* (p. 131) Their planetary bodies are returned to feed the Earth and Askokin vibrations feed the moon—but generally they serve only local cosmic purposes. Others may have formed a Kesdjan body and will be drawn into the corresponding spheres of such substances, at least for a limited time. Others might even be embodied as one or two-brained beings or suffer varied conditions of remorse, retribution and purgatory conditions. The highest possibility is to actualize those possibilities for which the three-brained beings were originally designed—of becoming Sacred Individuals worthy of assuming a role in the larger world order or of blending again into the Most Holy Sun Absolute. Beelzebub suggests that behind real "I" is God, not with a comb in his pocket, but as the Most Holy Sun Absolute. He depicts the ultimate possibility for human evolution, which is to be thought worthy *"... of uniting with the presence of our Most Most Holy Sun Absolute."* (pp. 765-6)

In his *Tales*, Gurdjieff provides more detailed discussions of the higher being-bodies and afterlife processes than those recorded by Ouspensky. In particular, Beelzebub explains the sacred Rascooarnos as *"... the separation of these diverse-natured 'three-in-one' formations from each other."* (p. 765) The Rascooarnos involve the separations of a human's different being-bodies—the planetary body, the Kesdjan body (astral body) and the higher being body—which occur at death and within afterlife realms.

Beelzebub explains what happens through the Sacred Rascooarnos:

> "Now it is necessary to explain to you in more detail in what successiveness the first sacred Rascooarno then occurred ... At first on the planet itself the 'second-being-body,' i.e., the body-Kesdjan, together with the 'third-being-body' separate themselves from the 'fundamental-planetary-body' and, leaving this planetary body on the planet, rise both together to that sphere where those cosmic substances—from the localization of which the body-Kesdjan of a being arises-have their place of concentration.

> "And only there, at the end of a certain time, does the principle and final sacred Rascooarno occur to this two-natured arising, after which such a 'higher being-part' indeed becomes an independent individual with its own individual Reason." (p. 765)

---

[35] Gurdjieff describes various processes by which individuals who have attained more advanced levels of the crystallization of their Kesdjan body can help to "materialize" the Kesdjan body of another being who has died, so that for a certain time period, the second individual is able to manifest some of the functions proper to the physical body. Mr. G. and Beelzebub describe how people might maintain a connection to an evolved teacher through having established a connection with his or her Handbledzoin (the blood of the astral body). In Beelzebub's Tales, "the sacred Almznoshinoo" is described in reference to the last supper of Christ, where the sharing of the body and blood of Christ with the disciples establishes a link between them which persists beyond physical death.

The first Rascooarno is the separation of both higher being-bodies from the planetary body. These then rise to that 'sphere' corresponding to their own nature—or their center of gravity of being. The higher being-bodies thus rise into the atmospheres of the planet, which provide the medium in which the radiations of the Sun and planets most easily convey their influences.

Beelzebub explains this subtle process involving the Kesdjan body in afterlife states:

> "And so, inconsequence of the fact that the body Kesdjan of the being is coated with those substances which in their totality make this cosmic formation much lighter than that mass of cosmic substances which surrounds the planets and is called the planetary atmosphere, then as soon as the body Kesdjan of the being is separated from the planetary body of the being (i.e., at death), it at once rises according to the cosmic law called 'Tenikdoa,' or as it is sometimes called the 'law of gravity,' to that sphere in which it finds the weight proper to it equally balanced and which is therefore the corresponding place of such cosmic arisings ..." (p. 728)

The Kesdjan body rises according to the 'law of gravity' to that sphere where *"it finds the weight proper to it equally balanced."* This broadens the familiar concept of gravity, as a force between material masses, to the concept of different substances having their own 'centers-of-gravity' –a place or realm to which they will be naturally drawn, or to which they will gravitate. The atmospheres are described as providing the ideal medium for planetary and solar emanations, radiations and influences; and the Kesdjan body is sustained by the second being-food, air, which contains the substances required for coating and maintaining it.

The Kesdjan, after the first sacred Rascooarno, rises into upper levels of the atmosphere or into other concentrations as related to the planetary sphere. An individual who has crystallized the Kesdjan body is thus granted further existence beyond the death of the material planetary body, although this existence is also time bound. Beelzebub explains that the body Kesdjan *"can exist in space only for a limited period, namely, only until the completion of the appointed movement of that planet, on which the given being had arisen, around its sun."* (p. 729)[35] This suggests that the Kesdjan body persists for only a year.

The Kesdjan body cannot exist long before it also decomposes and this is the second Rascooarno. As this time approaches, if the highest being body has not reached the required degree of Reason and is still dependent upon a Kesdjan body, it will search for a similar Kesdjan body to inhabit, in order to continue to exist for its further self-perfection. This *"Okipkhalevnian-exchange-of-the-external-part-of-the-soul"* or the *"exchange of the former being-body-Kesdjan"* is a process by whereby incomplete beings maintain their existence through the second Rascooarno. Beelzebub comments on this strange process:

---

[36] Gurdjieff's views on these subjects are similar to the claims made by the living Heart Master, Adi Da: "On March 20, 1993, Avatar Adi Da confirmed conclusively to His devotees: Swami Vivekananda's compassionate urge to be reborn in order to serve the West had created a unique conjunction with Avatar Adi Da's Divine Impulse to Manifest in the human realm, and it was this conjunction that provided the vehicle for Avatar Adi Da's incarnation as Franklin Jones." Adi Da describes this process: "The Deeper Personality Vehicle of Swami Vivekananda arose in the conditioned domain and provided the conjunction with Me (As I Am). That Vehicle was conjoined with My Very Being. Swami Vivekananda was given up completely, and the Vehicle became transparent to Me."

[37] Adi Da's explanations illustrate what Beelzebub describes as the 'okipkhalevnian-exchange-of-the-external-part-of-the-soul" or the "exchange of the former being-body-Kesdjan." Swami Vivekananda surrendered his astral vehicle for incarnation of the Divine Person of Adi Da. (Lee, 1998)

"Here, you might as well be told that your favourites also have, as it were, a similar representation about the 'Okipkhalevian exchange' and they have even invented a very clever name for it, namely, 'metempsychosis' or 'reincarnation' ... According to this fantastic branch of this theory of their 'science,' now called spiritualism, they suppose among other things that each of them already has a higher being-part or, as they call it, a soul, and that a transmigration must be occurring the whole time to this soul, i.e., something of the kind of this same 'Okipkhalevnian exchange' ... those fantastic souls of theirs, (are) only the fruits of their idle fancy ... nothing else but ... 'twaddle.'"
(pp. 767-8)

This strange process described by Beelzebub involves an individual inhabiting the Kesdjan body of another being in order to continue their existence—still within the sphere of the radiations of the sun and planets.[36 / 37]

Beelzebub's descriptions of afterlife possibilities and phenomena of the okipkhalevnian exchange of the external part of the soul, of reincarnation and recurrence, are very difficult to understand and elaborate, and raise many questions and issues. Such processes simply cannot be explained in words, "to slugs," who take the ephemeral for the real and imagine that they already know Mr. God himself with his comb in his vest pocket or sitting on his throne. Gurdjieff, in Ouspensky (1949), describes *"something like what people consider 'reincarnation' and 'recurrence'"* as occurring—particularly involving individuals with crystallized higher being-bodies returning to material existence.

Beelzebub explains that if the highest being-body has been formed but has not attained the required degree of reason and self-perfection required to return to the Sun Absolute, it will continue to live throughout the life of the solar system and will not decompose:

"... the higher being-body itself, being formed of crystallizations received directly from the sacred Theomertmalogos into the solar system within the limits of which the being arises and where his existence proceeds, can never decompose; and this 'higher part' must exist in the given solar system as long as it does not perfect itself to the required Reason." (p. 768)

The highest being body is formed from the Emanations of the Sun Absolute, the Theomertmalogos or Word God, and is *immortal within the limits of the solar system*. However, until this highest being-body is perfected, the individual remains within the solar system Ors.

Beelzebub explains that in the beginning, those highest being-bodies who had attained the required development of Divine Reason would pass directly on to the Most Most Holy Sun Absolute. However, after another cosmic catastrophe, which effected the larger Universe, these individuals ceased to have this possibility of blending again with the Sun Absolute. Instead, they passed on to the Holy planet Purgatory, described as *"the heart and place of concentration of all the completing results of the pulsation of everything that functions and exists in the Universe."* (p. 745) Purgatory is described by Beelzebub as the richest and most beautiful planet of the Universe, where the higher being bodies sense everything external in states of bliss and delight. However, although Purgatory is described, on one hand as a paradise, on the other hand, it is described as a *"hell."* Hell is the inner state experienced by the higher being-bodies dwelling there who understand the reality of everything existing and are able to perceive the Common Father who is so near, but who are unable to blend again with the Most Holy Sun Absolute. Thus, these higher being-bodies experience *"constant anguish, grief and oppression."* (p. 804)

The prospects for Hasnamuss individuals in afterlife states are not too promising. Recall that according to Beelzebub, Hasnamuss individuals are those who have not crystallized the Divine impulse of Objective Conscience. Further, they are subject to the seven *"Naloo-osnian-spectrum-of-impulses,"* which include such impulses as towards *"every kind of depravity," "irresistible inclinations to destroy the existence of other breathing creatures,"* the *"feelings of self-satisfaction from leading others astray,"* and so on. (p. 406) Their pathological manifestations cause all kinds of grief and suffering for others and eventually the Hasnamuss will face what Beelzebub calls *"serious-retributive-suffering-consequences."* Some of these individuals consist of only a planetary body but others have at least partially coated the higher being-bodies.

Beelzebub distinguishes four types of Hasnamuss individuals and outlines their afterlife fates. All four types experience varied afterlife states as determined by the actual nature of their actions and their consequences and the responsibilities pre-established for these being. Beelzebub explains:

> "For these four kinds of Hasnamuss-individuals ... the mentioned retributive-suffering-consequences are various and correspond both to the nature of each kind as well as to what is called 'objective-responsibilities' ensuing from the primordial providence and hopes and expectations of our COMMON FATHER concerning these cosmic actualizations." (p. 407)

The first type is a person who consists of only a planetary body and has formed neither a Kesdjan body nor a higher being-body. During the Sacred Rascooarno, he will be *"destroyed forever such as he is."* (p. 406) His planetary body will devolve into its elements and return to the Earth and subtle vital energies, the Askokin vibrations, will feed the Moon. Beelzebub explains that when this being dies, all of his impulses and sensations do not die at once, or simultaneously. Instead, he dies by thirds. Firstly, *"one of his brains"* or of the *"independent spiritualized 'locations'"* will die, then the second, and third. One by one, the independent brains *"cease to participate in his common presence."* Beelzebub also notes that after the final death, the *"disintegration-of-all-the-active-elements"* of the planetary body proceeds much more slowly than usual. As this occurs, there is an ongoing *"inextinguishable action ... of the mentioned 'sensed-impulses' he had during life."* This suggests a gradual repetition of impulses and sensations within the disintegrating psyche through the processes of death and the dissolution of the brains.

The second type of Hasnamuss-individual has formed a Kesdjan body, which has the property of *"Toorinoorino"*–defined as *"nondecomposition in any sphere of that planet on which he arose."* This type *"has to exist, by being formed again and again in a certain way,"* in order to eradicate a certain 'something' from his psyche and to continue to strive for self-perfection. He is unable to perfect himself without a planetary body and so he must be coated again and again in planetary bodies, even taking the forms of one and two-brained beings. This process will proceed until the Hasnamuss qualities have been eliminated from him. Beelzebub states: *"... he must constantly begin all over again in the form of another being of the planet ...."* (p. 409)

The third type has acquired a third being-body, which for Beelzebub, is what it means to have attained a soul. This is evident in his description:

> "The third kind of Hasnamuss-individual is the highest being-body or soul, during the coating of which in the common presence of a three-brained being this something arises and participates, but he also acquires the property of Toorinoorino, but this time

proper to this highest being-body; that is to say, this arising is no longer subject to decomposition not only in the spheres of that planet on which he had his arising, but also in all other spheres of the Great Universe." (p. 407)

The "something" which participates in the arising of the third being-body or soul, is the undesirable properties and qualities formed in the Hasnamuss individual. This being has attained a *"degree-of-cognition-of-one's-own-individuality,"* but is unable to evolve further until *"a certain something is entirely eradicated from his common presence."* This being is not subject to decomposition during the existence of the Great Universe.

Beelzebub explains that compared with the second type, *"the matter is still more terrible"* for the third type. This is because this type *"according to the foreseeing FIRST-SOURCED-PRINCIPLE-OF-EVERYTHING-EXISTING was predetermined to serve the aim of helping the government of the whole increasing World ...,"* and had a certain responsibility for his manifestations. (p. 409) The certain 'something,' the Hasnamus tendencies, can now only be eliminated as a result of *"intentionally actualized Partkdolg-duty"*–of conscious labours and intentional suffering. However, the third type of individual *"never loses the possibility of freeing himself"* from that *"certain 'something,'"* which participated in the formation and coating of the third being-body.

Beelzebub states that certain HIGHER-SACRED-INDIVIDUALS have allotted three planets of the Universe, in remote corners, as a place for the *"suffering existence"* of this higher order of Hasnamuss-individuals. These planets exist under the names of 'Remorse-of-conscience,' 'Repentance' and 'Self-Reproach.' The Hasnamuss individual, Lentrohamsanin who spread his false doctrines and is described as *"the chief culprit in the destruction of all the very saintly labors of Ashiata Shiemash,"* is one of the few inhabitants of the planet 'Retribution.'

The fourth type is the *"Eternal-Hasnamuss-individual."* This individual faces varied *"retributive-suffering-consequences"*–without chance of attaining real I or of blending again with the Most Holy Sun Absolute. Whereas the third type of Hasnamuss individual can at least still possibly be *"cleansed from this something,"* those undesirable qualities, the fourth type has lost such possibilities forever. As a special place for the continued, eternal existence of the fourth type, the higher Sacred Individuals allotted the planet *"Eternal-Retribution."* Beelzebub depicts their eternal state: *"The chief torture of the state of these 'highest being-bodies' is that they must always experience these terrifying sufferings fully conscious of the utter hopelessness of their cessation."* (p. 410) Certainly, this is a dismal fate with no end in sight until the dissolution of the Great Universe.

Beelzebub provides remarkable teachings about the subtle afterlife possibilities for the four types of Hasnamuss-Individuals–from dying by thirds, to repeated material lives even in the forms of one and two-brained beings, to Eternal Retribution or suffering without cessation!

7b. "A Particle of All that Exists"

In order to understand how a three-brained being embodies the whole of the "Megalocosmos," we have to consider the creation process elaborated by Beelzebub. Before creation occurred, *"nothing yet existed"* and the whole of the Universe was *"empty endless space."* The UNI-BEING CREATOR existed alone within the Most Most Holy Sun Absolute, but otherwise, the empty space was filled with the prime source cosmic substance of *"Etherokrilno."*

In the beginning, the Common Father Creator Almighty had changed the functioning of the sacred cosmic laws of three and seven, or the Triamazikamno and Heptaparaparshinokh, and directed the action of these forces from within the Sun Absolute into the empty spaces of the Universe. Beelzebub describes this first process as the *"Emanation-of-the-Sun-Absolute,"* or alternatively as the *"Theomertmalogos"* or *"Word God."* This process is similar to the book of Genesis, where the earth was empty and void, and the Will and Word of God initiates the creation process.

The "emanations" originate from the Most, Most Holy Sun Absolute, and *"began to act at certain definite points of the space of the Universe upon the prime-source substance Etherokrilno from which ... certain definite concentrations began to be concentrated."* (pp. 758-9) The world of emanations gives rise to Second order Suns, which then become established with their own laws of three and seven. In turn, the Second Order Suns transform their results and radiate their influences. A new generation of crystallisations of a different density are formed around the Second Order Suns, again out of the Etherokrilno. These Third order Suns are the planets, which began to group around the newly arisen Suns.

At this point, Beelzebub describes half of the force of the Emanation of the Sun Absolute as taken up by the initial creation processes, and now the other half begins to manifest within itself, which gave rise to *"similarities-to-the-already-arisen"* on the planets:

> "... after this, ...the actualization of the fundamental outer cycle ... ceased, and all the action of its functioning entered forever into the results already manifested by it, and in them there began to proceed its inherent permanent processes of transformation, called 'evolution' and 'involution'.

> "And then, thanks this time to a second-grade cosmic law ... the 'aggregation of the homogeneous,' there began to be grouped on the planets themselves, from the mentioned 'relatively independent' new formations named 'similarities-to-the-already-arisen,' yet other also 'relatively independent' formations." (pp. 758-9)

The outer cycle of creation ceased and the action of the forces entered into the processes of the involution and evolution of the "active elements."

According to Beelzebub, the results of these processes establish the *"Trogoautoegocratic principle"* –the reciprocal feeding of everything existing in the Universe. Everything feeds upon other elements and in turn becomes food in the cosmic exchanges of substances. Beelzebub describes the evolution of varied microcosmoses, cells, through different forms of vegetation, one and two-brained beings, up to the complex Tetartocosmoses, or three-brained beings, the *"men-beings."*

The men-beings on planet Earth are created and maintained by the same laws of Triamazikamno and Heptaparaparshinokh as embodied within the larger cosmos. This is the basis upon which human beings can perfect their higher being-bodies and assume larger cosmic purposes. Beelzebub explains firstly the triune nature of human beings and then the sevenfold:

> "When each separate 'higher-perfected-being-body' becomes an independent Individual and acquires in itself its own law of Sacred Triamazikamno, it begins to emanate similarly to the Most Most Holy Sun Absolute but in miniature." (p. 798)

> "... through each of them the cosmic substances arising in all seven Stopinders of the Sacred Heptaparaparshinokh could be transformed, and all of them ... besides serving as apparatuses for the Most Great Trogoautoegocrat, could have all possibilities for absorbing from those cosmic substances which are transformed through them what is corresponding for the coating and for the perfecting in each of them of both higher-being bodies; because each three-brained being arisen on this planet of yours represents in himself also, in all respects ... an exact similarity of the whole Megalocosmos ... but of course in miniature ... " (p.775)

At varied times, Beelzebub refers to three-brained beings as potentially becoming *"a particle of all that exists,"* (p. 163) or *"a particle though an independent one, of everything existing in the Great Universe."* (p. 183) Elsewhere, he describes humans *"as beings having in their presences every possibility for becoming particles of a part of Divinity ...."* (p. 453)

In the context of describing one of Saint Buddha's teachings, Beelzebub explains the most profound secrets of human potential:

> "This Most Great Foundation of the All-embracing of everything that exists constantly emanates throughout the whole of the Universe and coats itself from its particles upon planets-in certain three-brained beings who attain in their common presences the capacity to have their own functioning of both fundamental cosmic laws of the sacred Heptaparaparshinokh and the sacred Triamazikamno-into a definite unit in which alone 'Objective Divine Reason' acquires the possibility of becoming concentrated and fixed. ... certain parts of the Great All-embracing, already spiritualised by Divine Reason, return and reblend with the great Prime Source of the All-embracing ..." (pp.244-5)

Beelzebub explains that after Buddha's talk, the people misunderstood his message and began to believe that they already were such *"parts of the Most Great Greatness,"* even without performing any being-Partkdolg duty. They were *"convinced that they were already particles of Mister Prana himself."* (p. 246)

A soul is not given to a human being but must be acquired. Unfortunately, the cosmic catastrophes which occurred to the earth and the miscalculations around the organ Kundabuffer, led to the emergence of a strange breed on the planet, slugs, who according to Beelzebub are willing to believe any old tale. Humans have missed the mark and do not establish their own inner triangle or sevenfold nature, completing the inner octave to blend again with the Most Holy Sun Absolute or to assume other roles in the larger Cosmos.

In explaining the localization of a human's thinking centre in the *"cells-of-the-head-brain,"* Beelzebub explains that those individuals who perfect the highest being-body assume a similar role in relationship to the Sun Absolute:

> "... the 'cells-of-the-head-brain,' actualize for the whole presence of each of them exactly such a purpose as is fulfilled at the present time by the 'higher-perfected-bodies' of three-brained beings from the whole of our Great Universe, who have already united themselves with the Most Most Holy Sun Absolute ..." (p. 778)

Such independent Holy Individuals can serve larger cosmic purposes—a role initially conceived also for those three brained-beings on planet Earth. Unfortunately, your favorites ended up—because of the abnormal conditions of being-existence, the organ Kundabuffer and their strange psyches, and various cosmic catastrophes—behaving, living and dying more 'like dog' or nuts which become only fertilizer.

Imagine that, human beings are potentially similitudes of the whole, particles of the Great Universe, with deep hidden roots within vast dimensions of being and non-being. Behind essence is real I, behind real I, is God, or at least the Most Most Holy Sun Absolute. Beelzebub provides many strange and provocative talks for his grandson Hassein, about the hidden dimensions of those strange three-brained beings on planet Earth.

The notion of a particle is very profound. Ouspensky related Gurdjieff's discussion of dimensions to understanding the nature of a point:

> ... seven cosmoses related to one another in the ratio of zero to infinity. ...
> "The zero-dimension or the point is a limit. This means that we see something as a point, but we do not know what is concealed behind this point. It may actually be a point, that is, a body having no dimensions and it may also be a whole world, but a world so far removed from us or so small that it appears to us as a point." (1949, p.209)

The relation of "I" to "God" or the "Sun Absolute" is surely the relationship of the zero-dimension to the infinite and it is all tied up in seven dimensions.

8. Remembering, Forgetting
& the Inevitability of Death

> "... every man should strive to have his own "I" ..."
> G. I. Gurdjieff (1950, p.1201)

Humankind is in a terrible state, asleep to the realities of life, unable to perceive the real world, passively conditioned by the pleasuring of the stomach and sex organs, governed by a false consciousness system and bound only to serve local cosmic purposes–feeding the earth and moon. Humans' psychological illusions blind them to the horror of the situation and of themselves. Most central are the illusions of being properly conscious, of having real will and of knowing "I." Beyond these, humans hold the illusion that they all have eternal souls, about to experience the pleasures of paradise and heaven or live innumerable lives until they get it right, and once again know God–Mr. God himself, with his comb sticking out of his vest pocket.

Gurdjieff presents a dismal view of the reality and horror of the situation:

> Nature takes all measures to ensure that we shall live without seeing the terror, and that we should not hang ourselves, but live long; and then, when we are required, She slaughter us. (p. 1226)

Humans in quotation marks are slugs who can end up as only fertilizer. Humans do not have a soul, as such, but only the potential for achieving one. They must produce the necessary being efforts through work on self, the struggle to awaken, conscious labours and intentional suffering, and the fulfilling of their being obligations, in order for this potential to be realized. In this view, the only thing that is serious is the possibility of attaining "I," real I. Gurdjieff explains, by the title of Book III of his *"All and Everything"* series, that *The World is Real only then, when 'I AM.'* The I Am refers to the Particle, established in its own nature. Elsewhere, G. is quoted by Nicoll: *"Behind Real I lies God."* (1975, p. 1388)

Gurdjieff, as recalled by Ouspensky, always asked what is serious to a human in prison who is condemned to death, and then answered–to escape–to escape from the general law and to be free. In the light of the fourth way teaching, it is clearly evident that people normally turn around in circles of insignificant interest and insignificant aims, with no idea of what they are missing. Humans do not even realize that they are imprisoned, as slaves and slugs to Great Nature. At least, for one who encounters *the Work*, or *Beelzebub's Tales to His Grandson*, he or she can cultivate a more conscious attitude towards his or her slavery. This can initiate processes of self-study and self-remembering, experiences of the sacred being-impulses and the instinctual sensing of cosmic truths. The aim is to remember to be aware of the totality of ourselves within the present moment, within the depths of our being. Normally, humans are lost in forgetfulness and need to remember Self–as an emanation of the sorrow of the Common Father and as a particle of the Divine. Unfortunately, all of mechanical life puts the slugs to sleep, amusing them with pleasures and imagination, until they are fit food for the moon. Humans need to remember themselves always and everywhere, until they attain real I.

In *Beelzebub's Tales*, Gurdjieff ascribes a central role to the moon and the implanting of the organ Kundabuffer as causing latter psychopathology among those three-brained beings on planet Earth. In Views from the Real World, Gurdjieff elaborated on the Kundabuffer, the moon, and their significance:

> The moon is man's big enemy. We serve the moon. ... Kundabuffer is the moon's representative on earth. We are like the moon's sheep, which it cleans, feeds and shears, and keeps for its own purposes. But when it is hungry it kills a lot of them. All organic life works for the moon. Passive man serves involution; and active man, evolution. You must choose. (1975, p.198)

At the very end of his tales to his grandson, in a chapter entitled, *"The Inevitable Results of Impartial Mentation,"* Beelzebub explains one remaining route of escape for "your favorites:"

> "The sole means now for the saving of the beings of the planet Earth would be to implant again into their presences a new organ, an organ like Kundabuffer, but this time of such properties that every one of these unfortunates during the process of existence should constantly sense and be cognizant of the inevitability of his own death as well as of the death of everyone upon whom his eyes or attention rests.

> "Only such a sensation and such a cognizance can now destroy the egoism completely crystallized in them that has swallowed up the whole of their Essence and also that tendency to hate others which flows from it ..." (p.1183)

Beelzebub explains that only such an organ would break down the egoism crystallized in humankind and reveal the insignificance of *"all his favourite things."* Of course, Beelzebub notes that the organ Kundabuffer and human's psychological illusions prevent such cognition of *"these genuine terrors."* Humans have sown little and so shall they reap. Without the desire and struggle to remember self, a human does not attain real I and realize the larger possibilities for immortality, consciousness, genuine love and self perfection. The slugs can even serve higher cosmic purposes and blend again with the Most Most Holy Sun Absolute, although it may take a long time. Beelzebub's views and teachings on the nature of those unfortunate three-brained beings on planet Earth are as inspiring as they are horrifying.

About the Author

Christopher P. Holmes

Christopher P. Holmes was born in England, on October 7 1949, and raised in Ontario, Canada. He graduated with a B.A. from Carleton University, Ottawa in 1971 and a Ph.D. in clinical psychology from the University of Waterloo in 1978. He taught at York University, Downsview, Ontario over an eleven year period, amidst controversy over his investigations of mystical and spiritual psychology, science and psychic phenomena. He co-founded with Anita Mitra, three centers–the Institute for Mystical and Spiritual Science, Maple, Ontario, the Rainbow Centre in Toronto, and Zero Point in the Ottawa valley. Christopher has also worked for twelve years as a forensic psychologist with young offenders and adults within the Ontario Ministry of Corrections. He currently dedicates himself to furthering the aims of Zero Point-Institute for Mystical and Spiritual Science–currently in Kemptville, Ontario.

Dr. Holmes has studied widely in modern psychology and science, as well as in the mystical and spiritual traditions. In his view, the mainstream of modern thought is seriously misguided in dismissing the spiritual and soul nature of human beings, and in failing to explore the deep roots of human consciousness and the heart. Dr. Holmes explains that a science of soul and spirit must consider the physics, metaphysics and cosmology of consciousness. Most importantly, it involves self study and awakening through the alchemy of psycho-spiritual transformation.

Christopher was introduced to the Gurdjieff teaching while a graduate student in clinical psychology interested in the development of consciousness within psychotherapy and in the broader nature of human psychopathology. His early years of study were focused more on the Ouspensky version of the fourth way teaching, and it was only over the following twenty years that he began to fathom the depths of Gurdjieff's masterpiece *Beelzebub's Tales* and to apply the study of the sacred laws to the findings, theories and philosophy of modern science.

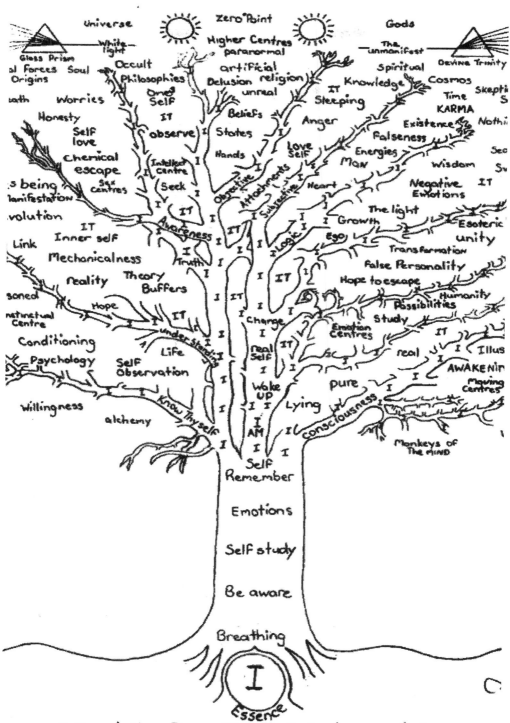

A Seed Has Been Planted And Now I Grow

Bibliography

Anderson, M.
The Unknowable Gurdjieff. Weiser, New York, 1962.

Baba Ram Das, (Alpert, R.)
Be Here Now. Lama Foundation, New Mexico, 1972.

Bakan, P.
Two streams of consciousness. In Pope & Singer (Eds.), *The Stream of Consciousness.* Plenum Press, New York, 1978.

Barker, E.
Letters from a dead man. Rider, New York, 1914.

Bawa. G.
The Mind is in the Heart. *Psychology Today.* Interview, April 1977.

Blavatsky, H.
The Secret Doctrine: The syntheses of science, religion and philosophy. Theosophical University Press, Pasadena California, 1888.

Bennett, J.
Gurdjieff: Making a New World. Harper & Row, New York, 1978

Commentary on Beelzebub's Tales to his Grandson. Columbe Press, England. 1977.

Witness. Omen Press, Tucson, Arizona, 1974.

A Spiritual Psychology. CSA Press, Lakemont, Georgia, U.S.A. (1974)

Bucke, R.
Cosmic Consciousness: A Study in the evolution of the human mind. Olympia Press, New York, 1972.

Butkovsky-Hewitt, A.
With Gurdjieff in St. Petersburg and Paris. Samuel Weiser, 1978.

Capra, F.
The Tao of Physics. Fontana/Collins, Great Britain, 1975.

Castaneda, C.
A Separate Reality. New York, Pocket Books, 1971.

Chia, M.
Taoist Secrets of Love: Cultivating Male Sexual Energy. Aurora Press, New York, 1984.

Chambers, D.
The Puzzle of Conscious Experience. *Scientific American.* Dec.1995.

Cohen, J., Phipps, J.
The Common Experience. Tarcher, Inc.,Los Angeles, 1979.

Collin, R.
The Theory of Celestial Influence. Watkins, London, 1980.

The Theory of Eternal Life. Shambhala, Boulder, 1984.

Cox, J.
Dialogues of Gurdjieff. Chan Shal Imi Society, Atlanta, Georgia, 1976.

The Death of Gurdjieff in the Foothills of Georgia. Stone Mountain, Georgia, Chan Shal Imi, 1980.

Crookall, R.
The Interpretation of Cosmic and Mystical Experiences. Attic Press, Greenwood, S. C., 1969.

DeRopp, R.
Warrior's Way: The Challenging Life Games. Delta Books, Dell Publ., New York, 1979.

Ey. H.
Consciousness: a phenomenological study of being conscious and becoming conscious. 1978.

Foster, D.
The Intelligent Universe: a cybernetic philosophy. Putnam & Sons, New York, 1975.

Gnostic Gospels.
Selections from *The Nag Hammadi Library.* Harper & Row, San Francisco, 1978.

Gold, H.
Secret Talks with Mr. G. IDHHB, INC., 1978.

Gurdjieff, G.
All and Everything: Beelzebub's Tales to His Grandson. Routledge & Kegan, London,(1959)1950.

Cited by Ouspensky, In Search of the Miraculous. 1949.

Life is Real only Then, When "I AM". E. Dutton, New York, 1975.

Meetings with Remarkable Men. Routeledge & Kegan, New York,1974 (1963).

Views from the Real World. Dutton & Co., New York, 1975.

The Herald of the Coming Good. Weiser, New York, (1974) 1933.

Hall, M.
Man: Grand Symbol of the Mysteries. Philosophical Research Society, Los Angeles, 1972/1956.

Hahn, T.
The miracle of mindfulness! Boston: Beacon Press, 1976.

Hesse, H.
Siddhartha. New Directions Publ., New York, 1951.

Holmes, C.
Within-Without from Zero Points: Book I: *The Heart Doctrine: Mystical views of the origin and nature of human consciousness.* Zero Point, Kemptville, Ontario, 2010.

Within-Without from Zero Points: Book II: Microcosm/Macrocosm: Mystical Views on the Origin of the Universe, the Nature of Matter & Human Consciousness. Zero Point, Kemptville, Ontario, Canada 2010.

The Slugs:" On G. I. Gurdjieff's Beelzebub's tales to his grandson. Zero Point, Kemptville, Ontario, Canada, 2010.

Horney, K.
Finding the real self: a letter with a forward by Karen Horney. *American Journal of Psychoanalysis.* 1949.

Hulme, K.
Undiscovered Country:
A Spiritual Adventure.
Little Brown, Boston, 1966.

James W.
The Principles of Psychology.
Holt, New York, 1890.

Psychology (Briefer Course).
Holt, New York, 1892/1972.

Varieties of Religious Experience.
New American Library, New York,
1958.

Jaynes, J.
The origin of consciousness in the
breakdown of the bicameral mind.
Boston, Houghton, Mifflin, 1976.

Jung, C.
Memories, Dreams, Reflections.
New York: Pantheon, 1963.

King, C.
The States of Human Consciousness.
University Books, New York,
(1922)1963.

Klinger, E.
Modes of normal conscious flow. In
Pope and Singer (Eds.), *The Stream*
of Consciousness.
Plenum, New York, 1978.

Leary, T.
The Politics of Ecstacy.
Paladin, New York, 1968.

Lee, C.
The Promised GOD-MAN is Here.
Ruchira Avatar Adi Da Samraj.
Dawn Horse Press, Middletown,
California. 1998.

Lilly, J.
The Center of the Cyclone.
Bantam, New York, 1972.

May, R.
Psychology and the Human Dilemma.
Princeton: Van Nostrand, 1964.

McNeil, E., Rubin, Z.
The Psychology of Being Human.
Canfield, San Francisco, 1977.

Mishra, R.
Yoga Sutras. Doubleday
Anchor Books, New York, 1973.

Moffatt, J.
But I'll Know My Song Well.
Zero Point Publications, Oxford Mills,
Ontario, 2002.

Narasimha, B .
Self Realization: Life and teachings of
Sri Ramana Mararshi.
Jupiter Press, Madras, 1976.

Natsoulas, T.
Consciousness. *American*
Psychologist. October 1978.

Needleman, J., Baker, G. (Eds.)
Gurdjieff: Essays and Reflections on
the Man and HisTeaching.
Continuum, New York, 1997.

Neisser, U.
Cognitive Psychology. Englewood
Cliffs: Prentice-Hall, 1966.

Nicoll, M.
Psychological Commentaries on the
Teachings of G. I. Gurdjieff and
P.D. Ouspensky.
Robinson & Watkins, London 1975.

Living Time: and the integration of the

life. London: Stuart & Watkins, 1971.

Nott, C.
Teachings of Gurdjieff: T
he Journal of a Pupil.
Weiser, New York, 1962.

Journey Through This World:

Meetings with Gurdjieff and
Ouspensky.
Weiser, New York, 1969.

Ornstein, R.
The Psychology of Consciousness.
Penguin Books, Markham,
Canada,1972.

Ouspensky, P.
The Fourth Way.
Vintage, New York, 1957.

The Psychology of Man's
Possible Evolution.
Vintage Books, New York, 1950.

In Search of the Miraculous:

Fragments of an Unknown Teaching.
Harcourt, New York, 1949.

The Strange Life of Ivan Osokin.
Penguin, Baltimore, 1947.

A New Model of the Universe.

A. Knopf, New York, 1969.

Tertium Organum: A Key to the

Enigmas of the World. Alfred Knopf,
New York, (1922) 1968.

Pagels, E. T
he Gnostic Gospels.
Vintage Books, New York, 1981.

Patterson, W.
Struggle of the Magicians: Exploring
the teacher-student relationship.
Arete Communications, Fairfax
California, 1998.

Voices in the Dark: Esoteric, occult
& secular voices in Nazi-occupied
Paris 1940-44. Arete Communications,
Fairfax, California, 2001.

Pearsall, P.
The Heart's Code: Tapping the
Wisdom and Power of our Heart
Energy.
Broadway Books, New York, 1998.

Pelletier, R.
Towards a Science of Consciousness.
Dell, New York, 1978.

Penfield, W.
The Mystery of the Mind.
Princeton, Princeton University
Press,1977.

Peters, F.
Gurdjieff Remembered. Weiser,
New York, 1974.

Boyhood with Gurdjieff.
Penguin Books, Inc., Baltimore, 1964.

Popoff, I.
Gurdjieff: his work on myself, with
others, for the Work.
Weiser, New York, 1969.

Powells.
Zen and Reality. 1961.

Pribram, K.
Self-consciousness and intentionality.
In Schwartz, G., Shapiro, D., (Eds.)
Consciousness and Self-Regulation.
Plenum Press, New York, 1976.

Rehner, J.
Diary of a Modern Alchemist.
George Allen & Unwin, London, 1974.

Gurdjieff in Action.
Allen & Unwin, London, 1980.

Ouspensky: The unsung Genius.
Allen & Unwin, London, 1981.

Robinson et al..
Nag Hammadi Library.
Harper & Row, San Francisco, 1981.

Sagan, C.
*Broca's Brain: Reflections on the
Romance of Science.*
Random House, New York, 1979.

Sartre, J.
Being and Nothingness.
New York: Washington Square
Press,1969.

Nausea.
New York: New Directions, 1964.

Sechehaye, M.
Autobiography of a Schizophrenic Girl.
New York: Grune & Stratton, 1951.

Speeth, K.
The Gurdjieff Work.
Berkeley, California, And/Or Press,
1976.

Friedlander, I.
Gurdjieff: Seeker of the truth.
Harper & Row, New York, 1980.
Strange, J.
A Search for the Sources of the Stream
of Consciousness, in Pope & Singer
(eds). *The Stream of Consciousness.*
Plenum Press,New York,1978.

Tart, C.
*Waking Up: Overcoming the
Obstacles to Human Potential.*
Shambhala, Boston, 1987.

(Ed.) *Transpersonal Psychologies.*
Harper & Row, New York, 1975.

States of Consciousness.
New York: E. Dutton, 1975.

et al., Eds. *Symposium on
Consciousness.*
Middlesex, England, Penguin Books,
1976.

Upanishads.
Selections from Prabhavananda &
Manchester,
Upanishads: Breath of the Eternal.
New American Library, 1965.

Vaysse, J.
*Towards Awakening: An approach to
the teaching left by Gurdjieff.*
Harper & Row, San Francisco, 1979.

Walker, K.
Venture with Ideas.
Samuel Weiser, New York,1965.

The Making of Man.
Routledge & Kegan Paul, London,
1963.

A Study of Gurdjieff's Teaching.
Award Books, New York, 1969.

Watson, J.
Behavior.
Holt, Rinehart & Winston, 1914.

Welch, L.
Orage with Gurdjieff in America.
Routledge & Kegan Paul, Boston,
1982.

Yogananda, P.
Autobiography of A Yogi.
Self Realization Fellowship. California,
1998.

Zero Point Publications
Box 700, Kemptville, Ontario, Canada K0G-1J0

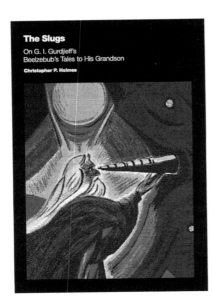

The Slugs
On G. I. Gurdjieff's
Beelzebub's Tales to His Grandson
Christopher P. Holmes

"THE SLUG"
On G. I. Gurdjieff's Beelzebub's Tales to his Grandson

Christopher P. Holmes

The Slugs provides an overview, explanation and interpretation of G. I. Gurdjieff's masterpiece Beelzebub's Tales to His Grandson, undoubtedly one of the most profound and mysterious books of the sacred literature in the modern world. The framework of ideas, claims and objective science offers a fundamentally alternative view of the nature of life, the origins and history of the Solar System and humankind, the nature of the human psyche and psychopathology, and a science of the soul. In the light of The Tales, most of modern thought and philosophy is so much 'pouring-from-the-empty-into-the-void.' The 'sorry scientists' of 'new format' have no conception of the great inscrutable mysteries of Nature and the subtle inner dimensions and alchemy of human beings. Beelzebub's Tales is a work not only of myth, allegory, history and fantasy, but about the secrets of 'objective science' and the psychology of the soul.

Gurdjieff's masterful Tales also provides a shocking portrait of the "strangeness of the human psyche" and explains how humans' essential consciousness and the divine impulses of faith, hope and love, passed into the 'subconsciousness,' while a 'false consciousness system' replaced it, crystallized around their egoism and associated unbecoming being-impulses. Beelzebub as a cosmic figure of higher reason observes the horrific "processes of reciprocal destruction," or war as periodically occurs on Earth, and asks how such phenomenal depravities come about and why humans cannot eradicate such an arch-criminal particularity in their psyche. The strange three-brained beings perceive reality "topsy-turvy," are mechanized to "see nothing real" and squander their sacred sexual substances solely for pleasure and their multiform vices. Beelzebub's portrayal of the "Hasnamusses," individuals who lack the Divine being-impulse of 'conscience,' the 'intelligentsia' and the 'crats,' provides vivid images of the psychopathology of the world's so-called 'elites' with their special societies or "criminal gangs," their "international five o'clocks" and "Hasnamussian sciences." The future of humanity is bleak indeed without the guidance of a being of such a higher intelligence as Beelzebub himself. The Slugs, like Gurdjieff's Tales, provides searing and illuminating insights into human psychopathology, the cause of war and the horror of it all.

The Author: Christopher P. Holmes is a mystic scientist and consciousness researcher, a clinical and forensic psychologist, and truth activist. He has studied the Gurdjieff work for over thirty five years and pursued broad investigations of human consciousness, the physics and metaphysics of creation, the mysteries of love and esoteric mystical teachings.

ISBN 978-0-9689435-4-0

www.zeropoint.ca

$21.95 Cdn 2nd Edition

GOD, SCIENCE & THE SECRET DOCTRINE
The Zero Point Metaphysics and Holographic Space of H. P. Blavatsky

Christopher P. Holmes, Ph.D. (Psych)

"... the Secret teachings ... must be contrasted with the speculations of modern science. ... To make of Science an integral whole necessitates, indeed, the study of spiritual and psychic, as well as physical Nature. ... Without metaphysics ... real science is inadmissible."
. P. Blavatsky, 1888

H. P. Blavatsky's *The Secret Doctrine* was published in 1888 and is relatively unknown in modern times. As it happens in this strange universe, Madame Blavatsky over a century ago anticipated numerous modern concepts concerning the creation of the Universe and the mechanisms of the laws of nature, including the holographic paradigm in psychology and physics. Blavatsky articulated the concept of the zero point or singularity origin of the Cosmos and of Sons, and a profoundly alternative view of the nature of the Aether and higher Space dimensions.

Blavatsky states: *"... 'material points without extension' (zero-points) are ... the materials out of which the 'Gods' and other invisible powers clothe themselves in bodies ... the entire universe concentrating itself, as it were, in a single point."* Dr. Holmes has grasped the profound meanings of this claim and related these ancient mystical teachings to the newest ideas in physics and science, and to explorations of human consciousness, spirit and soul, and the mysteries of the Heart. *God, Science & The Secret Doctrine* raises the ultimate question of the existence or non-existence of God—and what we mean by this term.

"While portions of this book are not easy going, Holmes plunges the reader into the deep places of the occult and the new frontiers of science to come up with a lucid and provocative book. It unseals many of the Secret Doctrines mysteries as it weaves the seeming opposites of spirit and science into a new synthesis. It is a must read for those wishing to understand the complex and seemingly impenetrable world of Helena Blavatsky alongside the newest ideas of quantum theory. Holmes has created something of his own tour de force in God, Science and the Secret Doctrine. His book is destined to serve as a guidebook for all those that follow." **Donna Brown,** The Esoteric Quarterly, Spring 2009, www.esotericstudies.net

ISBN 978-0-9689435-6-4

www.zeropoint.ca

$24.95 Cdn

WITHIN-WITHOUT from ZERO POINTS I

THE HEART DOCTRINE
Mystical Views of the Origin and Nature of Human Consciousness

Christopher P. Holmes

" ... "material points without extension" are Leibnitz's monads, and at the same time the materials out of which the 'Gods' and other invisible powers clothe themselves in bodies.... the entire universe concentrating itself, as it were, in a single point."

H. P. Blavatsky, The Secret Doctrine, I. Cosmogenesis, 1888

Modern psychology and science have been dominated by "the head doctrine"–the assumption that the material brain produces consciousness. In contrast, mystics claim that the origins of consciousness and Self are related to the mystical dimensions of the Heart. We are individual "eyes" or "I"s of "THAT," the divine unity within which we live, move and have our being. Mystical experiences involve penetrating various veils of nature which allow for the awakening of consciousness and the Heart, the realization of higher Space dimensions, and experiences of the unity of things within the inner life. Most importantly, human beings have a zero point centre and this is the means by which higher dimensional influences bring life and consciousness into the living being. These are the deep mysteries explored by the fool at the zero point.

Within-Without from Zero Points is an extremely unusual and provocative series which juxtaposes the most advanced concepts in modern science with mystical and spiritual teachings. It provides a sweeping scope of inquiry into the ultimate mysteries of consciousness, life, creation and God.

"My mission is to help uncover the forgotten, deep heart teachings of Jesus. ... The information you have gathered on the zero point has been a powerful validation of my own inner meditation practice and intuitions. Hence it has greatly enhanced my faith and the effectiveness of my meditation. Thank you so very much for your labors." **John Francis, *The Mystic Way of Radiant Love: Alchemy for a New Creation.***

"... if Christopher Holmes' articulation of 'the heart doctrine' had been restricted to citing and commenting upon those awe-inspiring teachings, he would have accomplished a great deal by establishing the foundation of an alternative paradigm to that which dominates contemporary approaches to the study of consciousness. However, when he introduces the mysterious concept of "the zero point," his arguments take on a level of significance which is, in my opinion, unparalleled in modern consciousness research. ..."
James A. Moffatt

ISBN 978-0-9689435-0-2
www.zeropoint.ca

$24.95 Cdn

UPCOMING

WITHIN-WITHOUT FROM ZERO POINTS II

MICROCOSM-MACROCOSM
Scientific and Mystical Views on the Origin of the Universe, the Nature of Matter & Human Consciousness

Christopher P. Holmes

" ... "material points without extension" are Leibnitz's monads, and at the same time the materials out of which the 'Gods' and other invisible powers clothe themselves in bodies.... the entire universe concentrating itself, as it were, in a single point." H. P. Blavatsky, The Secret Doctrine, I. Cosmogenesis, 1888

"... all the so-called Forces of Nature, Electricity, Magnetism, light, heat, etc., are in esse, i.e., in their ultimate constitution, the differentiated aspects of that Universal Motion. ... for formative or creative purposes, the Great Law modifies its perpetual motion on seven invisible points within the area of the manifest Universe." Madame H. P. Blavatsky, The Secret Doctrine, 1888

"It is necessary to notice that in the Great Universe all phenomena in general, without exception wherever they arise and manifest, are simply successively law-conformable 'Fractions' of some whole phenomenon which has its prime arising on the Most Holy Sun Absolute." G. I. Gurdjieff, 1950

Mystical accounts of states of Union, or unity with the world or universe on varied levels, attest to the fact that there is some kind of inner magic and alchemy going on within the inner cosmos of human consciousness—a metaphysics and physics to consciousness and the human heart.

Microcosm-Macrocosm explores the newest theories in physics and creation science—including materials on superstrings, higher dimensions, singularities, the quantum vacuum and the holographic principle. It also draws from ancient metaphysics—particularly The Secret Doctrine of H. P. Blavatsky (1888), esoteric Judaism and Kabbalah, and the cosmology and metaphysics of G. I. Gurdjieff. This is a challenging and provocative work with deep insights into the Divine Mystery teachings and a unique critique of modern science philosophy. It provides a shocking alternative view of the zero point origins of human consciousness and cosmos.

UPCOMING

WITHIN-WITHOUT from ZERO POINTS III

TRIUNE MONADS IN SEVEN DIMENSIONAL HYPERSPACE
Scientific and Mystical Studies of the Multi-Dimensional Nature of Human Existence

Christopher P. Holmes

Monads draws from the teachings of Madame Blavatsky, Kabbalah and Judaism, Gurdjieff, and a wide range of mystical doctrine about the multidimensional nature of human existence. Esoteric teachings identify the abode of the 'I' as within the human heart, where a triune Monad element is established within a Seven Dimensional Eternal Parent Space which underlies and sustains our normal physical four-dimensional space-time complex. Such ideas from mystical sources bear profound relationships to theories in advanced physics as to the nature of Space itself, quantum interconnectedness and higher dimensional superstring elements at zero point levels. A triune and sevenfold Monadic Essence spins a Web of Spirit, Soul and Matter within a Seven Dimensional Virual Reality out of the Aethers of the void and plenum, the quantum vacuum. In order to illustrate the necessity for such an alternative understanding of reality, this work examines evidences for out-of-body experiences, Sheldrake's fields of extended mind, enigmas posed by heart transplant patients and twin studies, and an interpretation of other paranormal investigations.

UPCOMING

WITHIN-WITHOUT FROM ZERO POINTS IV

A FOOL AT THE ZERO POINT
An Autobiographic Tale about the Strange Case of Professor Z, the Mysteries of Love and Ecstasies of the Heart & the Horror of It All

Christopher P. Holmes

Christopher, by the grace of God, will provide an autobiographical account of his life experiences, his psychical and mystical experiences, his life struggles and relationships, and an account of awakening to the horror of it all. This work includes materials on Christopher's struggles for academic freedom at York University, his twelve years of work in correctional centres as a forensic psychologist, his life and loves, and his awakening to psychopathology of the world elites with their plans for committing genocide against the human race.

ZERO POINT TEACHINGS
Selected Writings of Mystical Psychologist & Scientist

Christopher P. Holmes

The zero point teachings are a portal to awaken you to a higher dimensional experience of yourself and of the structure of reality--to view and experience the world in a magical and mystical way. The basic idea is that all living beings have a zero point centre within as related to the higher dimensional physics and metaphysics of the heart. This is the means by which "the Gods and other invisible powers clothe themselves in bodies"—as as explained by mystic scholar H. P. Blavatsky in The Secret Doctrine (1888). Just as scientists conceive that the universe grew from an infinitesimal singularity out of the quantum vacuum, so also, you also have such a hidden zero point or singularity condition--a singular I or point of supernal lux within the Heart. We emerge "out of nothingness" in some mysterious way unknown to modern science and contemporary understanding, and are an essential light and life element, or I, established within higher dimensional Space.

This selection is drawn from the www.zeropoint.ca website, an article series published within the online journal of www.esotericstudies.com and from Christopher's varied books and studies. It includes materials on the origin and nature of human consciousness, the mystery teachings of the heart doctrine, Kabbalah and The Secret Doctrine, modern holographic physics and quantum theory, a commentary on the psychopathology of humanity and the causes of war based on the teachings of G. I. Gurdjieff, book, movie and music critiques, and much more. Most importantly, it includes original socio-political and 9-11 writings and research, and the 'zero point' proposal for the human race to bring forth a new era of human justice and international law, instead of the archcriminal lawlessness and psychosis of the modern and past eras.

ISBN 978-0-9689435-7-1

$24.95 Cdn

ZERO POINT PUBLICATIONS
Box 700, Kemptville
Ontario Canada K0G-1S0
www.zeropoint.ca

Made in the USA
Lexington, KY
13 September 2012